HIDDEN IN PLAIN SIGHT

Cultural Expressions of World War II

Interwar Preludes, Responses, Memory

Phyllis Lassner, Series Editor

Hidden in Plain Sight

Jews and Jewishness in British Film, Television, and Popular Culture

Edited by
Nathan Abrams

Northwestern University Press | Evanston, Illinois

Northwestern University Press
www.nupress.northwestern.edu

Printed in the United States of America

10 9 8 7 6 5 4 3 2 1

Library of Congress Cataloging-in-Publication Data

Names: Abrams, Nathan, editor.
Title: Hidden in plain sight : Jews and Jewishness in British film, television, and popular culture / edited by Nathan Abrams.
Other titles: Cultural expressions of World War II.
Description: Evanston, Illinois : Northwestern University Press, 2016. | Series: Cultural expressions of World War II | Includes index.
Identifiers: LCCN 2016001861| ISBN 9780810132825 (pbk. : alk. paper) | ISBN 9780810132832 (cloth : alk. paper) | ISBN 9780810132849 (e-book)
Subjects: LCSH: Jews in motion pictures. | Jews on television. | Jews in popular culture—Great Britain. | Motion pictures, British—Social aspects. | Television programs—Social aspects—Great Britain.
Classification: LCC PN1995.9.J46 H53 2016 | DDC 791.436529924041—dc23
LC record available at http://lccn.loc.gov/2016001861

CONTENTS

ACKNOWLEDGMENTS

I would like primarily to thank Phyllis Lassner for encouraging and guiding this project from conception through to fruition. She believed in it and backed it from the start when others were unsure of the book's potential. I would also like to thank the contributors to the volume and the staff at Northwestern University Press, without whom there would not be a book. This book is dedicated to Danielle, Isabel Willow, and Jacob Leon (*fy nheulu i*), as well as Stanley and Elwood, with all my love.

HIDDEN IN PLAIN SIGHT

NATHAN ABRAMS

Introduction

British Jews have played a major role in the pioneering of the United Kingdom's film and television industries. They have been prominent in all of these media's branches and at all levels from the beginning. This participation has continued unabated since; indeed, if anything, it has increased in the twenty-first century, reaching perhaps unprecedented levels of visibility, particularly in the mid-2010s. Yet, given this important and historic role, it is surprising to write that, today, the role and representation of Jews and Jewishness in the celebrated and global Anglophone film and television industries of Britain is still a neglected field of study with only a few scholarly articles dedicated to exploring it. When it comes to film and television, Jews have been present, right in front of our eyes, yet their presence is not always made known, either by themselves or by scholars, hence the descriptor in the title of this book, "Hidden in Plain Sight."

Consequently, in contrast to the story of the Jewish contribution to cinema and television (both in front of and behind the camera) in the United States, which is well known, in terms of academic research, little has been written on the contribution to and representation of Jews in British film and television. While there are studies of other marginalized and underrepresented groups, from the perspective of race, gender, and sexuality, including blacks, women, and homosexuals, there has been surprisingly little interest in the place of Jews in British cinema and television. In fact, it seems that Jews have been written out of the histories of film and television in the United Kingdom and its constituent nations. Although British Jewry has been explored from a variety of perspectives, beyond literature and synagogue architecture, its cultural output has been virtually ignored. Despite the growth of film and television studies and Jewish studies, as of 2016 no extensive study with Jewish film and television as its primary focus had been published, even in light of the increased visibility of Jews and Jewishness in public and mass cultures. As a consequence, there is a dearth of published scholarship on the subject of Jewish film and television in the United Kingdom.

Furthermore, studies that have looked at Jewish film and television in the United Kingdom have often tended to focus on individual directors, films, and programs. Unfortunately, they are then treated in isolation, divorced from the British Jewish context from which they derived, almost to the point of being ahistorical. The scholarship surrounding Sandra Goldbacher's beautiful 1998 film *The Governess* is a case in point, as little of the scholarship about the film situates it in either a British film industry or Jewish community context.[1] Hence, despite these studies' insightful analysis, they unfortunately shed little light on how the peculiar context of Britain has shaped the production, circulation, and reception of British films and television programs. Conversely, when books have looked at British Jewish history, they have ignored film and cinema. It is striking yet illustrative that in his chapter "Art and Intellect" in his survey of British Jewish history, *The Club: Jews of Modern Britain* (1989), Stephen Brook completely ignores the film industry.[2] Until a study of Jews in British film and television is written, the picture of Jewish life in Britain in particular, as well as in the global creative industries in general, cannot be considered complete.

This is where the present collection steps in. In 2010 I called for further research on the subject of Jewish film in the United Kingdom.[3] Thankfully, this call was answered, and two years later I edited an issue of the *Journal of European Popular Culture* containing five essays exploring this theme.[4] With this present volume, the range has been widened not only by expanding the number of contributions but also by including television. Consequently, *Hidden in Plain Sight: Jews and Jewishness in British Film, Television, and Popular Culture* aims to rectify this neglect by offering insight into Jews and Jewishness in the history of British film and television. This collection of essays begins to redress this historiographical gap by bringing together, for the first time and in a single coherent volume, a range of original essays that address various aspects of Jews and Jewishness in British film and television from the period between the two world wars to the present. It is this overarching theme that ties the book together. It builds on previous studies to produce a corrective and contextual historical study that analyzes film and television in the United Kingdom in a way that is reflective of both the Jewish experience and its particularly *British* context. Furthermore, it does so on its own terms, without constantly comparing it to the United States, as if somehow Britain were some distant, less well off and less well known cousin.

In so doing, the individual chapters in the book present case studies of cultural representations, in the form of film and television, that respond to the years of crisis before World War II, the global war itself, and the Holocaust; to past and present memories and memorializations of the 1930s and 1940s; and to the legacy and collective memory of antisemitism in England that date back to the medieval period. Together, the chapters provide enriching interdisciplinary linkages from various perspectives and theoretical approaches that seek to answer the question: what differences do the linkages between various national crises of the 1930s, World War II, the Holocaust, and collective memory make to film and television in the United Kingdom?

The chapters demonstrate that, overall, even in those instances where the films and programs do not directly engage with the years of crisis before World War II, the global war itself, the Holocaust, or past and present memories and memorializations of the 1930s and 1940s, those events loom as an "indelible shadow," to use Annette Insdorf's memorable phrase, over British film and television.[5] British Jews operate in a post-Holocaust mode caught in a liminal status of a nation that was directly and proximately involved in World War II but which, largely, did not experience the Continental Holocaust. Furthermore, in terms of the production, circulation, and reception of those texts, British Jews are both defined by and define themselves in relation to the Holocaust and ongoing antisemitism in the United Kingdom today, and this is especially the case for contemporary audiences, seeking to make connections with a minority group that it does not, in general, understand.

This volume features a blend of more established as well as emerging and junior scholars, both in the United Kingdom and North America, who come from a variety of disciplines (literature, gender and queer theory, postcolonial studies, history, film studies, television studies, media studies, religious studies, Jewish studies, to name just a few). The book draws on the rich existing literatures of Jewish cultural studies as well as the newer work on the cultural production of Jewishness beyond the U.S. context. Each essay offers a close textual study illustrating the significance of the representation of Jews and Jewishness in British film and television.

The book's interest does not simply lie in those who study the United Kingdom and its constituent nations, but rather, it should be of interest to scholars of Jewish life everywhere. The U.K. film industry is historic, and the presence of Jews within it equally so; and, although Britain's empire may have declined, its global networks of distribution (in particular those via the British Broadcasting Corporation, or BBC) are still vibrant. Thus, despite the hegemonic presence of the U.S. film and television industries, especially in Jewish terms, their British counterparts still have much to teach us.

Jewish Pioneers and Entrepreneurs

The reason for this high level of activity was primarily because both the film and television industries admitted Jews by not denying their entry. The film industry, in particular, required minimal capital investment and was considered not only a passing fad but also somewhat disrespectable in comparison to other forms of culture, particularly the theater and literature. Consequently, it lacked the barriers to entry that other professions had erected. At the same time, alongside the commercial factor, was the lure of glamour and excitement.

The first key Jewish pioneer was George Berthold Samuelson. As a producer, Samuelson was an important and colorful behind-the-scenes presence in the making of British silent films. In 1910, he set up as Britain's first film renter with the Royal Film Agency. Four years later, he acquired Worton Hall studio and established the Samuelson Film Manufacturing Company. He went on to produce more than ninety movies, beginning with *Sixty Years a Queen* (1913).[6] Samuelson also left a legacy in the form of his sons, all of whom entered the movie business. Sydney, a cinematographer, was the most prominent, knighted for his services to the industry in 1995; Peter and Marc became active producers in the 1980s and 1990s.

One of the most important players in the British movie industry between the wars was Hungarian Jewish émigré Alexander Korda. Having worked in his native country, Austria, Germany, France, and United States, Korda in 1930 moved to Britain, where he established London Film Productions and later Denham Studios, the only British studio to model itself on its American counterparts. Under Korda's direction, many notable films were produced in the 1930s and 1940s. These included, among others, *The Private Life of Henry VIII* (1933).[7] Indeed, Korda was described as "Britain's only move mogul."[8] Korda, though, did not vaunt his Jewishness on screen; indeed, he systematically wrote Jewish characters out of his screenplays and promoted so-called English identity and values. Throughout his career, Korda desired to downplay, even conceal, his Jewishness to ensure his success in the British entertainment industries; in doing so, he unwittingly provided the model to be copied by other British Jewish filmmakers.

Michael Balcon was also responsible for transforming the British film industry into a much more modern enterprise. Initially in charge of Alfred Hitchcock's British movies before World War II, he continued to play a key part in British cinema after the war when he ran Ealing Studios, overseeing the series of films known as the "Ealing Comedies."

Elsewhere in the United Kingdom, Jews began to acquire and build movie theaters. In Aberdeen, Ernest Bromberg held movie-themed events at his the Palais de Dance from 1926 onward. He subsequently opened Aberdeen's first News Cinema in September 1936. Solomon "Sol" Levy also set up as an exhibitor, opening a number of movie theaters in Birmingham, where Oscar Deutsch, Victor Saville, and Balcon were also operating. In London, Phil and Sid Hyams pioneered "cine-variety"—an entire evening of entertainment, consisting of two films, a newsreel, music (an "organ interlude"), and variety acts featuring top artistes. They also built six palatial cinemas in some of London's dreariest neighborhoods, including the Gaumont State in Kilburn, in northwest London, which was Britain's largest cinema, with 4,004 seats.

A number of Jews also branched out from exhibition into distribution. Levy established a small rental company, Sol Exclusives. Gambling that U.S. movies would be popular with British audiences, he obtained the

Midlands' distribution rights of many movies, including those by D. W. Griffith. In 1919, Charles Moss Woolf and S. Freedman set up a small rental company, W and F Film Service, which distributed a blend of American and European features. By the end of the twenties, Gaumont-British had become Britain's first vertically integrated film company. It was run by the Ostrer brothers, led by Isidore.

Likewise, the presence of Jewishness in film and television also dates back almost to the inception of both industries. During its early years, images of Jews were fairly common on the screens of the fledgling film industry, largely because Yiddish was still a vibrant language in Britain. Judith Goldberg has estimated that approximately 130 feature films and 30 short Yiddish-language films were made between the years 1910 and 1941 and distributed to the United Kingdom; however, since most of them were produced in the United States, they tended to focus on American Jewish life.[9] Indeed, despite having a thriving Yiddish theater, no Yiddish films were produced in the United Kingdom.[10]

Jews and Jewishness on the Screen before World War II

The first *British*-made representations of Jews and Jewishness appeared in the silent shorts of the early twentieth century. Perhaps the first of these was *Petticoat Lane* (1903).[11] It documented the market located in the eponymous street in London's East End, an area notable for its sizable Jewish population, and thus surely featured Jews. Thereafter, fictional representations tended toward the crude and overtly antisemitic. The Jew was an "outsider" and "invader" to be feared. The large-scale immigration of Jews from Eastern Europe into Britain's cities had sparked widespread public alarm, leading to the Aliens Act of 1905, which required all "aliens" to register while in Britain. Two films from that same year, *The Alien Question* and *The Aliens' Invasion,* underlined how cheap foreign labor, which was frequently Jewish, was undercutting British workers and pushing them out of work.[12] The plot synopsis on the Internet Movie Database (IMDb) for *The Alien Question* states, "Jews, Russians, Poles and Germans come to London and force British artisans to emigrate to Canada," while that of *The Aliens' Invasion* is "English workmen are sacked and babies die because Jews come to England and accept low wages."[13] Four years later, preying on this fear of the "alien" (Jewish) other, *The Invaders* (1909) depicted foreign soldiers disguised as Jewish tailors.[14]

Explicitly racialized on film, "the Jew" was portrayed in such a fashion as to remove any sense of intragroup difference, whether in terms of religious observance, region, national origin, language, class and socioeconomic status, or politics. Thus he (I use the masculine pronoun deliberately) was typically swarthy, hunchbacked, hooked-nosed, and bald-headed, with oversize feet and protruding belly. This Jew was a subhuman, avaricious, unrefined, dishonest, greedy, venal, grasping, shifty and menacing cheat. He was either a greedy capitalist or, paradoxically, a violent, anticapitalist, radical reformer and/or dangerous subversive rebel. Such representations appeared in *The Robber and the Jew* (1908), *A Bad Day for Levinsky* (1909), and *The Antique Vase* (1913).[15] Representative of this group of movies was the review for *A Bad Day for Levinsky* in which the author stated, "One can scarcely commend this picture. . . . There is too much malicious feeling expressed in the fun and cannot but believe that this apparently holding up a certain people to scorn and making them the basis of a certain species of fun—which is anything but funny."[16]

Adaptations of British literary classics, featuring Jewish characters, emanated from both sides of the Atlantic and Europe at this time, as they were particularly popular. These films included multiple versions of *Oliver Twist* in 1907, 1909, 1910 (French), 1912 (two), 1916, and 1919 (Hungarian).[17] Various silent versions of *The Merchant of Venice* had been produced in France (1905), the United States (1908, 1912, and 1914), Italy (1911), and France (1913), before the first British adaptation was released in 1916 and followed by another in 1919.[18] In 1922, the series *Tense Moments from Great Plays* presented the court scene.[19] In addition, there were also productions of *Ivanhoe* in 1911 and 1913 (twice) and *Trilby* in 1915, which was reedited and subsequently reissued in 1917.[20] There were even spinoffs, including *A Female Fagin* (1913) and *Gwendolyn, The Sewing Machine Girl* (1914), the latter adapted from George Eliot's 1876 novel *Daniel Deronda*. Depending on the source text, these representations veered between the sensitive and the derogatory.[21]

During the 1920s and 1930s, this trend of literary adaptations continued. Films of this period included, as was to be expected given their popularity, further versions of *Oliver Twist, Jr.* (1921), *Oliver Twist* (1922,

1933), *The Merchant of Venice* (1927), *Trilby* (1923), and *Svengali* (1931).[22] But, overall, more sympathetic representations began to appear in the form of *General Post* (1920); two versions of *Disraeli* (1921, 1929), which joined an earlier one that had been made in 1916; *Daniel Deronda* (1921); *The Wandering Jew* (1923, remade 1933); *Motherland* (1927); *Loyalties* (1933); *Jew Süss* (1934)—on which more later; *Mr. Cohen Takes a Walk* (1935); and *Car of Dreams* (1935).[23] Lester Friedman commented that "the most popular historical Jew of the silent period is the nineteenth century's most famous politician, Benjamin Disraeli."[24] It is also certainly significant that the word "Jew" appeared in the titles of three of these films and thus would feature prominently in the films' promotion, including the marquee/signs above the cinema entrances. Furthermore, as Tobias Hochscherf notes, "Given that anti-Semitism and anti-alienism was common in British society their absence in films is somewhat surprising [in that] films did not feature stereotyped Jews posing a threat to British society."[25]

The reasons for this shift to more positive portrayals can possibly be attributed to the need to respond to antisemitism and/or because of the behind-the-scenes influence of Jewish personnel who entered the film industry between the two world wars.[26] Such Jews benefited from a United Kingdom–wide trend in which, the Jewish community s became more assimilated and significant than before World War I, taking advantage of the decline in Britain's manufacturing dynasties. Those Jews already involved in the British film industry were boosted by the arrival of a significant influx of German-speaking Jews. Certainly, after 1929, the vast majority of exiled film practitioners who migrated to Britain were Jewish. Many arrived in the United Kingdom following the introduction of sound in 1929 which, together with the stock market crash in the United States that set off the Great Depression, had had a shattering impact on the German film industry.[27] They were joined by more Jewish refugees from Nazism, including producers Hermann Fellner, Josef Somlo, and Emeric Pressburger, and actors Lucie Mannheim, Peter Lorre, and Elisabeth Bergner (the latter of whom moved from Germany in the 1930s, as did Anton Walbrook), joining those Jewish entrepreneurs, mentioned earlier, who had already begun to make a name for themselves.[28] Unfortunately, however, these exiles and émigrés created tensions within the industry, blending with the already existing xenophobia and antisemitism extant in British life, and despite the significance and scale of their contribution, they faced an ambivalent climate.[29]

It was around this time when the world's first formal high-definition public service television transmission began. Jews were present at this inception (having been involved with the BBC as far back as 1922, when it was broadcasting only radio). When, on November 2, 1936, the BBC sent its first broadcast from Alexandra Palace in North London, Jewish technician Isaac Schoenberg was in charge of the arrangements. At 3.30 P.M. that same day, the first BBC music program, which featured the BBC Television Orchestra conducted by Hyam Greenbaum, was broadcast. In 1936, the British mandate–operated Palestine Broadcasting Service began and lasted until 1947. The BBC made its first program in Yiddish in July 1942, and a Hebrew service (for Israeli listeners) was introduced in October 1949. Incidentally, the BBC's on-screen logo, which first appeared in December 1953, was designed and devised by Abram Games.[30]

According to Andrew Spicer, while "Jewish entrepreneurs did not control the pre-war British film [and television] industry, they did much to help shape it, providing the energy, ambition, financial acumen, willingness to take risks and vision essential in building a modern industry that was, despite severe difficulties, sufficiently robust to survive ferocious American competition."[31] In spite of the fact that the majority of the British film industry was run by non-Jews, the small but significant presence of Jewish entrepreneurs at its higher levels began to provoke the widespread notion that the British movie industry was controlled by Jews. The novelist Graham Greene wrote in 1939, for example, "How the financial crisis has improved English films! They have lost their tasteless Semitic opulence and are becoming—English."[32]

Hidden in Plain Sight

Having provided some prehistory of the role and representation of Jews in the pre–World War II British film industry, the book begins with Gil Toffell's consideration of *Jew Süss*, the Gaumont-British Picture Corporation's 1934 movie adaptation of Lion Feuchtwanger's 1925 novel *Jud Süß*. While British censors would not allow any film to openly criticize the German state, it was clear to both the British Jewish and mainstream British press that the historic events depicted in the narrative offered a pointed commentary on the Nazi policy of persecution of Jews. The task of his chapter is to trace this press reaction to understand the contours of the British Jewish reception of Lothar Mendes's *Jew Süss* film release. Toffell pays particular attention to the Jewish press, examining the distinctly Jewish concern with the film as an article of propaganda. Not only was alarm expressed that the film might disseminate antisemitic prejudice, but its potential to be read as a tendentious promotion of particularist interests was also a catalyst for anxiety. The unease associated with this latter factor should, it is argued, be understood in the context of the widely articulated contemporary belief that the cinema was a Jewish monopoly.

Several years later, novelist Phyllis Bottome published *The Mortal Storm* (1937), a story revealing and dramatizing the plight of Jews in Nazi Germany. Bottome joined forces with her compatriot, Claudine West, who had been working as a Hollywood screenwriter since the 1920s. Together these two British artists translated Bottome's novel into the 1940 blockbuster MGM film, directed by Frank Borzage.[33] In their chapter, Phyllis Lassner and Alexis Pogorelskin trace the origins and development of the screenplay, closely exploring the film and how it managed to illustrate the fate of German Jews under National Socialism but at the same time never directly mention the word "Jew." In so doing, their chapter widens the term "British cinema" to include the productions of "diasporic" British artists and writers in Hollywood just before and during the Second World War.

Back on the British side of the Atlantic, Harold French's *Mr. Emmanuel* (1944) is remembered primarily for being the only *British* commercial wartime feature film to deal exclusively with Nazi antisemitism.[34] In adapting his 1939 novel of the same title, Louis Golding retained much of its story pitting an elderly British Jew against a racist system that assumed he was a conspirator in an assassination plot simply because he was Jewish. However, scholars have generally dismissed its depiction of the Nazi persecution of Jews as being too tame and note that its late release date diluted its impact, given what was already known about the Holocaust in 1944. In his chapter, Lawrence Baron reveals a hidden dimension to the film, arguing that to those readers familiar with Golding's earlier works, in particular his "Doomington" saga, the movie possesses a more pronounced Jewish and Zionist subtext than has hitherto been recognized.

Following the Second World War, a contradictory approach can be detected. According to Jan Epstein, Jews were portrayed both more frequently and more realistically.[35] As evidence of this shift, she cites *The Rake's Progress* (1945), *It Always Rains on Sunday* (1947), *Ivanhoe* (1952), *Make Me an Offer!* (1954), *A Kid for Two Farthings* (1954), *The Bespoke Overcoat* (1955), and *Expresso Bongo* (1959).[36] However, these films sit uneasily alongside *Oliver Twist* (1948) and *Svengali* (1955).[37] Although nowhere identified as a Jew, Alec Guinness's portrayal of Fagin, with his bulbous hooked nose, has been described as a gross antisemitic caricature. Likewise, *Svengali* emphasized the role of the notorious Jewish hypnotist of *Trilby* (1894), even if the film did not explicitly refer to his Jewishness. Presented as a disgusting, filthy, foreign, and sinister presence, Svengali (Donald Wolfitt) preys upon the poor hapless Trilby played by the German actress Hildegard Neff (née Knef). As Margaret Stetz points out, Neff's "heavily accented speaking voice reminds spectators throughout of her German identity (an identity wholly out of sync with du Maurier's original notion of the character as French Irish) and magnifies the topsy-turvy effect of the central dynamic, in which an innocent German is now being victimized by a scheming Jew."[38]

But, even though World War II and the background of the Nazis' persecution of Jews in Europe was a recent and vivid memory, the pressure for Jews was to remain hidden, or at least to keep their heads down, in the postwar years. The British Empire was falling apart, and in the British mandate in Palestine, Jewish violence against the British authorities was reported in the British press on an almost daily basis. The advent of the Cold War added a new mood of surveillance and suspicion directed toward "alien" identity, further discouraging overt protests that raised the specter of difference. Furthermore, building a united Western front against communism and the Soviet Union required the urgent rehabilitation of West Germany. Such rehabilitation necessitated representing it as an ally in the minds of the British public, not only through political rhetoric but also through the medium of popular culture. Consequently, there were multiple reasons for British Jews to be circumspect in protesting cultural productions that defamed them as a group.[39]

Meanwhile, on television in the years immediately following World War II, as James Jordan has shown elsewhere, the Jewish presence was discernable.[40] During what was a key period in British television history, from 1946 until 1955, when the BBC still held a monopoly, Jews played a significant if underappreciated role in developing what was still a growing medium. They appeared on-screen in a variety of roles: bandleaders (Geraldo and Oscar Rabin), artistic performers (Alicia Markova, Gertrude Holtand, and Alma Cogan), variety entertainers and comedians (Cilli Wang, Harry Green, and Vic Wise); and actors (Abraham Sofaer, Miriam Karlin, David Kossoff, Sid James, Yvonne Mitchell, and Sydney Tafler). Jews also held prominent offscreen positions. Ronald Waldman and Brian Tesler were the BBC's heads of Light Entertainment. Wolf Mankowitz, Sid Colin, and Dennis Norden were employed as writers. And producer Rudolph Cartier was to U.K. television what Korda was to British film and cinema.[41] Their influence can be felt in the range of programs that presented, in some way, images of Jews and Judaism, including television's first engagement with the Holocaust.

Yet, despite this key Jewish presence, the BBC, by the 1950s a major institution in British life, still tended toward the "very white and gentile."[42] Thus, when, in 1954, the Independent Television Authority was authorized by Parliament, thereby breaking up the BBC's monopoly, Jews leaped at the chance to run independent franchises that competed with the BBC. They exploited the opportunities available to entrepreneurs following the profusion of new and independent television companies. Sidney Bernstein founded Granada TV. Elkan Allan became head of entertainment of Rediffusion Television from 1962 to 1965. John Jacobs became head of drama at Anglia Television in 1964. Cyril Bennett became controller of programs at London Weekend Television. Brian Tessler was director and program controller of Associated British Corporation (ABC) Television, and Sir Lew Grade became the joint managing director of Associated Television.[43]

Moving into the sixties, Michael Berkowitz explores the hidden, or subsurface, Jewishness of Michael Powell's *Peeping Tom* (1960).[44] While much has been written about this classic of British cinema, none of it has considered its Jewish origins or how the film can be read, if one knows the codes, as an implicitly Jewish film. Here Berkowitz offers a reinterpretation of *Peeping Tom* through its Jewish genealogy (Leo Marks) and the film's incorporation of secularized Jewish imagery. As he points out, little has been said about the bizarre content of *Peeping Tom*: its German protagonist, Mark Lewis (Karl Böhm), a London-based photographer obsessed with taking photos of nude women at the moment of their deaths. Jewishness is a major but cagey and unstated element of *Peeping Tom*, particularly in its potentially antisemitic and hence shocking representation of Lewis as a seducer and murderer of gentile women so soon after the Holocaust. Berkowitz explores the argument that, like Alfred Hitchcock's *Psycho* (1960), released in the same year, *Peeping Tom* invokes the Holocaust through obscure motifs.[45] Furthermore, although *Peeping Tom* is not based on any known murderer, the main character and the plot derive, in part, from the experience of the Jewish Leo Marks (whose name is similar enough to suggest a relationship with the lead character) who wrote the treatment and screenplay. Finally, Berkowitz argues that Marks's creation is related to his views of the British Jewish engagement with photography, as revealed in his autobiography, *Between Silk and Cyanide* (1998).

Switching to television, the 1960s represented, according to David Herman, a "golden age" for Jewish involvement.[46] This involvement was felt at every level, from the executives to producers, writers, and actors. It was on TV, he argued, "the real national theatre of post-war Britain, that Jews found their voice in British culture."[47] Such influential figures as Mike Leigh, Jack Rosenthal, Arnold Wesker, and Tom Stoppard all received their start during this period. The high point came in the late 1970s when television featured the names of Jacob Bronowski, David Elstein, Jack Rosenthal, Jack Gold, Jonathan Miller, Alan Yentob, Frederic Raphael, and Harold Pinter. As Herman put it, "television enabled a new generation of young Jews to find their voice."[48]

In this context, Gavin Schaffer in his chapter considers Jewishness in British television sitcoms. By this point, the Jewish community had become much more established into general British life, being much more financially stable, bourgeois, and assimilated despite continuing antisemitic prejudice. However, against a backdrop of increased immigration from the West Indies and the Asian subcontinent, in a climate of accelerated black and Asian immigration, official thought about how to tackle prejudice and discrimination, in general, still focused on the dangers of antisemitism, often as a precedent for understanding other forms of racism. In light of this context, Schaffer argues that the tendency to use Jewish/non-Jewish relations as a precedent was similarly common in the world of television situation comedy, as it provided the backbone for a series of 1960s sitcoms — in particular, those penned by Johnny Speight and Vince Powell and Harry Driver. Schaffer shows that, as was the case in politics, Jewish/non-Jewish relations offered a framework for articulating, understanding, and countering concepts of race, and they offered a comparatively safe way to begin to "work through" British race relations on television. Through a seemingly lighthearted lens, television sitcoms offered an outlet in which the "hidden" realities of British race relations could be articulated and exposed to public light. In so doing, these writers and their comedies significantly influenced the ways in which African Caribbean, Indian, and Pakistani immigrants were depicted in British comedy. As Schaffer says, "Jewish/non-Jewish relations seem to have been used to test the water of this particular kind of conversation." Thus we encounter a paradox: Jews were visible subjects of the sitcoms of the 1960s, while the "hidden presences" — the true objects of political and cultural anxiety for the white British mainstream — were actually Asians and blacks, yet, at the same time, sitcom Jewishness was absorbed (submerged, as it were) within a wider cultural lineage of non-Caucasian ethnic representations in British TV sitcoms that seemed to be happy to rehearse old stereotypes.

Nevertheless, the 1960s begins a period in which Jewishness enjoyed a greater visibility in British life. This visibility was evident in the cinemas, too, with a string of films featuring Jews, often "as equal members of a pluralist society."[49] They included *Hand in Hand* (1960), *Conspiracy of Hearts* (1960), *Sparrows Can't Sing* (1963), *The Barber of Stamford Hill* (1963), *Reach for Glory* (1963), *The Spy Who Came In from the Cold* (1965), *The Deadly Affair* (1966), *Ulysses* (1967), *The Fearless Vampire Killers* (1967), and *Oliver!* (1968).[50] The final two films were particularly significant. Whereas Roman Polanski imagined Jewish vampires, Carol Reed's *Oliver!* transformed Fagin (here played by Ron Moody) into a sympathetic, even likable, character (and in 2005 Polanski himself would revisit *Oliver Twist*, casting Ben Kingsley in the role of Fagin).[51]

The 1970s continued this trajectory. In *Sunday Bloody Sunday* (1971), John Schlesinger explored homosexual relationships and Jewish identity in trendy North London.[52] It was not only "an important breakthrough in the normalising of a Jewish character in a major film" but also a rare example in which a British Jewish director dealt with personal and autobiographical issues.[53] *The Odessa File* (1974), *Voyage of the Damned*

(1976), and *Monty Python's Life of Brian* (1979) also qualify as British Jewish films from this decade.[54]

In this context, Rachel Garfield's contribution to this book offers a bridge between the 1970s and the contemporary moment in which Jews became "outed" (in both senses of that term, as heralded by Schlesinger's *Sunday Bloody Sunday*). In the first half of her chapter, she explores the two "Jewish" television dramas of Jack Rosenthal, a key British screenwriter; namely, *The Evacuees* (1975) and *Bar Mitzvah Boy* (1976); she then moves on to compare them to the more recent television sitcom *Grandma's House* (2010, 2012), which foregrounds the homosexuality of its Jewish star and writer, Simon Amstell.[55] Playing a version of his real-life self, Amstell is a gay man who is well known in Britain for being just as public about his sexual identity as about his Judaism. Thus *Grandma's House* presents an interesting case study of how the role of sexuality intersects with British Jewish life in general and with this specific representation of Jewish masculinity in particular, shedding light on the hidden presence in British television of men who are both Jewish *and* gay. In so doing, Garfield adds a much-needed dimension based on class analysis, which is often missing from studies of British Jewry because Jews in the United Kingdom are stereotypically considered to be — incorrectly, as she points out — members of the middle and upper-middle classes.

During the 1980s, the major Jewish directors of this period — namely, Schlesinger, Mike Leigh, and Michael Winner — did not tend to insert any Jewishness into their films in any direct or explicit fashion. This was left up to either non–British Jewish directors or non-Jewish directors instead. Building on *The Fearless Vampire Killers*, *An American Werewolf in London* (1981) featured another Jewish monster in the form of a werewolf whose death is necessitated by the need to preserve the English order.[56] Another outsider was embodied by Ben Cross, who played the real-life Jewish Olympic sprinter Harold Abrahams in *Chariots of Fire* (1981). Ironically made by a non-Jew, it attempted to shed light on and challenge entrenched British antisemitism through its focus on a true story.[57] *Escape from Sobibor* (1987), which could in some senses be seen as a hybrid global made-for-television film though in other senses as a British one, not least as it indeed drew directly from the work of British writer-director Jack Gold, focused on the true events surrounding the escape of Jewish prisoners from the Sobibor death camp during World

War II.[58] It featured the actress Sara Sugarman, who would later go on to become a filmmaker in her own right, albeit making films with little explicit Jewish content. The film *Forbidden* (1984) was another international coproduction set within World War II.[59]

Erstwhile film director Mike Leigh announced, "Here's my Jewish play," in advance of the National Theatre's production of his *Two Thousand Years* in the fall of 2005. The declaration was striking, for until then Leigh had not been usually identified as a "Jewish" filmmaker or playwright. In his chapter, Donald Weber explores the meaning—and limits—of Leigh's representation of "Jewishness" in *Two Thousand Years* in light of a long habit of reticence, of self-consciousness among British Jewish writers, what the novelist Howard Jacobson calls the "stay schtum" tradition in British Jewish experience. Despite Leigh's apparent participation in what has been termed a British Jewish cultural-expressive revival in contemporary U.K. letters, Weber argues that Leigh's deeper, indeed more richly imagined, *Jewish* work is his 1996 film *Secrets and Lies*, a film about lost souls searching for family ties, roots, and some mode of heart-needy connection in a topsy-turvy multicultural Britain.[60]

Ultimately, Weber argues, Leigh's famously self-proclaimed "Talmudic" style of theater and filmmaking ("to raise questions and posit possibilities," in his own words) is more provocatively on display in *Secrets and Lies*. By the end of the movie, all the characters achieve what Weber calls a position of "Jewish" empathy, the ability to feel the hidden pain of others. "This is the life, ain't it?" exclaims Cynthia (played by Brenda Blethyn), gazing with (Jewish?) motherly pride upon her two daughters, one black and middle class, one white and defiantly working class, amid the tacky residue of her East End backyard, in a scene filled with Leigh's warmhearted signature blend of "Jewish" pathos and irony. In its curious restraint in exploring Jewish faith identity, *Two Thousand Years* remains Leigh's *British* Jewish play; in its deeply felt, empathic gestures and Jewish allusions (autobiographical and linguistic), *Secrets and Lies*, he concludes, is Leigh's more profoundly *Jewish* work. While Weber focuses on *Secrets and Lies* and *Two Thousand Years*, his approach could productively be applied to the entire corpus of Leigh's work, even those pieces that do not immediately present themselves as Jewish on the surface.

Leigh was taking advantage of a sea change in British Jewish confidence that had occurred in the early 1990s which marked a period of unprecedented postassimilatory Jewish confidence. Beginning with *Leon the Pig Farmer* (1992), discussed by Claudia Sternberg in her chapter, a wave of new British Jewish films emerged, mingling with films and television programs about other migrant and diasporic groups, in particular African Caribbean and subcontinental Asians, and their experiences in Britain, which — crucially — proved commercially attractive.[61] About two dozen Jewish-directed and/or Jewish-authored British feature films have been produced since the early 1990s and constitute part of a wider international surge and diversification of diasporic and Israeli Jewish cinema. Yet, at the same time, "continuity" became the keyword of the communal agenda as set out by the then chief rabbi, Jonathan Sacks, in 1993. The decline in numbers since the end of World War II, which saw a decrease of British Jewry by almost a third, shocked the Jewish establishment into fearing for the very survival of the U.K. Jewish community itself. Although mainland Britain had not been directly touched by the Holocaust, fear of the eradication of British Jewry through exogamy — intermarriage or "marrying out" — was considered to be (and still is for some) a clear and present danger. British Jewish film production reflected these fears, particularly in three films that, in their different ways, treated the issues of fertility, infertility, adoption, and interethnic dating.

Sternberg's chapter offers a critical reading of two British Jewish film comedies, *Leon the Pig Farmer* and *The Infidel* (2010),[62] both of which focus on protagonists whose ethnic identities have been "compromised" by donor insemination or adoption. In the former, the titular Leon Geller (played by Mark Frankel) discovers that his biological father is a Yorkshire pig farmer who is not Jewish, while in the latter, a Muslim finds out that he is adopted and that his parents were Jewish. Sternberg locates these comedies in a context of the late twentieth and early twenty-first centuries in Britain, in which the cultural implications of assisted reproduction have repeatedly occupied politicians, theologians, legislators, theorists, and the popular media. In the same period, ethnic diversity and multiculturalism have been celebrated as well as contested, and many narratives of identity formation and "belonging" have been produced against this backdrop. Sternberg discusses the filmmakers' humorous take on anxieties associated with Jewish genealogy, kinship, and masculinity and explores how the screen narratives respond to concerns about community survival after the Holocaust and in contemporary societies of "choice." Her analysis is situated within the wider context of migration and diasporas in Britain and the production of British Jewish films in the 1990s and the new millennium.

Meanwhile, Michele Byers's chapter examines the film *Suzie Gold* (2004), the eponymous protagonist of which is faced with the dilemma of marrying the seemingly "perfect" Jewish bachelor who will make her parents happy or the non-Jewish colleague who will make her happy.[63] Suzie's choice is located in a Jewish world that is imagined as different and socially and culturally separated from other parts of British society, and the film links that space of difference more explicitly to the experience of antisemitism, diaspora, and displacement that are a legacy of World War II. Byers explores the choices the filmmakers made in foregrounding experiences of Jewish difference and antisemitism in Britain and what this tells us about post-Holocaust British Jewish identity today.

Suzie Gold was made at a time when British Jewish culture was flourishing, a condition that was ongoing at the time of this book's publication. It is apparent in relation to prize-winning novels, such as Linda Grant's *When I Lived in Modern Times*, winner of the Orange Prize in 2000, and Howard Jacobson's *The Finkler Question*, which was awarded the Booker Prize in 2010; to the increasing popularity of such annual festivals as the Jewish Book Week and the U.K. Jewish Film Festival; to the institution of Jewish Studies courses at university level; and to the setting up of the annual U.K. Holocaust Memorial Day in 2001. As suggested by the title of the periodical *Jewish Renaissance*, launched in 2001, all of these achievements point to a new confidence and visibility among British Jews. This visibility also includes the annual Limmud conference, held in England, which attracts between two thousand and three thousand participants from around the world every year; various cultural organizations, art galleries, and the expansion of the Jewish Museum in London; and, finally and most recently, the setting up of JW3—a new Jewish Community Center for London in the fall of 2013. The year 2006 commemorated 350 years of continuous Jewish history in Britain since Jews were allowed to return following their expulsion in 1290. It was marked with scores of events, panels, and exhibitions to which even the then prime minister, Tony Blair, was invited and spoke.

The televisual element of this renaissance of British Jewish activity has included episodes of reality television as well as drama and comedy.

Sue Vice's chapter considers two contemporary British situation comedies in relation to their representation of Jews and Judaism. These are Jason Cook's *Hebburn* (2012) and Robert Popper's *Friday Night Dinner* (2011–).[64] In the former, the non-Jewish protagonist brings his Jewish wife to live with his Catholic family, while in the latter the eccentric Jewish Goodman family come together once a week for the eponymous meal, to the fascination of their non-Jewish neighbor. Vice explores the ways in which Jewish characters and Jewish religious and cultural practices are presented, in terms suggested by the notion of a British "emancipation contract," by which means the host nation's tolerance is won at the price of Jewish assimilation. While this has the effect in *Hebburn* that the customary sitcom staples of class and social discord come to replace comedy on the theme of gentile responses to Jews, *Friday Night Dinner* acts more subversively to present a Jewish view of British Christian life.

The book, in taking a chronological approach, concludes with Nir Cohen's chapter on a remarkable television drama serial broadcast in Britain in early 2011. Peter Kosminsky's *The Promise* is perhaps the first major non-Israeli fictional intervention into the ongoing Israeli–Palestinian conflict, dealing with the sensitive issue of Britain's historical responsibility in laying ground for it.[65] *The Promise* is particularly notable for emanating from the United Kingdom, a country which is currently being branded as the capital of the worldwide campaign to delegitimize Israel. Furthermore, since British Jewish film and television have hitherto avoided tackling this thorny issue head-on (the brief, tame references in *The Infidel* cannot be counted in this respect), it is remarkable that a British Jew produced this project. Indeed, *The Promise* created a heated and polarizing public debate in Britain when it was first aired. Initially offered to the BBC, it was eventually commissioned by and broadcast on Channel 4, a publicly owned but mostly commercially self-funded British television broadcaster with a reputation for innovation (it also produced *Friday Night Dinner*). While Cohen cites Kosminsky denying that the BBC "bottled it"—that is, it suffered from a failure of nerve—it would have been highly controversial if the state broadcaster, which is already accused of anti-Israel bias by elements of the British Jewish community, had decided to produce and air this particular series.

In his chapter, Cohen shows how Kosminsky uses two parallel yet intertwined narratives, in which the device of love and romance produces a system of surveillance but in which true love and affection are conspicuously absent. Kosminsky's vision of Israel and Palestine both in the 1940s and in 2005 is one in which the concept of love is often marred by violence and undermined by a national cause, and the only attachment allowed is that of a man to his land. Cohen also considers the portrayal of the British mandate, its role in the Israel–Palestine conflict, and the way it is remembered in modern-day Britain. Such an examination adds a much-needed dimension to the on-screen representation of Israel, particularly given how, in Britain, the topic is typically confined to nonfiction and documentary when shown on television.

The Future

This volume neither claims nor achieves comprehensive coverage, and there is still a long way to go. Some of the topics in this book are fairly well known while others have received little to no academic attention hitherto. Admittedly, there is an emphasis on fiction film and television rather than nonfiction in the volume. British Jewish women as producers, screenwriters, and/or directors are, unfortunately, not so much in evidence here, either, simply for reasons of space—something which should be rectified by future scholarship. Scholars should look at Sandra Goldbacher, Sara Sugarman, or the creators of *Suzie Gold*. Documentary, docudrama, and reality television (for example, Alan Sugar in the British version of *The Apprentice*) are still all up for grabs.[66] One could explore Robert Vas's important documentary *The Vanishing Street* about the Jewish community in the East End of London as a complement to those series that depict a fictional representation of the decline of that community.[67]

Given the extent and volume of Jews and Jewishness in British film and television, any collection on this topic can inevitably provide only a snapshot. *Hidden in Plain Sight: Jews and Jewishness in British Film, Television, and Popular Culture* is conceived as only the beginning, as there is so much more to be studied: individual films and programs, actors, directors and their oeuvres, production personnel, and executives. One example from cinema might be the writer Harold Pinter, author of innumerable screenplays (and even an occasional actor in films). Pinter's "hidden" identity as a Jew is no less significant than Leigh's. Other significant figures are Peter Sellers and his contemporary incarnation, Sacha Baron Cohen, both of whom crossed over from radio and television, respectively, into film. As Ali G in the immensely popular and influential *Da Ali G Show*, Cohen certainly represents a "hidden presence" as a Jew behind that series.[68] So, too, his "hidden presence" as a Jew is tremendously important to how the audience receives the antisemitic comic rants of the title character in the film *Borat* (a creation imported from the television program).[69] Many people on both sides of the Atlantic are more than familiar with Cohen's work. That list does not even include exploring the Jewish possibilities of texts that are not even explicitly Jewish but which may be read as such, including the *Carry On* franchise or James Bond and *Doctor Who* (both of which celebrated their fiftieth anniversaries in 2012 and 2013, respectively), and benefited from significant Jewish input.[70] It is with this goal in mind that I hope that when the next volume on this subject is written, we no longer need to deploy the term "hidden."

Notes

1. *The Governess*, directed by Sandra Goldbacher (London: British Broadcasting Corporation [BBC], 1998); (Culver City, CA: Sony Pictures Home Entertainment, 1999), DVD. See, for example, Lynette Felber, "Capturing the Shadows of Ghosts: Mixed Media and the Female Gaze in *The Women on the Roof* and *The Governess*," *Film Quarterly* 54, no. 4 (2001): 27–37; Antje Ascheid, "Safe Rebellions: Romantic Emancipation in the 'Woman's Heritage Film,'" *Scope: An Online Journal of Film Studies* 4 (2006), http://www.scope.nottingham.ac.uk/article.php?issue=4&id=124; Judith Lewin, "Semen, Semolina and Salt Water: The Erotic Jewess in Sandra Goldbacher's *The Governess*," in *Jews and Sex*, edited by Nathan Abrams, 88–100 (Nottingham, UK: Five Leaves, 2008); Helene Meyers, "Educating for a Jewish Gaze: The Close Doubling of Antisemitism and Philosemitism in Sandra Goldbacher's *The Governess*," in *Antisemitism and Philosemitism in the Twentieth and Twenty-first Centuries: Representing Jews, Jewishness, and Modern*, edited by Phyllis Lassner and Lara Trubowitz, 103–18 (Newark: University of Delaware Press, 2008).

2. A more recent example is Tony Kushner and Hannah Ewence, eds., *Whatever Happened to British Jewish Studies?* (London.: Vallentine Mitchell, 2012), which, in its section on culture, completely omits film and cinema (although there is some consideration of television).

3. Nathan Abrams, "Hidden: Jewish Film in the United Kingdom, Past and Present," *Journal of European Popular Culture* 1, no. 1 (2010): 53–68.

4. "Jews in British Cinema," special issue of the *Journal of European Popular Culture* 3, no. 2 (2012).

5. Annette Insdorf, *Indelible Shadows: Film and the Holocaust* (Cambridge: Cambridge University Press, 2003).

6. *Sixty Years a Queen*, directed by Bert Haldane (London: Barker, 1913).

7. *The Private Life of Henry VIII*, directed by Alexander Korda (London: London Film Productions, 1933).

8. Charles Drazin, *Korda: Britain's Only Movie Mogul* (London: Sidgwick and Jackson, 2002).

9. Judith N. Goldberg, *Laughter through Tears: The Yiddish Cinema* (London: Associated University Presses, 1983), 17.

10. Gil Toffell, "'Come See, and Hear, the Mother Tongue!' Yiddish Cinema in Interwar London," *Screen* 50, no.3 (Autumn 2009): 227–98.

11. No details are available for this film.

12. *The Alien Question*, directed by Alf Collins (London: Gaumont-British Picture Corporation, 1905); *The Aliens' Invasion* (London: Hepworth, 1905).

13. "*The Alien Question*," *IMDb*, accessed October 16, 2015, http://www.imdb.com/title/tt0486257/?ref_=fn_al_tt_1; "*The Aliens' Invasion*," *IMDb*, accessed October 16, 2015, http://www.imdb.com/title/tt2011272/?ref_=fn_al_tt_7.

14. *The Invaders*, directed by Percy Stow (London: Clarendon Film Company, 1909).

15. *The Robber and the Jew*, directed by Jack Smith (London: Robert W. Paul, 1908); *A Bad Day for Levinsky*, directed by T. J. Gobbett (London: T. J. Gobbett, 1909); *The Antique Vase*, directed by H. O. Martinek (London: British and Colonial Kinematograph Company, 1913).

16. Quoted in Patricia Erens, *The Jew in American Cinema* (Bloomington: Indiana University Press, 1984), 35.

17. *Oliver Twist*, directed by J. Stuart Blackton (New York: Vitagraph, 1907); *Oliver Twist*, directed by J. Stuart Blackton (New York: Vitagraph, 1909); *L'enfance d'Oliver Twist/Oliver Twist*, directed by Camille de Morlhon (Paris: Pathé, 1910); *Oliver Twist*, directed by unknown (New York: General Film Publicity and Sales, 1912); *Oliver Twist*, directed by Thomas Bentley (London: Hepworth 1912); *Oliver Twist*, directed by James Young (Los Angeles: Paramount, 1916); *Twist Olivér/Oliver Twist*, directed by Márton Garas (Budapest: Corvin Film, 1919).

18. *Le Miroir de Venise (Une Mésaventure de Shylock)/Venetian Looking Glass* was possibly the first film to be based on *The Merchant of Venice*, but since it is lost, this cannot be confirmed. See "*Miroir de Venise (Une Mésaventure de Shylock), Le*," *British Universities Film and Video Council*, accessed October 18, 2015, http://bufvc.ac.uk/shakespeare/index.php/title/av72472; *The Merchant of Venice*, directed by J. Stuart Blackton (New York: Vitagraph, 1908); *The Merchant of Venice*, directed by Barry O'Neil (New York: Thanhouser, 1912); *The Merchant of Venice*, directed by Philipps Smalley and Lois Weber (Los Angeles: Universal, 1914); *The Merchant of Venice*, directed by Gerolamo Lo Savio (Rome: Film d'Arte Italiana, 1911) [also known as *Der Kaufmann von Venedig* (Austria / Germany), *Shyloch, ó el mercador de Venecia* (Spain), *Shylock, ou le marchand de Venise* (France), and *The Merchant of Venice* (UK)]; *The Merchant of Venice* directed by Henri Desfontaines (Paris: Pathé, 1913); *The Merchant of Venice*, directed by J. Walter West (London: Broadwest Film Company, 1916); *The Merchant of Venice*, directed by J. Anson Dyer (London: Hepworth Picture Plays, 1919).

19. *Tense Moments from Great Plays*, directed by Edwin J. Collins, H. B. Parkinson, Challis Sanderson, and George Wynn (London: Master Film Company, 1922).

20. *Ivanhoe*, directed by J. Stuart Blackton (New York: Vitagraph, 1911); *Ivanhoe*, directed by Leedham Bantock (London: Zenith, 1913); *Ivanhoe*, directed by Herbert Brenon (Los Angeles: Universal / Independent Moving Pictures Co. of America, 1913). *Trilby*, directed by Maurice Tourneur (Fort Lee, N.J.: Equitable-World, 1915); *Trilby*, directed by Maurice Tourneur (Fort Lee, N.J.: Equitable-World, 1917).

21. *A Female Fagin*, director unknown (New York: Kalem, 1913); *Gwendolyn, the Sewing Machine Girl*, director unknown (New York: Biograph, 1914). More detail on these adaptations can be found in Erens, *Jew in American Cinema*, 68–70.

22. *Oliver Twist, Jr.*, directed by Millard Webb (Los Angeles: Fox, 1921).; *Oliver Twist*, directed by Frank Lloyd (Los Angeles: Jackie Coogan Productions, 1922); *Oliver Twist*, directed by William Cowan (Los Angeles, Monogram, 1933); *The Merchant of Venice*, directed by Widgey R. Newman (New York: DeForest Phonofilms, 1927) [its presentation of Shylock's "Hath not a Jew eyes?" speech was the world's first Shakespeare film with synchronized sound]; *Trilby*, directed by James Young (New York: Richard Walton Tully Productions, 1923); *Svengali*, directed by Archie Mayo (Burbank: Warner Brothers, 1931).

23. *General Post*, directed by Thomas Bentley (London: Ideal Film Company, 1920); *Disraeli*, directed by Charles Calvert and Percy Nash (London: NB Films, 1916); *Disraeli*, directed by Henry Kolker (New York: Distinctive Productions, 1921); *Disraeli*, directed by Alfred E. Green (Burbank: Warner Brothers, 1929); *Daniel Deronda*, directed by W. Courtney Rowden (London: Master Films, 1921); *The Wandering Jew*, directed by Maurice Elvey (London: Stoll Film Company, 1923); *The Wandering Jew*, directed by Maurice Elvey (London: Twickenham Film Studios, 1933); *Motherland*, directed by G. B. Samuelson (London: Reciprocity Films, 1927); *Loyalties*, directed by Basil Dean (London: Associated Talking Pictures, 1933); *Jew Süss*, directed by Lothar Mendes (London: Gaumont-British, 1934); *Mr. Cohen Takes a Walk*, directed by William Beaudine (London: Warner Brothers-First National Productions, 1935); *Car of Dreams*, directed by Graham Cutts and Austin Melford (London: Gaumont-British, 1935).

24. Lester Friedman, *Hollywood's Image of the Jew* (New York: Ungar, 1982), 11–12. See also Tony Kushner, "One of Us? Contesting Disraeli's Jewishness and Englishness in the Twentieth Century," in *Disraeli's Jewishness*, edited by Todd M. Endelman and Tony Kushner, 201–61; esp. 231–32 (London: Vallentine Mitchell, 2002).

25. Tobias Hochscherf, *The Continental Connection: German-Speaking Emigres and British Cinema, 1927–1945* (Manchester, UK: Manchester University Press, 2011), 118.

26. Jan Epstein, "Jewish Representation," in *The Encyclopedia of British Film*, edited by Brian McFarlane and Anthony Slide, 366 (London: BFI/Methuen, 2005).

27. Hochscherf, *Continental Connection*. .

28. Kevin Gough-Yates, "Jews and Exiles in British Cinema," *Leo Baeck Institute Year Book* 37 (1992): 517–41, at 518.

29. See Hochscherf, *Continental Connection* and Tim Bergfelder and Christian Cargnelli, eds., *Destination London: German-Speaking Emigres and British Cinema, 1925–1950* (New York: Berghahn, 2008). Although this has been explored by Hochscherf and Bergfelder et al., since their focus was on German-speaking émigré filmmakers in British cinema, the specific Jewish dimension was not explored to a significant extent.

30. Martin Jolles, "Jews and the BBC (1922–1953)," *JHSE Newsletter* 10 (May2004): 3–4, http://www.jtrails.org.uk/trails/Miscellaneous/articles/c-244/jews-and-the-british-broadcasting-corporation-1922–1953/.

31. Andrew Spicer, "A British Empire of Their Own? Jewish Entrepreneurs in the British Film Industry," *Journal of European Popular Culture* 3, no. 2 (2012): 117–29, at 122.

32. Graham Greene, *Spectator*, April 7, 1939, cited in *New York Review of Books*, September 21, 1995, http://www.nybooks.com/articles/archives/1995/sep/21/greene-anti-semitism/?pagination=false.

33. *The Mortal Storm*, directed by Frank Borzage (Los Angeles: MGM, 1940).

34. *Mr. Emmanuel*, directed by Harold French (London: Two Cities Films, 1944).

35. Epstein, "Jewish Representation," 366.

36. *The Rake's Progress*, directed by Sidney Gilliat (London: Rank, 1945) [in the United States, the title was changed to *Notorious Gentlemen*]; *It Always Rains on Sunday*, directed by Robert Hamer (London: Ealing Studios, 1947); *Ivanhoe*, directed by Richard Thorpe (Los Angeles: MGM, 1952) [there was also a TV series of the same name in 1958 (London: ITV), starring Roger Moore]; *Make Me an Offer!* directed by Cyril Frankel (London: Group 3, 1954); *A Kid for Two Farthings*, directed by Carol Read (London: London Films, 1954); *The Bespoke Overcoat*, directed by Jack Clayton (London: Warner Brothers, 1955); *Expresso Bongo*, directed by Val Guest (London: Val Guest Productions, 1959).

37. *Oliver Twist*, directed by David Lean (London: Rank, 1948); *Svengali*, directed by Noel Langley (London: George Minter Productions, 1955).

38. Margaret Stetz, "The Hate That Dared Not Speak Its Name: *Svengali*, Anti-Semitism, and Postwar British Heritage Cinema," *Journal of European Popular Culture* 3, no. 2 (2012): 155–67, at 163.

39. Margaret Stetz points out how these British productions compared unfavorably to those across the Atlantic in which the original Victorian offensive and antisemitic elements were excised by Hollywood directors and screenwriters who, more often than not, were likely to be Jewish (ibid., 157).

40. James Jordan, "Assimilated, Integrated, Other: An Introduction to Jews and British Television, 1946–55," *Jewish Culture and History* 12, nos. 1–2 (2010): 251–66.

41. See James Jordan, "What We Have Gained Is Infinitely More than That Small Loss: Rudolph Cartier and *The Dybbuk*," *Jewish Culture and History* 11, no. 1–2 (2010): 156–71.

42. David Herman, "Great Channel Swimmers," *Jewish Chronicle*, March 3, 2006, 27.

43. See "Television and Radio," in *Encyclopaedia Judaica*, 2nd ed., vol. 19, edited by Michael Berenbaum and Fred Skolnik, 594–96 (Detroit: Macmillan Reference, 2007).

44. *Peeping Tom*, directed by Michael Powell (London: Anglo-Amalgamated, 1960).

45. *Psycho*, directed by Alfred Hitchcock (Los Angeles: Shamley Productions, 1960); Nathan Abrams, "The 'Sub-epidermic' Shoah: *Barton Fink*, the Migration of the Holocaust, and Contemporary Cinema," *POST SCRIPT: Essays in Film and the Humanities* 32, no. 2 (Winter/Spring 2013): 6–19.

46. Herman, "Great Channel Swimmers," 27.

47. Ibid.

48. Ibid.

49. Epstein, "Jewish Representation," 366.

50. *Hand in Hand*, directed by Philip Leacock (London: Warner-Pathé, 1960); *Conspiracy of Hearts*, directed by Ralph Thomas (London: Rank, 1960); *Sparrows Can't Sing*, directed by Joan Littlewood (London: Carthage Films, 1963); *The Barber of Stamford Hill*, directed by Caspar Wrede (London: Ben Arbeid Productions, 1963); *Reach for Glory*, directed by Philip Leacock (London: Blazer Films, 1963); *The Spy Who Came In from the Cold*, directed by Martin Ritt (Los Angeles: Salem Films Limited, Paramount, 1965); *The Deadly Affair*, directed by Sidney Lumet (Los Angeles: Sidney Lumet Productions, 1966); *Ulysses*, directed by Joseph Strick (London: British Lion Films, 1967); *The Fearless Vampire Killers*, directed by Roman Polanski (Los Angeles: MGM, 1967); *Oliver!* directed by Carol Reed (Los Angeles: Columbia, 1968).

51. *Oliver Twist*, directed by Roman Polanski (Paris: R. P. Productions, 2005).

52. *Sunday Bloody Sunday*, directed by John Schlesinger (Los Angeles: Vectia / United Artists, 1971).

53. Quotation in Epstein, "Jewish Representation," 366.

54. *The Odessa File*, directed by Ronald Neame (Los Angeles: Columbia, 1974); *Voyage of the Damned*, directed by Stuart Rosenberg (Los Angeles: Avco Embassy, 1976); *Monty Python's Life of Brian*, directed by Terry Jones (Burbank: Warner Brothers-Orion, 1979).

55. *The Evacuees*, directed by Alan Parker (London: BBC, 1975); *Bar Mitzvah Boy*, directed by Michael Tuchner (London: BBC, 1977); *Grandma's House* for BBC TV (London: Tiger Aspect Productions, 2010 and 2012).

56. *An American Werewolf in London*, directed by John Landis (Los Angeles: Universal, 1981).

57. *Chariots of Fire*, directed by Hugh Hudson (London: Enigma Productions, 1981). For essays exploring the Jewishness of *Chariots of Fire*, see Nathan Abrams, "The Jew in the Gym: Judaism, Sports, and Athletics on Film," in *Jews in the Gym: Judaism, Sports, and Athletics*, ed. Leonard J. Greenspoon, 53–64 (West Lafayette, Ind.: Purdue University Press, 2012); Ellis Cashmore, "*Chariots of Fire*: Bigotry, Manhood and Moral Certitude in an Age of Individualism," *Sport in Society*, 11, nos. 2–3 (2008): 159–73.

58. *Escape from Sobibor*, directed by Jack Gold (New York: CBS, 1987).

59. *Forbidden*, directed by Anthony Page (London: Anthea Films, 1984).

60. *Leon the Pig Farmer*, directed by Vadim Jean and Gary Sinyor (London: Leon the Pig Farmer Plc, 1992).

61. *The Infidel*, directed by Josh Appignanesi (London: Infidel Films Limited, Slingshot, Met Film Ombudsman; developed in association with BBC Films), 2010.

62. *Suzie Gold*, directed by Ric Cantor (London: Green Wolf Films, 2004).

63. *Secrets and Lies*, directed by Mike Leigh (London: Thin Man Films, 1996).

64. *Hebburn*, directed by Christine Gernon (London: Baby Cow Productions, BBC Two, 2012); *Friday Night Dinner*, directed by Steve Bendelack and Martin Dennis (London: Popper Pictures/Big Talk Productions, Channel 4, 2011–2012).

65. *The Promise*, directed by Peter Kosminsky (London: Daybreak Pictures/Stonehenge Films, Lama Films; London: Channel 4 Television, 2011).

66. *The Apprentice*, (London: BBC, 2005–).

67. *The Vanishing Street*, directed by Robert Vas (London: BFI, 1962).

68. *Da Ali G Show* (London: Channel 4 Television, 2000–2004).

69. *Borat: Cultural Learnings of America for Make Benefit Glorious Nation of Kazakhstan*, directed by Larry Charles (London: Four By Two Productions, 2006).

70. For suggestive essays on some of these topics, see James Jordan, "The Wandering Who," *Jewish Quarterly* (Autumn/Winter 2013): 71–74; Nathan Abrams, "Is Doctor Who a Jew?" *Ha'aretz.com*, November 25, 2013, http://www.haaretz.com/israel-news/culture/leisure/.premium-1.560029; Nathan Abrams, "The Name's Bond. Ya'akov Bond," *Ha'aretz.com*, November 22, 2012, http://www.haaretz.com/jewish-world/jewish-world-features/the-name-s-bond-ya-akov-bond.premium-1.479770.

GIL TOFFELL

"Awaiting, with Some Anxiety"
The Jewish Response to Jew Süss *(1934) in 1930s Britain*

On a balmy June evening during the summer of 1938, Joe Louis—the world heavyweight boxing champion—stepped into the ring in the middle of a crammed Yankee Stadium and pummeled his archenemy, the German hero Max Schmeling, into submission in little more than two minutes. Famously, many of Louis's most devoted fans were Jewish, and listening on radios across the globe, they rejoiced. Schmeling had been feted by the Nazi Party, while the African American Louis was promoted as democracy's representative. With the clash-of-ideologies backstory and the explosive nature of the bout, distributors had little trouble selling the international rights to the film of the fight, and it was on British screens by early July. One of the most enthusiastic reviews was published in the *Jewish Chronicle*. As well as describing the piece as a "thrilling film," the politics of the event were made clearly evident. With Louis seen hammering his opponent "with blows that must agonise any Schmeling worshiping Nazi," readers were assured that the film "will be banned in Germany."[1]

While the Louis–Schmeling fight may be a major event in boxing history, the thirteen-minute film of the action has become—at best—a footnote in film history. For contemporary British Jewish visitors to the cinema, however, this footage offered something all too rare on British screens: an image of Nazism as a force that could be defeated. From 1933 to 1939, the British Board of Film Censors (BBFC) worked hard to ensure amicable relations with foreign nations. As such, in Britain, the most culturally significant mass communications medium of the era — the cinema — would remain remarkably free of denunciations of Hitler's regime right up to the outbreak of war. In a world in which cinematic crumbs such as the film of the Louis–Schmeling fight were seized upon for their anti-Nazi content, it thus seems remarkable that only a few years earlier what was reported as the most expensive film in British production history offered something of a critique of Nazi antisemitism.

In October 1934, the Gaumont-British Picture Corporation released *Jew Süss*, a historical tragedy starring Conrad Veidt as the eighteenth-century Stuttgart "court Jew" Joseph Süß Oppenheimer. As Jeffrey Richards asserts, during the early 1930s Gaumont-British had been determined to produce a film denouncing antisemitism.[2] Indeed, BBFC scenario reports record the company submitting two synopses overtly critical of political antisemitism for assessment by the censor in mid-1933. *A German Tragedy* narrated the ostracism of a brilliant Jewish doctor from German society following the imposition of Nazi legislation, while *City without Jews* explored the devastating cultural and economic consequences that befall a fictional contemporary Austria when the country's Jews face banishment. Both synopses were rejected by the BBFC as political propaganda, with fears raised that *A German Tragedy* "might easily provoke a disturbance"[3] given the strength of public feeling in regard to recent events in Germany.

Refusing to drop its commitment to putting out a feature dealing with the persecution of Jews, Gaumont-British submitted the scenario for *Jew Süss* to the BBFC in November 1933. Based on Lion Feuchtwanger's best-selling 1925 novel *Jud Süß* and having had a successful run in London as a 1929 stage production, it seems likely that its status as legitimate culture — together with its historical setting — helped protect the script from the censor's knife. Mainly concerned with toning down assorted expressions of sexual desire deemed too direct, the BBFC recommended only minimal amendments,[4] and the film went into production in early 1934 with the full financial weight of the company behind it. When completed, *Jew Süss* boasted a first-rate cast, finely detailed sets, and lavish costumes. With such production values, the film was guaranteed to attract significant critical attention, and every section of the British press — national, trade, local — devoted column space to reviews or photographic stills of notable scenes. Although notices were not uniformly gushing, many were extremely positive. Writing in the *Evening Standard*, a young John Betjeman declared it "undoubtedly the best film of the week" and praised Veidt's "outstanding performance."[5] Some of the most complimentary comments came in the Jewish press.[6] For the *Jewish Times* the piece was "one of the grandest films ever to be created,"[7] while the *Jewish Chronicle* labeled it "A Stupendous Production."[8]

For British Jews living during the interwar period, the significance of the exhibition of *Jew Süss* should not be underestimated. At that moment, Jewish communal concerns pertaining to the Nazi persecution of Jews and the turn to antisemitism by Oswald Mosley's British Union of Fascists might achieve sympathetic recognition on the national stage as a generalized non-Jewish public gained a deeper understanding of the victimization of Jews. Complicating any Jewish reception of the film, though, was the widely articulated contemporary stereotype that cinema was a Jewish monopoly. If *Jew Süss* were read as a tendentious promotion of particularist interests, it would fail the most elementary test of individualistic liberalism: universal relevance. A Jewish preoccupation with the non-Jewish majority's view of the film should thus be understood as integral to any assessment of its Jewish reception. Such concerns were clearly apparent in the output of the Jewish press, and unease with the film's potential status as propaganda was a notable feature of the discourse assessing it. To be sensitized to this minority orientation to majority opinion not only offers an understanding of the discursive context in which the consumption of *Jew Süss* took place but also provides an insight into what can be referred to as a British Jewish interwar "structure of feeling."

A Rare Moment of Criticism

As in Feuchtwanger's novel, the movie *Jew Süss* portrays the ascendancy, and brutal fall, of Joseph Süss Oppenheimer in the Württemberg court of Duke Karl Alexander. The story begins with Süss confessing his hunger for power to his loyal friend Landauer, explaining his desire to secure respect not just for himself but for all Jews. The opportunity for advancement soon presents itself when Süss ingratiates himself with Alexander through a gambling loan, and he quickly becomes incorporated into the duke's household. Proving himself an indispensable servant, Süss rises to the point where he is able to secure the release of a poor ghetto Jew falsely accused of ritual murder. However, this charmed existence is not fated to last, and following the death of his daughter Naomi — who falls from a high roof while attempting to escape the advances of the lascivious duke — Süss plots the duke's ruin. Although successful in his plan to sabotage the duke's attempts to do away with the Diet and grasp absolute rule, Süss becomes scapegoated during the inquiry into the affair and dies a tragic hero, reciting the Shema on the execution scaffold.

With eighteenth-century Württemberg as the film's setting, it is unsurprising that no direct reference to Hitler is made throughout. An absence of references to Nazism notwithstanding, the piece is described by Rachael Low as "loaded with obscure significance,"[9] and textual allusion to the contemporary position of German Jews is apparent at several moments, albeit delivered at an oblique angle. During the film's opening, a title card reads, "It was a time of universal intolerance and the Jews above all suffered oppression and boycott." As Susan Tegel has noted, the boycott was very much a tactic of Nazi antisemitism rather than earlier varieties,[10] and the embargo of Jewish shops in Germany had received significant attention in the British news media in the spring of 1933.[11] Further title cards refer to the unfinished nature of Süss's efforts in breaking down the ghetto walls, stating "his story lives." Perhaps most pointed is a sequence of dialogue between Süss and Landauer. Dismissing his friend's report of anti-Jewish persecution, Süss asserts, "Ach! Old fables . . . we are now in 1730!" To which Landauer responds, "They can do it in 1730, they can do it in 1830, they can do it in 1930!"

To what extent the import of such references was readily decoded, or proved too subtle for contemporary viewers, is now impossible to judge. What is clear is that both the mainstream and British Jewish press positioned the film as inevitably located within the context of the mounting crisis in Germany. Although mention of Nazism was provided in only a minority of reviews in mainstream British news sources, its relevance to *Jew Süss* was unambiguously stated. The *Observer* referred to the "present political situation in Germany" in its review, while the *Spectator* claimed, "But for Hitlerism, this film would perhaps, never have been made."[12] Interestingly, parallels with contemporary events were offered somewhat guardedly in appraisals of *Jew Süss* in the Jewish press. The *Jewish Times* gave some details about the persecution suffered by Feuchtwanger in Germany, while the *Jewish Chronicle* made reference to the film's "valuable lessons."[13] *Jew Süss*, it was claimed, "lays bare certain foundations of modern European popular opinion on which have been built the Jew hatred that we know today."[14] Why Germany was not singled out is ultimately unknowable, but, as we will see, much coverage of the film in the Jewish press was marked by a clear hesitancy.

It is somewhat paradoxical that some of the clearest discursive associations of *Jew Süss* with Nazi antisemitism came into being through accounts of its censorship in Austria. Shortly after its release in London, the film exhibited in Vienna. Quickly arousing the ire of both Roman Catholic groups and Austrian Nazis, it was removed a mere six days after its opening. Again, only a minority of British mainstream newspapers covered this development. The *Daily Mail* ran a few lines noting the proscription, though it was attributed only to Catholic disapproval.[15] The *Manchester Guardian* was somewhat more expansive, stating that there had been "considerable propaganda" directed against the film from "both Nazi and Clerical [*sic*] sources."[16] Also covering the story was the Jewish press. The *Jewish Chronicle* recorded the involvement of various reactionary groups — including National Socialists — and remarked on the irony of the situation, given the trouble Austrian distributors were having in getting their films shown in Germany,[17] while the *Jewish Times* added that the "scene in which Jew Suss is executed particularly provoked antisemitic demonstrations."[18]

Jewish Interest in *Jew Süss*

That the Jewish press was keeping a close eye on *Jew Süss* is not a surprise. Emerging in the 1910s and continuing through the 1920s and into the 1930s, a diverse Jewish cinema culture had developed in Britain. Yiddish-language film, Zionist film, and the ethnic romances and comedies that Hollywood produced, such as *The Cohens and the Kellys* and *His People*, were part of the Jewish leisure landscape during the period.[19] Tracking the production details of upcoming titles was a common feature of the entertainment pages of Jewish newspapers, and *Jew Süss* was subject to comment well before it reached cinema screens. In early 1934 the *Jewish World* reported on production developments and set design, noting "a complete replica of the Ghetto of Frankfort [*sic*] has been built."[20] The *Jewish Chronicle*'s interest went back even further. In 1928 the paper was reporting that film rights had been sold to Louis Blattner and that an anticipated production was expected to cost one hundred thousand pounds.[21] Following the passing on of rights to Gaumont-British, the same publication listed the film as the first item in a piece on upcoming titles in 1934. Addressing the reader as a distinctly Jewish consumer, it was stated that "Jewish patrons of the cinema will assuredly be intrigued by 'Jew Suss,' which is announced to be released in the autumn."[22]

Upon the film's release it was not only the Jewish press that believed Jews would be interested in the picture. Those areas of the film industry dedicated to marketing and exhibition clearly felt that there was a significant Jewish audience for *Jew Süss*. Both the *Jewish Chronicle* and the *Jewish Times* featured large pictorial advertisements announcing the film's exhibition at the West End's Tivoli Cinema. Three months after opening in central London, the film moved to local screens and the provinces, and it was again advertised in Jewish newspapers. In the *Jewish Times* one ad carried copy declaring that the film had been "praised in two continents," featured choice reviews — translated into Yiddish — from both London and New York–based newspapers, and listed the picture houses at which the film was screening.[23] The list of local cinemas exhibiting *Jew Süss* is itself instructional. Of the six at which it appeared in London, four were in neighborhoods with significant Jewish populations (Whitechapel, Stamford Hill, Dalston, and Hendon). The *Jewish Chronicle* also carried an advertisement for the screening of the film at Manchester's Piccadilly Cinema.[24] Only occasionally did a provincial cinema advertise in the paper, and when one did, it was inevitably to give notice of a production of particular interest to Jews.

It is perhaps worth dwelling on the character of a couple of the local cinemas at which *Jew Süss* was distributed, since viewing conditions at these locations could differ sharply from picture houses in non-Jewish areas. A few weeks after the film screened at the Ambassador Cinema in the London suburb of Hendon, the *Jewish Chronicle* marked the site's third birthday with a short article in which it was estimated that "about forty per cent of the patrons are Jewish."[25] This assertion was reflected in the entertainment program, and the piece went on to describe how the house organist had played the entirety of the Kol Nidre during a recent screening of *The House of Rothschild*.[26] Somewhat less genteel was the

Rivoli Cinema in Whitechapel. A Yiddish theater and boxing venue during a previous life, the Rivoli was located in the heart of Jewish working-class London. Several Yiddish films — including the famous *Yiddle with His Fiddle*[27] — as well as Zionist films depicting nation building in the Palestine mandate were shown there during the period. It was also something of a communal institution, and on High Holidays the auditorium transformed into a place of worship to accommodate the congregants of the tiny nearby synagogue unable to cope with the extra demand for religious instruction.[28]

Anticipated as an event on the Jewish social calendar and consumed in locations coded as Jewish spaces, the contours of *Jew Süss* as site of Jewish cultural consumption are beginning to come into view. Yet film reception is not wholly reducible to these extratextual factors of exhibition context, and as Henry Bial and others have argued, minority ethnic readings of cultural texts are frequently marked by specialist knowledge unavailable to majority audiences.[29] Reviewing the film in the *Jewish Times*, its editor Morris Myer remarked that while Cedric Hardwicke delivered a first-rate performance, "his Rabbi is a little gentile."[30] However, while Jewish audiences doubtless took interest and pleasure in the film's formal qualities for a host of reasons, my concerns are restricted to one area. Overshadowing the Jewish papers' coverage of the film was a keen awareness of its non-Jewish consumption. In addition to the straightforward appraisal of aesthetics (including script and acting quality, production values apparent in the mise-en-scène, and so on) evident in mainstream news titles, the Jewish press expressed concern *with* the majority's reception. By taking the perspective of the outsider, speculation over how gentile audiences would respond to the piece was articulated at various registers. This represented a signal moment in the animation of a specifically Jewish reception of the film.

A Declaration of Neutrality

A repeated trope in the Jewish press was the status of *Jew Süss* as a public object. Noting the piece's origin in Feuchtwanger's novel, the *Jewish Chronicle* referred to its transformation into a feature film as a rendering "into ultimate visibility."[31] Such a characterization was entirely accurate. Not only was the film reviewed extensively, but the presence of Prince

George (the future King George VI) at the London premiere ensured that a large crowd gathered in the Strand for the opening at the Tivoli Cinema, and the event received coverage in the news pages—rather than just the entertainment columns—of the mainstream press. The film also had a significant presence in public space through the display hoarding mounted on the exterior of the Tivoli. The design was felt worthy of an article in the *Kinematograph Weekly*, and under a photograph of the cinema's facade the decorations were described. Said to match the lavish interiors of the film, the design consisted of "a frieze richly embellished with plaster decorations in gold relief" that extended along the front of the theater. This frieze was accompanied by a mildly risqué still from the film—showing Conrad Veidt attending a bathing Benita Hume (as the Duchess Marie Auguste)—displayed across the entire facade, which was framed "in a setting richly adorned in relief work."[32]

As Jeffrey Richards has observed, the 1930s represented something of a high point in exhibition site film promotions.[33] Often imaginative and elaborate, billboards and displays in or around a cinema would typically reproduce some key aspect of a featured film; a spilling of the fictional world into reality. The promotional displays for *Jew Süss* at the Tivoli were designed and built by Suprema Publicity Service,[34] and the designers apparently decided to emphasize the opulence and decadence of court life and the high production values required to effectively re-create this spectacle. A common criticism of the film was its lack of popular appeal—even the staid and stately *Times* newspaper described the piece as slow[35]—and it thus seems probable that the display of the immediately hedonistic pleasures of rococo excess and sexual frisson was somewhat cynically utilized to entice a mass audience who might not otherwise be interested in this rather dour and literary production.

Although the trade press enthused about the promotional decorations at the Tivoli, not all the attention the cinema's eye-catching marketing strategy received was positive. Writing in the *Daily Herald*, the left-wing journalist Hannen Swaffer primly chastised "the film industry"[36] for the suggestive billboard of Süss conversing with the bathing duchess. While nothing in his article gives reason to believe that Swaffer's objections were motivated by antisemitism, it does warrant considering to what extent the public display of a Jewish figure interacting with an obviously flirtatious gentile woman might prove discomfiting to non-Jews, particularly those individuals with minimal sympathy for a Jewish presence in Britain. While the satirical magazine *Punch* did not discuss the Tivoli's marketing tactics, one article did concentrate on the physical space of the cinema following *Jew Süss*'s opening. In a supercilious piece listing Jewish-themed films recently shown at the Tivoli,[37] it was provocatively asserted that the location "must begin to Aryanise itself or it will be thought of as the abode of Hebraic eminence and idiosyncrasy."[38] For *Punch* the ongoing presence of ethnic difference had polluted the site, and if this undesirable mark were not to be made permanent, some purification had to occur. As much as *Jew Süss*'s overt presence in the public realm could confer legitimacy, then, this same visibility could be antagonistic enough to Jewry's enemies to provoke them into comment.

Given the social context of *Jew Süss*'s release, it is not wholly surprising that prior to the film's exhibition, the *Jewish Chronicle*'s film writer, "G. J.," expressed some doubt over the venture, noting that he or she was awaiting it "with some anxiety."[39] This apprehension was founded on the idea that the film's content would provide a catalyst for anti-Jewish sentiment. As the article continued, the film could, "if handled with anything but the most expert discretion . . . produce an impression upon the minds of the masses very different from that desired by authors."[40] While G. J. did not expand on what this impression might look like, it does not require much imagination to understand why the representation of a Jew as a cunning manipulator of powerful men could sound alarm bells. According to Tegel, Süss's life was subject to a variety of literary treatments during the nineteenth century, both philosemitic and antisemitic — the latter imagining Süss as a sexual predator.[41] This contradictory status continued into twentieth-century adaptations, with the Süss story variously presented on the Yiddish stage in New York under the direction of Maurice Schwartz in 1929[42] and used by Veit Harlan as the basis for his infamously antisemitic 1940 Nazi propaganda film.[43] Drawing on Wilhelm Hauff's 1837 novella of the same name, Harlan's *Jud Süß* would see him twice tried for crimes against humanity in the years following the war. Highly ambiguous, Joseph Süß Oppenheimer was a figure open to widely contrasting artistic interpretations.

It should also be remembered that only a few years previously, Jews on both sides of the Atlantic considered Cecil B. DeMille's *The King of Kings* a dangerous libel in its blaming of Jews for Jesus Christ's death.[44]

Indeed, the *Jewish Chronicle* branded the film "the lie of lies," conducting an ongoing campaign against the piece.[45] For the Jewish press, films featuring Jewish characters were generally to be welcomed, but this did not mean they did not contain a minatory aspect, and it was often regarded as wise to approach their exhibition with some caution. There was a sense of relief, then, when upon *Jew Süss*'s release it could be confirmed that it contained "nothing that could give rise to or intensify anti-Semitism."[46] Indeed, its depiction of Süss's honor and courage, and the irrational brutality of racism, were seen to offer "valuable lessons" and "throw open the whole ugly, disgusting mentality of persecution and mass hatred."[47] Far from presenting a threat to Jews, then, the film's highly public nature — its "ultimate visibility" — was to be welcomed. It was the condition on which the text's moral instruction could take effect.

Interestingly, the specter of antisemitic representations was not the only menace the *Jewish Chronicle* was glad to dismiss. Equally significant was the declaration that *Jew Süss* contained "nothing that could be classed as pro-Jewish propaganda."[48] Of great importance to the paper's reviewer was the quality of restraint apparent in the production, its "tact." This "tact" was attributed to directorial choice, with Lothar Mendes asserted to adopt "the method of the intelligent observing eye . . . ingeniously giving that impression of factual recording which . . . [is] . . . the best suited method to the subject."[49] Unfortunately, however, the finale of the film struck a wrong note, contrasting unfavorably with the composure of the overwhelming majority of the film. As the review continued, the gravity of the execution scene was "marred . . . by the incontinent howling of Suss's Jewish friends" that left the audience feeling "as though our bosoms had been roughly pummelled in a street row."[50] The *Jewish Times* was similarly dissatisfied with this ending, complaining that "the great wailing of the crowd" detracted from the self-possession of Veidt's performance.[51] Thus, for the Jewish press, the film was divided into two segments. The overwhelming majority of the film could be considered a success through its rejection of the manipulation of emotion; because the dramatic ending employed an appeal to affect, though, the final minutes were viewed as a failure. In distinction with some of the mainstream British press that unfavorably compared the bulk of film to the engaging American style of product but enjoyed the "Great Climax"[52] of the finale, the Jewish press saw virtue only in the aesthetic of detachment.

The Jewish press expressed the feeling that aesthetic austerity was the most appropriate form for this film. As such, its members liked the first eighty-five minutes, which many viewers found boring, but disliked the final five minutes, which were highly dramatic.

That a detached and austere aesthetic might be understood as an appropriate expressive mode for a film dealing with the subject of Jewish persecution should be understood within its specific historical context. In wide circulation at that moment was the perception that Jews were central to the business of film production. Such an idea could operate at various registers. More benign articulations merely noted the high numbers of Jews working in the trade. In the *Daily Film Renter*, for instance, several articles published around the time of the 1938 Jewish New Year recorded the significance of the holiday for the business. In addition to wishing readers a happy Rosh Hashanah, it was noted that the Wardour Street area of Soho (then the center of the London film industry) was lacking its customary bustle.[53] Somewhat more malevolent, however, was the meshing of the idea that cinema was seen to possess an almost supernatural power to exert influence over audiences with the antisemitic canard that Jews were in control of the entertainment industry and mass media.

That *Jew Süss* might be understood as an outcome of the prevalence of Jews in the film business was not a paranoid fantasy. At the beginning of 1934, the *Observer* published a piece titled "Judaism on the Screen [*sic*]" in which critic C. A. Lejeune lauded several upcoming productions featuring Jewish characters, stating, "In England and America the epics of Jewry have begun."[54] With a subheading to the article reading "The Significance of 'Suss' [*sic*]," *Jew Süss* was singled out for special attention, and production information (cast, set detail) was given along with quotes from the director, Mendes, and the assertion that the film could be read as "a protest of a whole race against barbarism."[55] At the end of the piece the writer expanded upon her theme of righteous propaganda, concluding:

> For nearly half a century they [Jews] have been using the motion picture as a mouthpiece for the ideas and interests of other races. It is not unreasonable that at last, now that the right moment has come, they should contemplate using it for the justification of their own.[56]

For Lejeune, then, to make sense of *Jew Süss* was to understand it as a collective Jewish response to Nazi persecution. *Jew Süss*, together with *The House of Rothschild* and the aborted Victor Saville project *Magnolia Street*, was part of what she saw as a wider propaganda strategy involving both U.S. and British producers to promote Jewish interests.[57]

It is clear that the Jewish press was quite aware of the circulation of such ideas. Indeed, shortly after its publication in the *Observer*, the *Jewish Chronicle* ran an article commenting on Lejeune's piece. Although greeted favorably — Lejeune's article is referred to as "excellent" — one senses some discomfit in the author, and Lejeune is said to merely "allege" (rather than state) that Jews are "using their own medium as a racial manifesto."[58] Ambivalence around the notion of film as Jewish medium was an ongoing feature of the *Jewish Chronicle*'s coverage of the issue, and as the 1930s developed, the newspaper's take on the matter shifted between contradictory positions. As Andrew Spicer has shown, the important role Jewish individuals played in the development of the film industry — in both the United Kingdom and the United States — is a matter of historical record.[59] That Jews could achieve success in such a prominent field was a source of pride for the *Jewish Chronicle*, and regular items detailed the achievements of assorted producers. Indeed, one piece on "Jewish film magnates" considered their "rise from obscure beginnings . . . a romance of the films in itself."[60]

Yet there was also significant investment in the idea that cinema had the power to corrupt and that Jews involved in the industry had a moral responsibility to curb film's deleterious effects. For example, in early 1931 the *Jewish Chronicle*'s editor used his column to condemn "undesirable films" in the hope that his "calling attention to the matter, would be useful, in view of the large influence, at almost every point, upon the cinema industry of Jews."[61] A few months later, a letter submitted to a "Los Angeles journal" by an anonymous "Hollywood Jew" was discussed at some length in the same paper. Denouncing "Jews who control the movie industry," the writer claimed that Hollywood's moguls were "engaged only in the feverish acquisition of wealth by pandering to the worst instincts of humanity."[62] Far from condemning such a position as objectively antisemitic, the editor again appealed to ethics, stating that "this call to Jews to behave justly . . . is but part of the Jewish mission."[63]

Guiding British understandings of Hollywood during the interwar years was a wider cultural debate that has come to be known as the "battle of the brows." While self-appointed spokespersons for a modernist intellectual elite—the "highbrows"—derided the cultural tastes and modes of living of those in the socioeconomic middle, "middlebrow" cultural producers and critics took issue with both the avant-garde pretensions of continental Europe and the profit-driven populism of the United States—instead arguing for a national British aesthetic able to eschew outright commercialism yet awake to public taste.[64] The aesthetic dispositions of the *Jewish Chronicle* were located well within the middlebrow band of the spectrum, and in the early 1930s the paper's comments on cinema aligned with this vision of the cultural landscape. For Dick Hebdige, the profound social and economic changes brought about in interwar Britain (namely, the growth of a lower middle class and the rapid expansion of consumer markets) were registered most keenly at the level of culture, and the United States—conceived as an alien force eroding British cultural and moral values—was understood to be the key catalyst of this upheaval.[65] It was from such a perspective that the editor of the *Jewish Chronicle* was to assert that "films sent across here from America were largely demoralising and disgusting, and designed to play upon the worst passions of those for whom they are provided."[66]

By 1932, however, increasingly vituperative attacks on an allegedly Jewish film industry appear to have become a feature of public discourse. Far from being merely the preserve of the political extreme right (the "Jewish-controlled" media was a mainstay of fascist propaganda), this notion was articulated at various levels of authority: culture, state, the church. In his poem "Naaman's Song," Rudyard Kipling transposed Hollywood for the biblical river Jordan and recounted the Syrian general Naaman's obstinate refusal to bathe in it when the prophet Elisha suggested it as a cure for his leprosy. Responsibility for the supposedly demoralizing influence of cinema was laid squarely with Jewish producers, with one line stating how Jordan's banks/Hollywood was "Commanded and embellished and patrolled by Israelites," and another sinisterly warning that "Israel watcheth over each."[67] Somewhat less cryptically, the Conservative M. P. George Hartland was in no doubt over who was to blame for the "ruin" of "millions of boys and girls in this country."[68] Elaborating on his conspiracy theory, he was recorded referring to "a syndicate of dirty American Jews—the Hollywood magnates; what fine English names most of them have got—who take damned good care they observe their own Sabbath [*sic*]."[69] Finally, both individuals and publications of the church were implicated in a series of calumnies. In a meeting of the General Assembly of the Church of Scotland, the Rev. T. B. Stewart Thompson was said to have delivered a diatribe on the Jews that included the information that "The Jew largely controls the places of amusement"; while it was also reported that Canon Patrick Palmer of Ilford, in east London, had referred to cinema as "Jewish filth" in an interview.[70]

All too often, then, antisemitism became a feature of debates and campaigns around film morality. Within this discourse American and Jewish alterity could coalesce, introducing some ambiguity into the identity of the cultural invader infecting vulnerable young British minds via cinema screens. In response to this development, the *Jewish Chronicle* directly challenged the blatant antisemitism of the worst offenders, designating, for instance, Canon Palmer's comments "Nazi language."[71] But the newspaper also seems to have become increasingly careful to moderate references to Jewish control of the industry, drawing a sharp distinction between the recognition of a prominence of Jewish production personnel and the notion of a coordinated Jewish film monopoly. The existence of this latter entity was readily questioned, voicing doubt that George Hartland M. P. possessed evidence for his assertions or—as we have seen—prefiguring Lejeune's suggestion of cinematic Jewish collective action with the adjective "alleged."[72] Any move by the Jewish press to read *Jew Süss* as a sober and considered presentation of reality, and not a tendentious piece of emotional manipulation, is thus wholly comprehensible. Given the context of a widespread belief in the idea of Jewish media dominance, any perceived deviation from an objective and neutral narrative within *Jew Süss* might risk a public dismissal of the piece as the special pleading of minority interests or, worse, attract the reputation of conspiratorial propaganda.

Historicizing a Politics of Representation

Whatever judgment the *Jewish Chronicle* reached, this could not stabilize or limit readings of *Jew Süss* proffered elsewhere in the British news media. Despite claims that the film evinced no pro-Jewish tendency, at least two mainstream British newspapers came to the opposite conclusion. Writing in the *Evening Standard*, John Betjeman considered *Jew Süss* "obviously a film of propaganda"; and as we have seen, the *Observer*'s C. A. Lejeune was an enthusiastic advocate for conducting Jewish defense through cinematic means, believing Jews to have "the clearest claim of all to a national drama of the screen."[73] Interestingly, Lejeune registered a distinction between "this new Jewish movement in the cinema" and the propaganda produced by Russia, the United States, or fascist governments. For her, the dividing line, or what she called Jewish propaganda's "odd and peculiarly characteristic quality," was in "its diffidence. It is the only deliberate propaganda on the screen that is reluctant to admit its authority."[74]

In an era in which English clergymen were denouncing cinema as "Jewish filth," it should, perhaps, have been less of a surprise that films dealing with antisemitism might be marked by hesitancy. The naïveté of liberal newspaper columnists aside, both film producers and the Jewish press seem to have been united in the recognition that in Britain one had to tread gingerly when dealing with Jewish communal concerns in film. It has long been recognized that one assimilationist strategy adopted by British Jews has been to define Judaism as a private matter.[75] Doubtless there is much to recommend this observation, and an instinct to bracket ethnic and religious difference has surely played a role in shaping the nature of a host of cultural texts produced by Jews. As Nathan Abrams has shown, unable to access a hyphenate "British-Jewish" identity, Jewish directors in Britain have opted to ignore Jewish themes, instead concentrating on "universal" narratives.[76] Nevertheless, it is important to be sensitized to fluctuations and developments animating the social imaginary. If Jews were understood to occupy a significant role in influencing the character of the interwar mass public sphere, then it seems productive to examine cultural consumption within the context of this belief. For some Jews, it was wholly desirable that film might act as a vessel to transport Jewish concerns into the gaze of a generalized public. What they had to reckon with was the risk contained in the moment of rendering a given production visible. This risk was fully recognized by Jewish newspapers and was explicitly reflected on. If, as Raymond Williams suggests, lived "structures of feeling" can be discerned in the cultural detritus of the past, a discomfiting social uncertainty appears as a signal characteristic of the everyday experience of Jews in interwar Britain.[77] Although we can never reconstruct the precise relationship between press discourse and actually existing audiences, it is clear that readers of the British Jewish press were addressed as a distinct kind of spectator in the writing about *Jew Süss*. Offered to them was a position—a space of habitation in the social field—from which reception of the film might be oriented. This position of reception was intrinsically contradictory—while a cinematic indictment of contemporary Jewish persecution was presented to offer some moral satisfaction to Jewish audiences, it was tempered by imagined projections of gentile consumption as potentially suspicious of the machinations of a Jewish film monopoly. As source material, the Süss story had historically been subject to opposing interpretations in various ideological contexts—as it would continue to be. It seems fitting that the Gaumont-British Picture Corporation's one intervention into the precarity of Jewish life drew on such a mercurial narrative.

Notes

1. "The Louis-Schmeling Fight," *Jewish Chronicle*, July 8, 1938, 53.

2. Jeffrey Richards, *Age of the Dream Palace: Cinema and Society in Britain 1930–39* (London: Routledge, 1984).

3. Scenario report for A German Tragedy, May 10, 1933, Scenario Reports 1933 file—BBFC-1-2 1933, Scenario Reports series—BBFC-1 1931–1949, British Board of Film Censors Collection fonds—BBFC, British Film Institute, London.

4. See Scenario report for Jew Suss, November 2, 1933, ibid.

5. John Betjeman, "A Great Thrill Film—Death in the Iron Cage," *Evening Standard*, October 6, 1934, 8.

6. Three British Jewish newspapers are referred to in this article. The *Jewish Chronicle* was founded in 1841 and was distributed nationally on a weekly basis. It had long conceived itself as the official voice of British Jewish interests: a subheading on the publication's masthead declared the paper "The Organ of British Jewry." The *Jewish Times* (*Di Tsait*) was a well-established Yiddish-language daily comprising about eight pages. Produced in the East End of London, it had a keen awareness of the political and cultural dispositions of its proletarian readership. The *Jewish World* was a weekly magazine-style publication. While it provided coverage of political events from across the spectrum, it cultivated a respectable socially conservative image. It ceased publication in 1934.

7. Morris Myer, "Film Triumph of Jew Suss," *Jewish Times* (*Di Tsait*), October 7, 1934, 2.

8. G. J., "'Jew Suss' at the Tivoli," *Jewish Chronicle*, October 12, 1934, 43.

9. Rachael Low, *The History of British Film 1929–1939: Film Making in 1930s Britain* (London: Allen and Unwin, 1985), 142.

10. Susan Tegel, "The Politics of Censorship: Britain's 'Jew Süss' (1934) in London, New York and Vienna," *Historical Journal of Film, Radio and Television* 15, no. 2 (1995): 219–44.

11. See Tony Kushner, *The Holocaust and the Liberal Imagination: A Social and Cultural History* (Oxford: Blackwell, 1994).

12. C. A. Lejeune, "Jew Suss," *Observer*, October 7, 1934, 18; Spectator quotation from Tegel, "Politics of Censorship," 227.

13. Myer, "Film Triumph," 2; G. J., "Jew Suss at the Tivoli," 43.

14. G. J., "Jew Suss at the Tivoli." 43.

15. *Daily Mail*, October 23, 1934, 11.

16. "Austrian Ban on 'Jew Suss' Film," *Manchester Guardian*, October 23, 1934, 12.

17. See "'Jew Suss' Banned," *Jewish Chronicle*, October 26, 1934, 29.

18. "Film Jew Suss Banned in Vienna due to Antisemitic Demonstrations," *Jewish Times (Di Tsait)*, October 23, 1934, 3.

19. *The Cohens and the Kellys*, directed by Harry Pollard (Los Angeles: Universal Pictures, 1926); *His People*, directed by Edward Sloman (Los Angeles: Universal, 1925). See also Gil Toffell, "Cinema-Going from Below: The Jewish Film Audience in Interwar Britain," *Participations: Journal of Audience and Reception Studies* 8, no. 2 (2011): 522–38, http://www.participations.org/Volume%208/Issue%202/contents.htm.

20. "Kinema, Gramophone and Broadcasting Notes," *Jewish World*, January 11, 1934, 17.

21. "Variety and Cinema News," *Jewish Chronicle*, February 3, 1928, 34.

22. "Some British Films for 1934," *Jewish Chronicle*, October 20, 1933, 43.

23. See *Jewish Times (Di Tsait)*, January 4, 1935, 8.

24. See *Jewish Chronicle*, January 11, 1935, 30.

25. "The Ambassador Hendon," *Jewish Chronicle*, February 22, 1935, 44.

26. *The House of Rothschild*, directed by Alfred Werker (Los Angeles: 20th Century Pictures, 1934).

27. *Yiddle with His Fiddle* [*Yidl mitn Fidl*], directed by Joseph Green and shot in Poland (Green-Film, 1936).

28. Toffell, "Cinema-Going from Below," 533.

29. Henry Bial, *Acting Jewish: Negotiating Ethnicity on the American Stage and Screen* (Ann Arbor: University of Michigan Press, 2005).

30. Myer, "Film Triumph," 2.

31. G. J., "Judaism on Screen," 43.

32. "'Jew Suss' Display at Tivoli," *Kinematograph Weekly*, October 11, 1934, 40.

33. Richards, *Age of the Dream Palace*, 21.

34. "'Jew Suss' Display at Tivoli,"

35. "Jew Suss," *Times*, October 5, 1934, 12.

36. Hannen Swaffer, "A Talkie on Itself," *Daily Herald*, October 16, 1934, 12.

37. In the twelve months prior to *Jew Süss*'s exhibition, *The Wandering Jew* and *The House of Rothschild* were both screened at the Tivoli.

38. Tegel, "Politics of Censorship," 227. As Tegel also noted, *Punch* had something of a reputation for an unsympathetic attitude to Jewish concerns.

39. G. J., "Judaism on Screen," 42.

40. Ibid.

41. Tegel, "Politics of Censorship," 222.

42. See Peter Bauland, *The Hooded Eagle: Modern German Drama on the New York Stage* (Syracuse, N.Y.: Syracuse University Press, 1968).

43. *Jud Süß*, directed by Veit Harlan (Berlin: Terra-Filmkunst, 1940).

44. *The King of Kings*, directed by Cecil B. DeMille (Los Angeles: De Mille Pictures Corporation, 1927);. Yael Ohad-Karny, "'Anticipating' Gibson's 'The Passion of the Christ': The Controversy over Cecil B. De Mille's 'The King of Kings,'" *Jewish History* 19, no. 2 (2005): 189–210.

45. "The King of Kings," *Jewish Chronicle*, December 9, 1927, 12.

46. G. J., "Judaism on Screen," 43.

47. Ibid.

48. Ibid.

49. Ibid.

50. Ibid.

51. Myer, "Film Triumph," 2.

52. "Great Climax," *Daily Mail*, October 8, 1934, 9.

53. "Wardour Street Gossip by 'Commentator,'" *Daily Film Renter*, September 24, 1938, 2; "Wardour Street Gossip by 'Tatler,'" *Daily Film Renter*, September 27, 1938, 2.

54. C. A. Lejeune, "Judaism on the Screen," *Observer*, January 7, 1934, 23.

55. Ibid.

56. Ibid.

57. Published in 1932, Louis Golding's *Magnolia Street* was a best-selling novel about Jewish and gentile interactions in working-class interwar Manchester. In 1934 it was adapted for the stage, playing at the Adelphi Theatre in central London.

58. G. J., "Judaism on Screen," 41.

59. Andrew Spicer, "A British Empire of Their Own? Jewish Entrepreneurs in the British Film Industry," *Journal of European Popular Culture* 3, no. 2 (2012): 117–29.

60. VEE, "Miscellany," *Jewish Chronicle*, May 17, 1929, 12.

61. The Editor, "Undesirable Films," *Jewish Chronicle*, March 20, 1931, 13–14.

62. "Jews and the Film Industry," *Jewish Chronicle*, October 9, 1931, 16.

63. The Editor, "Jews and the Films," *Jewish Chronicle*, October 16, 1931, 7.

64. For a recent discussion of the "battle of the brows" that makes extensive reference to film, see Lawrence Napper, *British Cinema and Middlebrow Culture in the Interwar Years* (Exeter, U.K.: Exeter University Press, 2009).

65. Dick Hebdige, "Towards a Cartography of Taste 1935–1962," in *Hiding in the Light*, by Dick Hebdige (London: Comedia, 1988), 45–76.

66. The Editor, "American Films," *Jewish Chronicle*, August 21, 1931, 6.

67. Rudyard Kipling, *Limits and Renewals* (London: Macmillan, 1932). The poem "Naaman's Song" accompanied a short story, "Aunt Ellen." The verse from which the second quotation is taken reads as follows:

> And here is mock of faith and truth, for children to behold;
> And every door of ancient dirt reopened to the old;
> With every word that taints the speech, and show that weakens thought;
> And Israel watcheth over each, and — doth not watch for nought . . .

68. The Editor, "Give a Dog a Bad Name . . . ," *Jewish Chronicle*, May 13, 1932, 7.

69. Ibid.

70. The Editor, "'Damn the Jew,'" *Jewish Chronicle*, June 10, 1932, 7; The Editor, "A Clergyman's Lapse," *Jewish Chronicle*, August 17, 1934, 6.

71. Editor, "Clergyman's Lapse."

72. Editor, "Give Dog Bad Name"; G. J., "Judaism on Screen," 41.

73. Betjeman, "Great Thrill Film," 8; Lejeune, "Judaism on Screen."

74. Lejeune, "Judaism on Screen."

75. See Nathan Abrams, "Hidden: Jewish Film in the United Kingdom, Past and Present," *Journal of European Popular Culture* 1, no. 1 (2010): 53–68.

76. Ibid. An example here would be Mike Leigh, the subject of Donald Weber's chapter in this book.

77. Raymond Williams, *The Long Revolution* (London: Chatto & Windus, 1961).

PHYLLIS LASSNER AND
ALEXIS POGORELSKIN

An Anti-Nazi Special Relationship

British Writing, Hollywood Filmmaking, and The Mortal Storm *(1940)*

During the 1930s, British writers, filmmakers, and actors were lured to Hollywood as both an asylum from the threat of war and to make films that guaranteed creative opportunities, international distribution, and acclaim far beyond what the cash-strapped British film industry could afford.[1] As the Nazi threat in Europe escalated throughout the decade and Britain was increasingly threatened, the cultural bridge that this artistic diaspora represented developed a political purpose. British artists were joining their nation's propaganda efforts to win the sympathy and support of the United States.[2] Phyllis Bottome contributed to that effort, determined to see her anti-Nazi transatlantic best-selling novel *The Mortal Storm* (1937–38) produced in Hollywood. A prime example of a work that is both eminently British in its creative origins and focuses on the Jewish question remains *The Mortal Storm* (1940), directed by Frank Borzage.[3] The production joined two British authors, Bottome and the principal screenwriter, Claudine West. Bottome made important suggestions to strengthen West's script that, for the first time in Hollywood or British film history, dramatized the plight of Europe's Jews under the Nazi regime.[4] This chapter will explore Bottome's political intentions and the complicated creative and political process that brought the novel to the screen. We will analyze the film's multilayered cinematic and narrative structures and lexicon to show how they represent intersections between Jewish and British vulnerability. The film served as a warning to Americans of what awaited them as World War II began. In effect, we will argue that a diasporic British cinema that constitutes an Anglo-American hybrid politicized Hollywood and expanded the production of British cinema as it reached across the Atlantic for American support.

If Bottome and her *Mortal Storm* enjoy any public recognition today, it is because of the Metro-Goldwyn-Mayer (MGM) studio's 1940 film adaptation starring Margaret Sullavan and Jimmy Stewart. Today a late night TV favorite, the film capitalizes on the stars' repeat performances in a trilogy of films as lovers struggling against the political and economic crises of the 1930s. Their first film together, in 1936, was a Universal Pictures production, *Next Time We Love*, a melodrama that established the appeal of their screen relationship, in which Stewart and Sullavan play a married couple who struggle to balance careers and keep the flame of their romance alive. The emotional intensity of this film sets the pace and tone for the three films produced by MGM in which they starred together between 1938 and 1940: *The Shopworn Angel* (1938), *The Shop around the Corner* (January 1940), and *The Mortal Storm* (June 1940).[5]

All of the films starring Stewart and Sullavan are easily classified as middlebrow in the sense that they were produced by major Hollywood studios for mass audiences and revenue. Each film is structured around key melodramatic plot points and follows familiar and comforting narrative arcs, with the lovers outgrowing their own restricted perspectives to achieve emotional and political wisdom. While MGM had to change potentially inflammatory elements of Bottome's *The Mortal Storm* to achieve wide audience approval, she did not disapprove, for she wanted nothing more than to make her anti-Nazi message accessible, clear, and persuasive to the largest possible audience. As we maintain, however, this accessibility adds a crucial critical dimension to both novel and film. Because Bottome's multifaceted political and cultural analysis is conveyed in both media through self-consciously designed narrative and cinematic experiments, they support and advance scholarly arguments for the complex sophistication of middlebrow cultural production.[6]

Bottome completed *The Mortal Storm* in 1937, having returned to Britain after residing in Germany and Austria for over a decade.[7] She knew the German threat firsthand but could not convince her fellow Britons of it. She wrote to a friend from the United States, where she had gone to lecture in 1938, that "a very large and important part of [England] is Fascist."[8] She warned another friend that "certain elements in the press . . . intend to spread . . . Nazi doctrine [with] great financial backing."[9] Bottome remained grateful to her publisher, Geoffrey Faber, who defied public opinion to publish the novel "when it was dangerous to do so."[10]

The Mortal Storm Crosses the Atlantic

There were several reasons why it was unlikely that a cinematic version of the novel could be made in Britain. First, the financially weak British film industry could hardly be expected to produce a film that required snow-capped mountain vistas. Second, the prevailing mood of appeasement created a potentially indifferent, even hostile, audience to a film that advocated intervention in European affairs. After residing in central Europe for a decade and a half, Bottome on her return to Britain found the "nonchalance of London" toward the Nazis "incomprehensible."[11] She encountered naïveté and ignorance across the political spectrum. Her conservative friends exclaimed, "Oh, but we like Hitler!" Her friends in the Liberal and Labour Parties expressed a measure of hope: "Perhaps Hitler will settle down and leave the Jews alone." One of Bottome's like-minded friends, another "premature anti-Nazi," wrote her that year, "I will soon be hanged and keep you a place next [to] mine at the lamp-post."[12] As these comments indicate, Bottome's compatriots considered hostility to Nazism in 1935 at best "premature," at worst cause for alarm, even retribution.

Another source of potential hostility to a film version of the novel lay with British producers themselves. Alexander Korda, for example, like the Hollywood moguls he was alleged to resemble, "desired to downplay, even conceal his Jewishness."[13] Korda went even further, according to Greg Walker, his biographer. He "did everything possible to obfuscate and elide" his Jewish identity.[14] Portraying Bottome's novel on-screen, particularly with its destruction of a Jewish family by the Nazis, would hardly contribute to such determined discretion. Korda did have one advantage for Bottome among British producers. He could be said to bridge British and American cinema, having joined the board of United Artists (UA) in 1936. From 1937 to 1939, he partnered with UA's most powerful board member, Samuel Goldwyn, precisely the years during which Bottome sought a Hollywood producer for her novel. Goldwyn, however, negated this option. He adamantly opposed the production of what Hollywood termed "message pictures." Goldwyn also shared Korda's attitude to his Jewish identity.[15] Michael Balcon, another British Jewish mogul, might possibly have bridged Anglo-American cinema to facilitate a production of *The Mortal Storm*, but he also proved problematic. Having worked at MGM, he quarreled with its head, Louis B. Mayer, and returned to Britain to run Ealing Studios in 1938. Because of the controversial nature of the novel, Bottome therefore began to pursue selling the movie rights on her own.

The United States beckoned for several reasons. The novel that defied public opinion in Britain and could even be "dangerous" to publish found a different reception in the United States. Bottome's American publisher Little, Brown reprinted it thirteen times in 1938, affording her an audience she would otherwise not have had. She lauded the results:

> *The Mortal Storm* has done far more than I ever dreamed of. I am told that it has definitely helped to check the spread of anti-Semitism in America. It is still a best seller and has brought many opportunities that I have never had before to impress . . . a far wider public.[16]

Her wider public included readers of the American magazine the *New Republic*, which published her biting essay "I Accuse," a denunciation of the British establishment for seeking to compromise with Hitler at the time of the *Anschluss*. Bottome contended that the British elites had sold out Austrian Jews. British publishers had refused to touch it. Bottome, convinced that isolationism amounted to a fool's errand, turned to another opportunity that the United States afforded—namely, that "most perfect medium the world has ever had" to deliver her message.[17] To her frustration, however, as of 1939, "not one of the big movie studios had yet dared to produce a straightforward anti-Nazi film."[18]

Bottome therefore determined to make her case for *The Mortal Storm* in person. Her campaign began almost as soon as she arrived in North America on her first lecture tour, October 1938 to May 1939, following the novel's American publication. She had previously sold another one of her novels, *Private Worlds* (1935), to the independent producer Walter Wanger, who brought it to the screen for Paramount in 1935. Because of debt and controversy over *Blockade* (1938), Wanger's film about the Spanish Civil War, he could not produce *The Mortal Storm*.[19] Another frustration was the failure of her literary agent, Ann Watkins, to interest a major studio in the novel. And so Bottome took matters into her own hands. With the escalation of Nazi persecution of the Jews, she believed that the subject of *The Mortal Storm* could not wait.

The Role of the American Jewish Community

The circuitous route to Hollywood ran through the North American Jewish community. Bottome spoke often to Jewish groups. Given the subject of *The Mortal Storm* and her work on behalf of Jewish refugees, she would have been a welcome speaker. Her denunciations of isolationism and growing antisemitism would have added to her appeal. She informed the Bishop of Chichester on the eve of departure for her first lecture tour, "My husband and I are leaving for America this week. We shall lecture from end to end of it in hope of stemming this rising tide of anti-Semitism."[20] Her talk at Toronto's Holy Blossom Temple proved instrumental in bringing *The Mortal Storm* to the screen. Its Rabbi, Maurice N. Eisendrath, one of the most socially engaged Jewish leaders in North America, offered to place his Hollywood connections at her disposal:

> I was exceedingly interested . . . that . . . your novel may be filmed. Is there anything that I can do to help you in this matter[?] . . . A number of the men in my congregation are very closely identified with the motion picture industry. In addition I know Rabbi Edgar Magnin of Los Angeles exceedingly well and he is on the most intimate terms with the people in Hollywood.[21]

Rabbi Magnin, the gregarious and charismatic "rabbi to the stars," counted a number of studio heads and executives among his congregants.[22] Most significant for Bottome, who sought an MGM production for her novel, Magnin was on intimate terms with Mayer, the mogul who ran Hollywood's then premier studio. On behalf of Bottome, her husband, Ernan Forbes Dennis, replied, "Would it be possible for you to send my wife an introduction to Rabbi Magnin so that we could meet him during the next few weeks while Los Angeles is our headquarters?"[23] True to his word, Eisendrath wrote to his fellow rabbi within the week:

> Early this fall we had the rare treat of having Phyllis Bottome on our . . . Forum. She is indeed a magnificent spirit and her message is a most challenging and timely one. You have no doubt read her "The Mortal Storm" and have found it an especially fine piece of work. She is now . . . trying to interest the motion picture people in filming this searching anti-Nazi story. I am amazed that it is necessary for her to do this, as I should think that they would be pleading with her so to do. I know of no recent piece of literature that . . . would make a more popular and exciting scenario. . . . I do hope . . . that you will use the great influence that you have with [those] people to interest them in this project.[24]

Magnin did indeed intercede with his congregant Mayer. He provided Bottome with a letter of introduction to the mogul and invited her to speak "in his beautiful temple."[25] But he assisted her ambivalently. Eisendrath had earlier noted Bottome's difficulty with Hollywood moguls: "I am amazed [at their lack of interest] as I should think that they would be pleading with her for the rights" to film the novel.[26]

Magnin understood why they were not. Mayer, for example, shared the same fear, regarding his Jewish identity as did Korda and other British producers.[27] According to Steven Carr, it would be box office disaster if the movies were perceived as "Jewish."[28] Jewish communities in the United States and Britain shared concerns that protests against Nazi persecution of Europe's Jews would encourage both harsher abuse and an antisemitic backlash by their own compatriots. But Magnin could not deny the sentiment among some leaders of the North American Jewish community that something had to be done about the Nazis. Mayer too faced certain pressures. He himself could no longer stand idly by after his rivals at Warner Brothers made the first openly anti-Nazi film *Confessions of a Nazi Spy* (1939). Warner's film, one of the first to address the Nazi phenomenon, confined itself to a spy ring in New York without ever mentioning Nazi policy and persecution directed at the Jews. Starting in March 1939, Bottome negotiated furiously with Mayer and others at MGM over possible terms of a sale of *The Mortal Storm*. Even so, she signed the contract with MGM only "at the last moment" before her departure for Britain.[29]

The Mortal Storm in Production

Magnin nevertheless remained involved. He advised Mayer and the film's producer, Sidney Franklin, not to hit the Americans over the head with what they already knew about Germany.[30] Overriding objections from the film's production team — including Bottome, who served as an unpaid consultant to MGM during the making of *The Mortal Storm* — Mayer forbade the word "Jew" in the script.[31] As a result, the film depicts the Nazis hounding and destroying a family of "non-Aryans."

Neither Bottome nor those who made the film accepted the studio head's prohibition without a fight. Claudine West had completed a version of the script in mid-July 1939. Bottome did not see a revised copy of it until early February 1940 when she was ostensibly recovering from exhaustion on her second lecture tour in the United States.[32] Using illness as an excuse, she had in fact placed herself at MGM's disposal during the filming of her novel in the winter and spring of 1940. Having seen West's script, she made several suggestions for additional scenes. She argued politely but firmly for the word "Jew" and for including one scene in particular from the novel where the young Rudi asks his father, "What is a Jew?" Bottome told Franklin that the answer to the question "is the crux of the book and the crux of the world today."[33] West embraced Bottome's pleas, trying with numerous versions of the "father-son scene," as she called it, to make Mayer budge.[34] He would not. Not even "non-Aryans" could be described as the bearers of so many of civilization's greatest gifts. Although Bottome's novel escaped Britain to find a studio buyer and acclaim in the United States, the film reached a line that the head of MGM would not allow it to cross. "Non-Aryan" in Hollywood proved to be almost as insurmountable as in the Third Reich.

The Mortal Storm on Screen

The film was released in June 1940, only two months before the Luftwaffe began bombing Britain. Starring Sullavan and Stewart, the film also featured Robert Young, Frank Morgan, Robert Stack, Bonita Granville, Irene Rich, and Maria Ouspenskaya. It succeeded in bringing the plight of Europe's Jews to the screen even as it danced around the question of their identity. Indeed, *The Mortal Storm* echoed the debate within the Anglo-American Jewish communities regarding the Nazis. Where Rabbi Eisendrath called for intervention and Magnin urged restraint in response to the Third Reich, *The Mortal Storm* bridged their differences with its evenly divided references to "non-Aryan" identity and its condemnation of the Nazi pseudoscience of race. The two concepts were linked because for the Nazis, non-Aryans—that is, Jews—constituted a subhuman race.

The film's political significance lay in part in its depiction of Nazi racism. *The Mortal Storm* opens on the day that Hindenburg appointed Hitler as Chancellor of Germany. Family celebrations on January 30, 1933, for world renowned physiologist Professor Viktor Roth's (Frank Morgan) sixtieth birthday are interrupted by news which only some at the table find disturbing. Professor Roth's clearly anguished wife, Amélie (Irene Rich), who is descended from an aristocratic Austrian family, and hence "Aryan," asks, "what about those who are . . . non-Aryan?," meaning her husband.[35] Mayer may have disallowed the word "Jew" in the film but the on-screen family retained its surname from the novel. "Roth" was unmistakably Jewish, as the film's plot confirmed. For example, a storm trooper addresses Professor Roth's daughter, Freya (Sullavan), as "Miss Roth," snarling, "You know your name doesn't sound very well to German ears." A Gestapo official makes the same point regarding Freya's "mixed" parentage: "You belong *in part* [emphasis added] to the German race." Confiscating her passport, he explains: "You have shown yourself unworthy to represent that race abroad." Freya's unworthiness stems from defending her father and his expertise. He had challenged a classroom full of Nazi students, by insisting that "science" had found "no difference in the . . . blood of the various races. . . . Scientific truth . . . cannot be altered to suit the policies of the hour or the clamor of immature hoodlums," he warned the hoodlums he faced. Freya breaks her engagement to her fiancé, Fritz Marburg (Robert Young), now a storm trooper, telling him, "You belong to this new Germany . . . that persecutes my people." Much of the audience must have recognized the identity of Freya's "people." If not, even a casual glance at the cheap version of the novel for sale in theatre lobbies in 1940 would have revealed "Jew," not "non-Aryan," as the Roths' identity.

The case of *The Mortal Storm* presents a paradox. What would seem most fundamental to the question of the Jew in British cinema is elusive in the film, occurring outside Britain and offscreen. Yet two British writers, Phyllis Bottome and Claudine West, collaborated to bring the plight of Europe's Jews and Britain's peril to that "most perfect medium," as Bottome termed it.[36] West, goaded by Bottome, managed the transition from print to silver screen. The surname Roth and the film's double-edged dialogue evaded Mayer's tremulous censorship. Image and narrative, to which we now turn, accomplished the same artful dodge.

Although the film was produced by MGM, an icon of American cultural power, *The Mortal Storm* embeds a very British message: that is, Britain's plea to the United States to join in defending democratic principles from Nazi onslaught. This combination, which we view as a hybrid cultural artefact, reflects the persona of Phyllis Bottome, whose parentage was British and American and who identified with both nations.[37] While Bottome's optimistic trust in bringing *The Mortal Storm* to the screen relied on the two nations' shared democratic values, this project would not be easy. There was, after all, no doubt that since the catastrophic losses of World War I, American tolerance for British prowar propaganda and sympathy for Europe's internecine conflicts were exhausted.[38] Although a generation had passed since the war, many forms of memorialization and antiwar sentiments had become firmly entrenched in British and American literature and culture.[39]

In its accessible narrative style that aligned it with middlebrow cultural production, the film dramatizes the combined concerns of its diasporic British writers, American director, and Central European production team[40] about Hitler's march toward world conquest. For example, a pair of Central European refugees, Hans Rameau (Ellis Anderson) and George Froeschal, joined Claudine West, adding the visual evocation of pre-Nazi German cinema to an MGM production. Seemingly distant from both Britain and the United States, both novel and film are structured as a German Jewish family epic. As director Frank Borzage explained,

> We're filming a human interest story of a family's disintegration. It just happens to have Nazi Germany as its background. Our picture won't have any "heavies" and it's not an attack on Ger-

> many. It's just a picture of what happens when a force like that arises. . . . We try to show the fanatic fervor that motivates [the brutality], but we don't excuse it.[41]

If Borzage is attempting to portray the film as a family melodrama, neutralizing the force of destruction, he overlooks his own achievement in wedding his story to the current political crisis. Despite Bottome's intentions, the MGM synopsis writer Helen Corbaley misread the novel and argued that *The Mortal Storm* was not political in its intent, "but a fair picture of the situation in Nazi Germany."[42]

In opposition to the Nazi ideal of racial purity, hybrid cultural identity informs the plot of *The Mortal Storm.* The affectionate mutual respect between the Jewish Roth and German von Rohn families is lacerated when Amélie's sons from her first marriage, Otto (Robert Stack) and Eric (William Orr) von Rohn, are seduced by a lethal form of unity—the Nazi drive for supremacist domination. Beginning as family crisis, the consequences of Nazi racist and sexist ideology metastasize into threatening destruction of all those men and women considered *Untermenschen* (subhumans) by Nazi ideology and its translation into the 1935 Nuremberg Laws. By charting the changing attitudes of its characters, *The Mortal Storm* shows that the will of the Third Reich can only be fulfilled by the bloody annihilation of individual and collective identity, difference, freedom, and interdependence. Dramatizing its opposition to this tyranny, the film combines middlebrow accessibility, classic melodramatic emotional acting styles, expressionist imagery, and black-and-white contrast to enact a plea for resistance. Having prided itself on its independent island status, Britain now required the support of the United States to withstand the threat of Nazi Germany. In contrast to MGM's 1939 sagas of Americana—the romantic historical epic *Gone with the Wind* and the heartland fantasy *The Wizard of Oz*—in *The Mortal Storm* the idea of homeland as a source of identity and belonging has no efficacy for the persecuted.[43] As the film's visual metaphors of impassable borders and threatening landscapes show, unless the United States joins Britain in combating Nazism, neither individual fortitude nor integrity can withstand the unified terror of Nazi oppression.

The urgency of collaborative resistance is dramatized in several scenes where Freya, the intrepid half-Jewish daughter of the Roths, joins political forces with the peasant Martin Breitner. Significantly, the film substitutes Martin's pacifism for his communist counterpart (named Hans) in Bottome's novel. While this tactic is easily interpreted as MGM's avoidance of censure for displaying communist sympathy, Martin's pacifism is not presented as a viable alternative. Instead pacifism is depicted critically.[44] Because his retreat from Nazi brutality to pastoral isolation is no safeguard, his mountaintop home becomes a politicized site, confronting American audiences with a parallel threat to their own heartland. As failed resistance to Nazi terror, Martin's pacifism, a form of isolationism, invites an argument for intervention. The argument is enacted in two echoing scenes wherein silence becomes an instrument of dissent, not of retreat. When storm troopers invade the Breitner home, instead of futile protests of innocence and ignorance, and despite brutal intimidation of their maid Else (Bonita Granville), Mrs. Breitner (Maria Ouspenskaya) cannily uses her silence to stonewall threats of violent retaliation. In another scene, in a ski tavern, Martin and Freya stand silently as everyone (including Otto, Eric, and Freya's fiancé) proudly sings MGM's version of the Nazi anthem. With stunning political impact, Martin and Freya are framed by sharp angles, facing left while everyone else faces right and raises their right arms in the Hitler salute. The camera work here supports the dissenters' perspective and confronts the enforcement of Nazi unity. What had been a "pact of eternal friendship" among Freya, Martin, and their closest friends, "signed with our own blood," is now ruptured by a blood brotherhood of racial supremacy. The silence of dissent transforms into action when racial ideology translates into violence and the schoolmaster, Mr. Werner, is beaten by storm troopers for refusing to salute or sing. Abandoning his pacifism to help Werner, Martin is also beaten as he intervenes. By the scene's end, as the horde of storm troopers overtakes the tavern, now a microcosm of Germany's transformation, possibilities for escape from Nazi oppression have been obliterated.

The film's gloomy but powerful message earned critical success but box office disappointment.[45] Bosley Crowther in the *New York Times*, noted that

> this picture turns out to be one of the most harrowing and inflammatory fictions ever placed upon the screen. . . . "The Mortal Storm" falls definitely into the category of blistering anti-Nazi

> propaganda. . . . But so violent is [Nazi] oppression . . . and so bitter and hopeless is the fate of [its victims] that even the spiritual satisfaction which might be derived from a story of heroic suffering is seriously impaired, especially in the light of current headlines. As propaganda, "The Mortal Storm" is a trumpet call to resistance, but as theatrical entertainment it is grim and depressing today.[46]

Although Crowther specifies Nazi terror, he complies with MGM's reticence by identifying the primary victim only as "those." But whereas the screenwriters visually gesture toward the Jewish subtext of "non-Aryan," Crowther fails to mention that Roth's prison armband is marked with a definitive if shadowy *J*. This encoded sign signals the film's expressionist method, with an intertwined but tense political text and context. The abbreviated *J* signifies MGM's approach and avoidance strategy of the Jewish story. While the *J* is visible, the full word "Jew" (or, in German, *Jude*) is never spelled out or articulated, and so as Roth recedes into the darkness of his prison, his back to the camera, the symbol is easily missed or dismissed. The film's oblique representation of Jewish identity and persecution also suggests tensions between the shared and professed humanistic values of British and American democracy and whether to intervene in the fate of European Jewry. The film's hybrid British and American teamwork parallels Britain's special relationship with its American cousins. Because the two nations' shared values included belief in national homogeneity and unity, portraying Jewish difference would represent an aesthetic and polemical challenge.[47] In fact, David Welky argues that to attack Nazism "as an anti-Semitic ideology . . . remained taboo" for Hollywood at the time.[48] Instead of resolving this challenge, *The Mortal Storm* expresses its concern for Europe's persecuted Jews in an encoded fashion. Jewish identity can be identified, but it remains unclear whether it can be integrated or acculturated into this film at this historical moment.

Representing "the torch of science," Viktor Roth teaches an ethos of open inquiry that Bottome associates with both the British empirical tradition and Jewish contributions to civilization. Roth's scientific conclusion, for which he is expelled from his university, is that "physiology has been unable to discover any differences between the races." While this statement confirms Crowther's analysis of the film as "blistering anti-Nazi propaganda," through its expressionist lighting, angles, and framing, it also confronts American audiences with the rampant racism and antisemitism in their nation's midst.[49] That this reminder could easily have alienated its audience there is no doubt. But the film assuages its audiences' reservations by inviting them to identify with Roth as his students celebrate his sixtieth birthday, honoring his scientific humanity. Establishing rapport with the audience, the film issues this invitation at the beginning when Roth's students award him a trophy bearing the figure of a torchbearer. His response also appeals to the audience: "Into your hands will fall the torch of science." The image of the torch permeates the film as an expressionist symbol of hope and a dystopian warning that myths of Aryan supremacy overtake rational discourse. Those myths are dramatized in a harrowing scene of book burning wherein great works of Western tradition are subjected to the torch.[50] The setting may be Germany, but the warning extends to the United States.

At the end of the film, as the camera pans the Roths' empty house, disembodied voices echo through the rooms from the short-lived birthday celebration. Anton Kaes describes the visual lexicon of German expressionist film that applies to this scene and others in *The Mortal Storm*: "harsh lighting that produces deep shadows cutting across a scene," rooms and domestic objects that register both their own two-dimensional artificiality and the characters' deep feelings, "mute signs that signify what cannot be put into words."[51] We hear echoes of Roth talking of tolerance and humor while the trophy fades into a shadowy reflection. As the scene ends, the perspective moves slowly from closed doors to footsteps in the snow. Expressionistically, whiteness ironically signifies annihilated innocence and a polemical shift from the hopes of humanistic enlightenment to the dire consequences of Nazism's dogma. At the same time, the film echoes with Viktor Roth's voice of reason and humanity. Bottome's polemical narrative is thus translated by Claudine West and Frank Borzage into a visual hybrid perspective. The film graphically depicts the values of accepting difference and warns its American audience about the consequences of not defending them.

The film's expressionism calls attention to Britain's diasporic cultural presence in Hollywood. Instead of MGM's typical romantic fantasies of self-discovery and restoration of social and ethical norms, *The Mortal*

Storm displaces the trust in communal traditions. Hervé Dumont asserts that Frank Borzage exploited conventions of popular melodrama to create "a platform . . . centered around basic psychological conflict" involving "everyday characters with whom everyone can immediately identify."[52] As we argue, however, these universalizing themes are transformed by the film's British-American confrontation with Nazi psychology and practices. In an illustrative scene, when Amélie Roth visits her incarcerated husband, expressionistic images and lighting denote the lethal promises of Nazism. Amélie's nighttime entrance and exit from the concentration camp are engulfed in a rainstorm in which ominous flashes of light expose the raindrops as composed of dust. The power that has reduced Germany's human landscape to dust is also exposed by the lightning, seen in the *Schutzstaffel* (SS) banner that flies high over the concentration camp tower. It was the SS that was charged with running the Nazi system of concentration camps. It was the SS that was subsequently charged with implementing the Final Solution. With metonymic implications, the camp has poisoned nature, the air the nation breathes, and therefore destroys any idea of the nation's purity.[53] The room where Amélie meets her husband is lit only enough to cast their shadows on the walls, which appear to close in on them, as though they have in essence already been squashed. Amélie's devotion to her Jewish husband has excised any value she may have had as a "superior" German Aryan woman.[54] A window reveals the fate that awaits them as individuals and as a nation. A circle of undifferentiated prisoners marches aimlessly past to be murdered by exhaustion.

Shifting shades of gray suggest how the couple's anguish must be encrypted to avoid inciting the wrath of the Nazi guards. In expressive concert with the film's palette, the couple's gentle voices and facial movements reveal what explicit dialogue cannot. While the Roths' expression of mutual love and respect is obvious, the scene's context reconfigures the meaning of "everyday characters." Love here is not destroyed by "basic psychological conflict" but by the political consequences of Nazi racial ideology. The enforcement of Aryan supremacism ensures that Viktor Roth must be annihilated solely for his Jewish identity and scientific empiricism, the combination of which defies Nazism's mythology. With this embedded argument, the film complies with and challenges both its self-imposed constraints and those of its audience. For racial supremacism does not only target the Jew. Roth's racially "contaminated" widow is forced into exile to save her life and those of their half-Jewish son and daughter. Freya's arrest and the confiscation of her father's scientific treatise encapsulate the Nazis' defensive war against intellectual inquiry embodied by the Jews. Resonating with an earlier image of storm troopers burning books by prominent German intellectuals such as Stefan Zweig, Albert Einstein, and Thomas Mann, the film argues that the German enlightenment is already in exile. By extension, the film's narrative of exile reverberates with that of British artists in Hollywood who defended their nation under attack. Creatively interweaving the interests of Britain and the United States, these artists adapted Bottome's polemical novel to argue that saving the Jews meant defending the enlightenment Nazi Germany was destroying.

In its representation of intercultural love and marriage, the film supports its own politically inflected British-American construction. This representation also combines love and marriage as a middlebrow subject and the film's cinematic experimentation. The Roths' marriage as an idyll of German–Jewish mutual love and respect is condemned by the Nazi dogma prohibiting *Rassenschande* (race defilement). In a critical parallel structure, the love between the Roths' half-Jewish, half-German aristocratic daughter, Freya, and the pacifist peasant, Martin, is portrayed as Germany's only possibility for redemption. As the young couple prepares to ski across a forbidding mountain pass to freedom, Martin's mother presents them with a traditional bridal cup on which their names will be engraved once they are married. Situated on a windowsill, as the last of a line of such family goblets, its symbolic position insists that the only possibility for a democratic German future lies in marrying political resistance to the acceptance and integration of cultural difference. Attesting to this marriage is the scene's interweaving of pastoral romance and anti-Nazi polemic. But just as the Roths are trapped by the immutability of Nazi doctrine, so Freya and Martin are prevented from crossing the border of Nazi Germany into the possibility of freedom. The film's ending and beginning bracket and parse the ambivalent opening frames, which introduce the conceit of a mortal storm. In painted images, dark clouds and thunderclaps threaten a picturesque landscape in which a German university town nestles cosily within gently sloped mountains. As the credits run, and the year 1933 is announced, a narrator proclaims,

"When man was new upon the earth he was frightened by the dangers of the elements [and responded,] I must kill my fellow man to appease angry gods. . . . How soon will man build a lasting shelter against his ignorance and fear?"

Dwarfed by ominous stone-faced mountains at the end, the couple's defiant love is doomed. A Nazi patrol, filmed as mirror images of the mountains, shadowing the tiny but intrepid figures, shoots and kills Freya.[55] The film ends with Martin carrying her body across the border accompanied by the singing of "Gate of the Year" by Minnie Louise Haskins: "Give me a light that I may tread safely into the unknown." The ending is fraught with all the film's textual and contextual tensions. Like Amélie and Rudi, even had they crossed the border safely, the film's 1940 production year warns that there can be no welcome awaiting anti-Nazi dissidents in Nazi-occupied Europe. This border, like the windows in the concentration camp scene and elsewhere, reflects the world as a Nazi prison. Yet within this unhappy ending, as the figure of Martin fills the screen, the film's dire warning morphs into a visual and spoken statement of hope. As Welky notes, "Stewart plays Martin without an accent[,] . . . making his every line ring with the tones of the American heartland."[56] Just as the pacifist peasant intervenes in the assault on the schoolmaster, carrying Freya's body across the border suggests that in assuming responsibility for the fate of Europe, the Americanized hero will act to defend the United States and help Britain fight against Nazi tyranny.

The Mortal Storm originated in the imagination of Phyllis Bottome, a British writer, who was inspired to write her novel by her passionate response to Hitler's plans for world conquest and what that meant for the Jews. The cosmopolitan production team, British writers conjoined with Weimar-era artistry, allowed *The Mortal Storm* to transcend the studio censorship that threatened to distort the message of Bottome's novel irrevocably. The novel and its film adaptation dramatize her interpretation of a relationship she viewed as crucial: the United States as Britain's necessary partner to defeat Nazism and to save the world's imperiled Jews. In one of the novel's most powerful scenes, Professor Roth teaches his son, Rudi, about Jewish contributions to civilization, without which modern democracy and culture could not have developed. Thus the novel and film conjoin the fate of the Jewish people with Britain, and by extension the United States, confirming the right of the two countries to call themselves democratic. In the end, diasporic cinema, British as well as European, brought the plight of the Jews to the American screen at least once on the eve of war. The hybrid identity of the film and those who helped produce it attest to the democratic identity Bottome would wish to affirm for both Britain and the United States.

Notes

1. See Estel Eforgan, *Leslie Howard: The Lost Actor* (London: Valentine Mitchell, 2010), 84, 95, 106–7 for a perceptive discussion of the British film industry in the period between the two world wars.

2. Phyllis Bottome to Robert Vansittart, December 10, 1939, British Library (London), (henceforth BL), ADD. MS. 88921/3/2, informing him of her appointment to the American division of the Ministry of Information. See also Nicholas Cull, *Selling War: The British Propaganda Campaign against American Neutrality in World War II* (Oxford: Oxford University Press, 1995), 38–56.

3. Controversy continues over Borzage's directorial role on *The Mortal Storm.* Victor Saville sued in 1941 to have his role as director acknowledged in the screen credits. Jimmy Stewart, one of the film's lead actors, maintained that he never saw Saville on the set. See Hervé Dumont, *Frank Borzage: The Life and Films of a Hollywood Romantic* (Jefferson, N.C.: McFarland, 2006), 284–301.

4. Not all of Bottome's suggestions were taken, however. In opposition to her, the studio insisted on substituting "non-Aryan" for "Jew," an issue to be discussed in this chapter.

5. *The Shopworn Angel,* directed by H. C. Potter. (Los Angeles: MGM, 1938); *The Shop around the Corner,* directed by Ernst Lubitsch (Los Angeles: MGM, 1940). Directed by the celebrated master of romantic comedy films, Ernst Lubitsch, *The Shop around the Corner* takes place in a troubled Budapest in 1940. Although Hungary would not be invaded by Nazi Germany until 1944, its fascist government was only nominally independent. Hungary's history of antisemitism showed that the nation shared many values with Nazism, but the nation's Jews were not rounded up and deported to Auschwitz until after Germany took over in March 1944. Despite this respite, the film suggests that in 1940, Budapest tingles with the tensions of both economic and political threats. Whereas Hitler promised Germany economic recovery and political glory, Lubitsch's Budapest still suffers from the Great Depression, and even the reconciled lovers cannot represent anything more than a romantic interlude.

6. Middlebrow studies is now a going concern, with the Middlebrow Network and scholarly studies of the subject. The vigorous network of scholars reevaluating and developing a new middlebrow aesthetic are situating it within modern literary and cultural history and are bringing serious critical attention to many marginalized writers, artists, filmmakers, and playwrights. Scholars in middlebrow studies are also recovering and reassessing works by major artists and writers that do not seem to cohere with their more critically acclaimed oeuvres. See the special issues of the journals *Modernist Cultures* and *The Space Between: Literature and Culture 1914–1945,* as well as Erica Brown and Mary Grover, *Middlebrow Literary Cultures: The Battle of the Brows, 1920–1960* (Basingstoke, U.K.: Palgrave, 2012).

7. Bottome published two editions of the novel. Faber and Faber, London, published the British edition in the fall of 1937. Little, Brown released the American edition on April 4, 1938.

8. Phyllis Bottome to Julian Lucas, 12 December 1938, BL. ADD. MS. 88921/3/1.

9. Phyllis Bottome to Locker-Lampson, 12 December 1938, BL. ADD. MS. 88921/3/1.

10. Phyllis Bottome, *The Goal* (London: Faber & Faber, 1962), 275.

11. Ibid., 258.

12. Ibid., 258.

13. Charles Drazin, *Korda: Britain's Only Movie Mogul* (London: Sidgwick and Jackson, 2002), 58.

14. Greg Walker, "The Roots of Alexander Korda: Myths of Identity and the International Film," in *Patterns of Prejudice*, vol. 37, no. 1 (2003) as cited in Nathan Abrams, "

15. Scott A. Berg, *Goldwyn: A Biography* (New York: Riverhead Books, 1998), 305, 337.

16. Phyllis Bottome to Locker-Lampson, 12 December 1938, BL. ADD. MS. 88921/3/1.

17. Phyllis Bottome to Professor Potter, 9 March 1939, BL. ADD. MS. 88921/2/1.

18. Ibid. See also Thomas Doherty, *Hitler and Hollywood, 1933–1939* (New York: Columbia University Press, 2013).

19. M. Bernstein, *Walter Wanger: Hollywood Independent* (Berkeley: University of California Press, 1994), 129–50.

20. Phyllis Bottome to Bishop of Chichester, September 19, 1938, BL. ADD. MS. 88921/2/1.

21. Maurice Eisendrath to Phyllis Bottome, February 14, 1939, BL. ADD. MS. 88921/3/3.

22. Neal Gabler, *An Empire of Their Own: How the Jews Invented Hollywood* (New York: Anchor Books, 1989), 280–81.

23. E. Forbes Dennis to Eisendrath, February 28, 1939, BL. ADD. MS. 88921/3/3.

24. Maurice Eisendrath to Edgar Magnin, February 28, 1939, BL. ADD. MS. 88921/3/3.

25. Phyllis Bottome to Maurice Eisendrath, 20 May 1939, BL. ADD. MS. 88921/3/3.

26. Eisendrath to Magnin, 28 February 1939, BL. ADD. MS. 88921/3/3.

27. Gabler, *Empire of Their Own*, 280–85.

28. Steven Carr, *Hollywood Anti-Semitism, A Cultural History up to World War II* (Cambridge: Cambridge University Press, 2001), 60–93.

29. Bottome to Eisendrath, 20 May 1939, BL. ADD. MS. 88921/3/3.

30. David Welky, *The Moguls and the Dictators* (Baltimore, Md.: Johns Hopkins University Press, 2010), 375.

31. Scriptwriter Claudine West subsequently had to obtain Mayer's approval for script revisions. He had overall authority over script content.

32. Phyllis Bottome to Sidney Franklin, 7 February 1940, University of Southern California Cinema Arts Archive. MGM File on *The Mortal Storm* (henceforth USC/MGM).

33. Ibid.

34. Various versions West presented to Mayer are found in the Margaret Herrick Library's script collection. Pogorelskin discusses this point in her "Phyllis Bottome's *The*

Mortal Storm: Film and Controversy," *Space Between: Literature and Culture, 1914–1945* 6, no. 1 (2010): 39–58; 42–45. Pam Hirsch's essay, "Authorship and Propaganda: Phyllis Bottome and the Making of *The Mortal Storm*," *Historical Journal of Film, Radio and Television* 32, no. 1 (March 2012): 57–72, at 62 refers to West's "writing and rewriting" the scene where Rudi asks his father, "What is a Jew?" to save it from MGM censorship. She does not cite the earlier essay on this point. Pogorelskin determined West's rewrites from studying those scripts. Whereas Hirsch focuses on negotiations within MGM to purchase Bottome's novel, Pogorelskin discovered significant pressure to purchase by the North American Jewish community.

35. All film citations of *The Mortal Storm* are to the MGM 1940 production attributed to Frank Borzage as director.

36. Bottome to Franklin, 7 February 1940, USC/MGM.

37. Pam Hirsch's fine biography of Bottome recounts her exposure to both cultures and political development as a result of her hybrid upbringing: *The Constant Liberal* (London: Quartet, 2010).

38. Cull discusses Britain's propaganda aimed at the United States in the late 1930s. In that decade, revisionist interpretations held that the British propaganda machine had lured the United States into the war in Europe against U.S. best interests.

39. Among the artists, writers, and filmmakers who expressed antiwar polemics were Ernest Hemingway, Robert Graves, and Virginia Woolf.

40. Sidney Franklin, an American Jew, who collaborated closely with Claudine West, the primary scriptwriter, produced the film. Victor Saville, who was British and Jewish, has received credit as director along with Frank Borzage, an Academy Award–winning director for *Seventh Heaven* (1927). Saville took over after Franklin found the news of Nazi atrocities and their filmic representation too painful. Because he was British and the United States was not at war, Saville's name could not appear in the credits under the U.S. Neutrality Act. Saville subsequently contested Borzage's role on the film; see Dumont, *Frank Borzage*, 289.

41. Quoted in Dumont, *Frank Borzage*, 288.

42. Helen Corbaley, "Synopsis of *The Mortal Storm*" (early 1939), Archive of the Academy of Motion Picture Arts and Sciences, Margaret Herrick Library, Los Angeles, as cited in Pogorelskin, "Phyllis Bottome's *The Mortal Storm*: Film and Controversy," *The Space Between*, 39.

43. Welky notes that the film's attacks on Nazism so differed from MGM's typically glamorous and "wholesome family fare . . . that it could not help but surprise moviegoers" (*Moguls and the Dictators*, 202).

44. Those who clung to pacifism throughout the war were not receptive to Bottome's critique, but there were other British writers, such as Storm Jameson and Rebecca West, who argued that war had become an urgent necessity with Nazi Germany on the march. See Phyllis Lassner, *British Women Writers of World War II* (Basingstoke, U.K.: Palgrave Macmillan, 1998).

45. *The Mortal Storm* made the *New York Times*'s Ten Best List 1940, Best Picture of the Month for June 1940, *Film Daily*'s Ten Best Pictures 1940, and the "Canadian Critics Best Selection of 1939–40," but audiences found it "far too depressing," and after a cost of $900,000, it earned only $4,000,000, a fifth of profits for *Gone With the Wind* (Dumont, *Frank Borzage*, 288, 301).

46. Bosley Crowther, "The Screen," *New York Times*, June 21, 1940.

47. For British wartime myths of national unity, see Angus Calder, *The People's War* (London: Cape, 1986). For British humanistic values in relation to its Jewish history, see David Cesarani, ed., *The Making of Modern Anglo-Jewry* (Oxford: Basil Blackwell, 1990). For analysis of American and British liberalism and the plight of the Jew, see Tony Kushner, *The Holocaust and the Liberal Imagination* (Oxford: Blackwell, 1994).

48. Welky, *Moguls and the Dictators*, 204.

49. Crowther, "The Screen," *New York Times*, June 21, 1940. Exiled German Jewish directors who brought German expressionist film style to Hollywood include Billy Wilder and Fritz Lang. For studies of expressionist style, see Marek Haltof. "From Gothicism to Demonism: A Literary Transition to German Expressionist Film," *S: European Journal for Semiotic Studies* 4, no. 3 (1992): 441–58. Thomas Elsaesser, "Time, Space and Causality: Joe May, Fritz Lang and the Modernism of German Detective Film," *Modernist Cultures* 5, no. 1 (2010): 79–105.

50. We wish to thank Kristin Bluemel for her incisive observation.

51. Anton Kaes, *Shell Shocked Cinema* (Princeton, N.J.: Princeton University Press, 2009), 84.

52. Dumont, *Frank Borzage*, 17.

53. According to Dumont, this was the first film replica of a concentration camp and was based on information from second unit director Richard Rossen, who had been interned by the Nazis in Austria (*Frank Borzage*, 296).

54. Gisela Bock theorizes that Nazi racial and sexual hygiene combined in policy and practice, leading to "racist sexism," the demand on "ethnically or socially superior women to have children they may not want," and "sexist racism," applied to socially or ethnically inferior women whose pregnancies were prohibited, "Racism and Sexism in Nazi Germany: Motherhood, Compulsory Sterilization, and the State," *Different Voices: Women and the Holocaust,* Carol Rittner and John K. Roth, Eds .(New York: Paragon, 1993), 161–86. 178.

55. Reflecting Bottome's more radical politics and the 1937 date of her novel, the original ending is more optimistic. Although Freya's lover, an avowed communist, is killed, she gives birth to his child in the Breitners' humble home (suggesting a crèche), leaves the baby to be raised with their humane values, and skis over the border to make her way to American freedom and her scientific career.

56. Welky, *Moguls and the Dictators*, 205.

LAWRENCE BARON

Mr. Emmanuel (1944)

A Belated British Film about Nazi Antisemitism

Harold French's *Mr. Emmanuel* (1944) holds the distinction of being the first and only wartime British commercial feature film to focus on Nazi antisemitism.[1] Adapted from Louis Golding's novel of the same title, the movie chronicles the perilous search by Isaac Emmanuel, an elderly British Jewish man, for the German mother of a half-Jewish German refugee boy whom he has befriended in England. Isaac fails to realize that merely inquiring about the wife of a Jewish dissident who had been jailed and killed by the Gestapo will attract the attention of the authorities. Instead, he naively expects his British citizenship to protect him from any harassment. Although Patricia Erens commended it for its unique depiction of a Jewish protagonist fighting against German persecution,[2] *Mr. Emmanuel* strikes scholars today as timid, considering what was publically known about the extermination of European Jews at the time of its release, and they take the view in hindsight that American and British filmmakers should have depicted and denounced the ongoing genocide more forthrightly. Commenting on Isaac being shocked when the Gestapo grabs his passport and slaps him in the face with it, Ilan Avisar sarcastically remarks that British audiences probably deemed this "a grave national insult—certainly something more offensive than the persecution of the Jews."[3] Estel Eforgan belittles "the groveling attitudes of the protagonist," which she ascribes to the "incomprehension and vacillation amongst older British Jews," who "had been so browbeaten all their lives about their inferior status as Jews that they seemed incapable of protest or action at this vital time."[4]

The producers of *Mr. Emmanuel*, however, assumed that the egregious mistreatment of its eponymous saintly hero would anger American and British audiences and critics when the movie premiered. The British press book proclaims that its story affords "a rare insight into a people and country held in the grip of a regime which led to the present world-shattering events" and underscores Germany's contempt for other nations with the poster tagline, "If you've ever had a British passport, see this film."[5] The American publicity campaign for the movie emphasized the indignation it would arouse: "If you're a liberal minded, big-hearted, tolerant American with a true love for your fellow men, then you're going to get mad at the villains in this picture."[6] The *Gloucestershire Echo* highlighted that the movie dealt with "the brutal treatment of the Jews by the Gestapo."[7] When the picture opened in the United States in January 1945, *New York Times* critic Bosley Crowther praised it "as the sharpest damnation of Nazi 'kultur' that the screen is likely to show for some time."[8]

To account for the contradictory past and present reactions to *Mr. Emmanuel*, one must remember that its restrained representation of the Nazi persecution of the Jews was typical of both British and Hollywood productions that tackled this subject matter. In the 1930s, the censorship guidelines that both film industries adopted closely resembled each other to ensure the distribution of English-language films on both sides of the Atlantic.[9] In practice this meant eschewing derogatory depictions of countries, ethnic groups, and religious denominations to avoid offending domestic advocacy groups and foreign governments, particularly when American neutrality and British appeasement were still each country's official policy toward German expansionism.[10]

After Britain entered the war and President Roosevelt incrementally shifted American policy from neutrality to assistance, British films such as *Pastor Hall* (1940) and *Pimpernel Smith* (1941) and American films such as *The Mortal Storm* (1940) and *The Pied Piper* (1942) attacked Nazi racism, either employing the generic euphemism "non-Aryan" to identify Jewish characters or portraying Jews among other groups as victims of Nazi persecution.[11] Only Charlie Chaplin's *The Great Dictator* (1940) dared to put Adolf Hitler's hatred of the Jews at the center of a motion picture.[12] The wartime agencies in both countries that regulated the content of motion pictures cautioned against singling out Jews as victims of Nazi barbarism, lest this attention substantiate German propaganda that the war was being fought to serve Jewish interests. The movie censorship boards in each country discouraged graphic depictions of Nazi atrocities that might repel audiences, demonize Germans, disseminate false atrocity reports (as happened in World War I), or weaken civilian morale. Those involved in the policing and production of feature films assumed antisemitic sentiment was widespread and avoided exacerbating it. They preferred to offer escapist entertainment to their audiences rather than depressing depictions of wartime atrocities.[13]

Even though Jews were disproportionately represented in the British film industry, they rarely used their productions to spotlight the plight of Hitler's Jewish victims. This tactic served several purposes. It publically subordinated their ethnic and religious backgrounds to their British citizenship. As Nathan Abrams has observed, Britain's concept of civic equality "has not warmly embraced the notion of the hyphenate identity as in the United States."[14] During the war, minimizing or neglecting the topic of Jewish persecution conformed to national censorship guidelines and preempted accusations that Jews in the film industry were exploiting their positions to pursue a parochial agenda. The hypersensitivity of Jewish filmmakers to having their loyalties impugned reflected awareness among those who were British-born of an undercurrent of antisemitism in the country and legitimate fears among émigrés that their alien origins cast a pall of suspicion over their true allegiances.[15]

As more news reports about German war crimes surfaced, a few filmmakers were emboldened to incorporate Nazi crimes against civilian populations into their movies.[16] A year after the "euthanasia" protest in Germany in 1941, the Hollywood screwball comedy *Once upon a Honeymoon* (1942) speculated that Jews in German camps were slated to be sterilized.[17] *Hangmen Also Die* (1943) and *Hitler's Madman* (1943) dramatized the reprisal executions of males over the age of sixteen that occurred in the Czech town of Lidice in June 1942;[18] whereas the British short *The Silent Village* (1943) transposed this scenario to a Welsh town.[19] In December 1942, the Allied Powers issued a joint declaration with the other countries belonging to the fledgling United Nations confirming that Germany was implementing "Hitler's oft-repeated intention to exterminate the Jewish people in Europe" and pledging "that those responsible for these crimes shall not escape retribution."[20]

Columbia Pictures' *None Shall Escape* (1944) was the only wartime American or British feature film to recognize that the Third Reich planned to eradicate the Jews of Europe.[21] It envisioned what a war crimes trial against the *Schutzstaffel* (SS) officer in charge of German racial policies in a Polish city would reveal. In one scene, a rabbi's clarion call for his fellow Jews to revolt rather than passively board a deportation train to certain death prompts the SS commander to order his troops to machine-gun the Jews down.[22] The movie became a box office success and received an Oscar nomination for best original story. The Communist Party newspaper the *Daily Worker* called it "the most militant indictment of anti-Semitism in the history of Hollywood."[23]

Unlike *None Shall Escape*, *Mr. Emmanuel* confined itself to critiquing the suppression of Aryan-Jewish mixed marriages and political dissidents in Germany during the 1930s. Like its American counterparts *The Mortal Storm*, *Address Unknown* (1944), and *The Seventh Cross* (1944), the film's prewar setting absolved it of the responsibility to extrapolate the genocidal potential of Hitler's persecution of the Jews into the future war.[24] These films shared being attenuated adaptations of popular novels. Viewers familiar with the novels probably perceived the sinister implications behind the less-than-explicit filmed versions, filling in details that had been deliberately deleted. Golding coauthored the script for *Mr. Emmanuel* with veteran screenwriter Gordon Wellesley, who already had penned several British anti-Nazi movies, most notably *Night Train to Munich* (1940).[25] Director Harold French had been churning out anti-Nazi films such as *Secret Mission* (1942) and *Unpublished Story* (1942) during the war as well.[26] While the film version of *Mr. Emmanuel* toned down the Jewish content of Golding's 1939 novel, it remained faithful to his convictions that Jews had achieved acceptance as fellow citizens in Great Britain and faced an implacable foe in Germany.

Louis Golding's Anglo-Jewish Identity and Politics

When Golding died in 1958, the *Jewish Chronicle's* obituary considered him "the best known novelist produced by the Anglo-Jewish community since Israel Zangwill."[27] The son of Jewish immigrants from Czarist

Russia, Golding grew up in Manchester and achieved fame with his "Doomington Saga," a series of books chronicling the generational conflicts within Jewish families residing in Manchester's Jewish enclave, where Jews and gentiles resided on opposite sides of the same streets but for the most part did not intermingle. Instances of hostility and occasional friendship and romance mark the relationships between the two groups. Golding inserted "doom" into his fictional name for Manchester to signify "not only the doom of the factory-hands in the factories and the clerks in its warehouses, but the doom of the Jews who live in its Ghetto, the doom that presided over their dispersal." [28] Despite interfaith tensions, he stressed that British Jews deeply loved their adopted country and had earned the equality granted to them by British law. In Golding's novel *Five Silver Daughters* (1934), May Silver founds a school located in the English countryside to Anglicize Jewish children from the urban slums in accordance with her belief that "Jews make a better job of being English than they make of being anything else in the world. . . . They've had more training in adapting themselves, to begin with. And I think that what they bring with them fits in better with the English idea."[29] The first chapter of *Mr. Emmanuel* tellingly begins with Isaac Emmanuel discovering that a swastika has been scrawled in chalk on the front door of his flat on Magnolia Street, but it ends with an anonymous fair-haired, blue-eyed gentile youth erasing it.[30]

To ensure that Jews would have gentile allies, Golding advocated intermarriage. His novels are replete with Jewish-gentile love stories that sometimes culminate in the non-Jew intervening on behalf of his or her Jewish mate. In *Mr. Emmanuel* Isaac receives a letter from his old friend, the former Rose Berman, "one of those Magnolia Street folk — they had been few — who had married on the opposite side of the street."[31] Having wed naval captain John Cooper and moved to a cottage in the countryside, she requests Isaac's assistance in caring for five German refugee boys while her husband is away. Here Emmanuel meets Bruno Rosenheim, the troubled youth whose Jewish father died at the hands of the Nazis and whose Aryan mother no longer sends him letters. When John returns, his support for offering his home as a respite for the boys is evident.[32]

Parenthetically, Golding based Bruno on Kaspar Nägele, a German Jewish teen whom he helped place with an English host family in 1937. Kaspar's gentile father, Reinhold, a modernist painter, had been banned from exhibiting in Germany but could have received permission to do so if he would have divorced his Jewish wife, Alice. The couple eventually escaped from Germany in 1939.[33]

Once Isaac announces his plans to search for Bruno's mother in Germany, the Coopers try to dissuade him, with John volunteering to be his proxy.[34] When Isaac's quixotic quest leads to his arrest, Elsie Silver, the prodigal daughter of his best friend, Sam, comes to his rescue by pressuring her lover, a high-ranking Nazi named Willi Brockenburg, to intervene. Thus, a liaison between a Nazi and a Jew becomes the deus ex machina that secures Isaac's release from imprisonment. As Gavin Schaffer has remarked, "Through intermarriage and greater tolerance, Golding clearly hoped that bonds would be rebuilt between religious and ethnic communities."[35] While such optimism supplied Golding with a romantic resolution of Isaac's dilemma, it hardly represented a realistic defense against the enmity arrayed against the Jews during the Holocaust.

Notwithstanding his confidence in interfaith marriages, Golding considered Jews a separate race bound together by a common ancestry, history, and religion. He firmly believed that most Jews possessed a vestigial memory of their collective past that compelled them to protect their vulnerable Jewish brethren in the present. Thus, the Jewish partners in interfaith relationships felt an instinctual solidarity with endangered Jews.[36] Isaac Emmanuel's anticipation that the ostracized Elsie Silver would use her Nazi connections to aid his search for Bruno's mother arises from Golding's idea of Jewish racial responsibility.[37] In the novel, Elsie's internal monologue over why she decides to help Isaac expressed a primordial obligation as much as it did personal gratitude to her childhood benefactor:

> As for race, she could no more detach herself from her father and mother, her grandfathers and grandmothers, her great-grandfathers and great-great-grandmothers than she could put on some other body and start walking about in it. With what was she a Jew, then? With whatever she possessed of virtue, every fibre of it. . . . It was the key by which she entered into herself. To be true to the Jew in her left her a tolerable human being, neither better nor worse than most. To be untrue was to be the

rat that leaves the sinking ship (though even once again the ship might not sink after all).[38]

As Elsie's line of reasoning discloses, Golding perceived Jewish solidarity as an extension of personal integrity. To betray a fellow Jew was to betray a part of one's self. Creative license excused him from explaining why five years of Nazi rule elapsed before Elsie acted on this sense of obligation.

Golding's lifelong concern over antisemitism heightened in the 1930s. He recalled hearing frightening stories about the pogroms from his parents, who had fled Russia on their account. Growing up in Manchester, he experienced being taunted by gentile peers with epithets such as "sheeny" and "Christ-killer" and resented as a conspirator from "the alien race" that had impoverished adolescent mine and factory workers. At Oxford, Golding encountered the snobbish antisemitism of traditional elites who politely denigrated the accomplishments of Jewish parvenus.[39] An inveterate traveler, he toured Germany in the early 1920s and 1930s and witnessed with dismay the emergence of a virulent racist strain of Jew hatred fueled by Germany's defeat, inflation, political polarization, and unemployment.[40] The book *The Jewish Problem* (1938), which credited Golding as its author to maximize readership but was largely written by Britain's preeminent Jewish historian, Cecil Roth, with assistance from the Anglican Church's pioneer of Christian-Jewish dialogue, James Parkes, echoed Golding's realization "that the Jewish Problem has been a Gentile Problem from the first decades in which it raised its baneful head."[41] The following year Golding reiterated its message in his own book *Hitler through the Ages*, construing Hitler as the latest incarnation of the antisemitic tyrants who had tormented Jews throughout history.[42]

Even before Hitler's accession to power, Golding endorsed immigration to Palestine as one way to shield Jews from current and future outbreaks of antisemitism, reconnect them with their heritage and homeland, and reinvigorate them as a people. In 1927 he visited Palestine for the first time and recorded his impressions in the book *Those Ancient Lands*, which was published the following year. Therein he rhapsodized about the revival of Hebrew as a colloquial language, the historical significance of ancient biblical sites, and the promise afforded by the new Zionist settlements in the British mandate. He appreciated the Zionist goal of transforming the Jewish people from a nation of financiers, intellectuals, merchants, and professionals into factory workers and farmers.[43] At the end of his travel memoir *The World I Knew* (1940), he wished for a peaceful resolution of the Arab-Jewish conflict over Palestine, whether it entailed establishing a binational state with the Arabs if their opposition could be overcome, a sovereign Jewish state, or a crown colony under British rule. For him, any of these outcomes would fulfill "a millennial dream" and heal "the agony of Central Europe."[44] Golding's expectations testified to his gradual shift away from his preoccupation with the social acceptance of British Jewry to coping with the dire exigencies of European Jewry.[45]

Mr. Emmanuel: From Novel to Film

As soon as publicity surrounding the British release of *Mr. Emmanuel* was distributed in the spring of 1939, Golding learned that its benevolent protagonist and malevolent Nazi antagonists would offend some readers. He sent a synopsis of the book to Charles Graves, a journalist who wrote for the proappeasement *Daily Mail*. Graves responded by commenting in his column, "Louis Golding, being a Jew and therefore anti-Hitler has tied the story up with Nazi Germany. As he describes the plot, it sounds very insulting to Germany. But perhaps he hasn't really been so remarkably virulent as he suggested."[46] In a subsequent letter to Golding, Graves claimed he had done him a favor: "In the meantime, I have, you may not be aware, done you a very good turn with all the anti-Hitler readers in this country."[47] Graves was referring to the growth of British interventionist sentiment in reaction to Germany's annexation of Czechoslovakia in March 1939 in flagrant violation of the 1938 Munich Agreement with Britain and France to respect Czech sovereignty.

Several weeks later Golding received a letter from Charles Jarrott, the general secretary of the nationalistic Royal Society of St. George, chiding him for having Isaac Emmanuel call himself English in the novel: "I grant he could have been British if he became naturalized—but I should be very grateful if you could tell me by what process he became an Englishman. It has been suggested to me that it is impossible for a Jew to be an Englishman because the English and the Jews are two totally different races. With this view I am personally inclined to agree." In the postscript, Jarrott incredulously wondered, "Surely Mr. Emanuel [*sic*] did not have an English passport?"[48] Although Golding's reply to Jarrott is not extant, he ironically might have agreed because he too distinguished between the English as a race and Britain as a state.[49]

Since *Mr. Emmanuel* sold well, Golding and his agents expected it would be adapted into a film, but they discovered that the timing of its publication before the outbreak of World War II dimmed the prospects of this happening. Within a week of the novel's release, his Hollywood agent, Henrietta Malkiel, cautioned against charging less than twenty-five thousand dollars for the movie rights to *Mr. Emmanuel*.[50] In July 1939, Bella Muni reported to Golding that her husband, Paul, had read the book and recommended to Warner Brothers that it be made into a motion picture. Unfortunately, the largely negative reception to the recently released *Confessions of a Nazi Spy* (1939) augured poorly for another feature film decrying Nazi fanaticism and racism. Bella lamented that "those subversive powers who are evidently very diligent in our beloved America too, have succeeded in partly, not entirely, intimidating the motion picture producers, and for the time being, at least they have decided to hold back production on anti-Nazi and Fascist pictures." She shopped the book in vain to an unnamed producer with the suggestion that casting George Arliss, who had won an Oscar in the title role of the British prime minister in *Disraeli* (1929), as Isaac Emmanuel might make the venture profitable.[51]

Why it took until 1943 for *Mr. Emmanuel* to become a viable movie project remains a mystery. The book was a commercial success in both Britain and the United States.[52] While the war itself generated sympathy for Jews as British soldiers and victims of persecution, it exacerbated domestic distrust of them as black marketeers, communists, foreign spies, and military shirkers.[53] Reluctance to mount a motion picture devoted primarily to Germany's persecution of Jews also stemmed from anxieties among Jewish citizens and refugees in the British film industry that such special pleading could lead to charges of dual loyalty.[54] Felippo Del Giudice of Two Cities Films ultimately acquired the movie rights for Golding's novel.[55] Del Giudice had fled fascist Italy for political reasons in 1933 and founded Two Cities in Great Britain in 1937 to produce films in London and Rome.[56] After enacting antisemitic laws in 1938, Italy subsequently prohibited Two Cities from making films there on the grounds that the studio had "a Jewish Board of Management."[57] Shortly after the outbreak of World War II, Britain temporarily interned Del Giudice as an enemy alien. To compensate for his foreign and religious origins, he, like many of his fellow Jewish expatriate filmmakers, accentuated his British patriotism in his public pronouncements and cinematic works.[58] He financed and produced some of Britain's most inspiring wartime films, including *In Which We Serve* (1942) and the morale-boosting *Henry V* (1944).[59] *Mr. Emmanuel's* plotline probably attracted him because it enabled him to tout the virtues of British democracy while denouncing the viciousness of Nazi antisemitism.

The movie begins with Isaac Emmanuel, played by the character actor Felix Aylmer, returning to his home on Magnolia Street after his retirement party from the Doomington Board of Guardians. Instead of being affronted by a swastika on his door as in the novel, he is greeted by amicable neighbors who want to see the pocket watch the board has awarded him in appreciation of his forty years of service. A dignified old man whose visage is silhouetted by pince-nez, an aquiline nose, and a goatee, he speaks English with a slight Yiddish inflection and looks credibly Jewish. After entering his darkened and quiet flat, he stares lovingly at a photograph of his deceased wife. His dear friend Sam Silver, played by Meier Tzelniker, stops by to inquire when he will be departing to visit his son in Palestine. Both in his accent and his appearance, the veteran Yiddish actor Tzelniker is more palpably Jewish than Isaac. The contrast between Sam and Isaac makes the latter, perhaps intentionally, seem more British. Sam advises Isaac to take a well-deserved vacation at his son's farm in Palestine. Isaac expresses less enthusiasm: "A new life: an old man sitting in the sunset on a bench against the wall." Upon receiving a request from Rose Cooper (Elspeth March) to help care for three German refugee boys boarding at her house in Sussex, Isaac exudes a renewed sense of purpose and informs Sam that he will assist Rose before embarking on the trip to Palestine.

What is striking about this opening scene is the mention of Palestine accompanied by the background melody of the Zionist anthem "Hatikvah" ("The Hope"). When Great Britain became the mandatory authority of Palestine in 1919, it pledged itself to fostering a Jewish national home in Palestine while respecting the civil and religious rights of the Arab Christians and Muslims who constituted a majority of its population. The British proposal of 1937 to partition the territory into separate

Arab and Jewish states generated violent Arab opposition. In 1939 Great Britain reversed its policy, electing to curtail Jewish immigration for the next five years and grant independence to a unified Palestine in ten years, when Jews would remain in the minority. This tilt toward the Arabs and Muslims in the British Empire aimed at securing their strategic support in the war against Germany.[60] Golding, or perhaps composer Mischa Spoliansky, a Russian-born Jewish émigré who had fled Nazi Germany, embedded "the hope" that Palestine could shelter Jews from oppression in the film's score.[61] "Hatikvah" serves as a subtextual message easily deciphered by Jewish audiences, but not necessarily by gentile ones. It recurs as a leitmotiv in subsequent scenes when Isaac is distressed: initially over how intimidated by the Nazi regime the Jews are in the Berlin pension where he is lodging and later when he is arrested by the Gestapo.

The cinematography for the scenes of the Coopers' home and environs provides a more hospitable mise-en-scène than Isaac's cramped apartment and the menacing circumstances that will envelop him in Berlin. The pastoral setting of the English countryside, the dwelling's spacious and sunlit rooms, and the joyfulness of the Cooper children identify the abode as a happy, safe place. The press book for the film highlights this cinematic strategy: "The background of the film is a vivid contrast of light and shadow, the peaceful, lovely English countryside standing out against the more subdued atmosphere of Doomington's Magnolia Street, the brittle luxury of Berlin's night resorts and drama of its sinister prisons."[62]

Within this cheery microcosm, young Bruno Rosenheim (Peter Mullins) looms like a dark cloud on an otherwise sunny horizon. When his peers receive letters from their German relatives, he gets none. Rose comments that "he's so worried about his mother." Bruno confides to Isaac that his father was a non-Aryan dissident who was beaten and killed by the Nazis and that he worries that the same fate has befallen his mother. During a birthday party for Bruno, the children sing "Oh My Darling Clementine." The refrain "you are lost and gone forever" mirrors Bruno's forebodings. He sneaks away into the night to the banks of a river. The children detect his absence and rush outside to find him. This scene segues into one of Isaac and a doctor discussing Bruno's health after his suicide attempt. Isaac comforts Bruno, but as he leaves the room, Bruno blurts out, "Next time it will be done properly." Isaac promises the boy he will go to Germany and inquire into the whereabouts of his mother if Bruno will pledge not to harm himself again.

Isaac proceeds to Germany under the ingenuous impression that his mission has no political implications and that his British passport will protect him from harassment. Arriving in a subway station in Berlin, he literally finds himself in the belly of the beast, with uniformed police, soldiers, and storm troopers milling about, Nazi pamphlets on display, and an enormous portrait of Hitler hanging above the exit to the street. At the pension where he is staying, the Jewish owner and guests fear his presence might cast aspersions on their allegiances. They suspect that they are being spied upon by an Aryan maid who was permitted to work for a Jew because she allegedly was more than forty-five years old. On a nearby street corner, Isaac meets a Jewish cigarette vendor who formerly had taught at the university in Berlin before being fired as part of the Nazi purge of Jewish faculty. Even the official at the Jewish Refugee Committee advises Isaac to return to England rather than arouse the suspicions of the police. Merely inquiring where Frau Rosenheim lives and identifying himself as English triggers a barrage of invectives from a doorkeeper in Bruno's old neighborhood: "This is a Jew's name. You say you are English! You are a Jew! Damn Jewish pig!"

Glimpsing the name "Elsie Silver" emblazoned on a nightclub marquee, Isaac hopes to enlist her in his quest. Golding's readers will recall that her father, Sam, was a former anarchist who had become wealthy during World War I and lost most of his money paying off the debts of a business partner. One of his daughters, Susan, married a Russian communist and participated in the Bolshevik Revolution. Elsie moved to Berlin during the Great Inflation, where she performed as a singer in a transvestite cabaret. She subsequently broke her father's heart by becoming the mistress of an influential Nazi named Willi Brockenburg, who claims she is an Aryan.[63] The stunning Greta Gynt, who was Del Giudice's mistress, plays the glamorous Elsie, and Walter Rilla, a German émigré who was placed under Gestapo surveillance for harboring pro-Jewish sentiments, plays the Nazi opportunist Willi.[64] Infatuated with Elsie, Willi calls her his "Jewish hellcat," but she reminds him that his compatriots know she's a "little Jew girl." He retorts that *he* decides who is considered Jewish. When Elsie receives a note from Isaac, she fondly recalls "old Emmanuel from Magnolia Street." Since she has been invited by Willi to a gala where he can flaunt Elsie in the faces of the Nazi leadership, she cannot meet with Isaac. At the ball, people whisper about her Jewish ancestry or snub her. Nonetheless, Willi's sway prevails as even Hermann Göring and Henrich Himmler treat Else cordially. The festive occasion, however, comes to an abrupt halt when the Nazi official in whose honor it was being held is assassinated.

The assassination serves as the pretext for the arrest of Isaac. His inquiries into the whereabouts of Bruno's mother have alerted the authorities to his activities. When he approaches the professor for advice on how to locate her, the professor instructs him to meet at a telephone booth around the corner. Inside the booth, the professor is petrified by a drawing sticking out of the phonebook and scurries away in panic. Isaac discovers it is a crude sketch of Hitler being hanged. Next Isaac naively goes to the police station to see if it has a current address for Bruno's mother in its files. That evening Gestapo agents descend upon his pension, pound on the door, roust him out of bed, and confiscate unsent letters he had written to friends back in England. He waves his British passport as if it were a talisman but symbolically gets smacked in the face with it by his captors.

Whatever illusion Isaac retains of rectifying this miscarriage of justice is dispelled by his encounter with the Nazi penal system. After being incarcerated for eight weeks without being charged, Isaac is summoned for an interrogation. A portrait of Hitler flanked by two swastika banners hangs behind the examiner. Isaac identifies himself as English and insists that the British Consulate be notified. The snarling examiner (Frederick Schiller) exclaims, "To us you are just a Jew!" He charges Isaac as a conspirator in the assassination plot because one of the confiscated letters was addressed to the "communist" Sam Silver. This guilt by association is not explained in the film. Only audience members familiar with the Doomington saga could make the connection of Sam to communism through his daughter Susan. Refusing to confess to a crime he did not commit, Isaac endures a beating by prison guards whose blows expressionistically appear as shadows on a wall in the manner of film noir to visually instill a sense of dread. Upon waking up, Isaac hears the din of inmates pounding on their cell doors as another prisoner is marched to his execution. The volley of gunshots serves as another harbinger of Isaac's presumed fate.

As the newspapers report the case against Isaac, Elsie Silver doubts he could be guilty of the charges. She intimates that she will withhold her affection if Willi does not persuade Göring to release Isaac, but he callously declares that "the fellow isn't an Englishman; he's just an old Jew." Elsie reminds him that "the English don't look at it that way." He storms out of her suite, but Elsie calmly tells her maid that he'll be back. In the interim Isaac attends another hearing where the real assassin, a man who obviously has been tortured, testifies to Isaac's collusion, but then retracts his statement in the face of Isaac's adamant denials. Shortly thereafter, Isaac witnesses the professor being led to his execution. Unbeknownst to him, Elsie's confidence in her feminine wiles ultimately is borne out. Willi returns twice, and each time she extracts more concessions from him. First, he arranges for a lawyer to convince Isaac to plead to a lesser charge in exchange for his release. Of course, Isaac steadfastly proclaims his innocence. Then Willi manages to get the indictment against Isaac dropped, resulting is his discharge from prison.

Some scholars erroneously argue that Elsie plays the role of the "good German" in contrast with the "bad Germans" who torment Isaac.[65] Avisar attributes her concern to her personal gratitude to him and defense of a fellow British citizen.[66] Considering how Nazi antisemitism is depicted throughout the film, audiences could logically infer that she was acutely aware of her precarious status as a Jew and correspondingly sympathized with Isaac. Golding's readers might recall Elsie's thoughts. At this stage in her development as a character, Elsie embodied the Jewish identity articulated by interwar British authors such as Golding, which Bernard Wasserstein describes as "a matter of retrospective loyalty, of warmth, a glow of fond remembrance rather than a burning bush that commands their present or shapes their future."[67] Golding subsequently deepened Elsie's Jewish consciousness in light of the persecution and decimation of European Jewry.[68] In *The Glory of Elsie Silver* (1945), Elsie loses her Aryan credentials when the German general she married dies on the Eastern Front and gets deported to the Warsaw Ghetto, where she participates in the 1943 uprising.[69] Though presumed dead, she resurfaces in *The Dangerous Places* (1951) on board the ship *Exodus* to Israel.[70] Upon retiring Elsie as a character in *To the Quayside* (1954), Golding named her his favorite creation because she began to redeem herself by rescuing Isaac and embroiled herself in "the tale of her people, the Jews, during the most critical events of their millennial history."[71]

Isaac makes one final attempt to find Bruno's mother after he is freed from prison. Elsie uses her connections to procure Frau Rosenheim's address. Played by Ursula Jeans, the woman he meets at the door insists her name is Heinkes, but Isaac persists in calling her Rosenheim until she admits that she once bore that surname but discarded it to be true to her German blood. She has married a zealous SS officer, as is evident by a Hitler portrait on the living room wall. Under the impression that Bruno had died because her husband had told her so, she is elated by the news that he is still alive. Outraged that his wife has deigned to speak to a Jew, let alone the notorious Mr. Emmanuel, Herr Heinkes (Friedrich Richter) acknowledges that he lied and burned subsequent letters from Bruno to erase "the last shameful remnant" of his wife's racial "pollution." Now he demands that she choose between her "Jewish brat" and her German husband. With mixed emotions, she casts her lot with her husband. A close-up of a swastika signals the finality of her disavowal of Bruno. Since Isaac cannot bring himself to tell Bruno that his mother has forsaken him, he reports that she is dead. By now, Bruno looks like any other English boy in his boarding school uniform and runs off to play soccer for the school team. He has gained a motherland even though he has lost his mother.

Popular and Critical Reception of the Film

The British press book for *Mr. Emmanuel* downplayed the Jewish content of the movie. It mentions Nazi antisemitism only in conjunction with Rilla's run-in with the Gestapo. Though differing from poster to poster, the taglines summarize the story line as that of "a gallant old gentleman who met strange adventures and a lovely woman in fulfilling his promise to a boy." The press book encouraged managers of theaters to organize discussions about whether Isaac was morally justified in lying to Bruno to insulate him from the more hurtful truth. The biographical sketch of Golding naturally lists the titles of his Doomington saga novels. An article about a samovar shown in one scene discloses that it was a family keepsake his mother brought to England when she fled Russia. A short press release recapitulates how Isaac "survives the hell upon earth his mission brings" to demonstrate that "the thing that matters is not race or creed or color but the essential tolerance and understanding between all men for the universal peace and brotherhood of mankind."[72]

Whether such coded or misleading publicity was necessary to overcome the hesitancy of viewers to deal with the discomfiting realities of Nazi antisemitism remains subject to debate, but some clues may be found in the polling results of a test audience that previewed the movie in July 1944, two months before its official premier. Eighty-five per cent of its members liked the film. Sixty per cent predictably selected Isaac as their favorite character. Bruno and Elsie were ranked second and third in popularity, respectively. One viewer enthusiastically endorsed the movie's message: "It is my contention that there should be more films of this nature. It might help to quell the racial prejudices, which unfortunately, exist is this country at the present time." Another smugly maintained, "It's a tribute to democratic living. I'm sure that this kind of picture portraying a worthy character, or characters, appeals to the public much more than the detective-cum-night club tripe that one sees so much of." Approximately a quarter of the audience applauded the film's realistic depictions of Nazi Germany, with one-sixth of its members finding the prison and interrogation scenes particularly effective. Despite their positive evaluations of the film, some of them thought Isaac's complacency about the risk he was running was implausible: "Surely he knew some of the workings of the Nazi system? Especially in connection with his own people."[73]

A quarter of those polled, however, expressed distaste for movies that dwelled on Nazi brutality, highlighted the plight of the Jews, propagandized against Germany, or reminded them of the war. Some of them simply were tired of stories about the suffering of Jews: "The Nazi bullying—we've had so much of it. We believe it happens." One frankly admitted, "Although I sympathize with the Jews, I'm afraid I don't like films about them." A soldier recounted how he "heard people complain of war news, and they look towards the pictures as a break from thinking of their loved ones." Along similar lines, another declared, "I don't want to be harrowed by Nazi beastliness. The war is harrowing enough." Only a handful of those who watched the preview denigrated it as "false propaganda." [74] A vocal but tiny minority of British citizens disrupted some screenings of *Mr. Emmanuel* by shouting approvingly whenever the Nazis mistreated Jews in general and Isaac in particular.[75]

The critical reception accorded the film in Great Britain and the United States was generally favorable. To be sure, some critics faulted the film for its slow pacing and sentimentality.[76] Many reviewers worried that the revelations emanating from Europe about the extent and nature of the German assault against the Jews would blunt the movie's appeal and impact. Contesting the latter claim, Peter Burnup opined, "The judgment is unsound, for it is precisely at this authentic hour of victory that the 'moral imperative' implicit in the film — admittedly the most distinguished of London's present week — is most urgently demanded."[77] Outraged over a reader's cavalier complaint that audiences were "getting tired of these Nazi horror films," Bosley Crowther defended his glowing review of *Mr. Emmanuel* on the grounds that it sensitively portrayed the personal tragedies Nazi bigotry inflicted on its victims without graphically exploiting the violence visited upon the Jews: "And in the heartbreaking disillusion of this old gentleman in a land of monstrous hate is revealed the grim scope of the malevolence that the Nazis have foisted upon the world."[78] The reviewer for *Time* speculated that the news reports might enhance the film's relevance: "But since history has made its horrors real, and the story is intelligently produced and extremely well played, it is one of the most affecting of anti-fascist screen melodramas."[79]

In June 1945, after the liberation newsreels and photos of skeletal survivors and piles of corpses left in the concentration and death camps were widely disseminated, *Mr. Emmanuel* received its national release in the United States and struck reviewers as outdated: "Had it come to the screen sooner it undoubtedly would have proved a sensation, but our minds and souls have been so repeatedly shocked with Nazi horror and tragedy the last few years, that *Mr. Emmanuel*, beautiful and heartbreaking as it is, comes as an anti-climax of sorts."[80]

Mr. Emmanuel deserves to be remembered as a touching British movie that was unique in its focus on Nazi antisemitism and a Jewish protagonist. It divulged that the Third Reich's racist ideology did not distinguish between native and foreign, assimilated and unassimilated, Jews. What it showed on-screen and what it concealed provide a portal into the mentality of British filmmakers and Anglo-Jewish authors of Golding's generation about what was considered appropriate fare for British audiences and what would pass the muster of wartime censorship. By 1944 Golding knew that a British passport could not ward off persecution, as was evident in Isaac's travails. Nevertheless, the movie muted Golding's growing awareness of the need for international Jewish solidarity and support of Palestine as a Jewish haven. Golding and director French exercised restraint and misrepresented the film in publicity to ensure its mass appeal. In hindsight, their self-censorship reduced *Mr. Emmanuel* to a curious exception to the corpus of British wartime films rather than a pioneering classic of Holocaust cinema.

Notes

1. Ilan Avisar, *Screening the Holocaust: Cinema's Images of the Unimaginable* (Bloomington: Indiana University Press, 1988), 102; Jo Fox, *Film Propaganda in Britain and Nazi Germany: World War II Cinema* (New York: Berg, 2007); James C. Robertson, *The British Board of Film Censors: Film Censorship in Britain, 1896–1950* (London: Croom Helm, 1985), 132.

2. Patricia Erens, *The Jew in American Cinema* (Bloomington: Indiana University Press, 1984), 169.

3. Avisar, *Screening the Holocaust*, 104.

4. Estel Eforgan, *Leslie Howard: The Lost Actor*, 2nd ed. (London: Vallentine Mitchell, 2013), 213.

5. *Mr. Emmanuel* Press Book, Louis Golding Papers (hereafter cited as LGP), Gen MSS 77, Box 2, File 26, Beinecke Rare Book and Manuscript Library–Yale University Library (hereafter cited as BRBML-YUL).

6. Fox, *Film Propaganda*, 144.

7. "Around the Cinemas," *Gloucestershire Echo*, November 21, 1944, 3.

8. Bosley Crowther, "*Mr. Emmanuel:* A Simple Film on Contrasts inside Germany," *New York Times*, January 8, 1945.

9. Fox, *Film Propaganda*, 141–44; Robertson, *British Board*, 145–58.

10. Gregory D. Black, *Hollywood Censored: Morality Codes, Catholics, and Movies* (New York: Cambridge University Press, 1994), 97–181; Thomas Doherty, *Hollywood and Hitler, 1933–1939* (New York: Columbia University Press, 2013), 16–17; Jeffrey Richards, "Controlling the Cinema: The British Cinema in the 1930s," *History Today* 33, no. 3 (1983): 16–17; Ben Urwand, *The Collaboration: Hollywood's Pact with Hitler* (Cambridge, Mass.: Belknap Press, 2013), 156–201; David Welky, *The Moguls and the Dictators: Hollywood and the Coming of World War Two* (Baltimore, Md.: Johns Hopkins University Press, 2008). For background on British appeasement, see Frank M. McDonough, *Neville Chamberlain, Appeasement, and the British Road to War* (Manchester, U.K.: Manchester University Press, 2010).

11. *Pastor Hall*, directed by Roy Boulting (London: Charter Film Productions, 1940); *Pimpernel Smith*, directed by Leslie Howard (London: British National Film Productions, 1942); *The Mortal Storm*, directed by Frank Borzage (Los Angeles: MGM, 1940); *The Pied Piper*, directed by Irving Pichel (Los Angeles: Twentieth Century Fox, 1942). For an excellent analysis of how early anti-Nazi films were edited to avoid violating the Production Code Administration guidelines, see Alexis Pogorelskin, "Phyllis Bottome's *The Mortal Storm:* Film and Controversy," *Space Between: Literature and Culture, 1914–1945* 6, no. 1 (2010): 39–57, as well as her chapter cowritten with Phyllis Lassner in this book.

12. *The Great Dictator*, directed by Charles Chaplin (Los Angeles: Charles Chaplin Productions, 1940). See Robert Cole, "Anglo-American Anti-fascist Film Propaganda in a Time of Neutrality: *The Great Dictator*, 1940," *Historical Journal of Film, Radio, and Television* 21, no. 2 (2001): 137–52.

13. Fox, *Film Propaganda*, 136–44. See also Steven Alan Carr, "Hollywood, the Holocaust and World War II," *Studies in Jewish Civilization*, vol.17 (Omaha, Neb.: Creighton University Press, 2006), 39–58; K. R. M. Short, "Hollywood Fights Anti-Semitism," in *Film and Radio Propaganda in World War II*, ed. K. R. M. Short, 149–55 (London: Croom Helm, 1983); Anthony Aldgate and Jeffrey Richards, *Britain Can Take It: The British Cinema in the Second World War* (Edinburgh: Basil Blackwell, 1994); Robert Murphy, *British Cinema and the Second World War* (London: Continuum, 2000); Robertson, *The British Board of Film Censors*, 128–32.

14. Nathan Abrams, "Hidden: Jewish Film in the United Kingdom, Past and Present," *Journal of European Popular Culture* 2, no. 2 (2010): 59.

15. Abrams, "Hidden," 59–62. See also Kevin Gough-Yates, "Jews and Exiles in British Cinema," *Leo Baeck Institute Year Book* 37 (1992): 517–41, at 540–41; Edward Marshall, "The Dark Alien Executive: Jewish Producers, Emigrés and the British Film Industry in the 1930s," in *New Directions in Anglo-Jewish History*, edited by Geoffrey Alderman (Boston: Academic Studies Press, 2010), 175–83; Tobias Hochscherf, *The Continental Connection: German-Speaking Emigres and British Cinema, 1927–1945* (Manchester, UK: Manchester University Press, 2011), 149–95.

16. For overviews on how Hollywood portrayed Nazis and the persecution of the Jews during World War II, see Sabine Hake, *Screen Nazis: Cinema, History, and Democracy* (Madison: University of Wisconsin Press, 2012), 32–65; Bill Krohn, "Hollywood and the Shoah, 1933–1945," in *Cinema and the Shoah: An Art Confronts the Tragedy of the Twentieth Century*, edited by Jean-Michel Frodon (Albany, N.Y.: SUNY Press, 2010), 149–71; and Urwand, *The Collaboration*, 202–30.

17. *Once upon a Honeymoon*, directed by Leo McCarey (Los Angeles: RKO Radio Pictures, 1942).

18. *Hangmen Also Die*, directed by Fritz Lang (Los Angeles: Arnold Pressburger Films, 1943); *Hitler's Madman*, directed by Douglas Sirk (Los Angeles: Producers Releasing Corporation, 1943). For more on the Office of War Information's decision to publicize stories such as Lidice but not the Holocaust, see Steven Casey, *Cautious Crusade: Franklin D. Roosevelt, American Public Opinion, and the War against Nazi Germany* (New York: Oxford University Press, 2001), 56–72.

19. *The Silent Village*, directed by Humphrey Jennings (Prague and London: Crown Film Unit, Czechoslovak Ministry of Foreign Affairs, Ministry of Information, South Wales Miners Federation, 1943); Matthew Lee, "The Ministry of Information and the Anti-Fascist Short Films of the Second War," in *Holocaust and the Moving Image: Representations in Film and Television Since 1933*, edited by Toby Haggith and Joanna Newman (London: Wallflower Press, 2005), 106–15, at 107.

20. *Wikipedia*, s.v. "Joint Declaration by Members of the United Nations," last modified September 2, 2015, http://en.wikipedia.org/wiki/Joint_Declaration_by_Members_of_the_United_Nations.

21. *None Shall Escape*, directed by André de Toth (Los Angeles: Columbia Pictures Corporation, 1943).

22. Lawrence Baron, "Trial by Audience: Bringing Nazi War Criminals to Justice in

Hollywood Films, 1944–1959," in David Cesarani and Eric J. Sundquist, eds., *After the Holocaust: Challenging the Myth of Silence* (New York: Routledge, 2012), 152–56.

23. David Platt, "A New Powerful Anti-Nazi Film," *Daily Worker*, April 8, 1944.

24. *Address Unknown*, directed by William Cameron Menzies (Los Angeles: Columbia Pictures, 1944); *The Seventh Cross*, directed by Fred Zinnemann (Los Angeles: Metro-Goldwyn-Mayer Studios, 1944).

25. *Night Train to Munich*, directed by Carol Reed (London: Twentieth Century Productions, 1940); *Wikipedia*, s.v. "Gordon Wellesley," last modified September 2, 2015, http://en.wikipedia.org/wiki/Gordon_Wellesley.

26. *Secret Mission*, directed by Harold French (London: Marcel Hellman Productions, Independent Producers, 1942); *Unpublished Story*, directed by Harold French (London: Two Cities Films, 1942); "Harold French Filmography: Director," *IMDb*, accessed October 23, 2015, http://m.imdb.com/name/nm0294094/filmotype/director.

27. "Obituary for Louis Golding," *Jewish Chronicle*, August 15, 1958.

28. Louis Golding, *The World I Knew* (New York: Viking Press, 1940), 16–18. For a discussion of the meaning of Doomington to Golding, see Gavin Schaffer, "Fighting Battles with History: The Novelist Louis Golding and the Story of the 'Doomington Wanderer,'" *Immigrants and Minorities* 24, no. 1 (2006): 77–83.

29. Louis Golding, *Five Silver Daughters* (New York: Farrar and Rinehart, 1934), 288.

30. Louis Golding, *Mr. Emmanuel* (New York: Literary Guild of America, 1939), 3–22.

31. Ibid., 23.

32. Ibid., 79–84.

33. Kaspar Nägele to Louis Golding, 7 September 1939, LGP, MSS 77, Box 2, File 26; "Kaspar Nägele's Family," 1940; Louis Golding Correspondence and Related Items, 1932–1944, Special Collections, Pennsylvania State University Library, University Park, Pa.

34. Golding, *Mr. Emmanuel*, 116–18.

35. Schaffer, "Fighting Battles," 83–84.

36. Ibid.

37. Golding, *Mr. Emmanuel*, 120–21.

38. Ibid., 345–46.

39. Louis Golding, *Hitler through the Ages* (London: Sovereign Books, 1939), 9–25.

40. Golding, *World I Knew*, 216–37.

41. Louis Golding, *The Jewish Problem* (Harmsworth, U.K.: Penguin Books, 1938), 11. For background on the book's real authorship, see Elisa Lawson, "'Scientific Monstrosity' Yet 'Occasionally Convenient': Cecil Roth and the Idea of Race," *Patterns of Prejudice* 42, no. 2 (2008): 209–27.

42. The cover of *Hitler through the Ages* emphasizes that it is an "entirely new book" to differentiate it from *The Jewish Problem*.

43. Louis Golding, *Those Ancient Lands: Being a Journey to Palestine* (New York: Alfred A. Knopf, 1928).

44. Golding, *World I Knew*, 337.

45. Joey Rubin, "Precarious Fringes of an Uncertain World: *To the Quayside* and Emanuel Litvinoff's European Jew," *Critical Quarterly* 53, no. 1 (2011): 62, 66.

46. Charles Graves, "I See Life," *Daily Mail*, May 1, 1939, 10.

47. Charles Graves to Louis Golding, 3 May 1939, LGP, Gen MSS 77, Box 2, Folder 24, BRBML-YUL.

48. Charles Jarrott to Louis Golding, 23 May 1939, LGP, Gen MSS 77, Box 2, Folder 24, BRBML-YUL.

49. J. B. Simons, *Louis Golding: A Memoir* (London: Mitre Press, 1958), 74–75.

50. Henrietta Malkiel to Louis Golding, 9 May 1939, LGP, Gen MSS 77, Box 2, Folder 24, BRBML-YUL.

51. Bella Muni to Louis Golding, 13 July 1939, LGP, Gen. MSS 77, Box 2, Folder 24, BRBML-YUL; "George Arliss Biography," *IMDb*, accessed October 23, 2015, http://www.imdb.com/name/nm0002183/bio?ref_=nm_ov_bio_sm.

52. "Books of the Week," *New York Times*, August 7, 1939," in LGP, Gen. MSS 77, Box 2, Folder 25, BRBML-YUL.

53. Tony Kushner, *The Persistence of Prejudice: Antisemitism in British Society during the Second World War* (Manchester, U.K. : Manchester University Press, 1989), 78–138.

54. Gough-Yates, "Jews and Exiles," 540–42; Abrams, "Hidden," 62.

55. Eforgan, *Leslie Howard*, 214.

56. Charles Drazin, *The Finest Years: British Cinema of the 1940s* (London: I. B. Taurus, 2007), 13–41.

57. Gough-Yates, "Jews and Exiles," 518–19.

58. Eforgan, *Leslie Howard*, 206.

59. Gough-Yates, "Jews and Exiles," 319; *In Which We Serve*, directed by Noel Coward and David Lean (London: Two Cities Films, 1942); *Henry V*, directed by Laurence Olivier (London: Two Cities Films, 1944).

60. Naomi Shepherd, *Ploughing Sand: British Rule in Palestine, 1017–1948* (New Brunswick: Rutgers University Press, 2000).

61. "Mischa Spoliansky: A Brief History," Mischa Spoliansky Trust, accessed October 23, 2015, http://www.mischaspoliansky.com/index.php/bio.html.

62. *Mr. Emmanuel* Press Book, LGP, BRBML-YUL.

63. Golding, *Five Silver Daughters*, 314–70; Golding, *Mr. Emmanuel*, 323–57.

64. Drazin, *Finest Years*, 23; *Mr. Emmanuel* Press Book, LGP, BRBML-YUL.

65. Fox, *Film Propaganda*, 144; Robertson, *British Board*, 132.

66. Avisar, *Screening the Holocaust*, 104.

67. Bernard Wasserstein, "Children of Magnolia Street," *Jewish Historical Studies* 38 (2002): 171–182.

68. Schaffer, "Fighting Battles, 79–80; Rubin, "Precarious Fringes," 55–56.

69. Louis Golding, *The Glory of Elsie Silver* (London: Hutchinson, 1945), 180–280.

70. Louis Golding, *The Dangerous Places* (London: Hutchinson, 1951).

71. Louis Golding, "To the Quayside: Goodbye to Elsie Silver," undated, LGP, Gen. MSS 77, Box 5, Folder 67, BRBML-YUL.

72. *Mr. Emmanuel* Press Book, LGP, BRBML-YUL.

73. *Mr. Emmanuel Audience Survey*, July 11, 1944, LGP, MSS 77, Box 2, File 26, BRBML-YUL.

74. Ibid.

75. Kushner, *Persistence of Prejudice*, 130.

76. Eforgan, *Leslie Howard*, 214.

77. Peter Burnup, "*Mr. Emanuel*," *MP Herald*, September 23, 1944.

78. Bosley Crowther, "Anti-Nazi Films," *New York Times*, January 14, 1945. Earlier in the war, Crowther had expressed his opposition to films that were too explicitly gory or prurient in depicting Nazi brutality and depravity: Bosley Crowther, "Atrocity Films," *New York Times*, October 24, 1943.

79. "New Pictures," *Time*, January 29, 1945, 94.

80. Sarah Hamilton, *Emmanuel* Touching Film," *Los Angeles Examiner*, June 6, 1945. See also OC, "*Mr. Emmanuel*: British Film Has Inside Germany Theme," *Citizen News*, June 29, 1945.

MICHAEL BERKOWITZ

Jewish Questions Lurking in *Peeping Tom* (1960)

All this filming isn't healthy.

—THE BLIND MRS. STEPHENS IN *PEEPING TOM*

No anti-Semite can begin to comprehend the malicious analysis of his soul which every Jew indulges every day.

—NORMAN MAILER, "RESPONSES AND REACTIONS IV"

Released in 1960, Michael Powell's *Peeping Tom* was considered to be smut.[1] One anonymous reviewer in the British Film Institute's *Monthly Film Bulletin* described it as a "*Sadiste*" film, deserving of scorn primarily due to Powell's unfortunate collaboration with screenwriter Leo Marks (1920–2001).[2] It was too puzzling, sexualized, and visually overpowering to be widely accepted by the public and especially by critics in the early 1960s.[3] The film was deeply disturbing to the reviewers because Powell and his émigré codirector on previous projects Emeric Pressburger had established themselves as one of Britain's most talented filmmaking teams: "Powell & Pressburger." Yet the film remains a fabulous testament to the creativity of both Powell and Marks. In 1994 Dilys Powell (no relation to Michael), critic for the *Sunday Times*, made a point of renouncing her initial disgust for *Peeping Tom*: "I find I am convinced that it is a masterpiece. If in some afterlife conversation is permitted, I shall think it my duty to seek out Michael Powell and apologise. . . . Reading now what I wrote in 1960 I find that, despite my efforts to express revulsion, nearly everything I said conceals the extraordinary quality of *Peeping Tom*."[4] She concluded by imploring readers to "see it (on TV) and spare a moment to respect the camerawork of Otto Heller." Although few are as explicit as Dilys Powell in revising their opinion, the tide surely has turned, and *Peeping Tom* is now held in lofty esteem.[5] Director Martin Scorsese and numerous other critics appreciate it as pathbreaking and a veritable "cornerstone in film history."[6] It today appears on many lists as one of the greatest films of all time.

Comprehension of *Peeping Tom* stands to be enhanced by recognizing its pronounced Jewish genealogy, as a number of secularized Jewish discourses are interwoven in the film.[7] Surely one may ask: is there evidence that contemporary critics and audiences understood it in this way? Initially, no. But over time, and especially through the interventions of scholars such as Laurence Rickels and Mark Lazar, who are more inclined to discern Jewish elements at play, it has come to be appreciated in this way. Such an approach focuses mainly on Leo Marks, as the writer of the story and screenplay. Although devotees of Powell, who treasure *Peeping Tom*, may find it hard to accept, the film was conceived by Marks, and it largely materialized according to his script. As British critic Luke Jennings has suggested, "Perhaps the best key to an understanding of *Peeping Tom* is *Between Silk and Cyanide*," Marks's memoir of World War II.[8] Indeed, Jennings may have erred on the side of caution. Marks's account is overtly and covertly drenched in *yidishkeyt* (Jewishness), so much so that *Peeping Tom* can be fruitfully explored as a "Jewish" and even, to a lesser extent, a "Holocaust" film. Such a perspective stands in contrast to the foundational work of Ian Christie and Laura Mulvey, neither of whom contemplate, even in passing, the importance of a Jewish ethnic identity for many people in the orbit of Powell and Pressburger, including the Jewish Pressburger himself (who was not involved in *Peeping Tom*).[9]

Revisiting the Film Itself

The film features Mark Lewis, played by Carl (or Karlheinz) Boehm, a subtly "German" photographer in London who identifies himself as having been born in the house he lives in and renting out the lower floor. He is obsessed with taking photos of women, preferably in the nude, at the moment of their death. Lewis murders the women with the end of a camera tripod fashioned into a bayonet. *Peeping Tom*, however, is not based on any known murderer or case. The main character and the plot derive from the imagination of Leo Marks as mediated by Michael Powell. Marks's creation stems, in large measure, from his desire to convey, to a general public, the mechanics as well as an appreciation of Freudian psychology, which is inextricably tied to the sense of Jews as outsiders held by both Marks and Sigmund Freud. Marks's reading of Freud roughly parallels the argument of John Murray Cuddihy's *Ordeal of Civility: Freud, Marx, Levi-Strauss, and the Jewish Struggle with Modernity* (1974). Cuddihy proposed that pressure on Jews, beginning in the nineteenth century, to strictly adhere to the manners and morals of gentiles in order to be accepted into European society at large prompted the Jews' "most original thinkers" to question the imperative of striving for respectability. "Instead, they developed challenging analytical ideologies which denied the validity and legitimacy of civil appearances and customs, claiming in their place the primacy of underlying motives and structures."[10] Similar to this line, one reviewer perceived *Peeping Tom* as "an unusually frank and non-judgmental portrayal of deviant psychology and sexuality. ([The murderer's] actions are not condoned, but he's more a tragic victim than a villain.) . . . The film asks questions and raises issues guaranteed to make nearly any audience uncomfortable."[11]

Laurence Rickels sees *Peeping Tom* as arising from a nexus between Nazism and psychoanalysis.[12] Lewis's horrific acts are shown as a consequence of his having been experimented upon by his biologist father, Professor A. N. Lewis (played, in a self-reflexive gesture, by Michael Powell himself), who was purportedly conducting an investigation of fear in children. David Lazar writes that the characterization of Professor Lewis recalls the notorious Dr. Josef Mengele, and hence the film, along with Alfred Hitchcock's *North by Northwest* (1959), "eerily suggest that any moral optimism to emerge from the defeat of Nazi Germany should be highly tempered."[13] According to Jann Matlock, "the biggest story is in terms of anxieties about replicating the dark sides of Nazi research through any kind of recording — film, tapes, or photos. What do we think Marks knew about Nazi scientists given safe status in Britain or the U.S. after the war? It's the father's place in that huge old house that gives me the creeps — more so than the son's photos (the murdering is the father's curse and legacy)."[14]

It was clear to Powell, upon getting acquainted with Marks in the late 1950s, that their collaboration would result in a movie that dealt expressly with Freudian themes. As soon as the deal for Marks's screenplay was secured, Marks reportedly asked Powell, "'Does the word scoptophilia mean anything to you?' to which Powell replied: 'Is it Greek?' 'Yes, it's Greek.' 'Love of looking? Urge to look?' 'Exactly: "the morbid urge to gaze" — a familiar term to alienists.' 'Hmmm . . . the morbid urge to gaze . . . *Peeping Tom*.'"[15] Powell also knew that the lead character was a takeoff on Marks himself. Herein lies a great contradiction: Powell found Leo Marks to be dazzling, attractive, delightful, brilliant, and cutting, albeit admirable. "Leo was an ideal creative partner," Powell recalled:

> He knew nothing about films or the theatre, but a very great deal about men and women. He was malicious, inventive and unshockable. In less than six weeks we had our draft script. *Our scoptophiliac, our Peeping Tom, turned out to be called Mark, of course, since Leo himself was the original scoptophiliac*. Mark works in the movies, as camera assistant and focus-puller on a big film in production at a major studio. He ekes out his slender salary by shooting front covers for pornographic magazines. His equipment is expensive and extensive. He uses a lot of film. He does his own developing and printing. He has his own projector and his own screen. His camera tripod has a concealed dagger in one of its legs. A distorting mirror locks into a slot above the lens. It is a murderous weapon. He is a camera fiend. He is gentle and sweet and attractive, and quite, quite mad.[16]

Yet the screen version of Marks was a sadistic, self-destructive killer as Powell slyly folded Leo Marks into his character, Mark Lewis.

Further revealing, in Jewish terms, was the original choice to play the lead character, photographer Mark Lewis: a European-born Jew, Laurence Harvey, whose career was cut short by his death from cancer at age forty-five.[17] "Mr. Harvey," according to Paul Gardner's obituary in the *New York Times*, "was a fastidious connoisseur of antiques, food and wine. His baronial manner, cheeky wit and upper-class British accent gave the impression that he was of aristocratic birth. But Mr. Harvey, whose real name was Larushka Misha Skikne, was born in Joniskis, Lithuania, of Jewish parents." Unusually for an obituary, Harvey also was recalled for his "arrogant manner." His personality "could freeze ice cubes." Gardner concluded that "Laurence Harvey will be remembered as the screen's most fastidious playboy who most mothers feared their daughters might marry — or be ruined by — during an afternoon in the country."[18] Michael Powell leaves no doubt that he was pleased with himself for casting Karl Boehm in the role after "losing" Harvey.[19] But, strangely, no interviewer thought to ask Leo Marks his feelings about Harvey being replaced by an actor with such different looks, temperament, and lineage. Harvey and Boehm actually appeared together two years later — as siblings — in the second film made with the "Cinerama" process, *The Wonderful World of the Brothers Grimm* (1962). Had Harvey played the part, it would have been easier for the audience and critics to read *Peeping Tom* as the "Jewish" film it was. Yet the film left Jewish traces nonetheless.

For example, in a scene late in *Peeping Tom*, Mark Lewis encounters the film's most overtly Jewish character, a Dr. Rosen (Martin Miller). Several clues allow us to read Rosen as Jewish. First, his name. Second, his profession: Rosen is described as an expert psychiatrist, who has been brought in by the police to help find the killer of Mark's second victim, Vivian (Moira Shearer), a vivacious extra murdered on the set of the feature film where Mark works as a "focus puller." Like Mark, Rosen also has a central European accent, if a bit more pronounced. The actor playing Rosen, Martin Miller (1899–1969), had played numerous scientists and doctors in television, film, and theater. He was also cast previously as a rabbi and a photographer. Born Rudolf Müller in Kremsier, Moravia — not far from the ancestral home of Sigmund Freud, in Austria-Hungary — he had made his career mainly in Vienna before escaping to Britain in 1940, not long after Freud himself came to London in 1938. Even though the character Dr. Rosen has elicited little comment, the casting of Miller makes the reading of him as a Jewish psychiatrist more convincing, adding to the hidden Jewish subtext lurking behind the film.

Leo Marks Uncovered

Kevin Jackson, writing in London's *Independent*, remarked that the script of *Peeping Tom* "is full of mischievous jokes" and "permeated with secrets." [20] A penetrating interview by Chris Rodley with Marks, published in the 2007 DVD edition of *Peeping Tom* acknowledges the layers of codes, cues, "play-acting," and misdirection in the film.[21] The importance of his Jewishness is raised by Marks but is not pursued by Rodley in his interviews, and Jewishness scarcely exists in the British discourse surrounding Powell and Pressburger. Yet, it is a hefty but protean element of *Peeping Tom*—in the film itself and Marks's cat-and-mouse games with Rodley. For an English Jew of his generation, Leo Marks was highly unusual in the extent to which he was willing to talk about and "perform" his Jewishness, a flesh-and-blood example of Judith Butler's notion of how Jews "perform" an imagined version of their ethnic identity.[22]

In his memoirs, with his frequent references to his Jewishness, combined with outbursts of risqué humor, which cannot be separated from his ethnicity, Marks presents the opposite of the stereotypical buttoned-up English Jew. Speaking of the women who worked beside him on secret codes, whom he credits with intelligence far superior to his own, Marks reveals that they were just as prone to use sexual references as were men. "Those dear girls," Marks wrote, "had produced samples of hard-core pornography which Marks & Co.," his father's bookshop, "would have hidden in a glass case on the fourth floor, surrounded by Bibles." One of their stanzas written for memorization by agents was this ditty:

> Is De Gaulle's prick
> Twelve inches thick
> Can it rise
> To the size
> Of a proud flag-pole
> And does the sun shine
> From his arse-hole?[23]

Describing his first encounter with "a wireless operator . . . [a] young man of Russian-Egyptian origin," Marks writes, "We both knew at a glance that we shared the Esperanto of being Jewish."[24] Among the pungent ingredients in this mix was their zeal for photography, which was associated with Jews, as was their interest in boxing as fans.[25] "Jewish" Esperanto to Marks meant a profession of universalism, yet it had a different significance among Jews themselves. There were Jews who felt some kind of solidarity with one another, who admitted to being Jews, and those who did not. Marks relished playing the game of figuring out who among the stuffy Englishmen he met had actually been born among "the chosen" and changed their names.[26]

Who was Leo Marks? A boiled-down synopsis, which barely does justice to his range of interests and accomplishments, begins with family background. His father was the founder and proprietor of the bookshop Marks and Company at 84 Charing Cross Road, which was the subject of the book by Helene Hanff and later a film adaptation, starring Anne Bancroft (1987).[27] Marks's memoir, *Between Silk and Cyanide*, details his exploits as a cryptographer for the British armed forces during the Second World War in the complex espionage and counterespionage operation based at Baker Street—about which there is little scholarship.[28] The first chapter, entitled "A Hard Man to Place"—the first of many double, triple, and quadruple entendres—begins:

> In January 1942 I was escorted to the war by my parents in case I couldn't find it or met with an accident on the way. In one hand I clutched my railway warrant—the first prize I had ever won; in the other I held a carefully-wrapped black-market chicken. My mother, who had begun to take God seriously the day I was called up, strode protectively beside me—praying that the train would never arrive, cursing the Führer when she saw that it had and blessing the porter who found me a seat. Mother would have taken my place if she could, and might have shortened the war if she had.[29]

Marks's reminiscence is similar to that of Robert Capa before his departure to cover the invasion of Normandy. The degree to which Capa articulates his Jewishness through his relationship with his mother has likewise been unnoticed and underappreciated by scholars.[30] For both Marks and Capa, beginning their stories with the image of their stereotypically overprotective *yiddische mames* (Jewish mothers), doting on their baby boys well into adulthood, was a way of marking themselves as Jews. For both, it was a literary equivalent of Brit Milah (also known as a bris, or circumcision).

Upon his interview for service in Special Branch with the "headmaster of the code-breaking school," a Major Masters, Marks was asked about his hobbies, to which he replied: "Incunabula and intercourse, sir."[31] After the war he mainly made his living as a writer — first as a playwright and then, most notably, as the moving force behind *Peeping Tom*. Several interviews reflect an atmosphere like the one recounted by Rodley:

> I first met Leo Marks in 1978, at his place. I remember a dark room, the smell of cigar smoke, and a face half in shadow, half in the dim light of a cluttered London mansion-block apartment. And then there was the rich, hypnotic voice, which seemed to emanate from the impossibly deep recesses of the studded leather armchair in which he sat: the voice of someone both understanding and enquiring. The encounter felt like some form of psychic surgery, during which it was difficult to tell exactly who was asking the questions, and who was providing the answers.[32]

Afterward, Rodley concluded that *Peeping Tom* was overwhelmingly the product of Marks's imagination. "Marks conceived the film, shot by shot, with alarming visual, as well as verbal, specificity. Nothing was left to chance, and little to interpretation. For those comforted by artistic intentionality, *Peeping Tom* is heaven-sent."[33] Rodley's point here is that Marks's authorship, not the direction of Powell, is more important for understanding *Peeping Tom* — and hence its Jewish subtext.

Jews and Pornography in Britain

An equally important and related subtext is Marks's complex historicizing of the Jewish engagement with photography, which is articulated more explicitly in his *Between Silk and Cyanide*. *Peeping Tom*'s "Mark Lewis" is not simply an everyman, a universal creature. He represents a connection between Jews and the history of photography, as one of *Peeping Tom*'s wellsprings is the history and mid-twentieth-century practice of photography as perceived by Marks. As one aspect of this history, Leo Marks toys with the overrepresentation of Jews in the making and peddling of pornography, with the protagonist serving as a distorted image of himself.

Pam Green (1929–2010), a talented actor, astute businessperson, "model," and art director, appears twice in *Peeping Tom* for Mark Lewis's photo shoots for pornography magazine publicity. As Milly, Green is not quite playing herself, but perhaps herself at an earlier stage of her career. She teases Mark with the words, "come on sonny . . . make us famous," and further requests that his photos avoid revealing her "bruises," received at the hand of her jealous fiancé.

When Lewis first appears at her door, she exclaims, "Well look who's here—Cecil Beaton!" Here is a joke within a joke. Mark was a nobody whereas Beaton was one of Britain's most famous "society" and royal photographers but who was seen as a phony by some of his fellow photographers and who was notorious as one of the few within the photographic world who expressed antisemitic views. Green is also aware that the taciturn Mark is not what he seems: "You're a puzzle and a half."[34]

Green was well known for her collaboration with former "glamour photographer" and later her husband, George Harrison Marks. Born George Harris Marks (1926–1997)—no apparent relation to Leo—Harrison Marks was said to be "a byword for the softest kind of soft pornography, a smut peddler who became a self-perpetuating legend. He was twice bankrupt, twice arrested and four times married, a vaudevillian at heart who pioneered porn in Britain and lived all his life in the same house where he was born."[35] Together Green and Harrison Marks founded the pornographic magazine *Kamera* (1957–1968), whose innocuous title resembled a number of other publications in this genre, in the guise of one-off magazines, such as *Art Advertiser and Studio News* and *Qt No. 62*. There is something of a tribute to Harrison Marks, who acted as a consultant on *Peeping Tom* and was on the set during filming.[36] When Mark is filming the outside of the newsagent shop where he plans to kill Milly upstairs toward the end of the film, he specifically shoots covers of *Kamera* featuring Green. Despite this blatant movie-within-the-movie with such specific clues, there has been little investigation of the particular Jewish role in pornography on both sides of the Atlantic.[37] While Mulvey is right that there is something vaguely pornographic about *Peeping Tom*, she does not appreciate how the history of pornography is played out in the film.

Engaging Jews and Photography

The characterization of Mark Lewis as the eponymous "Peeping Tom" is, on the one hand, a way to engage Freudian theory, and on the other, an inside joke, or a series of jokes, about Jews as Jews and Jews and photography. Marks was not a photographer, but he certainly knew their milieu. He was no doubt aware that from the 1850s to the 1950s, if one's picture was snapped for a price, there was a good chance that the person behind the lens was born a Jew.[38] It was more or less expected that photographers, and assistants in a studio, might be Jews — or some other kind of so-called foreigner — possibly Italian, French, Spanish, or Armenian. Jews in photography themselves often encouraged such ethnic obfuscation by adopting monikers that did not sound so, well, Jewish.[39]

Jews with cameras on tripods or around their necks enticed customers to have their photo taken, in public spaces, such as the grounds in front of Buckingham Palace and Trafalgar Square, and proceeded to sell them prints, postcards, albums, and buttons. Occasionally they were able to produce these goods on the spot. Up though the interwar years, Jews photographed the recently deceased, although this was not a standard practice in Judaism. Along with this practice, they encouraged the reproduction or enlargement of photographs of the dearly departed. Jews also helped institutionalize the photographic commemoration of more cheerful life-cycle events — above all, weddings. They were crucial in inventing the traditions of "class photos" and professional-quality "holiday snaps" in Britain.[40] Because photography was taken, without question, as a heavily Jewish field, Jews' participation was accepted in government-sponsored photographic expeditions, preservation efforts, and state-building projects. Jews were among court photographers, in Britain and elsewhere in Europe, since photography's inception. They advanced film and optical technologies, as individual inventors and as employees of major companies such as Kodak and Ilford, both of which were based in north London.[41] Despite persistent rumors to the contrary, George Eastman himself was not Jewish — he was, in fact, something of an antisemite. But he made exceptional arrangements for Jews he thought would be especially helpful to his business (such as Leopold Godowsky Jr., and Leopold Mannes, discussed later in the chapter).[42]

George Eastman was not a Jew, but an immense number of those operating in the realm of photography were. Yet few academics and critics who write about photography see any reason to comment on the significance of the skewed social composition of the field. The sparse attention to Jews who were central to the evolution and fortunes of photography in Britain exists in inverse proportion to extent to which these men and women affected the country's visual culture. They were so successful that almost nobody noticed.

Peeping Tom is one of the rare reflections on photography, as a medium, to confront its problematic relationship with respectability—which is inextricably tied to its Jewish past and contemporary connections.[43] Because photography was less than respectable, Jews were afforded entry into its field—as it was not typically the domain of upstanding Englishmen. It allowed for Jewish inclusion and, to a large extent, colonization of the profession. The fact that Jews and recent émigrés became central in almost every network concerned with photography, from its early days, also is crucial. Although Jews did not invent photography, they were among its chief purveyors and practitioners throughout Europe from the 1840s until the Holocaust.

Constructing Mark Lewis

Michael Powell's choice of an Austrian, Karl-Heinz (Carl) Boehm, had not been a part of Marks's script. Powell was intrigued, though, by Boehm's background in the arts and as the son of a well-known conductor, Karl, whose intensity of enthusiasm for Nazism had become a matter of controversy after the war.[44] Yet the vaguely Germanic "Mark Lewis" would evoke many of the stereotypes attributed to Jews overall and Jewish photographers in particular. (The slight lilt in his speech is never mentioned.) Even more important: there was an explicit reason why Marks wished to call attention to the questionable character of photographers. In *Between Silk and Cyanide*, in an episode central to his distinctive contribution to fortifying secret codes, Marks describes his need to enlist the efforts of photography firms. Either the code would be printed, photographically, on silk—or the agents would be compelled to swallow a cyanide capsule. The very title of his memoir reflects this practice. The photographers, though, did not want to undertake the work because they thought it would cost too much to produce, and they also were afraid that it would not turn out right. Although Marks presented this assignment as a matter of life and death for those in the field, many of the London (Jewish) photographers he met seemed unmoved. His initial, callous treatment at the hands of several photographers may have helped inspire his negative, wildly exaggerated tale of "Mark Lewis."[45] Marks related in one of his final interviews with Rodley how

> I knew nothing whatsoever about photography, but every single code had to be printed onto silk, and they were all different. Although they knew how to mass-produce maps on silk, this was a technique. So I became obsessed with photography, and even more obsessed by how to persuade photographers to work around the clock so that every agent could have a code printed on silk that was unique to him, or her. That is why *Peeping Tom* became a photographer.[46]

Mark Lewis is not in a position to shirk responsibility to his nation, but he repeatedly betrays the trust of those around him: Dora (Brenda Bruce), the prostitute who is his first victim (whose phlegmatic line, "It'll be two quid," opens the film); Vivian, whom he entices to meet him secretly, supposedly to make a short film featuring her dancing that would advance her career; Milly, the porn "model"; and especially Helen Stephens (Anna Massey), a librarian who lives with her mother downstairs from his apartment.

Helen longs to be an author of children's books, and she has indeed written one — inspired by her acquaintance with Mark. It is entitled *The Magic Camera*. It would show the world as perceived through the eyes of children. "The camera is owned by a little boy who is terrified of grown-ups," Helen tells Mark. "But when he looks in his magic camera he sees grown-ups as they were when they were children . . . and he isn't frightened any longer." A stage direction notes, "CLOSE SHOT of Mark listening, engrossed." Helen continues, "And one day he gives his camera away to a little boy who is even more frightened of grown-ups than he was — and do you know what he finds?" Another stage direction: "*The little boy opposite her* [Mark] *shakes his head*." Helen concludes, "That when he looks at grown-ups without his camera he can still see them as they were when they were children. And that means he's grown up himself."[47] Helen's "Magic Camera" is strikingly similar to the lie detector, as a diagnostic instrument, in the expert hands of David Mischler in Marks's play of the same name.[48] "I run a few clinics," Mischler says, describing a major part of his vocation. "The children who come to them have [had] a lot of trouble growing up. Now it's no good asking what the trouble is . . . we'd be lucky to get half the truth — so the machine takes a picture of their minds at work. Every thought — every impulse — every problem they have — comes out on that picture — the machine misses none of their worries . . . — because *this* is what it was built for."[49]

The viewer of *Peeping Tom* realizes, and so, eventually, does Helen, that her fantasy is an inversion of the monstrous experiments Professor Lewis performed on his son. She informs Mark that she has found a publisher interested in the book but that the press insists that the photography will be too difficult and costly to execute. "This is the problem," Helen explains to Mark. "The children who read the book will want to see the pictures the camera takes — but the publishers say they're impossible to photograph, and suggest drawings . . . but I don't agree."[50] Helen, then, has a problem roughly parallel to that of Leo Marks while he was with Special Branch. Mark expresses his sympathy and promises that he can figure out how to do the work. Near the end of the film Helen inscribes a copy of her manuscript for Mark: "From One Magic Camera which needs the help of another." Helen's mother also had been the victim of betrayal: the culprit was not a photographer or photography publisher but an ophthalmologist. She blames herself, though, because she "let a man operate on her" despite having no "faith in him." It is this blind woman — a substitute analyst and *yiddische mame* — who comforts Mark, who sees into Mark and asks: "What's troubling you? You'll have to tell someone," and implores him, "you need help."

Leo Marks and Jewish Integrity

Marks was no stranger to playing around with Jewish stereotypes, and he was particularly attuned to those who attempted to evade their Jewish origins. While on assignment in Cairo in 1945, he chanced to run into the comedian Jack Benny, with whom he wound up spending a memorable hour. Marks states that they had nothing in common, but Benny was intrigued to know how Jews in Britain felt about the war. He asked, in particular, what Jews were contributing to the war effort. "We'd created," Marks said,

> the best black market in the whole of Europe, and those of us who were anxious to avoid military service, which I estimated to be much more than 99 per cent, were responsible for a major

> scientific discovery. With the help of two Harley Street doctors we'd found a way to deceive our medical examiners by producing sugar in our urine when ordered to pass water. And when we were told to wait two hours in the presence of an orderly and then pass some more, our urine retained its sugar! This ensured a medical certificate which guaranteed exemption from military service.[51]

Benny turned serious for a moment, hoping that there was not a kernel of truth in Marks's story. "He was sure the vast majority of Jews realized that this was their chance to fight the greatest anti-Semite of all time."[52] Marks responded by telling another joke, which Benny immediately retold to his wife when she joined them, to Marks's utter delight. For anyone to have his own joke "stolen" by Jack Benny was a tremendous honor. At the close of the evening, Marks was thrilled that Benny had "given me an experience which I could dine out on for the rest of my life if anyone would believe it." "*Thank you, Jack Benny*," he wrote to himself, "for giving me a month's holiday in the hour we spent together . . . *Thank you for letting me be Groucho, though I'm a Marks without brothers, and for listening with an inner ear when I spoke about Uncle*." That is, although Benny made it seem that he took Marks's story about his uncle evading conscription at face value, he knew it was an artful dodge. "*And thanks for not being ashamed of being proud of your race. I wish I had the courage to be one of the troops you're here to entertain but even you can't work miracles except on the stage*." To his account, Marks adds the aside: "And just for the record, the drinks were on him."[53] This moment in Marks's memoir recalls that one of the core elements of Jack Benny's stage persona was his stinginess, a takeoff on the "cheap Jew" stereotype. Marks makes sure to testify that things are not always as they seem, especially as they seem to be on stage.

Color and Genre

Beyond the authorship of Marks, the shocking effect of *Peeping Tom*'s story line was facilitated by the studio's choice of color technology combined with the cinematography, which also can he better understood through appreciating Jewish historical strains in photography. The rawness in *Peeping Tom* was enhanced by its pioneering use of Eastmancolor, a process derived from the invention of Kodachrome by Leopold Mannes and Leopold Godowsky Jr., both of whom were the sons of eminent Jewish musicians. George Eastman was not Jewish, but everybody in the world of photography knew that Kodachrome was the brainchild of "Man and God"—Mannes and Godowsky. The fact that Leo Godowsky's wife was the sister of George and Ira Gershwin meant they were well known in the world of show business as well as classical music.

The movie begins with a visual joke about color film. Mark Lewis is secretly filming Dora, the prostitute who is to become his first victim. The view we see is from his viewfinder, in full color. He tosses a recognizable yellow box into a rubbish bin, Cine-Kodak Plus X film for a 16mm camera. However, we later see him watching the film in his home cinema in black and white. Who, then, is the cameraman: the cinematographer Otto Heller or the protagonist Mark Lewis?

While it is little wonder that Powell and Pressburger garner a great deal of attention in the scholarship on color motion pictures,[54] there is an important point to be made about the use of color in *Peeping Tom* under the control of cinematographer Heller, who has not generated much interest in film studies. Heller had a distinguished career in Hungary, Austria, and elsewhere in Europe before fleeing the Nazis in 1939. Having worked on a huge range of films, he certainly knew how to make a fictional film look like a documentary. He developed great expertise at shooting with low light and was known for improvising technical changes to his cameras while working.[55] For all of its gothic and sensationalistic wellsprings, *Peeping Tom* is largely a realistic film. This realism contributed substantially to it being so terrifying. It is also important to recall that another one of Mark Lewis's activities throughout *Peeping Tom* is his unhidden effort to produce and direct a documentary about himself. *Peeping Tom* mirrors Mark Lewis's movie, for which we see selected portions and are aware—from the sounds noticed by Mrs. Stephens—that he spends hours every night watching film.

In some respects, what Heller achieved for *Peeping Tom* in 1960 was similar to the role of Eliot Elisofon for John Huston's *Moulin Rouge* (1951). Elisofon is barely recognized for his spectacular work in both photography and cinema. Writing about his experience for *LIFE* magazine, Elisofon explained:

> There have been experiments in color in films, but in almost all instances these effects have been delegated to ballet scenes, music hall acts, dreams and nightmares and other unreal situations. It always seemed to me that color is and could be part of the expression of the film and could contribute very definitely to storytelling. . . . The visual research that came first was simply to make still color pictures of as many situations similar to the film as possible.[56]

Even though it may be true that color was everywhere by 1960, the way it was deployed in *Peeping Tom* took viewers by surprise. Upon its release in the United States by Astor Pictures, an ad in *Variety* (December 1961) lauded its excellent "photography and color," which was part of what made it distinctive, especially for the "horror film" genre.[57]

Color feature films, even more than movies generally, have a culturally Jewish pedigree. Four points may be made about the relationship between color motion picture film technology and the process used in *Peeping Tom* of Eastmancolor. First, the background of the inventors of Kodachrome, Mannes and Godowsky—as classical musicians and American Jews, attuned to currents in popular culture in the 1920s and 1930s—was critical in prompting their belief in the possibility of reproducing a full spectrum of color through optics and chemistry.[58] Second, the rudimentary state of color motion pictures before 1920, in particular, helped inspire a paradigmatic shift to proto-Kodachrome.[59] Third, there is a closer relationship between Kodachrome and other color motion picture technologies than is acknowledged in the historiography.[60] And fourth, there is more to say about the role of Jews, photography, and the genesis of discrete genres of "the movies" beyond the origins of Hollywood's so-called studio moguls. Their background as photographers was a decisive influence on the work of such cinematographers as Elisofon and Heller and such directors as Ernst Lubitsch and Stanley Kubrick. The fact that photography itself was in large part a Jewish field had an impact on the development of color motion picture film.

Even in the film's second coming, few critics and scholars have understood or appreciated the "color" of *Peeping Tom* in its historical context. Dan Whitehead in *Total Film* states that "the move to HD [high definition] shows the master's [Powell's] work, particularly his carefully considered use of *gaudy* Eastmancolor, which smears the screen with a queasy red and green glow, the depravity of the '60s Soho writ large."[61] Eastmancolor did not require the hot, bright lights of Technicolor. The characters, except for the porn models, are not heavily made up. They appear remarkably natural. In the film *Eye of the Beholder* produced for the special edition of *Peeping Tom*, Martin Scorsese refers to Eastmancolor as having a "nasty edge." What seemed "nasty" to Scorsese was, however, disturbingly "real" for its time.

The Business of Hollywood Is Business

Along with technical aspects of *Peeping Tom* that are inextricably connected with distinctively Jewish histories of photography and cinema, the film's business history illuminates how Jewish ethnic identity and networks allowed the film to be produced and impacted upon its reception and interpretations. Although it is commonly assumed that Jewishness was toned down in British films, this is not necessarily the case — as a number of popular Crazy Gang vehicles, such as *A Fire Has Been Arranged* (1935) and *Gasbags* (1941), feature Yiddish shtick.[62] Brian McFarlane describes Anglo-Amalgamated Productions, the studio that made the film and distributed it in Britain, as "a small but resourceful production/distribution company" that was "set up in 1945 by two energetic and astute businessmen, Nat Cohen and Stuart Levy."[63] Starting with "low-budget thrillers for the bottom half of the double-bill, and, gambling shrewdly on new talents," Levy and Cohen "showed themselves cleverly attuned to changing market demands, until, in 1969, they were swallowed up in ABPC/EMI."[64] The work of Anglo-Amalgamated was also an important precedent for *Peeping Tom*, as its "earliest productions were half-hour features . . . with plotlines that attested to the unceasing vigilance of Scotland Yard, and with portentous introductions by Edgar Lustgarten. By the 1960s these had given way to hour-long thrillers drawn chiefly from the works of Edgar Wallace and made at the austere studios at Merton Park."[65] There was something of Jewish realism in their work, which the defensively prickly *Jewish Chronicle*, the self-styled voice of British Jewry, might see as antisemitic.[66] Yet the films of Anglo-Amalgamated may also be regarded as revealing the courage to develop unconventional subjects that were nevertheless familiar and may have been less than flattering to Levy and Cohen's own tribe.[67] Before Powell became smitten with Carl Boehm and decided to cast him as Mark Lewis, it probably was assumed by the studio that the lead would be a younger version of Sydney Tafler, who was often thought to be Jewish (which he was) and from London's East End, in the studio's previous films. Laurence Harvey, mentioned earlier, fit the bill perfectly. The choice of Boehm was possibly the greatest departure from Leo Marks's authorship of the film, as there is no hint in his script of Lewis being tall, blond, good-looking, and with a detectable German accent. The lines are those of Marks, but the goy (Boehm)—son of a Nazi, no less!—was all Powell.

Related to the strong Jewish identification of the studio that produced *Peeping Tom* is a story distorting the film's reception, which makes its heads—rather than the critics—the major culprits in causing the near demise of Michael Powell's career. This version charges that Levy and Cohen, being most concerned with chasing after "honours," dumped the film prematurely. Powell himself and some later critics argue that Nate Cohen took to heart the threats that he would be finished in the movie business if he did not withdraw the film. Finished, that is, before being granted a knighthood. Cohen (sometimes Cohen and Levy) reportedly made the crucial decision to pull the film from distribution in Britain and not send it abroad.[68] "A few days after *Peeping Tom* opened in 1960," Alexander Walker recalled in 2000, "the late Robert Clark, the head of Associated British Pictures Corporation, in whose ABC cinemas *Peeping Tom* was showing, told me at a Variety Club lunch: 'We've put Nat in the doghouse until he gets rid of that piece of pornography.'" Walker claims that "the officers of the Variety Club . . . feared their chances of appearing in the honours list would be jeopardised by association with such a film," and snidely quips, "Nat Cohen died without ever getting a knighthood."[69] The assumption by some critics in retrospect is that had *Peeping Tom* remained in British theaters for a longer period, eventually public opinion would have overruled the critics' wrath in 1960. But this assumption is questionable.

Perhaps the time was not yet ripe, in Britain, for the masses to embrace *Peeping Tom*. To be sure, Alfred Hitchcock's *Psycho* (1960) succeeded at the box office a few months later, but Robert Bloch's story was not nearly as intellectually demanding and complex as *Peeping Tom*. Set in the western

United States, it did not strike as close to the British bone as did *Peeping Tom*, despite it being a product of British émigré director Alfred Hitchcock. Bloch had a penchant for puns; Marks, excruciating brain-teasing puzzles. Interestingly, Bloch (1917–1994), who is said to have attended a Methodist church and was a draft dodger during World War II, was exactly the type who would have been a prime target of Marks's humor.

To understand the studio's level of comfort with the film, it also is significant that Cohen and Levy allowed *Peeping Tom* to have some fun at the expense of Anglo-Amalgamated. The light comedy film set where Mark Lewis works could very well be one of its own. In one scene a phone rings in the director's office, prompting someone to shout, "Anglo wants in!" Perhaps the nastiest cut of all is that Mark Lewis aspires to be a film director. In his own production room cinema he has had a director's chair made with his name on it. It is, after all, Mark Lewis's and Leo Marks's movie.

It is unmistakable that Cohen and Levy were front and center when the film was released—their names were prominent in much of the film's publicity. Interestingly, Anglo-Amalgamated press announcements were largely consistent with the current critical reception of the film: "Brilliantly scripted by Leo Marks, it is claimed by Anglo to be the most intensely dramatic and intriguing thriller ever produced in a British studio."[70] They also sought to underscore that the "colour" of the film made it spectacularly distinctive. That the studio was unequivocally behind Powell and Marks should not be underestimated.

Nat Cohen's death in 1988 seems to have registered little notice in Britain, but the *Los Angeles Times* remembered him as "the cockney butcher's son who became the movie executive behind such hits as *Darling* and *Murder on the Orient Express*." He had

> entered films at age 25 and rose to become chairman and chief executive of EMI, Britain's largest film producer in the 1970s. Under his leadership EMI produced a series of madcap box office hits with names such as *Carry on, Sergeant* [1958] and *Carry On, Nurse* [1959]. His production successes included not only light entertainment but such socially aware movie as *Billy Liar* in 1963 in which Julie Christie was discovered opposite Tom Courtenay.[71]

Significantly, *Peeping Tom* was not mentioned. Had Cohen lived a few more years, however, that film would likely have been the first item in his obituary. Rather than insinuations that Jews destroyed Powell's reputation and willfully obliterated *Peeping Tom*, most credit should be given to a "Marks without a brother," without whom *Peeping Tom* would never have been conceived.

Notes

I am indebted to my colleague Jann Matlock for going way beyond the call of duty in helping me with this piece. Most of the best parts are either hers or things that were prompted by her comments.

1. *Peeping Tom*, directed by Michael Powell (London: Michael Powell [Theatre]; London: Anglo-Amalgamated Film Distributors, 1960). Comments by Hal Erickson and Mark Deming from Movie Guide website, accessed October 26, 2015, http://www.powell-pressburger.org/Reviews/60_PT/PT07.html. The screenplay was republished with an interview by Chris Rodley as Leo Marks, *Peeping Tom* (London: faber and faber, 1999).

2. "*Peeping Tom* (1960)," *Monthly Film Bulletin*, 27, no. 316 (May 1960): 65.

3. For the reception of *Peeping Tom* in the United States, see Kevin Heffernan, *Ghouls, Gimmicks, and Gold: Horror Films and the American Movie Business, 1953–1968* (Durham, N.C.: Duke University Press, 2004), 115, 126–32.

4. "Dilys Powell's Film of the Week: Peeping Tom," *Sunday Times*, June 1994, posted on Movie Guide website, accessed October 26, 2015, http://www.powell-pressburger.org/Reviews/60_PT/PT03.html.

5. David Ehrenstein, "Is the Filmgoer the Murderer? Michael Powell's Notorious Film Is More Gruesome than its Reputation, but More Ingratiating as Well," *New Times LA*, 1999, posted on Movie Guide website, accessed October 26, 2015, http://www.powell-pressburger.org/Reviews/60_PT/PT14.html.

6. Largely due to the efforts of film scholars Ian Christie and Laura Mulvey, and Movie Guide website host Steve Crook, who modestly describes himself as "just an admirer of the works of [Michael] Powell and [Emeric] Pressburger," there is an abundance of handy comment on the *Peeping Tom*. Most of this, unsurprisingly, centers around its producer and director, Michael Powell (1905–1990). See "The Powell & Pressburger Pages," Movie Guide, accessed October 26, 2015, http://www.powell-pressburger.org/Members/Steve.html; "Michael Powell and Emeric Pressburger: Pure Genius," Movie Guide, accessed October 26, 2015, http://www.powell-pressburger.org/; Ian Christie, *Arrows of Desire: The Films of Michael Powell and Emeric Pressburger* (London: Faber and Faber, 1994) and Ian Christie, ed., *Powell Pressburger and Others* (London: British Film Institute, 1978), esp. 53–62; Pressbook for "Martin Scorsese Presents Michael Powell's *Peeping Tom*" (undated, most likely 1995), accessed May 2013, http://www.rialtopictures.com/FTP/ZIP_britnoir/PeepingTomPressbook.pdf; Ehrenstein, "Is the Filmgoer the Murderer?" See also Laura Mulvey, "*Peeping Tom*," Criterion Collection, accessed October 26, 2015, http://www.criterion.com/current/posts/65-peeping-tom. Scorsese quoted in Jeffrey M. Anderson, "Peeping Tom," Combustible Celluloid, accessed October 26, 2015, http://www.combustiblecelluloid.com/peeping.shtml.

7. Some of the leading interpretations may be seen as complimentary to this perspective. See, for example, Linda Williams, "When the Woman Looks," in *Essays in Feminist Film,* edited by Mary Ann Doane, Patricia Mellencamp, and Linda Williams, 83–99 (Frederick, Md.: American Film Institute Monograph Series, 1983); Elena del Rio, "The Body of Voyeurism: Mapping a Discourse of the Senses in Michael Powell's *Peeping Tom,*" *Camera Obscura* 15, no. 3 (2000): 115–49.

8. Luke Jennings, "The Masterspy of Acton Town," *This Is London,* January 8, 1999, posted on Movie Guide website, accessed October 26, 2015, http://www.powell-pressburger.org/Reviews/Leo/Leo.html.

9. Interviews in "Eye of the Beholder" (Julie Cohen, 2005), a documentary featuring Ian Christie, Laura Mulvey, Martin Scorsese, and Thelma Schoonmaker, included in the special edition reissue of *Peeping Tom,* directed by Michael Powell (1960; London: StudioCanal, 2007), DVD.

10. John Murray Cuddihy, *The Ordeal of Civility: Freud, Marx, Levi-Strauss, and the Jewish Struggle with Modernity* (New York: Basic, 1974), ix.

11. Mark Deming, "All Movie Guide Reviews," Movie Guide, accessed October 26, 2015, http://www.powell-pressburger.org/Reviews/60_PT/PT07.html.

12. Laurence A. Rickels, *Nazi Psychoanalysis: Volume II, Crypto-Fetishism* (Minneapolis: University of Minnesota Press, 2002), 112–16.

13. Mark Lazar, introduction to *Michael Powell Interviews,* edited by Mark Lazar, x (Jackson: University Press of Mississippi, 2003).

14. Jann Matlock, e-mail message to author, March 29, 2013.

15. Michael Powell, *Million-Dollar Movie: The Second Volume of His Life in the Movies* (London: Heinemann, 1992), 393.

16. Ibid., 396, emphasis added.

17. Bertrand Tavernier, "An Interview with Michael Powell" [1968], in Lazar, *Michael Powell Interviews,* 37, 63; David Thompson, A *Biographical Dictionary of Film* (London: Andre Deutsch, 1994), s.v. "Harvey, Laurence, 1928–1973," 319.

18. Paul Gardner, "Laurence Harvey, Screen Actor, Is Dead at 45," *New York Times,* November 27, 1973, http://query.nytimes.com/mem/archive/pdf?res=F20C12FB3E5D127A93C5AB178AD95F478785F9.

19. Tavernier, "Interview with Michael Powell," 63.

20. Kevin Jackson, "Don't Look Now: *Peeping Tom* Revolted Critics in 1960; Now It Is a Classic; But Then the Man Who Wrote It Is not Quite as he Seems" *Independent,* October 22, 2011, http://www.independent.co.uk/arts-entertainment/dont-look-now-1320277.html. The screenplay was republished with an interview by Chris Rodley in Leo Marks, *Peeping Tom* (London: Faber and Faber, 1999).

21. "Leo Marks Interviewed by Chris Rodley, 1998," publication included in the 2007 special edition DVD of *Peeping Tom,* 11. Similar comments are made by other critics, such as Jennings.

22. Judith Butler, "The Charge of Anti-Semitism: The Risks of Public Critique," in *Prophets Outcast: A Century of Dissident Jewish Writing about Zionism and Israel,* edited by Adam Schatz, 357–70 (New York: Nation Books, 2004).

23. Leo Marks, *Between Silk and Cyanide* (London: HarperCollins, 1998)38.

24. Ibid., 74–75.

25. Ibid., 75, 89, 94.

26. Ibid., 59.

27. Helene Hanff, *84, Charing Cross Road* (New York: Grossman, 1970); *84 Charing Cross Road*, directed by David Jones (Los Angeles: BrooksFilms/Columbia, 1987).

28. "Ninety per cent of the WT [Wireless Telegraphy] records handed over to C [Secret Intelligence Service] have been destroyed, and the code department's records scarcely exist." Leo Marks, *Between Silk and Cyanide: A Codemaker's War, 1941–1945* (Glencoe, Ill.: Free Press, 1999), 599.

29. Ibid., 1.

30. Robert Capa, *Slightly Out of Focus* (New York: Henry Holt, 1947), 6.

31. Marks, *Between Silk and Cyanide*, 2.

32. "Marks Interviewed by Rodley, 1998," 11.

33. Ibid.

34. Susan Sontag emphasizes the mysterious nature of photography in her *On Photography* (Harmondsworth, U.K.: Penguin, 1978). See also Bernd Hüppauf, "Modernism and the Photographic Representation of War," in *Fields of Vision: Essays in Film Studies*, edited by Leslie Devereux and Roger Hilman, 94–126 (Berkeley: University of California Press, 1995).

35. Tony Sloman, "Obituary: Harrison Marks," July 10, 1997, *Independent*, http://www.independent.co.uk/news/people/obituary-harrison-marks-1249894.html.

36. "Tom, Michael and George," November 2, 2010, BBC Radio 4, accessed June 2013, http://www.bbc.co.uk/programmes/b00vkws5 (program no longer available).

37. Nathan Abrams, "Triple-exthnics," *Jewish Quarterly* 196 (Winter 2004), www.jewishquarterly.org/issuearchive/articled325.html?articleid=38; Nathan Abrams, "Kosher Beefcakes and Kosher Cheesecakes: Jews in Porn—An Overview," in *Jews and Sex*, edited by Nathan Abrams, 147–68 (Nottingham, U.K.: Five Leaves, 2008).

38. In a personal communication to the author, September 27, 2009, William Meyers wrote, "Lucjan Dobroszycki [a leading scholar of Polish Jewry] once told me that if you had your portrait taken in Central or Eastern Europe any time before World War II it would probably have been taken by a Jew—even if you were the Czar."

39. For an exception to rule—an Italian who actually was an Italian—see *Oscar Marzaroli: Photography 1959–1968* (Edinburgh: Bourne, 2010).

40. Salman Stemmer, interview transcript no. 116, Refugee Voices collection, Wiener Library, London, 24, 29–31, 43.

41. Robert J. Hercock and George A. Jones, *Silver by the Ton: The History of Ilford Limited, 1879–1979* (London: McGraw Hill, 1979). Unfortunately, there is no comprehensive history of Kodak's operations in Britain.

42. A related urban myth is that the late Linda McCartney (née Eastman) was a descendant of George Eastman. There is no relation, and Paul's first wife was Jewish.

43. One can also consider the film *The Governess* from this perspective. See Michael Berkowitz, *Jews and Photography in Britain* (Austin: University of Texas Press, 2015), 11–14.

44. Powell, *Million-Dollar Movie*, 398–99; Michael Kater, *The Twisted Muse: Musicians and Their Music in the Third Reich* (New York: Oxford University Press, 1997), 63–65.

45. Marks, *Between Silk and Cyanide*, 261–62.

46. "Introduction: Leo Marks Interviewed by Chris Rodley, 1998," in Marks, *Peeping Tom*, xiv.

47. Marks, *Peeping Tom*, 96.

48. *The Lie Detector* was performed as *The Best Damn Lie* in 1956–57. It premiered at the Richmond Theatre and later was staged at London's Winter Garden Theatre. Its central character is David Mischler, an American, apparently a psychologist whose specialty is solving crimes and helping patients — especially children — overcome trauma.

49. *The Lie Detector*, act 1, scene 1, line 4.

50. Marks, *Peeping Tom*, 96.

51. Marks, *Between Silk and Cyanide*, 376.

52. Ibid.

53. Ibid., 377–78.

54. See Sarah Street, *Colour Films in Britain: The Negotiation of Innovation 1900–1955* (London: Palgrave-Macmillan, 2012); Sarah Street, Elizabeth Watkins, and Simon Brown, *British Colour Cinema: Practices and Theories* (London: Palgrave Macmillan, 2013).

55. "Otto Heller," *Česko-Slovenská Filmová Databáze*, accessed October 26, 2015, http://www.csfd.cz/tvurce/27790-otto-heller/; Duncan Petrie, "Otto Heller," BFI Screenonline, accessed October 26, 2015, http://www.screenonline.org.uk/people/id/518832/.

56. Newsletter-circular from Stanley Rayfield, January 19, 1953, "RAZZLE-DAZZLE OF TOULOUSE-LAUTREC (5 color pages): The Painter's Raffish Existence Is Shown in Glowing Color Film," 66.10, Elisofon, Series 9, About Elisofon, 1949–1959 (2 of 3), Harry Ransom Center, University of Texas, Austin.

57. Heffernan, *Ghouls, Gimmicks, and Gold*, 130–31.

58. Leopold Godowsky Jr., interview by Alan Green, April 16 [and] 30, 1971, transcript, American Jewish Committee, Oral History Library, New York, **P, Oral Histories, Box 27, No. 2, New York Public Library (NYPL), tape 1, pp. 39–41.

59. Ibid.

60. Ibid., 77–78.

61. Dan Whitehead, "*Peeping Tom*: Special Edition; Smile, You're on Candid Camera," in *Total Film: The Modern Guide to Movies*, January 21, 2011, http://www.totalfilm.com/reviews/blu-ray/peeping-tom-special-edition-1 (site discontinued), emphasis added. Dilys Powell, in her reappraisal cited earlier, got it quite right.

62. *A Fire Has Been Arranged*, directed by Leslie S. Hiscott (London: Twickenham Film Studios, 1935); *Gasbags*, directed by Walter Forde and Marcel Varnel (London: Gainsborough Pictures, 1941).

63. Brian McFarlane, "Anglo-Amalgamated Productions," BFI Screenonline, accessed October 26, 2015, http://www.screenonline.org.uk/film/id/839029/.

64. Ibid.

65. Ibid.

66. Andrew Roberts writes that the filmography of Sydney Tafler (1916–1979), who starred as a shady Jew in several Amalgamated movies, "raises questions as to how Jewish characters were depicted in post-war British cinema . . ." There was, however, no antisemitic intention whatsoever. It is just that the stories being told were not necessarily flattering to their Jewish characters. See Andrew Roberts, "Tafler, Sydney (1916–79)," BFI Screenonline, accessed October 26, 2015, http://www.screenonline.org.uk/people/id/1389560/index.html.

67. Heffernan notes the significance of the release of two "horror" films by Anglo Amalgamated at that time, *The Black Museum* (1959) and *Circus of Horrors* (1960); Heffernan, *Ghouls, Gimmicks, and Gold*, 128–30.

68. Alexander Walker, "Don't Blame the Critics," March 17, 2000, *Guardian*, http://www.guardian.co.uk/theguardian/2000/mar/17/guardianletters4.

69. Ibid.

70. "Big Anglo Premiere for 'Peeping Tom,'" trade ad in *Daily Cinema*, March 28, 1960, http://www.powell-pressburger.org/Reviews/60_PT/TheMyths.html.

71. "Passings: Nat Cohen, Film Producer," *Los Angeles Times*, February 11, 1988, http://articles.latimes.com/1988–02–11/news/mn-41859_1_nat-cohen.

GAVIN SCHAFFER

"You Don't Cure a Problem by Sweeping It under the Carpet"

Jews, Sitcoms, and Race Relations in 1960s Britain

Despite ongoing antisemitism, British Jewry was, by the 1960s, a generally settled, secure, and integrated community. Nonetheless, in a climate of accelerated black and Asian immigration, governmental thinking about how to deal with prejudice and discrimination continued to focus on the precedent of Jewish/non-Jewish relations. I will use the example of Jewish representation in 1960s television comedy to illustrate how this happened within the specific frame of humor, arguing that the ostensibly lighthearted representation of Jews and Jewishness significantly informed the ways in which black and Asian people were shown in British comedy. Jewish/non-Jewish relations formed the basis of humor in a series of 1960s sitcoms, notably in the work of three comedy writers: Johnny Speight, Vince Powell, and Harry Driver. Given that these writers went on to focus much of their work on black/white relations in Britain, I question whether and how their early approaches to Jewish/non-Jewish relations informed their thinking. Specifically, I assert that the long-standing political culture of "hiding" racial anxieties was exposed by comedy, as it strove to say the unsayable and give open voice to the quiet realities of British race relations.

Immigration and Anxieties: Contexts

Very few Jews migrated to Britain in the wake of the Second World War. Aside from a tightly controlled and ungenerously managed scheme that allowed a tiny number of Holocaust survivors to join families already resident, no attempt was made to provide shelter in Britain for the European Jews who had survived the war but were now homeless.[1] Britain had provided refuge for some Jews fleeing Nazi Germany before the war, but strictly on its own terms.[2] In the wake of the conflict, this selective compassion was not repeated. As Britain looked to rebuild, foreign workers were sought, but Jewish Holocaust survivors were not considered to be suitable labor migrants. Instead, Britain attempted to recruit hundreds of thousands of central and eastern European workers to support its heavy industry.[3] Holocaust survivors, it was thought, would not be sufficiently robust to engage in this sort of labor. Moreover, the British government perceived Jews as inherently urban and feared an increase in domestic antisemitism should the number of Jews in Britain be allowed to increase further.[4]

British attitudes toward Jews in the postwar period were, of course, shaped by responses to the Holocaust and, in particular, by broadcasts of camp-liberation footage.[5] Taken as a whole, however, these responses were complex and did not amount to the unequivocal climate of sympathy that one might expect. Long-standing currents of British antisemitism ensured an ongoing undercurrent of anxiety about Jewish culpability and tendencies to exaggerate suffering, ideas fueled by increasing British exasperation about Zionist conduct in Palestine.[6] Postwar Jewish terrorism in the Yishuv, targeted at British soldiers, caused fury. In 1947, anti-Jewish riots in Britain were triggered by the bombing of the King David Hotel.[7]

Despite persistent and ongoing currents of antisemitism, British Jews were becoming increasingly settled and established in this postwar period of minimal Jewish immigration. Jewish presence in Britain preceded the post-1880 Ashkenazi influx by hundreds of years, so that some British Jews were well established in Britain at the fin-de-siècle. However, most of Britain's Jews had come in this late-nineteenth-century wave, fleeing poverty and persecution in Russia.[8] These Jews were second- or even third-generation immigrants by the 1930s. Thus the eighty thousand Jews who were allowed refuge in the face of Nazi antisemitism stepped into increasingly confident and settled communities. In the postwar period, the bulk of London's Ashkenazi Jews were moving out of their impoverished East End homes, into the suburbs of outer London.[9] While the persistence of postwar antisemitism should not be underestimated, in many senses these Jews were yesterday's immigrants, mostly born in Britain, settled, and politically well represented.[10]

Prior to the Second World War, Jewish immigration had always been highly controversial and contested. Anxieties abounded about the impact of these Jews on the character of the nation.[11] In the face of the Third Reich, opposition to Jewish immigration focused on fears that more Jews would cause more antisemitism, leading to the kinds of "problems" being experienced in Germany arising in Britain.[12] Such fears permeated much of Britain's political classes but were driven in particular by the rise of Oswald Mosley's British Union of Fascists in the early 1930s.[13] In the postwar period, fascist groups struggled to maintain a foothold, undermined by associations with Nazism and the shame of wartime internment, and by the strong-arm activities of antifascist vigilantes.[14] In this climate of antifascism, where Jews were no longer immigrating in any great numbers and were dispersing into broader British society, the political issues of Jewish immigration receded into the shadows of British politics. Postwar British anxieties about immigration would not focus on Jews but instead on black and Asian immigrants and minorities.

Black and Asian people had lived in Britain for hundreds of years by the time that the *Empire Windrush* docked in Tilbury in 1948.[15] Nonetheless, the arrival of a few hundred Caribbean ex-servicemen on this particular vessel is often heralded as a starting point of immigration, the beginning of multicultural Britain.[16] This particular myth has vexed a series of immigration historians and theorists, mainly because it serves to silence pre-1948 British black history. But its use as a starting point of British multiculturalism is equally pernicious in terms of silencing those histories of British multiculturalism which orientate around white immigrant communities. As Panikos Panayi has pointed out in his recent book, *An Immigration History of Britain*, the development of British multiculturalism needs to be understood in terms of hundreds of years of history, encompassing the mass immigration of Irish and Jewish migrants, among others.[17] Indeed, the precedents set in dealing with these earlier migrations often shaped postwar responses to black and Asian migrants.

Accelerated black and Asian migration to Britain after the Second World War produced a climate of concern with strong parallels to earlier anxieties about Jewish immigration.[18] The same fascist fringe that had railed against Jews in the interwar period refocused its campaigning in the postwar on opposition to black and Asian immigration.[19] As had been the case regarding the Aliens Act 1905, the British government, fueled by its own prejudices, used public anxiety to justify restrictive immigration law, enacting the Commonwealth Immigrants Act 1962 to stem the flow of black and Asian migration. Both of these laws were underpinned by ostensible nonracism and hid their true intentions. The 1905 act did not actually mention the Jews who were its main target, while the Commonwealth Immigrants Act made no reference at all to color.

Government interest in migration was not, in the 1960s, only focused on restriction. When Harold Wilson's Labour government was elected in 1964, it came to power with no appetite to reverse the restrictive legislation of the previous administration. It did, however, move toward ameliorative race relations legislation as another plank of policy toward immigrants and minorities. Wilson's government saw the handling of immigration, Shamit Saggar has contended, as a "limitation-integration equation."[20] Immigrant numbers would be controlled, but moves would also be made to outlaw various forms of racial discrimination. This agenda was addressed in the form of the Race Relations Act 1965, legislation designed to help existing immigrants to settle successfully in Britain.[21] This act (bolstered by a stronger version in 1968) outlawed racial discrimination in public places such as restaurants (and from 1968 in employment and housing). It also rendered criminal the incitement of racial hatred.[22] While, as might be expected, such legislation was focused on the protection of Britain's black and Asian populations, looking at the parliamentary debate surrounding the new law reveals more complicated political intentions. In reality, the new antidiscrimination law emerged as much from concerns about antisemitism as from any anxieties about racism toward black and Asian communities, a mixed agenda which tells us much about the importance of longer-standing immigration experiences in shaping the history of British race relations. When it was discussed in the House of Commons, many of Britain's parliamentarians supported the Race Relations Act because they continued to see a need to protect Jews from fascist aggression. Barnett Janner, the Labour member of Parliament (MP) for Leicester North West, told the Commons that his experiences visiting former concentration camp inmates convinced him of its necessity, while other MPs too voiced their support in these terms.[23]

These concerns do not reveal an exclusive interest in protecting Jews so much as a recognition that there was similarity (in terms of the consequences of racism) between the contemporary experiences of black and Asian people and the history of antisemitism. Dingle Foot, the solicitor general, explained the legislation in terms of a desire "to prevent arising in this country in relation to the coloured immigrants the kind of situation which arose in relation to the Jews in this country in 1935 and 1936."[24] Similar ideas were voiced in the media. For example, the *Spectator* noted that new law needed to be directed equally against "Nigger baiters and Jew baiters."[25]

More broadly, the parliamentary focus on Jews also helped illuminate difficult questions about using race relations as a concept in law and society. Many parliamentarians were concerned that legislation to prevent racial discrimination would not cover Jews at all (because of confusion about whether Jews were a race). Antony Buck asked the attorney general to clarify "precisely how the Jews are brought into this Bill? Is it by race? Is it by the words 'ethnic,' 'race,' or 'colour'? What definitions are to be put on those words?"[26] It was important because Jews, to Buck's mind, were the ones who required protection from this legislation, which he feared may not include them:

> It is quite extraordinary, when one realises that what concerns most of us more than anything else is the possibility of anti-Semitism, that it should not have been made absolutely clear that Judaism and anti-Semitism is caught by Clause 1.[27]

These concerns reveal a broader recognition that the language of race relations had the potential to contribute to the problem as well as solve it. When was it appropriate, this debate questioned, to consider people as members of distinct racial groups? After all, the language of the Aliens (and the Commonwealth Immigrants) Act indicated that it was not. And if communities could not be described in this way, how could they be discussed at all — even when the issue was how to protect them? Ultimately, how should a society deal with race relations in a period that was trying hard to articulate itself as postracial?[28] Here, comedy provided an answer and a precedent.

British Television Comedy: Giving Voice to Racial Anxieties

While awkward discussions were taking place in Parliament about the meaning of race and racism, British television comedy was less cautious. It developed a clear position about how to deal with racial conflict, a position informed by experiences and principles relating to the representation of Jews. While anxieties about Jews in real life were generally hidden (outside the marginal Far Right), comedy gave these concerns unparalleled voice, and it could do so while hiding behind the defense that jokes, by their nature, were not to be taken seriously. To illustrate the point, this section will now explore the work of three of Britain's most successful sitcom writers from the 1960s and 1970s: Johnny Speight, Vince Powell, and Harry Driver. Writing alone, Speight produced the most successful sitcom of the 1960s, the BBC's *Till Death Us Do Part*, as well as other successful comedies including *Curry and Chips*.[29] Working together as a team (until Harry Driver's untimely death in 1973), Powell and Driver wrote a string of successful comedies for Britain's independent channels in the same period, including *Love Thy Neighbour*, *Mind Your Language*, and *Never Mind the Quality, Feel the Width*.[30] In both cases, these writers foregrounded racial themes in their work, writing successful and controversial comedies about racial difference on the basis that they were only joking. Moreover, it is arguable that the approach adopted toward race relations by both sets of writers was significantly informed by their early work on Jews.

British comedians approached racial conflict in a different way than British politicians did. As we have seen, in British politics, race relations were consistently dealt with by stealth, as politicians attempted to address what they perceived as a problem without speaking openly about race. For British politicians, race and racism were an embarrassing business. No leading politicians wanted to be presented as prejudiced, and those who did speak openly about the need for racial restriction became marginalized political pariahs. However, in British television comedy, things that were otherwise hidden could be revealed. In this arena, issues that were muffled and muted in politics were openly and loudly discussed.

We should not be surprised that comedy provided a vehicle for more open discussion of issues that were perceived as awkward or embarrassing in other arenas. As Sigmund Freud observed, jokes can provide a social opening to say the unsayable and give voice to positions that people might not want to defend in serious discourse.[31] In her recent study of comedy, Alenka Zupančič argued in this context that jokes provide a unique opportunity to voice anxieties and express our fears: "things that really concern us, things that concern the very kernel of our being, can be watched and performed only as comedy."[32] Central here is the ability of jokers to distance themselves from the point they are making. While a politician has to stand by his or her every word, comic performance at its essence carries the potential for what Salvatore Attardo described as "decommitment," the right to distance the joker from a different, serious position.[33] As regards the handling of race relations, this ability to "de-commit" becomes extremely important, for reasons that Michael Billig makes clear: "Teller and recipient can deny that they are racist; they can protect their own sense of their non-racist selves by claiming that they are just joking."[34] Key to this strategy is the creation of comic "fools." In the comedies that are considered in this section, lead characters assume positions that enable audiences to feel superior, to construct the comic protagonists as "fools."[35] Opinions and theories from the mouths of fools are easily disavowed by writers and audiences alike. In the cases of some of the comedies here, writers and producers went so far as to argue that the presentation of a view from their "fool" was tantamount to guiding audiences into opposition. This position was frequently taken by the writers and producers of *Till Death Us Do Part* regarding views expressed by the show's protagonist, Alf Garnett. For example, the BBC's head of Light Entertainment told the media that support from Alf was "the kiss of death" for any political cause.[36]

That the comedic treatment of difficult and embarrassing issues (such as race relations and immigration) was able to get into the homes of the British public at all was due to the technological explosion of television in the postwar period.[37] By 1961, 75 percent of British households owned a television set, a figure which had risen to 91 percent by 1975.[38] This rise in television ownership made watching television Britain's most common leisure activity by the 1960s and, unsurprisingly, drove forward both the variety and quantity of television production.[39] Put simply, by the 1960s Britons were glued to their television sets, as the BBC and independent channels vied for their viewing attention. The effect of this output on the thinking of the British public has been a long-standing matter of debate across a range of academic disciplines. At its core, this is an argument about what impacts television had on its audiences, and specifically about the ability of the technology to alter the views of the public. Without doubt, politicians and other activists became extremely concerned in the 1960s about the power of television to influence, an anxiety that was epitomized in Britain by the campaigning of Mary Whitehouse's National Viewers and Listeners Association, as well as by the increased attention paid to television by Britain's political parties.[40]

However, then and now, television theorists have been considerably more reticent about the power of the medium to influence, arguing often that audiences make what they want from television programs and do not easily imbibe messages or beliefs in any obvious sense.[41] Despite this no-doubt sage theoretical cautioning about the limited power of television, it remains reasonable to argue that television did hold the potential to have some influence over its public in the postwar period. The BBC (after 1955, the "duopoly" of the BBC and ITV) retained control of the images that were broadcast into Britain's homes, and the stories and the values of its programs became a core part of Britain's social life. However, this is not to say that the makers of British television set out constantly to change the thinking of the public. In fact, television rarely set out to give didactic lessons, which were perceived as likely to turn off audiences. Instead, as John Ellis has argued (following Freud), the influence of broadcasting should be seen in terms of its seemingly insatiable inclination to "work through" social issues.[42] The coverage of race relations offers one good example of this tendency. In weekly television schedules, issues of race were "worked through," both in news and current affairs programming and in drama. Through this coverage, a certain approach toward racial difference and racial conflict was adopted on television, wherein stories and characters were used to argue against racism and in defense of racialized communities (messages that were frequently tempered and undermined by unwitting authorial prejudices). But, as in the political arena, in these other genres argument about race was mostly hidden within the narrative. In contrast, comedy facilitated the emergence of a different kind of approach. In this transgressive genre, racial differences were openly entertained and racial conflicts "worked through" on a weekly basis.

Till Death Us Do Part

The first situation comedy to foreground this kind of open discussion was Johnny Speight's *Till Death Us Do Part*, a groundbreaking sitcom initially broadcast on the BBC between 1965 and 1968 and then again between 1972 and 1975.[43] The program oriented itself around the lives of the working-class Garnett family in the East End of London and focused in particular on the father of the family, Alf Garnett (played by Jewish actor Warren Mitchell). The character of Alf was written and performed to be the ultimate "fool." He was an angry, ignorant man with reactionary political views, underwritten by chauvinism and racism. As described in the *Financial Times* in 1967, Alf was

> the rampaging, howling embodiment of all the most vulgar and odious prejudices that slop about in the bilges of the national mind. Whatever hidden hates, irrational fears and superseded loyalties stand in the way of our slow stumble toward a more civilised society, Alf Garnett is the living, blaspheming expression of them. He is everything most hateful about our national character—xenophobic, illiberal, racist, anti-Semitic, toadying, authoritarian.[44]

Although Alf was constructed as the ultimate fool, Speight was quick to argue that Alf was no fictional bogeyman. Instead, he explained to a journalist for the *Evening News*, the character represented a very real constituency of Britons. "Go in any pub and you'll hear uninformed people arguing in a biased way about a subject they know nothing about. They're all Alf Garnetts."[45] Whatever the basis for Speight's creation, Alf's almost instant popularity was undeniable. *Till Death* soon became the most-watched program on British television.[46] After its initial demise in 1975, it spawned two further spin-off series, while Alf (as a solo character) continued to be performed in one-off programs up until Speight's death in 1998.[47] Although Speight's idea had supposedly been that viewers would watch Alf and be appalled by his views, in reality responses were (as we might expect) considerably more complex. Whether loved as a fool or a hero, Alf Garnett became the comic favorite of a generation.

One of the most controversial aspects of Garnett's character was his unflinching hostility toward black and Asian Britons. Using racist language and nasty stereotypes, Alf railed against black presence in Britain. However, while story lines about black and Asian people drifted in and out of the series, the issue of Alf's Jewishness was ever present and set the tone for the program's stance towards race. Jokes about Alf's Jewishness emerged early in the first series, in an episode entitled "Intolerance." In this story, Alf visits the doctor and is treated by a new physician, who is black, much to Alf's displeasure. Returning home, he tells his son-in-law Mike (Anthony Booth), "Old Kelly's gone away on holiday again, an [*sic*] left some sambo in charge down the surgery." Drawn into discussion about why the color of the doctor's skin was important, Alf tells his family, "Primitives ain't they? That's what they are. Primitives. Course they ain't had the education like what we've had, that's the trouble." Responding to Alf's prejudice, his daughter, Rita (Una Stubbs), and son-in-law tell him that he shouldn't have racist views of this kind because he is Jewish, an allegation that provokes Alf to fury. Having been told that his grandfather was "Solly Diamond," a Jewish fishmonger, and that he has a Jewish nose, Alf replies, "I ain't Jewish, I tell you, there's nothing Jewish about me. That nose, it's more Roman, that is." This episode concluded with Alf throwing his eggs and bacon at Mike, and past him through the open window, in anger at the suggestion that as a Jew he should not be eating them in the first place. Four episodes into the series, the die was now cast. Alf's racism would always be answered by the accusation that he himself was a Jew. Indeed, this was a joke made in the series time and again. In one 1972 episode, a cab driver apologizes to Alf for making antisemitic comments after having realized he "was Jewish." In 1974, Alf's wife tells him that his father "couldn't get a Jewish girl to marry him, and so I suppose, out of desperation, he married your mother." All the while, Alf becomes angrier and angrier at the suggestion.

Alf's consistent explanation for the rumors of his Jewishness was that his grandfather had needed to pretend to be a Jew to succeed in business in the East End of London. He tells his daughter, "He only changed he's name to Solly Diamond for business reasons. You wanna get on up in that Whitechapel you're better off, changing your name to Jewish and makin' out you're one of 'em."[48] This explanation underscored the joke-play engaged by Speight and Warren Mitchell in this story line. An

East Ender himself, Speight would have known well the familiar story that immigrant Jews Anglicized their names to avoid persecution and improve their life chances. Here, mischievously, this history was reversed amid the "fool's" idea that being Jewish was a help, not a hindrance, in East End life. This joke was compounded by Mitchell's own Jewishness. Having played stereotypically Jewish characters prior to his role as Alf Garnett, this irony would not have been lost on many of the audience members.[49] They could gain extra pleasure from the humor of watching a Jewish actor playing an antisemite accused of being a Jew and fiercely denying it.

The idea of playing with who was and was not a Jew (and how much this mattered) lay at the heart of Speight's handling of the issue of race. In a 1974 episode, Rita challenged Alf about why, when he was questioned about his Jewishness, he always reacted as if he had been "accused . . . of being something awful." Clearly, to Alf, the issue was one of essential and crucial difference, a point illustrated in another episode from 1968. In this earlier episode, Alf goes to donate blood, providing him with an opportunity to espouse his views about biological human differences. Seeing a black man making a donation, Alf expresses incredulity that this blood was the same as "white" blood, complaining, "they ought to label it . . . black blood for your blacks . . . and white blood for your whites." Again, thinking about Jewishness and the Jewish body lay at the center of Alf's understanding. Commenting on the world's first heart transplant patient, a Jewish South African man named Louis Washkansky, Alf argued that the man's failure to survive with his new heart was rooted in the essential differences between the Jewish and non-Jewish body:

> See . . . Your Washkanski [*sic*] was a Jew . . . an' if your doctors had . . . had a Jewish heart to put in him . . . he'd have been alright. . . .'Cos his body would accept that you see. . . . Well, I mean . . . of course they're gonna reject a Christian heart . . . because it isn't what they call Kosher. I mean, the same way a Christian would reject a Jewish heart . . . annit?[50]

The roots of Alf's thinking, and his role as "the fool," are laid bare here. To Alf, discredited notions of racial difference held sway, even when they ran in direct contrast with medical knowledge. But the fact that the idiocy of his racial positions was so frequently articulated in relation to Jews and Jewishness begs further questions. Perhaps, as had been the case in the evolution of Britain's race relations policies more generally, the issues of Jewish settlement and antisemitism were seen as the ultimate precedent, from which attitudes toward black and Asian immigrants could and should be extrapolated. And perhaps, in the mind of Speight and the BBC, this precedent was similarly seen as significant when it came to explaining how prejudice should be confronted in fictional form. Responding to a disgruntled viewer (who complained that the "Blood Donor" episode was racist), Huw Wheldon, the managing director of BBC Television, asserted:

> To say that Alf Garnett's view of "coons" and giving blood donations to coloured people confirms that Britain has nothing to offer immigrants is like seeing THE MERCHANT OF VENICE and concluding that anti-Semitism is rife in the Home Counties.[51]

Here, the BBC made the case that precedent relating to dealing with racism was being followed, rooted in long-standing, tried and tested handling of lighthearted Jewish representation. Jewish/non-Jewish history not only illuminated a pathway for dealing with racism but also privileged Jewish responses to racism as significant in informing the broader tapestry of race relations. For Warren Mitchell, his own Jewishness was of considerable importance to his decision to take on and perform the role of Alf Garnett. He explained, "As a Jew I've always been aware of racial prejudice."[52] *In Till Death Us Do Part*, "working through" Jewish/non-Jewish relations in comedy helped set out boundaries for wider race relations humor, geared toward making fools of those who believed in racial difference, challenging the euphemisms and whispering that framed political discussions of race relations. In 1967, another comedy about Jewish/non-Jewish relations, *Never Mind the Quality, Feel the Width* (written by Vince Powell and Harry Driver), began on Associated British Corporation (ABC) television, continuing for six "series" (the British equivalent of "seasons" in American television) until 1971.

Never Mind the Quality, Feel the Width

Powell and Driver began their careers as comedy writers when one of their sketches was used by Harry Worth as part of his *Here's Harry* comedy show in 1960, and they soon became regular contributors to Worth's program.[53] After working as story line writers for the northern soap opera *Coronation Street*, the pair wrote four series of their own sitcom, *George and the Dragon*, for the independent channel ABC between 1966 and 1968. During this period, Powell and Driver decided to pitch a new idea to a number of television companies for a sitcom centered around the relationship between two London tailors, one Jewish and one Irish Catholic. Having initially suggested the show to Frank Muir at the BBC, Powell and Driver agreed to make a one-off play, which was broadcast as part of ABC's *Armchair Theatre* series in 1967.[54] Despite offers from ATV and the BBC, Powell and Driver decided to sell the series to ABC, which was soon to merge with Rediffusion before becoming Thames Television.[55]

The premise of *Never Mind the Quality, Feel the Width* was that the relationship between a Jewish and a Catholic tailor was inherently ripe for comic transgression. The two characters, Manny Cohen (played by John Bluthal) and Patrick Kelly (played by Joe Lynch), were walking, talking racial stereotypes, each ascribed with the traits popularly attributed to Jews and Irishmen and supported by a group of similarly stereotypical coreligionists.[56] Patrick Kelly was constructed as happy-go-lucky, heavy-drinking, and unambitious. Typically, in one episode, he tells Manny, "I'm happy enough so long as I have enough money in my pocket for the odd packet of cigarettes, a few jars and a bit of skirt." Meanwhile, set in contrast, Manny Cohen oozed supposedly Jewish traits. Manny tells a friend that he did not see active service in the Second World War because he suffered from "cowardice," and Manny inflates his life jacket as a precaution when on a flight to Rome. His lack of masculinity meant that he was a forty-six-year-old virgin who had to telephone his overbearing mother if he was not home by half past eleven at night. Indeed, Manny's mother was a Jewish stereotype in her own right. When she thought Manny was courting a non-Jewish woman, she told him that she would give him as a wedding present "an invitation to my funeral."

While stereotypes abounded, *Never Mind the Quality* no doubt saw itself as sending a positive message about Jewish/non-Jewish relations.

Aside from the constant joking about race, Manny and Patrick were presented as extremely close friends. Racial humor was presented as a marker of acceptance; a point clarified by actor Powell in his autobiography, wherein he explained how, in his view, racial name-calling was a natural part of British working life in this period:

> A Welshman was Taffy, a Scotsman a Jock, an Irishman a Paddy, an Italian an Eyetie, a Chinaman a Chink, a German a Kraut and a black man a Sambo. These names were used not as insults but as a matter of course and were said and received with good humour.[57]

Ultimately, Manny and Patrick's relationship was rooted in kindness and acceptance. Indeed, such was the good-natured atmosphere of the program that it was selected and broadcast as ITV's entry to the First International Christian Television Festival in 1969.[58]

What was important, as far as the writers were concerned, was that serious bigotry resulted in defeat. While it was fine to make jokes about difference, real belief in racial types was shown to be foolish. Thus when Manny's mother stops him from seeing his non-Jewish girlfriend, it turns out that she was both a convert to Judaism and a millionaire. Moreover, when Patrick is so sure of Manny's cowardice that he tries to tease him into enlisting to fight in the Six-Day War of 1967, Manny tricks his friend into believing that he had really gone to fight, and Manny gets the last laugh as Patrick is forced to mourn his fictional death. Thus, as with *Till Death Us Do Part*, *Never Mind the Quality* "worked through" race relations by emphasizing the folly of racial thinking.

But key to both shows was also the idea that it was entirely appropriate and legitimate to joke about race. In *Never Mind the Quality*, even more so than *Till Death*, the idea that discussion of racial difference should be silenced was attacked time and again. This attack was rooted in the belief of all the authors concerned that the discussion of race relations was being proscribed by politicians and that stifling such discussion would ultimately have a negative effect on British society. This idea played out in *Never Mind the Quality* on numerous occasions, nowhere more clearly than in one episode in the fourth series, entitled "Without Prejudice." In this episode, Manny berates Patrick for calling a member of his church congregation "a Sambo." Patrick's response (which resonated clearly with Powell's quotation) was that name-calling was natural and healthy. He tells Manny that he is "too sensitive" and that "every man in the world has a bit of prejudice in him." To prove the point, Patrick sets Manny up on a blind date with a black woman. Hypocrite to the core, Manny runs away when he realizes that his date is black, thus proving Patrick's point that hidden prejudice was more dangerous than name-calling. Patrick, the name caller, turns out to be the least bigoted. After all, he tells Manny, he treated "Sambo just the same as I treat anyone else."

For the sitcom audience, the lesson from this story was clear. It was better to keep things out in the open, to disclose inner thoughts and joke about prejudices, than it was to pretend they did not exist and then act in a hypocritical manner. Through their comic creations, Speight, Powell, and Driver promoted open discussion and speech and attacked what they saw as the hypocritical "political correctness" of British race relations. In this spirit, Speight told the *Evening Standard* newspaper, "You don't cure a problem by sweeping it under the carpet. You have to talk about it."[59]

What is particularly interesting, from my point of view, is that Jewish/non-Jewish relations seem to have been used to test the water of this particular kind of conversation. Both Speight and the team of Powell and Driver soon abandoned Jewish themes in favor of comedy that focused on black/white relations in Britain. Speight, in 1969, wrote *Curry and Chips*, a sitcom centered around the integration into Britain of a Pakistani-Irish immigrant, played by the blacked-up Spike Milligan, for London Weekend Television. Powell and Driver's next successful sitcom was *Love Thy Neighbour*, which ran for seven series between 1972 and 1976. *Love Thy Neighbour* dealt with white/black British relations through a story about two neighboring couples in which the men, one white and one black, worked in the same factory.[60] The story focused on the prejudices of the white male neighbor, Eddie Booth (played by Jack Smethurst). Booth was deeply unhappy about having black neighbors and was openly racist toward them, especially to his male black neighbor and colleague Bill Reynolds, played by Rudolph Walker.[61] While the two wives tried to keep the peace, Eddie and Bill fought each other in episode after episode, the invariable outcome of which was Eddie's humiliation. Following the precedent set by *Till Death Us Do Part* and *Never Mind the Quality, Feel the Width*, bigotry always leads to defeat, a fact which made Eddie Booth seem like the biggest loser on British television. One journalist observed, "I can't think of anyone currently on the box who loses so consistently as Eddie."[62]

The precedent of the bigot always losing was not the only thing that *Love Thy Neighbour* borrowed from *Never Mind the Quality*. In many ways, the two series were extremely similar, even to the extent that plots were swiped from one and reworked into the other. For example, in one 1969 episode of *Never Mind the Quality*, the story centers around Manny being a friend of the Jewish actor David Kossoff, claiming that he could persuade Kossoff to play a charity benefit on his behalf. When the actor fails to turn up, Manny launches into a searing attack of Kossoff's character, only to be confronted by the arrival of Kossoff after all. Reworking Manny's behavior as Bill Reynolds's, *Love Thy Neighbour* followed exactly the same story line, only replacing the Jewish Kossoff with the black British comedian Charlie Williams.

The comparisons between the two series ran deeper than the borrowing of story lines. While ostensibly both were presented as an opportunity to have an innocent laugh at the silliness of prejudice,[63] in actuality they were long-standing demonstrations of an authorial desire to "work through" race relations. Both offered the analysis (like *Till Death*) that prejudices were better voiced than silenced and that bigotry always led to defeat. But both also championed the idea that prejudice was only a surface tension, under which lay human kindness and fraternity. In the final reckoning, both Manny and Patrick, and Bill and Eddie, were the best of friends. Going through life together, they worked and played in the same communities, ultimately tied to each other. In *Love Thy Neighbour*, this closeness was particularly notable. The two protagonists not only worked together and lived side by side, but their wives had children at the same time, in the same hospital. Covering this story line, Powell and Driver presented the two men in the hospital with their wives, affectionately holding each other's baby, an idealized picture of racial harmony, where love and fraternity lived alongside the "natural" desire to make innocent jokes about race.

This approach to race relations—indeed, the approaches to race relations in all of the programs discussed here—was highly problematic, and it is not my intention to present this comedy work as a force for good in British postwar history. While Speight did believe that his comedy served an ameliorative function, Powell and Driver were more circumspect, generally justifying their interventions on the grounds that they did not do "any harm."[64] But for good or ill, what these programs did do was open up discussion about race relations and give voice to this discussion in a particular frame. This frame legitimized the open stating of difference and the validity of racist name-calling and making racist jokes. Whether or not audiences got the point, this frame also made clear that people should be friends, whatever their ethnicity, and trivialized the idea of deep-seated racial differences. In this world, real bigots always lost, and love conquered all.

But what is most interesting is that this "working through" of race in British comedy heavily utilized Jewish/non-Jewish relations in its early stages, as if this terrain were safer and easier to engage. Here, hidden concerns about Jewish/non-Jewish relations came to the fore, in the process providing a precedent for similar concerns about black/white relations. Why was this the case? Perhaps it was felt that while antisemitism was far from absent from 1960s and 1970s Britain, British Jews in this period were safe and settled (and thus ready to become the butt of jokes) in a way that black and Asian communities often were not. Perhaps the horror of the Holocaust led writers to look for new lighter ways to give voice to Jewish/non-Jewish relations, so that these stories were prioritized in this period of British comedy. Or, perhaps the whiteness of Jewish/non-Jewish relations created a perceived safer ground for joke telling, less controversial and inflammatory. Ultimately, whatever the reasoning, comparisons to British politics are striking.

What comedy did openly, politics did quietly. In both, concerns about Jewish/non-Jewish relations drove agendas in a period wherein it would be expected that black and Asian immigration would take the spotlight. That this was the case points to the need for historians to reconsider the history of British immigration in the postwar period, and more generally. This is a history wherein the anxieties about white immigration — Jewish, Irish, and from continental Europe — continued to inform debate and discussion. If Britain became more multicultural in the postwar period, it is because immigration itself had from the start been truly multicultural. In the postwar period, worries about Jewish integration and settlement continued both in politics and in culture to take center stage.

Notes

1. The scheme in question was known as the Distressed Relatives Scheme, run from the Home Office. For details see Louise London, *Whitehall and the Jews, 1933–48: British Immigration Policy, Jewish Refugees and the Holocaust* (Cambridge: Cambridge University Press, 2000), 266–69; Tony Kushner, *The Holocaust and the Liberal Imagination: A Social and Cultural History* (Oxford: Blackwell, 1994), 229–38.

2. Britain provided refuge for about eighty thousand European Jews, who were allowed entry mostly in the period between Kristallnacht (November 9, 1938) and the beginning of the Second World War (September 1, 1939). See Tony Kushner and Katherine Knox, *Refugees in an Age of Genocide: Global, National and Local Perspectives during the Twentieth Century* (London: Frank Cass, 1999), 126–71; Bernard Wasserstein, *Britain and the Jews of Europe* (Oxford: Oxford University Press, 1988).

3. For details of these worker schemes and their exclusions, see Diana Kay and Robert Miles, *Refugees or Migrant Workers? European Volunteer Workers in Britain, 1946–51* (London: Routledge, 1992); John Tannahill, *European Volunteer Workers in Britain* (Manchester, U.K.: Manchester University Press, 1958).

4. David Cesarani, *Justice Delayed: How Britain Became a Refuge for Nazi War Criminals* (London: Heinemann, 1992).

5. See Tony Kushner, "Belsen for Beginners: The Holocaust in British Heritage," in *The Lasting War: Society and Identity in Britain, France and Germany after 1945*, edited by Monica Riera and Gavin Schaffer, 226–47 (Basingstoke, U.K.: Palgrave Macmillan, 2008).

6. See Kushner, *The Holocaust and Liberation Imagination*, 205–69. See also Gavin Schaffer, *Racial Science and British Society* (Basingstoke, U.K.: Palgrave Macmillan, 2008), 96–106.

7. Tony Kushner has argued that the motivations behind rioting were rooted in longer-standing tropes of British antisemitism. See his "Anti-Semitism and Austerity: The August 1947 Riots in Britain," in *Racial Violence in Britain 1840–1950*, edited by Panikos Panayi, 149–68 (Leicester, U.K.: Leicester University Press, 1993).

8. See Todd Endelman, *The Jews of Britain 1656–2000* (Berkeley: University of California Press, 2002); Lloyd Gartner, *History of the Jews in Modern Times* (Oxford: Oxford University Press, 2000).

9. See David Cesarani, "A Funny Thing Happened on the Way to the Suburbs: Social Change in Anglo-Jewry between the Wars, 1914–45," *Jewish Culture and History* 1, no. 1 (1998): 5–26.

10. See Geoffrey Alderman, *The Jewish Community and British Politics* (Oxford: Clarendon, 1983).

11. Schaffer, *Racial Science and British Society*, 11–14. See also Sharman Kadish, *Bolsheviks and British Jews: The Anglo-Jewish Community and the Russian Revolution* (London: Frank Cass, 1992); Bernard Gainer, *Alien Invasion: The Origins of the Aliens Act of 1905* (London: Heinemann, 1972).

12. See Richard Bolchover, *British Jewry and the Holocaust* (Cambridge: Cambridge University Press, 1993).

13. See Richard Thurlow, *Fascism in Modern Britain* (Stroud: Sutton, 2000); Thomas Linehan, *British Fascism, 1918–39: Parties, Ideology and Culture* (Manchester, U.K.: Manchester University Press, 2000).

14. On the struggle of postwar fascists to regain their political reputation, see Gra-

ham Macklin, *Very Deeply Dyed in Black: Sir Oswald Mosley and the Resurrection of British Fascism after 1945* (London: I. B. Tauris, 2007). For antifascist vigilante activity, see Morris Beckman, *The 43 Group* (London: Centerprise, 1993).

15. See Peter Fryer, *Staying Power: The History of Black People in Britain* (London: Pluto, 1984); Ron Ramdin, *Reimaging Britain: 500 Years of Black and Asian History* (London: Pluto, 1999).

16. For example, see Mike and Trevor Phillips, *Windrush: The Irresistible Rise of Multi-Racial Britain* (London: Harper Collins, 1998); Randall Hansen, *Citizenship and Immigration in Post-War Britain: The Institutional Origins of a Multicultural Nation* (Oxford: Oxford University Press, 2000).

17. See Panikos Panayi, *An Immigration History of Britain: Multicultural Racism Since 1800* (Harlow, U.K.: Pearson, 2010).

18. See Anne Kershen, *Strangers, Aliens and Asians: Huguenots, Jews and Bangladeshis in Spitalfields, 1660–2000* (London: Routledge, 2005).

19. For example, Oswald Mosley stood as a candidate in Kensington North in 1959 in the wake of the Notting Hill riots of 1958.

20. Shamit Saggar, *Race and Politics in Britain* (London: Harvester Wheatsheaf, 1992), 77.

21. Erik Bleich, *Race Politics in Britain and France: Ideas and Policymaking since the 1960s* (Cambridge: Cambridge University Press, 2003); James Hampshire, *Citizenship and Belonging: Immigration and the Politics of Demographic Governance in Postwar Britain* (Basingstoke, U.K.: Palgrave Macmillan, 2005).

22. Gavin Schaffer, "Legislating against Hatred: Meaning and Motive in Section Six of the Race Relations Act of 1965," *Twentieth Century British History* 25, no. 2 (2014): 251–75.

23. See 716 Parl. Deb., H.C. (5th ser.) (1965) 1029–64. See also Norman Fowler, "Grave Difficulties of Section Six," *Times*, September 1, 1969.

24. Dingle Foot quoted in 711 Parl. Deb., H.C. (5th ser.) (1965) 1047.

25. *Spectator*, January 15, 1960.

26. Antony Buck quoted in 711Parl. Deb., H.C. (5th ser.) (1965) 1029–30.

27. Ibid.

28. Numerous scholars have explored the survival of racial concepts in postwar Britain. See Marek Kohn, *The Race Gallery: The Return of Racial Science* (London: Jonathon Cape, 1995); Bob Carter, *Realism and Racism: Concepts of Race in Sociological Research* (London: Routledge, 2000); Paul Gilroy, *Between Camps: Nations, Cultures and the Allure of Race* (London: Penguin, 2000); David Theo Goldberg, *Racist Culture: Philosophy and the Politics of Meaning* (Oxford: Blackwell, 1993).

29. *Till Death Us Do Part* (London: BBC, 1965–1975); *Curry and Chips* (London: London Weekend Television, 1969). See Gavin Schaffer, "Till Death Us Do Part and the BBC: Racial Politics and the British Working Classes 1965–75," *Journal of Contemporary History* 45, no. 2 (2010): 454–77.

30. *Love Thy Neighbour* (London: Thames Television, 1972–1976); *Mind Your Language* (London: London Weekend Television, 1977–1986). *Never Mind the Quality, Feel the Width* (London: ABC Television, 1967–1971). See Sally Shaw, "'Light Entertainment' as Contested Socio-Political Space: Audience and Institutional Responses to *Love Thy Neighbour* (1972–76)," *Critical Studies in Television* 7, no. 1 (2012): 64–78.

31. Sigmund Freud, *Jokes and their Relation to the Unconscious* (London: Routledge and Kegan Paul, 1960).

32. Alenka Zupančič, *The Odd One In: On Comedy* (Cambridge, Mass.: MIT Press, 2008), 182.

33. Salvatore Attardo, "Violations of Conversational Maxims and Cooperation: The Case of Jokes," *Journal of Pragmatics* 19, no. 6 (1993): 537–85,cited from M. Billig, *Laughter and Ridicule: Towards a Social Critique of Humour* (London: Sage, 2005).

34. Michael Billig, "Humour and Hatred: The Racist Jokes of the Ku Klux Klan," *Discourse and Society* 12, no. 3 (2001): 285.

35. See Orrin Klapp, "The Fool as a Social Type," *American Journal of Sociology* 55 (1949): 157–62, cited from Billig, *Laughter and Ridicule*.

36. *Daily Mirror*, January 20, 1968.

37. See Raymond Williams, *Television, Technology and Cultural Form* (London: Fontana, 1974).

38. These figures are striking when one considers that fewer than 10 percent of Britons possessed a television set in 1951: John Williams, *Entertaining the Nation: A Social History of British Television* (Gloucestershire, U.K.: Sutton, 2004), 14.

39. See Mark Donnelly, *Sixties Britain: Culture, Society and Politics* (Harlow: Pearson, 2005), 77; Rob Turnock, *Television and Consumer Culture: Britain and the Transformation of Modernity* (London: I. B. Tauris, 2007), 194–97; Arthur Marwick, *The Sixties: Cultural Revolution in Britain, France, Italy and the United States c. 1958–c. 1974* (Oxford: Oxford University Press, 1998), 792.

40. See Lawrence Black, "Whitehouse on Television: The National Viewers' and Listeners' Association and Moral and Cultural Politics," in *Redefining British Politics: Culture, Consumerism and Participation 1954–70*, edited by Lawrence Black, 105–38 (Basingstoke, U.K.: Palgrave, 2010).

41. See John Fiske and John Hartley, *Reading Television* (London: Methuen, 1978), 193; Jonathon Bignell, *An Introduction to Television Studies* (London: Routledge, 2004); David Morley, *Television, Audiences and Cultural Studies* (London: Routledge, 1992); Stuart Hall, "Encoding and Decoding in the Television Discourse" (Centre for Contemporary Cultural Studies Occasional Paper, September 1973); and David Morrison, "Cultural and Moral Authority: The Presumption of Television," *Annals of the American Academy of Political and Social Science* 625 (2009): 116–27.

42. John Ellis, *Seeing Things: Television in the Age of Uncertainty* (London: I. B. Tauris, 2002), 79–80.

43. In between the two series, Speight wrote two *Till Death* films: *Till Death Us Do Part*, directed by Norman Cohen (London: Associated London Films, British Lion Film Corporation, 1969); *The Alf Garnett Saga*, directed by Bob Kellett (Los Angeles: Columbia Pictures Corporation; London: Associated London Films, 1972).

44. *Financial Times*, January 18, 1967.

45. *Evening News*, September 30, 1966.

46. See Schaffer, "*Till Death Us Do Part* and the BBC," 471–72.

47. ATV made the spin-off *Till Death* in 1981, before the BBC reclaimed the format in its *In Sickness and in Health*, which ran between 1985 and 1992. After the end of this program, Mitchell appeared as Alf in shows such as *An Audience with Alf Garnett* in 1997 and *The Thoughts of Chairman Alf* in 1998. The series also spawned many international versions, including *All in the Family* in the USA. For analysis see Christina von

Hodenberg, *Television's Moment: Sitcom Audiences and the Sixties Cultural Revolution* (London: Berghahn, 2015).

48. In a later episode ("Paki-Paddy," broadcast February 28, 1974), Alf claimed that his neighbors had constructed his family as Jews so that they had people to bully. "They didn't have any real Jews down this street—so they made out we was Jews . . ."

49. For example, Mitchell had played the role of Spencius in *Carry on Cleo*, directed by Gerald Thomas (London: Peter Rogers Productions, 1964).

50. This idea was revisited in the first episode of *In Sickness and in Health* (broadcast September 1, 1985), wherein Alf elaborated that Washkansky's body rejected a "black" heart. This was in fact untrue, as the donation to Washkansky was made by a white woman, Denise Darvall.

51. Hugh Wheldon to HG Leyshon, January 29, 1968, Caversham, File T16, 727, BBC Written Archives Centre, Reading, U.K.

52. Warren Mitchell quoted in Jonny Speight, *Alf Garnett: Till Death Us Do Part Scripts* (London: Woburn, 1973), 17.

53. Vince Powell, *From Rags to Gags* (Essex: Apex, 2008), 104.

54. Muir was assistant head of Light Entertainment at the BBC during this period. *Never Mind the Quality, Feel the Width*, Armchair Theatre, Series 7, Episode 4, broadcast February 18, 1967. *Till Death Us Do Part* began in a similar manner, as a one-off play on the BBC's *Comedy Playhouse*, broadcast July 22, 1965.

55. Powell, *From Rags to Gags*, 128–39. This was a decision, Powell recalls, which led to Frank Muir, at the BBC, telling him he would never work for the corporation again.

56. In choosing the names "Cohen" and "Kelly," Powell and Driver were probably consciously referencing Harry Pollard's 1926 film *The Cohens and Kellys*, which explored Jewish–Irish relations in the United States.

57. Powell, *From Rags to Gags*, 208.

58. Note on Series, CJN Martin, February 25, 1972, Box 3996148, Independent Television Authority Archive, Bournemouth University Library Special Collections.

59. Speight quoted in *Evening Standard*, May 20, 1996.

60. *Love Thy Neighbour* was broadcast by Thames Television.

61. Shaw, "'Light Entertainment' as Contested Socio-Political Space," 70.

62. Mary Malone, *Daily Mirror*, December 13, 1973.

63. Vince Powell remembered *Never Mind the Quality* in these terms: "Both John Bluthal and Joe Lynch kept us laughing with Jewish and Irish jokes. This was before political correctness was ever thought of" (Powell, *From Rags to Gags*, 141).

64. Jack Smethurst interview about *Love Thy Neighbour* in *Daily Express*, May 9, 1975.

RACHEL GARFIELD

From *The Evacuees* to *Grandma's House*
Class, Sexuality, and Jewish Identity on British Television, 1975–2012

My focus here is televisual representations of Jews in the United Kingdom from two significant periods in British Jewish history that draw an intergenerational arc from the Second World War to the present in terms of collective memory and adherence to notions of community and religion. Specifically, I will argue that the sitcom *Grandma's House* (2010 and 2012) represents a significant shift in self-representation, away from the mimetic[1] idea of Jewishness in relation to Jewish ritual and its place within the community, as seen in Jack Rosenthal's *The Evacuees* (1975) and problematized in his *Bar Mitzvah Boy* (1976). Ultimately, however, a form of continuity is restored in *Grandma's House* in terms of working-class representation, against the ongoing rags-to-riches, inner-city-to-green-suburb narrative that is still dominant in relation to British Jewry and which also feeds into the long-standing antisemitic discourse of all Jews being rich. Since the Rosenthal plays in the 1970s, British film and television, where it has deigned to represent Jews, has been dominated by visions of upper-middle-class concerns, as portrayed in such films as *Suzie Gold* (2004; discussed in a later chapter) and *Sixty Six* (2006).[2] *Grandma's House*, therefore, represents a welcome broadening out (in the dual senses of the word) of the experience of British Jewry on TV.

The Evacuees and *Bar Mitzvah Boy*: Jack Rosenthal and Postwar Jewry

Jack Rosenthal (1931–2004) was a prolific and important playwright in the United Kingdom, particularly on TV, where many of his plays were broadcast. Arguably his most fondly remembered plays are his "Jewish" ones written in the late 1970s: *The Evacuees* and *Bar Mitzvah Boy*. Both of these "Jewish plays" can be read as encapsulating British Jewry of the period. Whereas *The Evacuees* represents the memory of the adults of the 1970s—the threat of war and the fear of the Nazis that had an ongoing impact into their adulthood—*Bar Mitzvah Boy* echoes the voice of the 1970s present of that same generation seeing the future through the attitudes of the thirteen-year-old protagonist and the desire of that younger generation to put the past behind them.

In *The Evacuees*, two boys, Danny and Neville Miller (played by Gary Carp and Steven Serember, respectively), are evacuated with their whole class in September 1939 from working-class Manchester to St. Anne's, a northwest English coastal resort and a more economically affluent area than Blackpool—the usual holiday destination for the Manchester working classes. This difference is an important factor, as will be analyzed shortly. Sue Vice points out the desolation given to the landscape as a backdrop to the teacher trying to get the boys temporary homes and the gradual loss of morale throughout the day. The unwelcoming response of the inhabitants of St. Anne's is mirrored in this vision of the landscape, as opposed to the warmth and conviviality portrayed of the poverty-stricken cobbled Manchester streets. The inversion of usual associations (happy seaside vs. sad city poverty) is laid out here to powerful effect and introduces a theme that continues throughout the play. Vice also explains the structure of the editing; the crosscutting that builds the contrast between the home life and the evacuation that is so important to the viewers' understanding of the boys' experience.[3] This crosscutting holds throughout the play, positing the two families as binary oppositions in terms of class as well as ethnicity. The boys' family is portrayed as close and loving in contrast to the foster parents who are withholding and distant disciplinarians, which may also have class inflections. The story is portrayed through the boys' eyes, and in their eyes the St. Anne's foster parents are cruel. Their cruelty revolves around two aspects, both equally devastating for the boys: the foster parents will not show them their mother's letters and they also deprive the boys of good food, even food sent by their mother.[4] Both signs of withholding love are translated in the minds of the foster mother herself as being cruel to be kind, of disciplining the children for their own good, in sharp contrast to the Jewish family, which, it is implied, would not understand those terms of reference.

The issue with food is possibly the most memorable and signals contrasting cultural values on child rearing. The boys habitually eat standing up by the table while the two adults are seated. No chairs are provided for them. This scenario famously has its dramatic climax when the boys are forced to eat a single pork sausage on their plate, while their foster parents are digging in to their more tasty and fulsome meals. The camera lingers on the discomfort of the boys chewing the pork, obviously fighting their desire to repel the *treyf* (nonkosher) meat from their mouths. Thus the boys are shown to be both physically and metaphorically outsiders to the gentile Englishness of their temporary home: the unwelcoming dining room table highlights the breakup of the (partly absent) Jewish family unit — crosscut again, as Vice points out, with the empty chairs in the Manchester home.[5] It also posits the middle class as normative Englishness, and hence something to which the working-class Jew should aspire.[6]

Rosenthal specifically sets up the gentile English as having a distinct set of rules that is presented as excluding and unempathetic compared to the Jewish family. However, although the explicit exclusion comes from the non-Jews, this is not a one-way street. There is an implicit metanarrative of Jewish criticism of the cold, unwelcoming non-Jewish home that sends a strong message to the Jewish viewers of the unwelcome world beyond the community: trust is only to be extended to those within the Jewish community — even those within one's own regional Jewish community, as exemplified by a subplot wherein a Cockney boy is evacuated into Manchester and is goaded into fighting with the locals. The message of distrust has several roots. For example, the foster mother trying to erase the boys' mother from memory by hiding the letters could be seen within the history of Jewish children being snatched from Jewish homes and brought up as non-Jews within Jewish cultural memory.[7] More directly, however, by the 1970s, reference to the Second World War evoked the threat of the Holocaust in British Jewry and may well have served to remind the community in the 1970s of the times when they were beleaguered but survived and to reinforce the idea that only within Jewry can they feel safe.

Finally the younger of the two sons confesses to his mother what has been going on. She immediately takes action, returning them to the warmth of the Jewish home. There is a long crane shot of the mother and boys skipping and laughing through the bombed-out streets with a jolly song of the period playing, "Everything Is Tickety-Boo."[8] Another inversion is used to powerful effect: the implication of this scene is that their world is back to rights even if the rest of the world is not. The contrast of the happiness portrayed amid the misery of war serves to accentuate the message that a Jewish home that is split up is tantamount to ruin. The family would rather face death in the blitz and keep spiritually and emotionally warm than be certain of life in the coldness of the gentile English parlor. Back home the father lights the Hanukkah candles with the family around him, bathing in the glow of their light, singing a Hanukkah song, the family sitting around the table; the boys are valued, playing with their friends, being in the shelter, and bickering with their grandmother. The implications are clear: Jewish working-class community equals warmth whereas gentile middle-class Englishness is cold and hostile. It also reinforces Jewish nostalgia while positing normative Englishness as middle class and so achievable through class mobility to Jews. The foster mother's exclamation of self-justification to her husband, after the boys have gone, throws into relief the contrasting visions of child rearing operating within these different cultures: "I taught them respect. I wouldn't say that was cruel. I call that love. That's what I call it. Their love is not love at all. Too much love . . . that's what's cruel . . . I asked her to let me adopt them officially!" It thus sets up clear divisions between working-class Jewish and middle-class gentile English values whereby the hermetic Jewish life is left intact and Judaism as the "glue" of togetherness is reinscribed as the warm glow of a Jewish childhood.[9]

This is a Jewishness that does not take the Jewish law of Halacha too seriously but maintains the rituals that draw the family together and hopefully nurtures the social inwardness that ensures endogamy, such as kosher food and lighting Hanukkah candles. Vice discusses authenticity and memory in her analysis of *The Evacuees*, arguing that the viewers' responses to the play demanded authenticity and while Rosenthal had said the play was about memory, this view diverged with historians' accounts in some of the detail.[10] Nonetheless, in my view this play was pivotal in actually producing the cultural memory of the Jewish community in the 1970s and, it is important to note, supplying the responses and answers to its sense of history of itself: as well as winning four industry awards, it earned "encomia from Wolf Mankowitz, Jeremy Isaacs and Anthony Andrews," who were all significant public figures at the time.[11] The message to the community was clear: stick together, stay within the community, do "Jewish things," and ensure Jewish continuity. This is the message to the older members of the community, many of whom were perceiving the collapse of a consensus that coalesced around the idea of a middle ground in British Jewry, which arguably had never really existed but was now gaining in public awareness.[12]

The 1970s were a time during which Jewish marriage was falling drastically; fascist activity was rising, and the British public was just beginning to turn away from unquestioning support of Israel in the long buildup to the invasion of Lebanon.[13] The Orthodox synagogues were losing their supremacy on the Board of Deputies of British Jews as the then chief rabbi allowed the Liberal movement to include its representatives. Significantly, this action caused the Union of Orthodox Hebrew Congregations to walk out in protest in 1971.[14] In the light of these new issues, the codes in *The Evacuees* may have resonated as warnings to a community that felt itself to be fracturing and less secure from within. Despite having survived the threat of Hitler, an older section of the community still feared annihilation through exogamy, as exemplified through the popular epithet within British Orthodoxy that "marrying out" was "finishing Hitler's work."

So what happens when the children of *The Evacuees* grow up and start to watch their children come of age? While the aforementioned "Jewish glue" is also inscribed into *Bar Mitzvah Boy*, the terms are being renegotiated by the son (who, chronologically speaking, could be the son of the boys who had been evacuated in the *Evacuees*). *Bar Mitzvah Boy* play takes place in the contemporary moment of the 1970s when it was written. This postwar evocation is of a Jewish community that is Jewish in private yet British subjects outside the home but which, nonetheless, socializes almost exclusively within the Jewish community (as exemplified in the play itself). Rosenthal could not have known the prescience of this play when he wrote it in 1976, but since that time — between 1970 and 1989, according to Geoffrey Alderman — the Jewish community polarized dramatically: membership of the "black hat" Orthodoxy (as opposed to the more moderate and modern Orthodoxy of the United Synagogue) doubled and that of Progressive Judaism increased by a fifth.[15] Keith Kahn-Harris and Ben Gidley also talk of the turning point in British Jewry when the community shifted to a discourse of insecurity, and one of the two core reasons for this shift into fear politics was a concern with Jewish continuity (the other being antisemitism) even while assimilation was at its most successful.[16] A key trigger in their view was the Six-Day War of 1967, which, while seeming to be a miracle showing how precarious Jewish safety was, also underlined the common fate of world Jewry. As Kahn Harris and Gidley state, "Paradoxically then, Jewish security, a secure sense of belonging engendered by the success of the assimilation project, provoked a need to reinforce communal identification."[17]

Bar Mitzvah Boy takes place in a 1930s nameless London suburb.[18] It focuses on the dysfunctional members of the protagonist's family, who are all expectantly dealing with the impending bar mitzvah to take place the following day. All fulfill some kind of stereotype; the mother is a worrying martyr; the father hides behind his newspaper; the sister is withholding toward a boyfriend she does not respect, seeing him as a doormat. This is a very different depiction of family life than the earlier one in *The Evacuees*, where the family is warm and loving. This family is marked by mutual neurosis and of a love that exists despite the irritations — because love is bound to duty. That evening and the following morning, the bar mitzvah boy, Eliot (Jeremy Steyn), looks around at the men in his family (father, sister's boyfriend, grandfather) and decides he does not want to follow any of them into manhood. He does not respect them. He wants something else. In the synagogue, when he is called up to say his portion of the Law, instead of going up to the bimah to accept the accolade from the community and read the Law that defines him in their eyes as an adult, he makes a decisive act — in the synagogue — in front of the community and to everyone's considerable consternation: he walks out.

Unbeknownst to his family, who are dealing with their grief in their own ways, Eliot goes to the park and teams up with Denise (Kim Clifford), a gentile girl from his school, responding to her questions about bar mitzvahs. She likens it to wearing a bra or getting her period, but he is not interested, so she leaves — reinforcing an experiential split between Jews and gentiles, men and women. During the opening sequence, Denise had asked, "What's he mean? 'Marks his passage'? Is it rude?" Another boy, Squidge (Mark Herman), replies, "It's something Jewish. What Jewish boys do. You wouldn't understand." Denise, suspicious, is still not assuaged, "It *sounds* rude."[19] The gendering of the insider/outsider dichotomy is as noticeable as the cultural, although unstated. This event of the bar mitzvah is clearly one that happens only to males. They parade it with a slight swagger, never fully explaining to the girl, preferring to keep it as a secret and male rite of passage. While they are knowingly acting out their desire for ethnic "insiderism" in this scenario, they are also acting out their male bonding. The lewdness of the phrase emphasizes the exclusion of the woman and the sexualized nature of the banter or even flirtation, metaphorically flexing their manly muscles (in contrast to the other males in the play). Denise phones Eliot's sister out of spite, to pay him back for being boring. His sister goes to find him in the park. He is on a swing and puts on a Mickey Mouse mask — mirroring his doubts about the authenticity of adult life: the mask of the child hiding the reluctant adult behind. There is an additional overlay here of metaphor at this transformative moment — of going back to childhood innocence; the empty playground; the indecision of what to do, swinging back and forth in his head as well as literally.

Significantly, women are his confidantes. Denise is the first confidante, the outsider to whom he chooses to explain himself, as so many of his generation chose to do as adults by marrying "out,"[20] although she has nothing at stake and leaves. The other confidante is his sister, wheedling out of him his reasons: "but they're not men though that's the point," he states, emphatically, referring to the male members of his family. This may have been a poetic preview and judgment on what was at stake for the postwar community: the models of masculinity were being constructed through the shifts in representation from the *Evacuees* to *Bar Mitzvah Boy* to *Grandma's House*. These were the changes at the interface of assimilation as the community took on the mores of Englishness and refer back to a much older fear of the feminized male Jew. The more recent *Grandma's House* inverts this fear through the self-reflexivity of Simon Amstell and his on-screen character, both of whom are out and gay Jewish men (which I will discuss in more detail in the next section).

Within the contemporary assimilative worldview, the middle-class ambitious professional would be the aspiration.

It may also have been a comment on the community as a whole. Membership of an Orthodox synagogue has little intrinsic value to this community, other than ensuring the fact of belonging. The day-to-day observance that is so important to Orthodox Judaism itself means little, hence the wavering boy. However, the laissez-faire Orthodoxy of these "three-times-a-year-Jews,"[21] who tend to observe the positive rather than the negative commandments, is possibly as much a source of the boy's disappointment as the failed masculinity of the men as he perceives it, and in the logic of the play the two are intrinsically interconnected. In the moment of crises, the mother says to the father, "you're never *doing* anything," to which the father shouts, "I go out to work, earn the money. What else am I meant to do?" "That's it, you don't even know," she ripostes. He can only see the duty of fatherhood in very narrow economic, breadwinning terms, and nothing else: his wife is as disappointed in his passivity in relation to the world as is his son. The passive adherence to community or religion that his father represents has also had its day. That is, the idea of a religion that is observed mainly because it is expected of him by the community, not one that is actively and keenly felt or sought after by the individual, according to the logic of the play. Thus he has lost his potency, in contrast to the Jewish father in *The Evacuees*, who valiantly puts out the fire and is seen through the mother's eyes as the loving father and good husband and who fulfills the ritual of lighting candles. This shift in expectation of one's relationship to religion is in part a generational shift of the growing assimilation of Jewry from the post-World War II era to the 1970s and beyond, from the small world of the community to the larger world of the middle-class professions, accessed through education, or, put another way, from the mimetic ideal of Jewish life, as carried down the generations, to the self-chosen instability of contemporary subjectivity as exemplified by Simon Amstell in *Grandma's House*, to be looked at later. In the end, Eliot performs the reading of the Law outside of the community: in the park he stands on his head and recites his Torah portion with his sister as witness as proof of his manhood outside of the synagogue (and as hinted at when metaphorically flexing his muscles at the outset of the play). What this pivotal moment represents is *not* the moment he leaves the "community," but rather the moment he questions the terms his parents have set him about what kind of community he can expect, and what kind of manhood, compared to the kind of community he might desire or the kind of man he would desire to become. He cannot quite break away completely yet, which is why, significantly, he recites the portion to his sister, saving his true feelings for her, and not to Denise.

In this act Eliot embodies the metaphor of the upside-down world he and the future represent to the postwar generation, where the individual can flout the Law with impunity from the wider congregation — where marrying out is, if not the norm, then at least usual and openly practiced. In this way, the vision of British Jewish life, understood as a safe and natural home, as it was envisaged earlier in the postwar era, is significantly questioned. The normative Jewish life, as a kind of middle-of-the-road Jewishness that still clings to the idea of mainstream Orthodoxy in a three-times-a-year way, is also questioned through this final gesture. The self-chosen bar mitzvah act is the arbiter of change to a community that has Friday night dinner and attends the Orthodox synagogue on High Holidays and celebrations, where "marrying out" brings shame on the family and socializing internally is the expectation. What was a rite of acceptance and belonging conferred by the community to the individual now in effect becomes a rite of choice — or not — a personal decision of the individual and his journey into manhood. In this evocative and important moment in the play, the British Jewish community, in line with the broader trends, makes a generational leap, rejecting the social contract of the postwar generation that puts the social above the individual and joins the neoliberal individualistic narrative of freedom and choice.[22]

Grandma's House and Contemporary British Jewry

Grandma's House builds on the legacy of Jack Rosenthal in his presentation of a complete Jewish world. It similarly borrows the trope of parading the fractured family. It is a sitcom that relies on stock Jewish characters: the guilt-inducing nagging mother ("the stitches I had, giving birth to you" to which her son responds in a defiant gesture of refusal, "they must have healed up by now"); the benign schlemiel but much-loved grandfather, who does not say much, overpowered by the women in the family, just wanting an easy life; the way the family revels in everyone knowing everyone's business. In these ways *Grandma's House* does the same joke work that we have seen earlier in Rosenthal's plays. It can also been seen within the framework of Ivan Kalmar of "embarrassed Jewish Individuals" or "eji's" who trumpet their uneasy relationship to their Jewishness at every turn and use their social ambivalence to gain "social purchase."[23] As its title indicates, *Grandma's House* takes place exclusively on the property of the grandmother of the central character, Simon (played by Simon Amstell), and his younger cousin, Adam (Jamal Hadjkura). Members of the family congregate within her house during each episode. Each week focuses on a set of interweaving everyday dramas that draw out the vulnerabilities of each member of the family, their defensive competitiveness, and the social ambivalence of the two grandsons.

Grandma's House constitutes a multiple shift in self-awareness of the Jewish community in the United Kingdom. First, it represents an acknowledgement of double consciousness in Jewish identity. Second, it betrays a sense of Jewish subjectivity that is performative, or in a constant state of flux, rather than relying on mimesis through tradition. Third, it shows disregard for an "authentic" Jewish experience that is so important to Rosenthal's plays. Finally, Simon Amstell, the writer and star of this television program, is a gay man, who is well known in Britain for being just as public about his sexual identity as about his Judaism. The naturalized gay sexuality of Amstell's character — whose on-screen family revels in stories of his unrequited love life — represents a miasmic shift in Jewish masculinity since the period of Rosenthal's plays, as well as a wider acceptance in British culture of both gays and Jews. This sitcom also is important in the return to a working-class Jewish experience that has been largely absent in U.K. TV representations since Rosenthal's plays and offers a recuperative reading of Jewry that eschews the narrowness of the stereotypical upper-middle-class professional, bringing back an older stereotype of the Jewish taxi driver, who earlier featured in *Bar Mitzvah Boy*. It also takes place in a similar type of house to the earlier play.

The sitcom is essentially a vehicle for Amstell, who was born in 1979 in Gants Hill and has appeared in TV comedy since childhood. He is also a well-known stand-up comic in the United Kingdom. To be clear — Simon Amstell is a real person who is a comedian. In *Grandma's House* he is acting a character called Simon Amstell who, the audience is led to believe, is a fiction but who often references a TV career history that the audience knows happened to the real, pre–*Grandma's House* Amstell. Thus reality and fiction are blurred, making for a contemporary take on the subject who has no authenticity. The audience can never tell who the real Amstell in the fiction is, nor who is the real character in the comedy. This is another differentiating factor from Rosenthal's plays that is indicative of a shift in Jewish self-identity. Vice discusses the desire for authenticity in the audience responses to both plays discussed here by Rosenthal.[24] Such keenly felt desire for an authentic representation is rendered redundant in the reception of *Grandma's House*. A *Jewish Chronicle* reviewer, for example, acknowledged that this comedy was a subjective construction that does not necessarily define the whole community, nor did it worry about the burden of representation:

> Jewish viewers might squirm as they recognize something familiar in Simon's grandparents, mum, aunt and nephew who kvetch and bicker over the dinner table together. Whether you enjoy it or not will depend on how you feel about Amstell's geeky, angst-ridden persona.[25]

Interestingly, despite the doubling of the real and the fictional in the construction of Simon in the series, in interview Simon states that it was really important to him and David Swimer, his cowriter, that it was authentic. However, they did not imply authenticity in Jewish terms, instead as revealing "true" feelings.[26]

In the TV series (as possibly in reality) Simon struggles to redefine his career as a serious writer or actor, against his family's aspirations for him to become a popular TV celebrity. They were happy with his role as a talk show host and want him to continue on that track. Some of the gags in *Grandma's House* rely on his previous performances on TV, and his real life as a TV presenter is part of the conceit of the fiction in the sitcom. His previous career in real life on TV is one of the ways of situating contemporary subjectivity that is a site of flux, reinvention, and desire through the doubling, as will be explained shortly. This subjectivity-in-flux differentiates the Jewish subject from that of *The Evacuees* through *Bar Mitzvah Boy* to *Grandma's House* in an incremental way. Whereas the *Evacuees* offers a stable idea of Jewish identity that knows what it is and who it wants to be (it is a safe, protective, warm environment), *Bar Mitzvah Boy* begins to ask the question of what it is to be Jewish; or how one might want to be Jewish, but finds an equilibrium in compromise (in that Eliot celebrates his bar mitzvah but on his own in the park). *Grandma's House*, in contrast, offers no equilibrium but instead discomfort as normative, and with no redemption.

In its lack of visible and active Jewish ritual or formal involvement, *Grandma's House* shows a contemporary development away from the postwar British middle-of-the road type of mainstream Judaism as depicted in the Rosenthal plays, a Judaism that was more about an idea of community than Orthodoxy.[27]Adherence to religion and the role of the ritual in the shaping of the community as Jewish is central to the self-representation of postwar Jewry, as represented in the longevity of *The Evacuees* and *Bar Mitzvah Boy*.[28] In *Grandma's House*, in contrast, there is no adherence to religious ritual or reference to ritual, the synagogue, or formal community in this series as such. Jewishness is embedded in its use of language, such as Yiddish, as well as its cultural mores. In series (season) 1, episode 3, for example, Jewishness is alluded to, *inversely*, through the outrage of the family when Auntie Liz (Samantha Spiro) wears a crucifix in a desperate attempt to try to get her son into a Catholic school.

It is significant that *Grandma's House* is set in the northeast London suburb of Redbridge, which has had a long-standing working-class connection with the East End. Gants Hill, which is where the sitcom is specifically set, was known by the wider community in Redbridge as the "taxi driver belt," so it is no surprise that Simon's grandfather, Bernie (Geoffrey Hutchings), had been a taxi driver. The move out of the East End was precipitated in part by relative affluence and aspiration but also by bomb damage and postwar slum clearance.[29] Yet, Redbridge Jews generally were overwhelmingly employed in "distribution and services"[30] with little of the cultural or economic capital that marks the much more affluent, professionalized northwest London suburbs.[31] Nonetheless, by the 1970s, Redbridge had the largest population of Jews in Europe, and while Vice has identified the TV location of *Bar Mitzvah Boy* as Willesden, in my teenage Jewish circles in Redbridge, we (and there were others too) all believed it to be set in Gants Hill.[32] However, this community has been much reduced from dominance to marginality and concomitantly become increasingly culturally impoverished by the moving of cultural institutions from central London to the less accessible (for those in east and northeast London) middle-class suburbs of northwest London.

The extent of the invisibility of the nuances of class and geography in the Jewish community is exemplified by the fact that none of the reviewers of the first "series" (or "season," as Americans would call it) of *Grandma's House* recognized the particular locale of northeast London Jewry. For example, Jonathan Margolis, an ordinary Ilford Jewish viewer, wrote how his wife exclaimed, "Oh my good gawd, that's Clayhall," when the first exterior of the suburban semidetached house was shown. "Don't be so daft," he said. "It'll be west London somewhere. It always is. You know Ilford doesn't exist to the creative classes."[33] *Grandma's House*, therefore, represents a counterhegemonic Jewry that is little known outside the northeast London Jewish community itself. The professional northwest London of the Jewish professional classes is dominant in contrast to the northeast because the stereotypical picture of contemporary Jewry is one of bourgeois suburbia (rather than working-class suburbia and the stereotype of an inner-city working class). This current misrepresentation is bound up with the visibility of the Jews in the media (as journalists and commentators), coupled with the persistent stereotype of the Jewish professional (in particular, the doctor or lawyer).

However, it can be argued that it is also the way in which there is a disjunction between the notions of working class and Jewish: the connection between the terms and the historic connection to the East End of London, which has long been associated in popular memory with Jewish life for a particular historical period. It is central to the rags-to-riches journey of the many immigrant communities inhabiting this part of London, including that of the Jewish community: the East End is where that journey starts, and the affluent suburbs are where that journey ends. Working-class Jews in the United Kingdom are generally associated with the former struggle of grandparents and great-grandparents in the East End of London or Cheetham Hill in Manchester that is romanticized from a position of middle-class assimilated safety. It sits alongside an older stereotype of the poor peasant in the shtetl and the myth of progression to wealth and assimilation in the present. The idea of Jews as middle class is completely naturalized in contemporary Britain. Jews themselves reinforce this misconception, which, in turn, often blinds them to the reality of the breadth of contemporary British Jewry. Yet, the importance of Rosenthal in the British Jewish imaginary is a testament to this history of recent working-class Jewry running well into the 1970s, and now, as we can see, it returns again.

Despite the ostensible comforts of family and tradition that one might expect it to offer, *Grandma's House* is not a comfortable home. It is a home that Simon keeps coming back to but also keeps trying to escape from. He sits in the discomfort, reveling in his ambivalence. This is not a new ambivalence, it is just that we are allowed to see it more clearly in the gaps between what is known and what is presented on-screen. That is the hovering other in the series: the impossibility of either belonging or not belonging, the radical lack of certainty. Amstell's inability to be at home in the familial house with his family may well be underpinned by his sexuality. In Jewish Orthodoxy, to be gay is to be profoundly unaccepted and *in the closet*. Orthodoxy largely sets the overall tone for the U.K. Jewish community just as heteronormativity is the orthodoxy within the wider non-Jewish community in the United Kingdom. This difference can be usefully contrasted with the Rosenthal plays, wherein the familial equilibrium is always restored in the end and is predicated upon the traditional nuclear family. It may be that through the reinvention of Jewish life without the community—as it is represented in *Grandma's House*—Amstell's sexuality does not threaten the normative hegemonic Jewish values of a certain type of Jewish masculinity so central to Jewish continuity and Halacha that revolves around synagogue life.[34]

The insertion of the doubling—of Simon playing himself and Simon's interior life—is what allows the series to sidestep the patronizing sneer of the assumed normative middle-class white voyeur. We are asked to identify with the dilemmas with which Simon is faced; we see the family through his loving—even while ambivalent—eyes rather than our own. The doubling in *Grandma's House* is worked through several devices: the main conceit is the self-reflexivity of Amstell playing himself, which is directed at the viewers. There is also the misrepresentation between the self on-screen, whom the viewer never sees but who is alluded to again and again, such as the confident, cocky, famous real-life Simon and the self-doubting schlemiel we see before us. This misrepresentation, in turn, is played out through the portrayal of the difference between his mother's expectations of him and his own aspirations.[35] The members of his family are not interested in his aspirations and ridicule him for them when he forces them to take notice. He tries again and again to confer his interior world on them, to no avail.

It would be an obvious link to turn to the double consciousness, as formulated by W. E. B. Dubois, of the black subject who is conscious of the self of the African American and the self of Africa, his diasporic consciousness that speaks to the difference he is made to feel from the norm in the United States.[36] This link could be an explanation for the desire of Amstell to play himself. In playing himself, there opens up a gap that can reveal the dilemmas that are not his alone to own but that form part of the formation of otherness, of any otherness but specifically here of Jewishness in a performative repetition that reconstitutes the British Jewish subject in our time, the return of the repressed, hysterical, Other.

The performative doubling celebrates a heterogeneous disjunction and arises out of a continued lack of comfort, despite the assumed assimilation. The heterogeneous disjunction allows for critique and a questioning of the self as well as a performativity that produces the subjectivity formed through the dialogue between the real and the fiction. In the U.K. sitcom, through the main character, Simon Amstell, an interior life is conveyed that is not usual to the form of sitcom: Simon Amstell is trying to grow up. Through the interior dilemmas he expounds, which revolve around being taken seriously, about making a contribution (to art and culture), and particularly about negotiating between the members of his inward-looking family (with his grandmother as the matriarch) and the world outside the community, he speaks to dilemmas at the crux of contemporary everyday experience in the Jewish community and possibly timeless dilemmas of immigrant communities.

The heterogeneous disjunction is played out through one of the central themes of *Grandma's House*, which is the desire Simon feels to do something great, something that makes a difference. It speaks to the price that has to be paid in class mobility and in the notion of the Jew as arriviste, which goes to the heart of the intersection of race and class that runs through this program and the desire to assimilate. His family, in the piece, mocks the self-importance that they see in this desire. In their ridicule they reveal their lack of confidence in his world, in the scope of the world he desires as well as the need to rise in the shadow of his glory as they would see it from the eyes of the community: to *schep naches*. For example, when they ask him what his play is about, he answers that it is "about the struggle for truth and beauty against the powers of inauthenticity and dullness." His sister and mother immediately assume he's talking about Clive (James Smith), his mother's fiancé, who is an annoying boor in Simon's eyes but a point of comic relief to the audience as a foil in manhood to Simon himself. Their world is small, Jewish, and based in the home, in the concrete, but Simon's is big and outside the home in a way that reiterates as well as constitutes his sense of inadequacy as a Jew and his desire is for elevation: he fears their smallness pulling him back, back into being merely the talk show host, or more hilariously opening an information technology (IT) room in the local school.[37]

The tension is clear: his family members who reside completely in their Jewish working-class world do not desire the transcendence through culture as does Simon, who knows what the culture of the gentile intelligentsia offers (not to be confused with the slur, from antisemitic non-Jews, of the Jewish intelligentsia as an exclusionary and revolutionary elite): Ben (Iwan Rheon), the desiring male (desired by Simon), who cannot be heard either literally nor metaphorically by the family, is rendered as a whispering shadow in one hilarious episode (series 3, episode 1) wherein the family members struggle to hear him speak beside their own bellowing conversation style. The call of the middle-class, gentile world is too faint for them to hear. They can hear Clive, the loud, working-class, non-Jewish macho man, as they could hear the middle-class Jewish voice coach, Deborah Adler (Pam Ferris), but a middle-class non-Jew is a bridge too far. In the doubling and the gaps, it exposes Simon's doubts about life, but these doubts offer a radical ambivalence and contradiction. It is a paradox that makes him pertinent.

To return to the central plank of my argument: it is the process of comedy, not the subject of comedy, that really matters. In the final analysis, what marks *Grandma's House* as a transformative and radical sitcom that has something to say to contemporary Britain has to do with the difference between tragedy and comedy as exemplified in the difference between *Grandma's House* and, say, *Friday Night Dinner* (which debuted in 2011 and was still on air at the time this book went to print). *Friday Night Dinner* works from the particular to the universal. It speaks for everyone. In the ongoing childish pranks that the two sons endlessly play on each other there is a universal assumption that at heart "we are all like that really," that is, they are only being human. Conversely, *Grandma's House* works from the universal to the particular. Simon Amstell's grandiose pretensions are grounded in the particular of his family life: his family that grinds him down. He is speaking from the particular—his flaws, doubts, and ambivalence—yet the unshakable belief in himself despite it all makes him more than human so that in the end, we do not think less of him, despite his flaws, we think more of him for his intentions, which lends it a transformative value.

What do these self-portrayals say about the transformations of the Jewish community in the United Kingdom in the last few generations and the condition of being a Jew in Britain today? *The Evacuees* nostalgically harked back to a Jewish community that had been lost by the 1970s, if it ever was really thus. There is no self-shame or self-consciousness in *The Evacuees*. However, in *Bar Mitzvah Boy*, outsiders are brought in as a neutral foil that reveals the perceived awfulness of the Jewish home in stark contrast to the portrayal of the outsiders to Jewry in *The Evacuees*. By the time of *Bar Mitzvah Boy*, many of Eliot's generation had made choices that were different from those of their parents, either away from the middle-of-the-road Judaism or away from their class through upward mobility via the state education system of that time. But its vision of the duty of the Jewish family exists in a way that is much closer to the paradigm in *Grandma's House*. As such *Bar Mitzvah Boy* could be seen as a bridge between these visions of Jewish life in the United Kingdom, not in terms of class, which in this scenario represents continuity, but in terms of the message portrayed (or constructed) in what community might mean: from the warm glow of nostalgic warmth of the 1940s to the hyper–self-critical mood of claustrophobia and shame in the 1970s that still survives today.

Class is a theme that has run through these texts as an important factor in representations of Jews on British television. According to Jon Stratton, the Jewish sitcom in the United States waned at precisely the moment that Jews became middle class.[38] However, since Stratton wrote this in 2000, there has been a reemergence of Jewish sitcoms. Perhaps, then, the importance of *Grandma's House* is that, given Stratton's argument, it signals an incompleteness to the assimilative project for Jews and in relation to class. If, as Vincent Brook suggests, sitcoms "are a barometer of 'society's values,'"[39] then *Grandma's House* signifies a shift away from the so-called postwar British Jewish consensus to say much about the shifts in collective identifications since the Second World War within the contemporary British Jewish community.

Notes

1. I am using this term as "a way of producing the effect of identity through a Jewish tradition," as discussed by Vikki Bell, "Mimesis as Cultural Survival: Judith Butler and Anti-Semitism," in *Theory Culture and Society*, edited by Vikki Bell, 141 (London, Thousand Oaks; New Delhi: Sage, 1999).

2. *Sixty Six*, directed by Paul Welland (London: Working Title, 2006).

3. Sue Vice, *Rosenthal* (Manchester, U.K.: Manchester University Press, 2009), 168–76.

4. This term "foster parents" is a loose term, as they are merely the people who took in the evacuees for the duration of their evacuation.

5. Vice, *Rosenthal*, 170.

6. Institutions such as the Jews Free School, Jewish Board of Guardians were established in part to "introduce to foreign aliens Jews English middle class values." Juliet Steyn, *The Jew: Assumptions of Identity* (London: Routledge, 1999), 75.

7. Geoffrey Alderman states that many Jewish refugee children were fostered by non-Jews, and "some were lured or lulled into Christianity while others were exploited as substitute domestic servants." Geoffrey Alderman, *Anglo-Jewry: A Suitable Case for Treatment* (London: Royal Holloway and Bedford New College, University of London, 1989), 299.

8. Vice, *Rosenthal*, 171.

9. Even when the youngest son nearly burns down the house by relighting the Hanukkah candles just before bed, the love is not diminished and the punishment barely there — in direct contrast to the punishment inflicted on the boys when they get beaten up through no fault of their own in St. Anne's.

10. Vice, *Rosenthal*, 73.

11. Ibid., 168.

12. See David Cesarani, "How Post War Britain Reflected on the Nazi Persecution and Mass Murder of Europe's Jews: A Reassessment of Early Responses," *Jewish Culture and History* 12, no. 1–2 (2010): 95–130. There has never been a consensus; however, Geoffrey Alderman in his pamphlet cites the turbulence that was caused by the ascension of a representative of the progressive synagogues to the Board of Deputies and the subsequent exit of the Union of Orthodox Hebrew Congregation that heralded a profound rift that still existed at the time of writing the pamphlet (Alderman, *Anglo-Jewry*, 5).

13. Alderman, *Anglo-Jewry*, 4.

14. Ibid., 5.

15. Ibid.

16. Ben Gidley and Keith Kahn-Harris, *Turbulent Times: The British Jewish Community Today* (London: Continuum, 2010).

17. Ibid., 27.

18. Both North West and North East London have been claimed.

19. Quoted in Vice, *Rosenthal*, 176.

20. Marriages in synagogues fell drastically, from more than 2,000 in 1970 to 1,250 in 1978 and to 1,075 in 1982. By 1989 the number was down to 1,057. See Geoffrey Alderman, *Modern British Jewry* (London: Clarendon Press, 1998), 328.

21. This term refers to those who only attend synagogue on the High Holidays.

22. Shifts in political allegiance of Jews from 1974 to 1987 moved significantly toward the Conservative Party within British Jewry. In fact, Alderman found, "Jews have proved somewhat more Conservatively inclined" than their non-Jewish equivalents, which could have something to do with perceptions of (or actual) anti-Zionism within the Labour Party (Alderman, *Modern British Jewry*, 344–45).

23. Ivan Kalmar, *The Trotskys, Freuds and Woody Allens: Portrait of a Culture* (Toronto: Penguin, 1994), 199. See also Jon Stratton, *Coming Out Jewish* (London: Routledge, 2000), 297.

24. Vice, *Rosenthal*, 168.

25. Alan Montague, "Wincing with the Amstells," *Jewish Chronicle*, August 4, 2010, http://www.thejc.com/arts/arts-features/36463/wincing-amstells.

26. Quoted in Nick Fiaca, "An Interview with Simon Amstell," *TV Choice*, August 3, 2012, http://www.tvchoicemagazine.co.uk/interviewextra/simon-amstell-grandmas-house. Amstell added, "I was really terrified, after spending so much time trying to make the scripts as authentic, heartfelt and real as possible, that I might go in and screw the whole thing up with my horrific acting."

27. The term "community" has been widely problematized across disciplines. In this context I am referring to a definition in Gidley and Kahn-Harris of community "as a self-conscious though by no means unified entity whose members interact in Jewish institutions" (*Turbulent Times*, 7). For critiques of the term "community," a key foundational text is Benedict Anderson, *Imagined Communities: Reflections on the Origin and Spread of Nationalism* (London: Verso, 2006); see also Paul Gilroy, *Between Camps: Nations, Culture and the Allure of Race* (London: Allan Lane, 2000). My own work has been profoundly questioning of those terms, such as my video work "So You Think You Can Tell" (2000).

28. These two TV plays have been reissued recently in a BBC DVD.

29. Todd Endelman, *The Jews in Britain 1666–2000* (Berkeley: University of California Press, 2002), 230.

30. "Redbridge Jewish Survey 1977–78," *UK Data Service*, accessed October 28, 2015, http://www.esds.ac.uk/findingData/snDescription.asp?sn=1512.

31. According to recent statistics from the American Jewish charity Met Council, "there are almost a quarter of a million Jewish people in New York who live in households with incomes under 150% of the Federal Poverty Guideline. These 244,000 poor people represent 15% of the 1.66 million Jewish people in all Jewish households in the New York area." "Jewish Poverty FAQs," Met Council, accessed February 23, 2013, http://www.metcouncil.org/site/PageServer?pagename=About_Jewish_Poverty_FAQs (no longer available).

32. Jessica Elgot, *Jewish Chronicle*, October 1, 2009.

33. Jonathan Margolis, "Let's Hear It for . . . That Place in Essex," *Jewish Chronicle*, August 12, 2010, http://www.thejc.com/comment-and-debate/comment/36722/lets-hear-it-for . . .-place-essex. Clayhall is an area of the London Borough of Redbridge, very close to Gants Hill, with similar demographics.

34. An exploration of the intersectionality of race, class, sexuality, and gender incorporating the insights of Daniel Boyarin and Daniel Izkovitz, among others, would be part of a longer study that is beyond the scope of this chapter. It would be particularly rewarding to develop this subject in relation to British Jewish identity.

35. Interestingly, given usual cultural narratives of marriage, here his mother's expectations are not for him to be married, thus normalizing his homosexuality: his expectations of himself are to be creatively fulfilled and in love.

36. W. E. B. Du Bois, *The Souls of Black Folk* (New York: Gramercy Books, 1994).

37. This is the subject of series 1, episode 6, when Simon's aunt arranges for him to open the local college media room where his cousin is studying but without asking his permission. Simon sees this as beneath him. His aunt sees it as a way of gaining social power in her milieu and sees him as an ungrateful snob. More generously put, she cannot also understand him turning down work when he is in need of it, whereas he would rather not work than demean himself—another class split.

38. Stratton, *Coming Out Jewish*, 292.

39. Vincent Brook, *Something Ain't Kosher Here: The Rise of the "Jewish Sitcom"* (New Brunswick: Rutgers University Press, 2003), 3.

DONALD WEBER

Peckhlach
Mike Leigh's British Jewish Soul

In the fall of 2005 the award-winning British filmmaker and playwright Mike Leigh mounted his *Two Thousand Years* at the Cottesloe Theatre in London, at the invitation of the National Theatre's director, Nicholas Hytner. "Here's my Jewish play," Leigh asserted with a characteristic blend of the impish and impudent, introducing the published version of the play. "I've been threatening to do it for years, but I haven't felt ready until now, when I'm well into my sixties."[1] I explore the relation between Leigh's self-proclaimed "Jewish play" and, until recently, the long tradition of British Jewish reticence in the realm of literary and cultural expression. "I think I've come out of the closet to do this play," Leigh confessed in an interview during the play's sold-out run,[2] using the telling language of exposure, of feeling "outed," by revealing his hitherto undeclared ethnicity in public. Leigh is more usually associated with a rich archive of films exploring how everyday people struggle for dignity under degrading social and economic pressures imposed by 1980s Thatcherism, as in *High Hopes* (1988), or comic-tragic films about outsiders searching for some zone of balance in a world felt to be whirling out of control, as in *Naked* (1993).[3] "So Mike Leigh Is Jewish After All," ran the headline in the U.S. Jewish newspaper the *Forward*, announcing the ethnic "confession" of *TTY*.[4] In light of this revelation, I will ask the following questions: What is the meaning of Leigh's self-outing in *TTY*? What are the play's larger cultural-political meanings?

How does Leigh represent Jewishness on stage? Above all, what is the relation between Leigh's overtly "Jewish" play and the often fraught tradition of British Jewish self-consciousness: the long-nourished habit, on the part of British Jewry, of keeping quiet, of remaining hidden, of not calling attention to itself?

In answering these questions, I offer a brief overview describing the history of British Jewish reticence; I then describe the current cultural scene of a revived, in fact an energized, Jewish culture of performance in contemporary Britain (of which Leigh's play participates); next, I offer an engaged critique of *TTY*, highlighting what might be called the limits of Leigh's representation of Jewish identity; and I conclude the chapter with a brief reading of Leigh's masterpiece, *Secrets and Lies* (1996), a movie about the need to search for "roots" and "identity" in contemporary society. *Secrets* is Leigh's exemplary *Jewish* film, a more apt representation of what Leigh has described as the "Jewish spirit in my work."[5] Mike Leigh's "Jewish" soul remains more powerfully—indeed, most provocatively—revealed, not in his self-styled "Jewish play," but rather in his deeply moving film about lost souls searching for family ties, for a way of salving the pain of living in a topsy-turvy multicultural Britain, where everyday people, feeling apart and uprooted, seek alternative modes of filiation, of connecting with a tribe to call their own.

Contexts: Overturning the Legacy of "Stay Shtumm"

"In England," observes the Jewishly obsessed narrator (named Philip) in Philip Roth's 1990 novel *Deception*, "whenever I'm in a public place, a restaurant, a party, the theater, and somebody happens to mention the word 'Jew,' I notice that the voice always drops just a little."[6] By turns enraged and bewildered, fascinated and disgusted with what he perceives to be the self-muting habits of a tame British Jewry, the fictional Philip longs to return to his true homeland, New York City, which, in his view, is a heimisch territory inhabited, in his American Jewish fantasy, by "Jews with force . . . Jews with appetite. Jews without shame. Complaining Jews who get under your skin. Brash Jews who eat with their elbows on the table. Unaccommodating Jews, full of anger, insult, argument, and impudence."[7] Feeling uprooted in London, Roth himself spoke harshly of his experience as a "de-territorialized" Jewish writer-intellectual living half of each year in England. As he explained in a 1988 interview, in conjunction with the publication of his "memoir" *The Facts*, "what's driving [British] society isn't dramatized with anything like the turbulent intensity that animates America . . . the intensity that's generated by the American historical drama of movement and massive displacement, of class overspreading class, region overtaking region, minority encroaching on minority."[8]

At some level, it would seem, Roth's portrait of a relatively static British culture during the mid-1980s amounts to a projection, the displaced writer imposing his American (New York?) identity, born of imagined new world turbulence, marked by social upheaval and ethnic tensions, onto the British literary landscape. However, around the same time (if not sooner, perhaps beginning with the publication of Salman Rushdie's *Midnight's Children* in 1980) a vibrant literary scene was emerging in Britain centered on cosmopolitan London, belying Roth's premature assessment. Indeed, contemporary Britain now sounds with a rich aural-multicultural mix: an array of diverse voices, conjured by writers who take the vexed yet often comic story of global migration and "new world" adjustment to the "West" as their subject. And strikingly, perhaps in response to — or (more likely) as part of — the noisy babel of voices currently animating literary Britain, a rising generation of British Jewish writers, filmmakers, artists, musicians, and the like is now being heard. Indeed, Jewish culture in contemporary Britain is thriving.

Despite this recent outpouring in celebration of British Jewry's emergence in the culture — an arrival predated by a rich literary history, which includes such figures as Arnold Wesker, Bernard Kops, and Harold Pinter, among many others — at some level there remains an ingrained wariness expressive of a long history of accommodation, of self-effacement on the part of British Jews, in response to the pressures of what might be called "Anglicization." "In England the price of toleration was Englishness," recalls the British literary critic A. Alvarez, about the psychic and emotional costs of achieving British citizenship; "the only way to be English is scrupulously to obey the customs of the country."[9] A poignant version of this core British Jewish dilemma is heard in eleven-year-old Jonah Summerfield's poem, recited before a gathering of dignitaries — including then Prime Minister Tony Blair — at a ceremony in June 2006 celebrating 350 years of British Jewish life:

Am I Jewish or English?
This keeps me in confusion.
I'm both, you see, that's my final conclusion.
Judaism is my religion, I make it so, clearly.
I adore England, I love it so dearly.[10]

In earnest, if tempered, adoration of his homeland, the young poet keeps faith with generations of British Jews conscious of the assimilatory pressures associated with the host culture. In this respect, Maurice Samuel's 1952 memoir, *The Gentleman and the Jew,* about growing up as an immigrant son in early twentieth-century Manchester, registers the unalloyed, unironic embrace of "Englishness" for a generation of British Jewry: "Among us Jews, as I remember vividly," Samuel recalls, "the attitude toward England was one of intense admiration, respect, gratitude, and affection."[11]

In his brief speech, Prime Minister Blair seized the exemplary story of Jewish citizenship to score political points. Referring to the relatively smooth history of Jewish assimilation into British life, Blair offered an implicit moral contrast between British Jewish patriotism and the charged matter of "integration"—as the debate over acculturation is termed in Britain and Western Europe—among newer immigrant communities, perhaps in light of the approaching first anniversary of the July 7, 2005 ("7/7") bombings in London, carried out by British-born, alienated second-generation sons of (mainly) South Asian descent. Speaking of British Jews, Blair noted "how it is possible to retain a clear faith and a clear identity, and at the same time be thoroughly British. As the oldest minority faith community in this country, you show how identity through faith can be combined with the deep loyalty to our nation."[12] Like Asian Americans in the United States, here Jews are now presented as Britain's "model minority," exemplary of how the immigration-integration process should work.

In the robust if politically charged atmosphere of contemporary Britain—above all, in the linguistic babel of multicultural London, where the majority of Britain's three hundred thousand Jews live—questions of affiliation and identity have taken an urgent turn. In this respect, along with other minority groups, contemporary Jewish writers and critics are reimagining their relation to "Englishness," where "English," problematically in this account, is linked to histories of whiteness and power and is thus associated with a shameful history of British antisemitism and imperialism, including the expulsion of the Jews from England in 1290 and subsequent parliamentary actions limiting Jewish immigration.

"Jews are taking advantage of that discussion," noted historian Todd M. Endelman, about British Jewry's participation in twenty-first-century debates in the United Kingdom around multiculturalism. As a result, according to Matthew J. Reisz, a former editor of the *Jewish Quarterly*, the distinguished journal of British Jewish literary and cultural life that has been in publication for more than sixty years, writers now "move in and out of Jewish identity as one part of their British identity." Jewish stories, Reisz observes, are "being told very well, and unapologetically . . . in a completely unselfconscious way," as "part of a wider British conversation"[13] about faith identities, the multivocal definitions around the meaning of being "British." "The story of our finely tuned accommodations to English culture is a fascinating one," asserts the prizewinning novelist Howard Jacobson, "sometimes tragic, often heroic, always funny, and never less than urgent beneath a quiescent surface. It is time we told it."[14]

What stories are Jewish writers telling in the twenty-first century? According to Bryan Cheyette, "A sense of marginality and in-betweenness has led to an extraordinary growth in the inventiveness and originality of British Jewish literature since the 1980s."[15] Whether in response to the so-called British multicultural explosion, or as a result of embracing their identity as British Jews, or in an effort to claim (along with other best-selling "ethnic" writers) some of the literary cachet garnered by representing "exotic" subcultures to a general audience—as in the vogue for South Asian writers such as Hanif Kureishi, Zadie Smith, Monica Ali, and Gautam Malkani—British Jewish writers no longer seem quite so reticent. They are getting mouthy, raising their Jewish voices unabashedly, in the process overturning the tradition of "Stay shtumm."[16] As mentioned earlier, one surprising voice among this emergent Jewish-identified chorus is that of Mike Leigh. Should Leigh, belatedly, now be ranked among the "new" Jewish literary artists (a rising generation that includes Adam Thirwell, Naomi Alderman, and Francesca Segal, among others) in contemporary British culture? How does the matter of "Jewishness" find creative expression in the sociopolitical-affective world of Mike Leigh?

Mike Leigh's "Jewish" Play

At some level the long history of British Jewish self-consciousness accounts for the mixed response to *Two Thousand Years*, Leigh's insider portrait of a three-generation North London Jewish family in spiritual and political crisis. Watching this intimate family drama staged *in public*, Jewish audiences felt—for some, uneasily—that they were in effect eavesdropping, overhearing their deepest anxieties voiced out loud, on a stage filled, in novelist and critic Linda Grant's telling description, with "Shouty Jews."[17] What happened to the kibbutznik dream of a socialist Israel? Leigh seems to lament. "What does it mean to you to be Jewish?" asks Josh (Ben Caplan), the spiritually adrift son and grandson, searching for the answer to this familiar cosmic question (*TTY*, 52). Significantly, *TTY* ultimately provides no answers; rather, it poses this urgent question regarding spiritual identity to prod its implied Jewish audience toward self-critical reflection.[18]

What accounts for Leigh's long silence with respect to engaging Jewish themes? Why the desire to assemble only "Jewish" actors and talk out loud about the spiritual, political, and emotional condition of contemporary British Jewry? To a packed and at times truculent audience at Jewish Book Week in February 2006, Leigh spoke of wanting to direct Jewish actors in his "Jewish" play, especially after seeing the 2003 production of Kwame Kwei-Armah's *Elmina's Kitchen* at the National Theatre. "When I saw that," Leigh explained, "I thought, 'Ping!' I could do the ethnic equivalent for me. . . . After all, I've always thought that, just as it's wrong for white actors to black up to play black people, it's a bit odd to have non-Jewish actors play Jews. Often, the results are unbelievable."[19]

Looking back, we might say that Leigh, born in 1943, has tended to draw on his Manchester Jewish upbringing as a middle-class doctor's son, growing up in the working-class district of Salford, for his particular way of seeing and feeling the world. "Manchester Jewish," he styles it, "a very special condition, with its own abrasive sense of humour."[20] Indeed, his self-described double consciousness as "an insider and an outsider, all at once" in the 1940s and 1950s instilled a profound empathy for the struggling working-class souls who tend to populate his movies, wounded and adrift in the brutalizing landscape of 1980s and 1990s Thatcherite Britain.[21] His acid-dipped Mancunian Jewish outlook thus nourished a biting ironic-comic sensibility that has marked Leigh's achievement for many years on both stage and screen.

In addition to Jewish Manchester, Leigh was shaped by his membership in the Labor Zionist Habonim (literally, "the builders") youth movement, itself a response to the tragedies of modern Jewish history, above all, the Holocaust and the founding of the state of Israel. He attended summer camps before eventually visiting Israel in the late 1950s. Leigh's brief sojourn to Israel profoundly influenced his creative process, especially his famous "collectivist" practice as director. "Having that leadership experience," Leigh subsequently reflected, "was great and has absolutely informed not only how I am but also how I've worked. Everybody was open and democratic and working together towards a goal, a spirit of which goes right the way through my productions and the way I work."[22] Working intensely with a company of handpicked, committed actors, Leigh and his utterly devoted "disciples" develop characters embedded in the social fabric of British life as they imagine story lines, often via the fruits of improvisation, drawn from the actors' own experiences, or narratives distilled from the lives of others familiar to the actors. As the group's organic center of consciousness, only Leigh knows the outcome of the characters' linked stories; after months of collaboration and rehearsal, Leigh drafts the final script, which is then scrupulously followed and eventually staged (or filmed) without further revision. Tellingly, Leigh has described this much-discussed but still mysterious method as "a rebbe surrounded by Talmudic students, talking things out." He seeks "in a Talmudic way, to raise questions and posit possibilities."[23] As the critic John Lahr nicely observes, "The question mark is what Leigh's films are all about."[24]

In the case of *TTY* the key soul-searching question is voiced by the young, self-vexing Josh, who asks his grandfather Dave (John Burgess), a former Habonim pioneer, now disillusioned with the conservative turn, circa 2004, of Israeli politics under its then prime minister Ariel Sharon, "What does it mean to you to be Jewish?" This cosmic question hovers over the play, an uneasy specter haunting the *Guardian*-reading, middle-class British Jewish family living in material comfort in leafy Cricklewood, a somewhat upscale North-West London suburb. Always obsessed with achieving the "authentic," Leigh has maple-clean IKEA furniture grace the spacious living room, while familiar Matisse and Picasso prints adorn the walls — perhaps his wicked comment on the family's parvenu taste, a dig at their middle-class assumptions regarding comfort and style. At curtain's rise the family is sprawled about, reading in their respective spatial niches: father Danny (Allan Corduner) is absorbed by an article in the *Guardian* (the newspaper of choice for liberal, socially conscious families such as the one depicted onstage) on Israel; his wife, Rachel (Caroline Gruber), is reading a book; their son, Josh, surrounded by books, is already imaged as aloof, immersed in his own world of learning.

The core political-psychological drama enacted in *TTY* involves Josh's unanticipated religious "turn." In an early vignette we witness his methodical, exaggerated preparation, it turns out, for laying [wrapping] tefillin (phylacteries): first he closes the curtains of the conservatory; he places the ritual objects (straps to wrap around his arm attached to small square boxes containing parchment inscribed with Hebrew prayers) carefully on the couch; slowly, he rolls up his shirtsleeve, then hesitates, keeping his left arm suspended. Are these the furtive actions of a closeted drug addict about to shoot up? Perhaps for non-Jews in the audience, this seems to be what Josh is preparing to do. But no, it turns out that Josh is an uncertain, partially awakened Jew struggling with his "faith identity." The exaggerated performance of religious ritual ends abruptly. In Leigh's detailed stage directions, Josh "picks up a prayer book, opens it, pauses, and puts it down. Then he *tears* the phylacteries from his head and from his arm, takes off the skull cap, turns back to the conservatory, and opens one curtain a little. He stares out at the garden. Pause. Blackout" (*TTY*, 19; emphasis added). A familiar character type in Leigh's cinema, Josh represents, in Leigh's own words, one of "a long line of philosophical guys . . . who feel deeply but articulate very little of what they are thinking."[25] Josh's conflicted performance of Jewish ritual acts out a scene of spiritual yearning tempered by shame; his abrupt gesture — the tearing away of the phylacteries and the peering through the shrouding curtains — bespeaks (betrays?) his own uncertain faith. Has his anxious desire of observance been exposed? Has he been seen? Outed? What is he staring out at? Josh's actions generate a series of urgent questions, but curiously, *TTY* never really probes the sources of Josh's apparently soul-wrenching religious crisis.[26]

When we next see Josh, he has "come out," so to speak, much to his parents' chagrin and mystification. Just returned from holiday, the parents find Josh praying with a siddur and wearing a yarmulke. Leigh's richly comic exchange is, onstage, played as farce:

> DANNY: I don't understand, Josh. It's beyond me. It's unbelievable. It's like having a Muslim in the house.[27]
> RACHEL: Danny!
> DANNY: Alright, then, a Martian!
> JOSH: I'm still me — I haven't changed.
> DANNY: Of course you've changed!
> JOSH: I haven't!
> DANNY: Well, what's that thing on your head?
> RACHEL: We still love you, Josh.
> DANNY: Of course we do.
> JOSH: It's not a thing, it's a *capple* [*sic*].
> RACHEL: Look, Josh: we go away for two weeks; we come back, and — this . . .
> DANNY: What I want to know is . . . what's it all about? What's been going on? Where's it come from?
> RACHEL: Josh?
> JOSH: It comes from me. (*TTY*, 20–21)

Many British critics felt they were "eavesdropping on a north London dentist and his uneasy family" (as Sheridan Morley put in the *Daily Express*). "It feels so true," Alistair Macaulay wrote in the *Financial Times*.[28] These comments echo earlier critics who speak of the "near anthropological precision"[29] of Leigh's films, which tend to explore the spiritual plight of the British working and middle classes. For Linda Grant, eavesdropping on Leigh's "shouty Jews" provided a rare shock of recognition: "Watching the play as a Jew, I was aware that what was dramatized on stage was an argument that had been going on for some time inside my own head and among friends and family. It was as if one's own internal contradictions were being conveniently staged for you."[30]

"Jewishness is not at the heart of English culture," claims Howard

Jacobson. "This is one of the things cultured Jews in England feel every time we write or make a play or music."[31] Yet for British Jewish audiences, watching *TTY* appears to have provided a long-desired release, perhaps even some *relief* from the repressions of "Stay shtumm" and the long-nourished habits of British Jewish reticence. For two hours on stage the noisy spectacle of Leigh's "shouty" Jews—real Jewish actors performing *as* "Jews"—enabled British Jewry to lighten its historical baggage of habitual self-effacement, to ease the burden of their cultural *peckhlach*, the packages heavy with self-consciousness and anxiety over cultural difference that they have been carrying—schlepping—around for 350 years.

In Leigh's imaging of the play's contemporary British Jewish family, their activist daughter Tammy (Alexis Zegerman) keeps faith with her parents' former social justice–concerned Jewish selves, although she comes home to Cricklewood with politically conservative Tzachi (Nitzan Sharron), her Israeli boyfriend—who is tough, realistic, and, above all, emotionally stable. In this respect Leigh seems to be having some impish fun, contrasting the shouty unhinged family with the quietly assured Israeli, schooled in realpolitik. Along with Josh's troubling Orthodox turn, Tzachi embodies yet another insult to their North London peacenik, anti–West Bank settlement ethos.

But the fraught emotional center of *TTY* remains Josh's apparent crisis of faith, his posing of the cosmic question, "What does it mean to be Jewish?" For the most part Ben Caplan's moody performance as Josh nicely captures this young man's tormented journey, from sullen sourness and unfocused rage to the small but moving final scene of chess playing with his father. In his restless search for belief (or is it to escape the family's constant wailing about his failed intellectual promise?), he keeps entering and exiting the front room; he sends himself away in contrapuntal anger or annoyance, to the literal edges of the stage, to the psychic margins of British Jewish family life.[32] "I JUST WANT SOME PEACE!" Josh screams (*TTY*, 84), perhaps Leigh's own ironic-comic referencing of Israeli politics, political issues about which he has recently become embroiled. But if Josh were to become a true *frummer* (pious/observant), a *ba'al tshuvah* (a returnee to observant Judaism), would not his newly awakened "faith identity" with respect to Middle East politics alienate him from his grandfather's and parents' liberal position? If so, then Leigh's play would, in effect, enter dangerous territory, a troubled "no-go" zone of the British

Jewish defense of political Zionism, a deeply sensitive issue for Jews who follow the *Guardian* and its perceived anti-Zionist point of view. In this respect, for all its "shoutiness," *TTY* chooses not to explore or draw out an implied, potential generational debate over Israel and troubling contemporary political issues for an awakened British Jewry.

What, ultimately, is the source of the pain and disillusionment driving Josh's alienation? Is it his perception of the hypocrisies of British Jewish liberalism? The slackening of political and religious hope? The failed promise (ca. 2005) of Israel betrayed by Sharon and his ruling Likud Party's West Bank settlement policies? The soullessness that is the underside of the governing party in Britain's politics known as "New Labour"? In contrast to his biting film satires, such as *High Hopes* (1988), which render the soul-deadening effects of Thatcherite-afflicted Britain, Leigh never makes his Jewish family's dilemmas of ethnic identity—local and cosmic—clear.[33] Even grandfather Dave's ungenerous verbal picking at Josh's fresh, if uncertain, orthodoxy—he keeps calling him "rabbi," much to Josh's irritation—only highlights the play's mysterious, unaccountable omissions. If, according to the critic Ian Buruma, the use of "conversation as a form of evasion" characterizes a key aspect of Mike Leigh's dramatic art,[34] the evasions at the heart of *TTY* highlight the play's thinly constructed characters—each merely mouthing a "position" rather than embodying a lost, yet searching Jewish soul. By contrast, what if Josh channeled the dangerous, if nonetheless deeply empathic, figure of Johnny in *Naked*, whose relentlessly punning voice and ferocity of character register profound spiritual torment? And unlike, say, Maurice Samuel's host culture genuflections a half century earlier, there is little respect, gratitude, or affection toward the motherland in Leigh's hero. As *Times Literary Supplement* reviewer John Mullan shrewdly observed, "It is uncomfortably likely that Leigh himself is not much interested in any details of faith; he just needs to represent a tormented search for purpose."[35]

Leigh himself confessed to a telling disinterest concerning the question at *TTY*'s thematic, metaphysical core. Asked why he did not focus more on Josh's religious conversion, Leigh replied, "but actually I've got nothing to say about it."[36] In this respect *TTY* seems more inclined to show how this severely dysfunctional yet hilarious family stirs itself from spiritual inertia (much like the family in *Secrets*) so they can "get on with it"—the ultimate struggle of modern life voiced over and again by Leigh as his core subject—get on, that is, with their stymied, if vibrantly shouty, North London Jewish lives.

For grandfather Dave, wheezing from emphysema in his chair, he assuages his political pain through nostalgia for the old Habonim cause and the utopian dream—perhaps still attainable—of a democratic Israel, despite his rage against current Israeli political policies; for activist daughter Tammy, it's the dream of a better future through acts of social justice and education; for dentist father Danny, it is salvation through joking (a familiar Jewish mode of survival); for mother Rachel, it is the family as a latter-day "homeland," the only *heimisch* (homey) place left in her ruptured, unstable world.[37] For the late-arriving drama queen sister Mash (Samantha Spiro), her self-absorption is a mode of survival and evasion (although here I agree with most critics and find Samantha Spiro's manic, "operatic" performance over the top). For his own part, Leigh wants us to understand their respective survival strategies as small but potentially redemptive gestures at love, as ways lost (Jewish?) selves, spiritually unmoored in what he perceives to be Blair's soulless Britain, manage to hang on, to get on with it.

In the end, the most profound gesture in the play turns out to be Josh's; it is a subtle moment of filial empathy, expressive, it seems, of Leigh's deepest vision. No longer wearing a yarmulke (unnoticed by his family, and for some reason not explained in the play, Josh has removed the visible sign of his faith identity), Josh and his father discuss the ravages of the recent Hurricane Katrina (JOSH: "Makes you realize how vulnerable you are. One minute you exist. Next minute, gone."); Danny cracks another joke; father and son play chess:

> JOSH: Come on, Dad.
> DANNY: Whose go is it?
> JOSH: It's yours. (*TTY*, 118, 119)

In the end, Josh moves from angst-ridden alienation to filial empathy. Is this what Leigh means, ultimately, by *TTY* as his "Jewish play"? Perhaps. But his own substantial power of empathy, the signature Leigh blend of acerbic satire and profound understanding of human nature, is more richly on display in *Secrets*, which, ultimately, is a deeper representation of Mike Leigh's "Jewish" soul.

Secrets and Lies: Mike Leigh's Hidden "Jewish" Film

Secrets and Lies is about a young black woman's search for her birth mother and the dysfunctional white family she meets and—by the revelation of her blood relation—disrupts and ultimately helps heal. Leigh explained, "I wanted to do a film that in some way was about the need we all have to deal with our roots, to assert our identities and to know who we are, and to share and be truthful."[38] In its deeply empathic exploration of the human heart, *Secrets* leaves us with a series of unlikely reconciliations, resulting in filial bonding across race and class; in the process the film therapeutically enacts the lifting of a family's long-repressed, unspoken grief and long-held secrets, thus enabling their collective pain, born of silence and repression, to break through, so that the work of collective healing can begin.

In this respect, *Secrets* might be considered Leigh's more deeply *Jewish* work: Jewish, that is, in its "tragic-comic" tones (the "Jewish" influence that Leigh invariably acknowledges when asked about his relation to Jewishness), its sounding of the human heart, above all in its soul-searching powers of empathy.[39] Leigh reveals his own "Jewish" heart through the figures of Maurice Purley (Timothy Spall), the portrait photographer; Hortense (Marianne Jean-Baptiste), the black middle-class optometrist in search of her birth mother; and Cynthia (Brenda Blethyn), Maurice's devoted sister and, as is revealed, Hortense's white working-class mother, who possesses long-buried resources of mother love. Both by vocation and in their deepest nature, Maurice and Hortense are defined by an ability to see others clearly, with compassion, and to enable others to see themselves and thus the larger world more clearly as well. "Hortense and Maurice," writes J. Hoberman, "are both professionally engaged in helping people to see."[40] Edward Trostle Jones adds, "Maurice as a photographer exhibits craft in his chosen art and enormous empathy as well as real respect for the people he captures on film."[41] Above all, the three main characters possess an aching desire to unburden, to release their own stopped-up reservoirs of love, and the need to be loved. "Leigh's goal," suggests Morris Dickstein, "is to expose the buried humanity of each of these characters by having them face up to the secrets that have poisoned their lives and alienated them from each other."[42] Each character thus speaks on behalf of Leigh; and each, perhaps, represents a core aspect of Leigh himself as he plays the role of an empathic "lay" analyst for a troubled postwar gentile Britain; he listens attentively, from the heart, to the social-psychological ills of the nation, exploring its psychic condition.[43]

We observe this ability to attend to the buried pain of others from the beginning. The portrait photographer Maurice — modeled, apparently, on Leigh's Russian immigrant grandfather Mayer Leibermann, who made a modest living as a portraitist in Leigh's native Salford — is cast as a figure of boundless empathy.[44] Thus at some level the figure of Maurice seems to channel Leigh's still vivid Jewish family memories. As Gary Watson notes, "it is clear that Leigh's artistic project in some way resembles Maurice's, most strikingly, of course, in its preoccupation with those aspects of life that give cause either for lamentation or celebration, that make us either sad (and tearful) or happy (and smiling)."[45] Patient, encouraging, coaxing smiles from his sometimes resistant clients, Maurice ("Morris"?) is able to capture the essence of their humanity, revealed through his art of portraiture. Yet his personal life is filled with pain and despair and thwarted love, the neurotic center of Purley family tsuris that resides in its evasions, symptoms of the secrets it withholds and the lies it tells: their repressions and denials prevent the necessary release of honesty that, in Leigh's vision, is the only way their messy lives can "get on with it."

At its core, then, *Secrets* examines, with keen and compassionate eyes, a fraught emotional landscape. In this respect Hortense embodies, as an optometrist, an instinctual ability — call it another mode of empathy — to help others achieve clarity of (in)sight. As Leigh explains, "Hortense is in the business of seeing. So it resonates throughout the film, this whole thing of what we are, what we really are, how we appear to other people, how other people perceive us."[46] In an important scene between white mother and (as yet) unacknowledged black daughter, shot in one long eight-minute take, Cynthia and Hortense sit side by side in an empty coffee shop and unearth the past — and with it, the truth of Hortense's maternal history. During an intense, revelatory exchange, Cynthia moves from earnest denial to the dislodging of a fragment of long-buried memory and eventually to a shocked recognition and ultimately loving acceptance of her long-repressed, literally unimaginable mixed-race daughter.[47] In the process Cynthia — therapeutically, we might say — gains access to her past; her repression lifted, she now "sees" what has happened to the daughter she chose to give up at sixteen. As a result of Hortense's revelation, Cynthia gains a palpable confidence, a stronger sense of self and self-worth. At the same time, Hortense enters an alternate family history, moving from loss (at the beginning of the film she attends the funeral of her black surrogate mother, which prompts Hortense's search for her biological mother) into the fold of the dysfunctional Purleys, who eventually readopt her. In each case mother and daughter — as well as Cynthia's other daughter, the constantly scowling Roxanne (Claire Rushbrook), also born out of wedlock — begin to see their collective intertwined histories more clearly.

Like his older sister Cynthia, who more or less raised him as a child, Maurice possesses a reservoir of love and empathy without an object because his wife, Monica (Phyllis Logan), who longs for a child but cannot conceive, balks at his sexual attentions; shut down emotionally, she refuses to feel and instead projects all her private misery onto Cynthia and displaces her desires onto material things, on vivid display amid the middle-class order and taste of her home in the suburbs (a long-standing Leigh obsession, most famously skewered in the 1977 television play *Abigail's Party*[48]). At the end of *Secrets*, during a twenty-first birthday party for Roxanne hosted by Maurice and Monica, all the Purley family secrets and lies are, at last, revealed: the truth of Cynthia's hidden daughter; the identity of Roxanne's father; the sad fact of Monica's infertility. Leigh assigns Maurice the movie's most important observation: "Secrets and lies! We're all in pain! Why can't we share our pain? I've spent my entire life trying to make people happy, and the three people I love the most in the world hate each other's guts. I'm in the middle. I can't take it anymore!"[49]

Calming down after this poignant confession, Maurice turns to Hortense and says, "Welcome to the family." Maurice breaks the collective tension in a weary voice that registers a comic tone of Jewish ironic understatement. Maurice's "Jewish" voice seems even more strikingly on display when he asks Hortense about her daily commute from where she lives in Kilburn (in northwest London) to the factory somewhat far away in the East End (symbolic, in Leigh's implied allusion, of where Jewish immigrants began their upwardly mobile journey in Britain) where she supposedly "works" with Cynthia (before the truth of her blood connection comes out, Cynthia initially had introduced Hortense as her co-worker). Maurice observes, "It's a bit of a schlep, isn't it?"

At this moment Maurice seems positioned as a hidden Jew in *Secrets*.[50] Moreover, if we accept the Leigh "method" of his actors inhabiting, indeed virtually *becoming*, their characters during weeks of rehearsal and improvisation before the final script is settled on and the filming begins, then Maurice appears to declare his ethnicity, to "out" himself as a "Jew" through his coded, "insider" question to Hortense, even if the familiar Yiddish word "schlep" has, for the most part, acquired a universal meaning. At some (buried, instinctual) level, that is, Maurice speaks, and thus feels for Hortense's imagined (by him) daily "schlep," *as if* he were a Jew. Still, Maurice figures as "Jewish" in *Secrets* not in his verbal slip into the *mamaloshen* (mother tongue) but rather as a character able, in Ray Carney's observation about Leigh's core vision, "to go out of ourselves, to leave our own ways of understanding behind and inhabit genuine otherness."[51] By the end of *Secrets*, it seems, virtually all the characters approach this condition of (Jewish) empathy. And in light of such empathic engagement, we can, perhaps, imagine the hovering magical presence of Mike Leigh himself, orchestrating the human drama before us, "with his full beard and deep, expressive eyes . . . like a wonder-working Hasidic rabbi, able to examine the most intimate secrets of the soul."[52]

By contrast, however, in its curious reticence, its refusal to sound the spiritual-religious-political crises it announces at the beginning, Leigh's self-described "Jewish play" *Two Thousand Years* feels more like his *British* Jewish play. That is, the charged emotional debates around Jewish identity that lay at the heart of *TTY* feel constrained, under the pressure, conscious or not, of British Jewish self-censorship. In the end, *TTY* feels weighed down by its own *peckhlach*, the cultural baggage that haunts the psychic and emotional landscape of the British Jewish soul. Ultimately, Leigh is not able to achieve in his British Jewish canvas the depth and richness and complexity of character and crisis — of characters *in* crisis — that he captures so powerfully in his strongest movies.

For example, in contrast to the anarchic-liminal figure of Johnny (David Thewlis) in Leigh's masterpiece *Naked*, a figure who, in Leigh's own account, "keeps changing colours . . . a man of ideas and passions and frustrations, and positives and negatives . . . he *has* to be a character who constantly confuses and surprises us,"[53] Josh's crisis of faith in *TTY* and its (potential) unsettling aftereffects remain unexplored. Ironically, Leigh's *Jewish* soul finds its deepest expression covertly—indirectly—through those searching outsiders and tragicomic family situations that engage him in his films rather than in his self-proclaimed "Jewish" play. Coming out, imagining Jews in contemporary Britain, Leigh's art is tangled up in the limits of ethnicity, above all by the mystery of representing faith identity itself. For all its *heimische*, familiar insider "shoutiness," *TTY* struggles to display what remains *unspeakable*, under repression, in British Jewish culture.

To be fair, *TTY* was apparently rushed onto the National Theatre stage in the fall of 2005, its title and subject matter shrouded, veiled until the last moment. Given his famous creative-dramatic "Talmudic" method, Leigh may not have been able to fashion the depths of his actor's characters, to flesh them out in all their self-vexing complexity. Nevertheless Josh, who represents the core drama of the play, never emerges full-bodied in his crisis of Jewish identity, and thus the play ultimately feels static, arrested at the level of Jewish situation comedy. "There is an interesting gap," writes Elena Lappin, "between Leigh's unerring ability to outfit these people with as much Jewish paraphernalia as possible [recall Leigh's famous "anthropological precision"] . . . and his inability to place them at the core of a real human drama."[54]

That curious "gap"—the bounded threshold at the level of character, of plot, of theme—may explain the still unfinished quality—noted by some reviewers—of *TTY*. In the end *TTY* remains profoundly "*British* Jewish": even with all the shouting, with all the invocation of exotic Yiddish, the play feels reticent, safe. By the end of *Secrets* we feel drained and exhilarated. "This is the life, ain't it?" exclaims Cynthia, gazing, with motherly pride, upon her two daughters, each differently fathered, one black and middle class, one white and defiantly working class, amid the tacky residue of her ramshackle East End backyard, in a scene filled with Leigh's warmhearted signature blend of "Jewish" pathos and irony. Thus, in the example of Mike Leigh at least, when it comes to telling Jewish stories from the heart, we need to remember that, in the case of an often tight-lipped British Jewry, the impulse to lower the voice, what Philip Roth calls "British rules of dignified restraint,"[55] is sometimes latent, at times under repression, a *British* Jewish habit born of a lifetime of keeping quiet.

Notes

Thanks to Nathan Abrams for his careful reading of the manuscript and his many helpful suggestions, which improved the essay in innumerable ways.

1. Mike Leigh, *Two Thousand Years* (London: Faber and Faber, 2006), v (hereafter cited in text and notes as *TTY*). Interestingly, Hytner is Jewish and from Manchester as well.

2. Viv Hardwic, "Unscripted Sensation," *Northern Echo*, December 29, 2005, http://northern-echo.vlex.co.uk/vid/unscripted-sensation-77479788.

3. The literature on Mike Leigh as filmmaker is vast. On his relation of his film archive to British identity, see Ewa Mazierska, "Family, Social Class and Politics in the Films of Mike Leigh," in *Relocating Britishness*, edited by Stephen Caunce, Ewa Mazierska, Susan Sydney-Smith, and John K. Walton, 71–87 (Manchester, U.K.: Manchester University Press, 2004).

4. Nicole Taylor, "So Mike Leigh Is Jewish After All: But Is It Good for the Jews?" *Forward*, December 2, 2005, updated April 14, 2015, http://forward.com/articles/2382/so-mike-leigh-is-jewish-after-all-but-is-it-good-f/.

5. Stephen Applebaum, "Interview with Mike Leigh," *Jewish Chronicle*, November 4, 2010, http://www.thejc.com/arts/arts-interviews/40700/interview-mike-leigh. In this interview, which includes a conversation about Leigh's boycotting a planned trip to Israel and the West Bank in protest against the Israeli government's treatment of Palestinians, Leigh describes his work as "inescapably Jewish": "The films are comic and tragic, there's always two sides to a thing, and all of that—in that sense there's a Jewish spirit in my work."

6. Philip Roth, *Deception* (New York: Simon and Schuster, 1990), 83.

7. Ibid., 204.

8. Jonathan Brent, "What Facts? A Talk with Roth," *New York Times Book Review*, September 25, 1988, 3. Significantly, Roth's imagining of a multicultural England in the same interview needs serious revising, in light of the migration since the early 1990s, East to West, notes Roth: "The wholesale colonization of England's major cities by third world immigrants—and only little more than half a century after those cities had been colonized by tens of millions from the impoverished classes of eastern and southern Europe—is unthinkable."

9. A. Alvarez, "A Double Bind," *New York Review of Books*, December 16, 2004, 76. For rich historical-cultural overviews of British Jewish life, see Todd M. Endelman, *The Jews of Britain, 656 to 2000* (Berkeley: University of California Press, 2002); Tony Kushner, *British-Jewry since 1066: Place, Locality, Memory* (Manchester, U.K.: Manchester University Press, 2009).

10. "Blair Leads Commemoration of Jewish Resettlement in Britain," *European Jewish Press*, June 15, 2006, http://www.ejpress.org (article no longer available).

11. Maurice Samuel, *The Gentleman and the Jew* (New York: Knopf, 1952), 10. "English Jews make a huge contribution to the cultural life of this country," reflects Howard Jacobson, "but rarely as Jews, rarely making overt reference to their Jewishness. Implicitly, we feel we shouldn't. And our highest achievement is to pass as English."

Elizabeth Manus, "Howard Jacobson," *Something Jewish*, last modified September 15, 2004, accessed October 30, 2015, http://www.somethingjewish.co.uk/articles/1185_howard_jacobson.htm.

12. Jonathan Petre, "Blair Praises Jews' Contribution to Britain," *Daily Telegraph*, June 14, 2005, http://www.telegraph.co.uk/news/uknews/1521214/Blair-praises-Jews-contribution-to-Britain.html.

13. Todd M. Endelman and Matthew J. Reisz, conversations with author, June–July 2006.

14. Howard Jacobson, "Now We Are 350," *Jewish Quarterly* 201 (Spring 2006), http://www.jewishquarterly.org/issuearchive/article85b0.html?articleid=181. For a superb mapping of the recent British Jewish literary scene, see Ruth Gilbert, *Writing Jewish: Contemporary British-Jewish Literature (1990-Present)* (London: Palgrave, 2013).

15. Bryan Cheyette, "On Being a Jewish Critic," *Jewish Social Studies* 11, no. 1 (Fall 2004): 48.

16. I borrow this phrase from the novelist Howard Jacobson, who writes about his experience growing up Jewish in 1950s Manchester: "'Stay shtumm' ["stay quiet"; a variant of the Yinglish "sha, still"] was the advice given to me when I was growing up. Don't draw attention to yourself. If we feel safer today than we did sixty years ago, there remains a conviction of precariousness, a sense that it is better not to rock the boat." Howard Jacobson, "There Is an Obduracy in Anti-Semitism," *New Humanist*, last modified May 31, 2007, accessed October 30, 2015; https://newhumanist.org.uk/articles/723/there-is-an-obduracy-in-anti-semitism.

17. Linda Grant, "Mike Leigh Comes Out," *Guardian*, April 18, 2006, http://www.theguardian.com/film/2006/apr/18/theatre.religion. In light of the "stay shtumm" "tradition," Leigh mentions in the introduction, "Those of us who escaped from our Jewish background have usually spent most of our adult lives keeping quiet about our Jewishness, at least in public" (*TTY*, v). In a subsequent interview Leigh reflects, "Deciding to do *TTY* constituted a massive decision to come out, in a certain sense, to stop hiding." Mike Leigh, *Mike Leigh on Mike Leigh*, edited by Amy Raphael (London: Faber and Faber, 2008), 8. In a 2012 profile, the actor Samantha Spiro, who plays sister Mash in *TTY*, reflected about her experience in that play: "'For a lot of us [in the cast],' says Spiro, 'that was our first experience of playing Jewish—it was like a big coming-out. I'd never professionally been in a room with just Jewish people before.'" Spiro continues, with respect to taking on Jewish parts, "'Some of the parts I definitely didn't want to play . . . here you try to brush it [Jewishness] under the table and be a part of the establishment.'" After playing Sarah Kahn in the revival of Arnold Wesker's *Chicken Soup and Barley* in 2011, Spiro reflected, "It was definitely the Jewish year . . . I did think at one point: gosh, I'm really Jewish!" Brian Logan, "Samantha Spiro: 'I Was Never an Ingénue,'" *Guardian*, March 11, 2012. From 2010 onward, Spiro also featured in Simon Amstell's Jewish sitcom, *Grandma's House*, http://www.theguardian.com/stage/2012/mar/11/samantha-spiro-interview.

18. Yet, the printed version of *TTY* includes a substantial glossary of Yiddish words and phrases spoken in the play—perhaps another index of Leigh's "self-outing" as a Jew for gentile British audiences, a declaration of his insider culture linguistic facility.

19. Aleks Sierz, "All My Work Has a Certain Jewishness in It," *Daily Telegraph*, April 17, 2006, http://www.telegraph.co.uk/culture/theatre/drama/3651660/All-my-work-has-a-certain-Jewishness-in-it.html.

20. Ibid. Other famous Jewish sons of Manchester include the novelist Howard Jacobson and the playwright-screenwriter Jack Rosenthal.

21. Mike Leigh, interview with Graham Fuller, in Mike Leigh, *Naked and Other Screenplays* (London: Faber and Faber, 1995), xi.

22. Leigh, *Mike Leigh on Mike Leigh*, 6. For the shaping influence of Leigh's experience in Israel for his creative practice, see Michael Coveney, "The Spirit of Habonim," *Jewish Quarterly* 199 (Autumn 2005), http://www.jewishquarterly.org/issuearchive/articlec944.html?articleid=149.

23. Quoted in James Inverne, "Like Having a Muslim in the House," *Jerusalem Report*, October 17, 2005.

24. John Lahr, "This Other England," *New Yorker*, September 23, 1996, 50–54, at 50. Lahr goes on to describe Leigh's unique method of collaboration: "Leigh's process is a kind of treasure hunt, in which his collaborators bring stuff back from their lives and pick over it with the director to make up a story whose general parameters are growing in Leigh's mind but which is unknown to the group" (54).

25. Leonard Quart, "Going Beyond Despair: An Interview with Mike Leigh," *Cineaste* 28, no. 1 (Winter 2002): 39. In addition to Josh, there is also Cyril in *High Hopes*, directed by Mike Leigh (Toronto: BFS Entertainment, 1988), and above all Johnny in *Naked*, directed by Mike Leigh (New York: Criterion, 1993).

26. "Instead of exploring what happens when a fairly complacent, secular group of people are challenged by someone demanding a deeper sense of meaning and purpose," remarks Toby Young, "*TTY* ends up being yet another opportunity for Leigh to vent his rage at the lower-middle-class social climbers." Toby Young, "Below Par," *Spectator*, October 1, 2005, 58.

27. In light of the ongoing debates in Britain over integration, and only one year after the London bombings of July 2005, virtually every reviewer of *TTY* felt compelled to repeat this locally charged line.

28. *Theatre Record*, September 10–23, 2005, 1170, 1168.

29. Lee Ellickson and Richard Porton, "I Find the Tragicomic Things in Life: An Interview with Mike Leigh," *Cineaste* 20, no. 3 (January 1994): 11.

30. Grant, "Mike Leigh Comes Out"http://www.theguardian.com/film/2006/apr/18/theatre.religion. Leaving the packed Warwick Arts Centre, where I watched the play in March 2006, I overheard two women's fresh reactions: One confessed to being "emotionally drained"; the other found it "spot on."

31. Manus, "Howard Jacobson."

32. In his review of the play's U.S. premiere, Charles Isherwood wrote, "Josh's faith is treated more or less as a running gag. . . . An intriguing subject, but Mr. Leigh engages it only obliquely." Charles Isherwood, "No Yarmulke, Please, We're Assimilated," *New York Times*, February 8, 2008, E3.

33. *High Hopes*, directed by Mike Leigh (London: Skouras Films, 1988).

34. Ian Buruma, "The Way They Live Now," *New York Review of Books*, January 13, 1994, 10.

35. John Mullan, "You Can't Argue with That," *Times Literary Supplement*, September 23, 2005, 18.

36. Quoted in Golda Zafer Smith, "Mike Leigh Comes Out," *Jewish Renaissance* 5, no. 1 (October 2005): 8.

37. In this respect, Dave's rage, spurred by the shame he feels for Israeli policy, echoes Mike Leigh's: "Dave: I'll tell you what I'm ashamed of. I'm ashamed of Jewish racists . . . I am ashamed of all those Jewish arse-lickers in Margaret Thatcher's Cabinet. And, I'm afraid to say, I'm ashamed of what's happened to Israel" (*TTY*, 51–52). Ruth Gilbert briefly discusses *TTY* in a chapter titled, "Belonging and Division: British-Jewish Reflections on Israel," in her *Writing Jewish*: "Leigh has not often written explicitly about Jewishness, so *Two Thousand Years* provides an interesting insight into his background" (89). In light of Dave's rant, Leigh has lent his own name to Independent Jewish Voices (www.ijv.org.uk), a group gathered to protest current Israeli policies. So far it has collected hundreds of signatures of prominent British Jews in the arts. When asked in recent interviews whether he has any desire to return to Jewish themes, Leigh has emphatically said no: "BENJAMIN CARDULLO: Do you regret not having explored your Jewishness on film, which you have done in the theatre? LEIGH: I don't regret it, and should I wish to do it, I will." Benjamin Cardullo, "'I Call My Films Subversive': A Conversation with Mike Leigh," *Literature/Film Quarterly* 39 (2011): 28. Asked by Stephen Applebaum about any future project connected to Jewish themes, Leigh replied, "It's extremely unlikely it will be a further investigation into matters of a Zionist nature." The array of British Jewish voices around the debates over Zionism, the fact and fate of Israel, and Jewish identity can be overwhelming. Among them Linda Grant's stands out for its clarity and reasonableness. See, for example, her reflections on Independent Jewish Voices at its founding, in February 2007: "The dismissive consensus among those not currently open to the ideas expressed in the IJV manifesto was that its signatories [among them, Mike Leigh] wished to dissociate themselves from the mainstream of Jewish life and its embarrassing adherence to Zionism. . . . I can't speak for the intentions of the IJV, but if their collective membership wants to have any impact on the majority of the non-*Guardian* reading British Jews, they need to take the conversation to the places where Jews are: in the synagogues, at their youth groups, in their voluntary organisations. They need to acknowledge the central role that Israel plays in contemporary Jewish life, how it is now part and parcel of Jewish identity." Linda Grant, "Other Voices, Other Lives," *Guardian*, February 7, 2007, http://www.theguardian.com/commentisfree/2007/feb/07/othervoicesotherlives. What would the family portrayed onstage in *TTY* think? Would they be card-carrying members of the IJV? Regarding Tammy, Leigh's more recent *Happy-Go-Lucky*, about a flighty but supremely dedicated elementary school teacher named Poppy (Sally Hawkins), suggests a deeper exploration of the daughter's instinctual caring sensibility. *Happy-Go-Lucky*, directed by Mike Leigh (Santa Monica, Calif.: Miramax, 2009).

38. Mike Leigh, "Mike Leigh's Original Features," in Leigh, *Naked and Other Screenplays*, xlii.

39. Laura Miller captures Leigh's particular empathic vision perfectly: "Leigh's movies have a startling richness, the product of a ruthless eye working in concert with an expansive heart, an all-too-rare combination of biting satire and deep humanism." Laura Miller, "Listening to the World: A Conversation with Mike Leigh," *Salon*, September 16, 1996, http://www.salon.com/1996/09/16/interview960916/. Leigh's "Jewish" sensibility, I argue, is more richly on display in a film such as *Secrets and Lies* (1996) than in *Two Thousand Years*. Other Leigh films—for example *Naked* (1993) or

perhaps *Career Girls* (1997)—might also be usefully included in discussing the matter of empathy and the performing self as aspects of Leigh drawing on the "Jewish spirit" for his imagination; in my view *Secrets and Lies* reveals the "hidden presence" of Leigh's "Jewishness" on film more suggestively, through a mode of indirection. In this respect, the film *represents* Leigh's particular *British* mode of encoding Jewishness.

40. J. Hoberman, "Sweet Mysteries of Life," *Village Voice*, October 1, 1996, 64.

41. Jones continues, "These attributes also characterize Leigh's career and surely never more impressively than in *Secrets and Lies*." Edward Trostle Jones, *All or Nothing: The Cinema of Mike Leigh* (New York: Peter Lang, 2004), 109.

42. Morris Dickstein, "New Cinema: The Next Generation," *Partisan Review* 64 (1997): 111.

43. On the matter of "empathy" and Jewish modes of imagination in American Jewish popular culture, see Donald Weber, "The Limits of Empathy: Hollywood's Imagining of Jews circa. 1947," in *Key Texts in American Jewish Culture*, edited by Jack Kugelmass, 91–104 (New Brunswick, N.J.: Rutgers University Press, 2003).

44. Michael Berkowitz, in his contribution to this volume, demonstrates how portrait photography was, historically, a profoundly Jewish profession.

45. Gary Watson, *The Cinema of Mike Leigh: A Sense of the Real* (London: Wallflower Press, 2004), 132.

46. Leigh, *Mike Leigh on Mike Leigh*, 272.

47. "We see the memory literally flood Cynthia's face as she breaks down into compulsive sobs." Kenneth Turan, "The Case for Mike Leigh" [1996], in *Mike Leigh: Interviews*, edited by Howie Movshovitz, 7 (Jackson: University Press of Mississippi, 2000).

48. Originally a play performed at the Hampstead Theatre but later aired as a play on the BBC in 1977 as a "Play for Today," *Abigail's Party* helped launch Leigh's career and established his reputation as a biting satirist of the aspiring middle class in Britain. In Buruma's phrasing, "Leigh often displays a kind of horrified delight in the tawdriest aspects of English life" ("Way They Live Now," 8).

49. "There is usually a climactic scene in every story," observes Buruma about the plot structure of Leigh's work, "a horrible family row, a chaotic explosion of repressed emotion, sometimes relieved by an instance of tenderness. These scenes are theater, but with the dangerous edge of reality" (ibid., 7). *TTY*, for all its "shoutiness" and moments of family crisis, ending in the salving tenderness of father and son playing chess, ultimately lacks such a signature "Leigh" moment.

50. Interestingly, Timothy Spall plays a less ambiguously figured Jew in the comedy *Reuniting the Rubins* (2010), where he is cast as Lenny Rubin, the head of the Jewish family who tries to reunite a dysfunctional family on the eve of Passover so that the ailing matriarch Gran Rubin, (Honor Blackman), can regain her health. *Reuniting the Rubins*, directed by Yoav Factor (London: Balagan Productions, 2010).

51. Ray Carney, *The Films of Mike Leigh: Embracing the World* (Cambridge: Cambridge University Press, 2000), 22.

52. Turan, "Case for Mike Leigh," 7.

53. Leigh, "Mike Leigh's Original Features," xxxix.

54. Elena Lappin, "All in the Family," *Tablet*, September 28, 2005, http://www.tabletmag.com/jewish-arts-and-culture/theater-and-dance/48206/all-in-the-family-4. Lappin is quite brutal in her review of *TTY*: "And so it's final curtain time; you applaud because

it was certainly as much as fun as visiting just any Jewish family, but as you walk out of the theatre you feel utterly cheated. After months of the supposedly meticulous process which led to the creation of this play, Mike Leigh's Jewish family consists of cardboard figures with political opinions but without souls."

55. Philip Roth, *The Counterlife* (New York: Farrar, Strauss and Giroux, 1986), 335.

CLAUDIA STERNBERG

From Pig Farmer to Infidel

Hidden Identities, Diasporic Infertility, and Transethnic Kinship in Contemporary British Jewish Cinema

Leon the Pig Farmer (1992) and *The Infidel* (2010) are examples of the ethnic diversification in British cinema that gained momentum in the 1980s, resulting in the increased on-screen visibility of Jewishness and Jewish characters during the 1990s and beyond.[1] This visibility is narratively constructed as relational. *Leon* places contemporary British Jewishness in comical juxtaposition to a dominant culture cast as gentile, rural, and English, whereas nearly twenty years later, *The Infidel* teases out issues of Jewish locatedness and identity within urban British multiculture. It does so by humorously activating post-9/11 and post-Zionist sensitivities and relating "the Jew" to Britain's most marked constituent of the first decade of the 2000s: "the Muslim." Relationality, however, is also expressed historically and generationally *within* the British Jewish diaspora. It is the interplay between these relations that is my focus here. My reading supports the wider argument that *Leon* and *The Infidel* embrace the normalization of Jewish visibility while at the same time—tongue-in-cheek—draw attention to historical and communal legacies which account for a specifically "Jewish" negotiation of a place in culturally diverse Britain. Central to the two narratives is the motif of hidden ethnic identities that will ultimately out. Paradoxically, the Jewish body remains a site of cultural and social inscription, but its reproduction becomes a vehicle for negotiation.

Leon and *The Infidel* are constructed as comedies of identity in which the male protagonists experience the destabilization of their previously unambiguous ethnic and religious selves due to unexpected revelations about their parentage and descent. The eponymous Leon Geller (Mark Frankel) is an attractive, if slightly awkward, young Jew, who discovers that his parents had sought assistance from a fertility clinic due to his father's low sperm count. As it turns out, Leon's two brothers were conceived through artificial insemination of their father's sperm, whereas in Leon's case, his mother had accidentally received sperm from the donor Brian Chadwick (Brian Glover), a pig farmer. In contrast, in *The Infidel*, a Muslim minicab driver, Mahmud Nasir (Omid Djalili), is clearing the home of his recently deceased mother and finds out that he was adopted as an infant. Upon pursuing the matter further, he learns that he had been placed for adoption by Jewish birth parents.

The two films derive humor from these revelations, but they are only the starting point for further complications. Leon leaves North London to meet the sperm donor and his family in the remote northern English village of Lower Dinthorpe in Yorkshire. The Chadwicks warmly welcome Leon and eventually seek to accommodate his Jewish difference by acts of assimilation. Leon, in turn, tries to take on pig husbandry, but when assisting the local veterinarian during the insemination of sows, he inadvertently fills a syringe with sheep semen. As a result, a crossbred pig-sheep is born and has to be hidden from Brian, who, according to the vet, "don't like no-one messing with his pigs." Mahmud of *The Infidel* learns that his biological father lies dying in a Jewish care home, but he, a Muslim, is barred from seeing him by a rabbi (Matt Lucas) who acts as the old man's guardian. To break down the rabbi's resistance, Mahmud turns to Lenny (Richard Schiff), an expatriate American Jew, hoping that this disaffected divorcé can teach him the ways of being and acting Jewish. At the same time, however, Mahmud is under pressure to support his son Rashid (Amit Shah), who is about to get married. Rashid's fiancée is the stepdaughter of Ashrad Al-Masri (Igal Naor), an Islamist cleric from Egypt, who demands assurance that his diasporic future in-laws are devout and "proper" Muslims.

While *Leon* and *The Infidel* have family plots and include ethnically marked weddings, food scenes, and generational squabbles, it is notable that the films avoid the recurring themes of interethnic romance, the vagaries of intermarriage, clashes between traditionalism and modernity, or the struggle for female or homosexual emancipation. Rather, they build their narratives on a divergence between biological and social parenthood. The films offer a humorous take on the charged terrains of (in)fertility and adoption and thus, by implication, address questions of reproduction, genealogy, and kinship. Such questions are interlinked with old and new discourses of religion, race, and ethnicity, eugenics and "purity," social and genetic engineering, assimilation and mixing, and the physical and cultural survival of minority ethnic communities. These discourses relate to specific histories and "diverse bids for control over reproductivity."[2] Control mechanisms can include internal group restrictions or invasive and destructive practices imposed from the outside. Among the latter are policies of forced adoption or child removal, compulsory sterilization, and ultimately genocide, policies which have featured across the histories of ethnic and social minorities, indigenous peoples, and victims of wartime occupation. Reproductive choices, possibilities, and limitations also signify on the level of religious law and doctrine and in community history and memory; they are debated by society at large and regulated by the (secular) state, often with reference to the larger fields of human rights and the ethics of science. Religious leaders, minority activists, legislators, and service providers position themselves in response to them when supporting groups or individuals. Last but not least, the discourses and histories of reproduction play a role in the theorization of culture and appear as theme and metaphor in cultural representations, as it is the case in the two popular films examined in this chapter.

Alys Eve Weinbaum sees *reproduction* as "a highly condensed sign that performs ideological work."[3] She places reproduction alongside Raymond Williams's keywords of modernity; for her, "competing understandings of reproduction as a biological, sexual, and racialized process became central to the organization of knowledge about nations, modern subjects, and the flow of capital, bodies, babies, and ideas within and across national borders."[4] In a more narrowly defined understanding of Jewishness as an embodied experience, Howard Eilberg-Schwartz states that "ideas about how Jews reproduce themselves physically have always provided ways of thinking about how Jews remake themselves culturally."[5] *Leon* and *The Infidel* are not intended to represent the social reality of infertility treatment and adoption or to offer a commentary on bioethics. Yet the compromised conceptions of Leon and Mahmud and the films' various incongruous transformations actualize, by narrative design, some of these competing understandings and associated knowledges, which include traces of premodern religious signification as well as pointers to postethnic performativity. The films also employ their genealogical models as a means through which the history and contemporary position and condition of British Jewry are critically discussed.

The Gametes of Galut: Biological and Social Kinship in *Leon the Pig Farmer*

In Judaism, becoming Jewish is possible through formalized conversion. However, as Eilberg-Schwartz points out, most Jews are the "products of genealogy. Certain kinds of sexual unions produce Jewish children; others do not. . . . A Jew is a person born a Jew."[6] According to the combined logic of biological and ethnoreligious genealogy, therefore, a commitment to procreation and the acceptance (or at least awareness) of restriction on reproductive choices forms the basis of Jewish communal and thus cultural continuity. In *Leon the Pig Farmer*, the protagonist is confronted with a number of threats to Jewish self-preservation through reproduction, ranging from infertility and the irregularities of his own descent to the (genealogical) implications of having either no or a non-Jewish partner.

In the first scene in which the Geller family openly discusses the insemination, Leon's mother, Judith (Janet Suzman), exclaims, "What did you want us to do?" She evokes God's commandment to be fruitful and multiply (Genesis 1:28, 9:1, 9:7, and 35:11), the importance of which is reinforced in biblical and Talmudic texts by the exclusion of infertile men from marriage and the possibility of divorce after ten years of childlessness.[7] Three decades earlier, Leon's father, Sidney (David de Keyser), would have faced the general social stigma of infertility and its threat to family lineage as well as the specter of a scriptural tradition of potentially limited participation in community and domestic life. More important, however, would have been the modern histories of persecution and the Holocaust on the one hand and of assimilation and secularization on the other, which continue to have a significant impact on the understanding of a need for procreation defined as Jewish. Religious and ethnohistorical discourses blend in the explicit pronatalism of Israel and among Haredi Jews,[8] but they also inform non-Haredi diasporic communities whose numbers are contracting due to an aging population, low birth rates, outmarriage, and a decline in group affiliation. The awareness of the effect that genocide had on the Jewish population also remains acute and is manifest in demographic analysis as well as post-Holocaust thought. For Jewish philosopher Emil Fackenheim, after Auschwitz, "even a mere collective commitment to Jewish group-survival for its own sake is a momentous response."[9] "To cease to be Jews (and to bring up Jewish children)," Fackenheim asserts, "would be to abandon our millennial post as witnesses to the God of history."[10] It is against this legacy of a disappearing people that the title character of *Leon* is (or assumes to be) constantly pressured into marriage and fatherhood and, during the first half of the film, suffers anxieties about his own fertility and — thus — communal underperformance. To accentuate collective expectations, screenwriters Gary Sinyor and Michael Normand use the ploy of giving voice to an opinion-rich North London Jewish community by including a number of — usually unsolicited — verbal interventions.

In light of the reproduction imperative, rabbinical authorities have responded positively to advances in science, and — with some variation — approved of ways that improve chances of procreation and support domestic happiness. For example, the prohibition of "spilling seed" (Genesis 38:7–10) has been waived for fertility testing and treatment, and there "is usually no [Orthodox] Jewish objection to homologous artificial insemination (AIH), provided there are safeguards to ensure the sperm of the husband is being used."[11] In the film, Judith states that her sons should be proud because they "were one of the first in the country." Leon reads out a (Jewish) newspaper article from 1960 about the Geller story, which duly celebrates the couple's success to conceive and fulfill "one of the most positive commandments in the Jewish religion, to procreate," indicating both rabbinical and communal approval. It is insemination *by donor*, however, that is revealed as having taken place in the case of Leon, if unintentionally, and it is the presence of a third party that puts conventional family genealogy at risk. Hirsh summarizes the respective position within Orthodox Judaism during the 1990s, the period of the film's production: "Orthodox objections to donor insemination (DI) are based on the subterfuge created by the treatment. The false registration of a father is seen as dishonest and unlikely to create a foundation suitable for child rearing due to the confusion of paternal inheritance and genealogy"; furthermore, "in terms of the technique of DI, the analogy with veterinary methods is considered undignified."[12] The aforementioned medicocultural concerns of subterfuge, confusion, and dishonesty are activated in the film for serious and comic effect. In an ironic twist, the socially silenced practice of fertility treatment becomes less of a concern for the family than its potential "hidden" effects.

After the Gellers have become aware of the donor insemination, two implications of this intervention are referred to in the film's dialogue. Sidney exclaims, "My God, it's rape! They raped my wife!" to which Leon responds, "Dad, I think that's a bit much. At worst it's adultery." From a clinical or secular perspective, donor insemination would not bring associations of either rape or adultery, but religious debate over the use of third-party sperm and whether it constitutes a form of extramarital and therefore adulterous intercourse dates back to "Talmudic and medieval discussions on '*generation sine concubito*.'"[13] While Judaism does not render children born out of wedlock illegitimate, according to rabbinical law, the offspring of a married Jewish woman and a (Jewish) man other than her husband would be considered a *mamzer*, who would face social restrictions with regard to Jewish marriage (as would the mamzer's children into the tenth generation). Mamzers can also be created through—equally illicit—incestuous unions. Reproductive technologies have reinvigorated discussions about mamzerim and forbidden relationships,[14] and one recommendation has been to circumvent inadvertent incestuous insemination by the use of "non-Jewish" sperm. The "non-Jewishness" of Brian's sperm rules out mamzer status, but it prompts another concern relating to Leon's identity, which is also expressed by Sidney: "Is he Jewish?"

Judith reproaches her husband for calling their son's Jewishness into question on account of the erroneously administered sperm of the Yorkshire farmer, and Leon himself stresses the principle of matrilineal descent as determining a person's Jewishness.[15] Despite this Halachic reassurance and his cultural Jewish self-identification, however, Leon is compelled to investigate his biological descent, which brings him face to face with his own and his family's Other: the extended Chadwick family. Brian, well into his fifties, affirms his English rootedness and ties to the land through his farm, which was established in 1867, a period of increased general but also Jewish representation in British politics (through the Jews Relief Act of 1858 and the Reform Act of 1867). Chadwick's enduring virility is demonstrated through a relaxed body culture, casual conversations about human and animal sexuality, and the fact that he shares his table not only with his attractive current wife, Yvonne (Connie Booth), but also his two ex-wives. Brian is constructed as antithetical to the anxious, excitable Sidney, whose inconspicuous suburban lifestyle and net curtain business render him as weak as Leon, whose feelings alternate between intrigue, desire, and abjection in his encounter with gentileness, the latter being coded as physical, assertive, and untouched by the self-consciousness and angst of the Ashkenazi Jewish diaspora.

Additionally, a crude parallelism of assisted animal rearing and donor insemination is constructed in the film by making Brian a farmer and linking up the practicalities of breeding with Leon's humiliation at his parents' fertility clinic as well as the risk of "human error" that can lead to subterfuge and even, in the filmmakers' imagination, interspecies reproduction. As befits the comic take on Jewish custom, Leon seeks rabbinical advice on the pig-sheep, only to find that the two rabbis consulted expose the incompatibilities of positions within a diverse Judaism: the American-accented Progressive rabbi sees before him the materialization of "kosher hams," symbolizing the (impossible) integration of sameness and difference. By contrast, the strictly Orthodox rabbi, featuring an exaggerated Jewish accent, is unable to resolve the "difficult question" of reproductive manipulation and xenogenesis, which exemplify the unprecedented possibilities of the modern present.[16] The rabbis' learned confusion differs little from the diverging viewpoints expressed by the other Jewish characters who exercise social control over Leon's private life. Their divided opinions externalize one of Leon's further concerns with regard to mixing, namely, the implications of his relationship with Madeleine (Maryam D'Abo), the non-Jewish woman he literally bumps into after his visit to the fertility clinic who personifies the allure of a(nother) forbidden relationship.

In line with the film's principle of maximizing Jewish discomfort, circumstances and the new relations pose a constant challenge to Leon's religious observance and sensitivities. His biological father turns out to be a *pig* farmer and entices him to impregnate sows in rural Yorkshire. Leon is expected to masturbate for a sperm test in a glass-paneled high-rise building overlooking London and has intercourse with Madeleine during her period, which carries the association of ritual impurity. He endures the Chadwicks' fondness of pork and Madeleine's appetite for lobsters,[17] and last but not least models Jesus Christ on the cross for his artist-lover's Church of England stained glass windows.

Leon is, therefore, both Jewish and not Jewish enough, and the film invites the (Jewish) spectator to sympathize with and be amused by his twofold anguish. At the same time, it shows that Madeleine is and remains ignorant of Judaism and expresses no interest in Leon's life, family, or community. Her surface-level ethnophilia is simply a rebellious gesture directed at her offscreen father; Madeleine feels attracted to Leon because "Daddy hates Jews." While such unmitigated negative racialization appears outdated in the 1990s, the father's attitude is nevertheless suggestive of surviving residues from a long history of British antisemitism. In the twentieth century, it included xenophobia and anti-immigration legislation; political and physical racism inspired by fascist ideologies; ambivalent responses to refugees, Holocaust survivors, and the State of Israel; and, last but not least, an upper-class tradition of social restrictions and exclusion. Conversely, Brian's philosemitism, while as uninformed as Madeleine's ethnic infatuation (he refers to the movie *Ben-Hur* [1959] as his educational source and mistakenly associates the Qur'an with Judaism), is motivated by his admiration for "the way Jews believe in the family." As representatives of British majority culture, Madeleine and the Chadwicks are barely aware of British Jewry as an *actual* presence with whom they share a national history, nor can they relate to the Jewish diaspora's collective memory of scapegoating and persecution, the uncertainties of assimilation, or concerns about (self-inflicted) communal decline.

Leon humorizes this ignorance and discrepancy in a number of ways. When Brian says to Leon that "it's good to have you home," the incommensurability of homes, views, and lifestyles is underlined rather than negated. The Chadwicks attempt to increase Leon's comfort by making their home more like that of the Gellers. They adjust their home decor; change their spoken and body language; develop new attitudes toward family, gender, and nation; and engage with such American Jewish classics as Leo Rosten's *Joys of Yiddish* (1968) and Philip Roth's *Portnoy's Complaint* (1969). The Chadwicks thus try to perform Jewishness, but Leon points out their lack of a socially acquired essence: "Look, you're just fulfilling stereotypes. You don't understand the fundamental concept of guilt. Without guilt it's meaningless. Guilt isn't a word, it's . . . it's a way of life." The complexity of Jewish guilt runs through the film, from its images of the crucified (Jewish) Christ and suggested breaches of the covenant (deferred procreation, non-Jewish semen, a non-Jewish partner) to a more abstract "persistence of a certain reflectiveness, an inability to take things for granted, a continuously nagging sense of difficulty and problem."[18]

Leon purposely merges biological, religious, and cultural elements and undermines any possibility of a hermetic logic of Jewish descent. At the same time, the film also employs these elements to illustrate the need of and capacity for self-irony and self-assertion among British Jews in a largely oblivious wider culture. The flawed reproduction plot serves as a conceit to playfully juxtapose stereotypically Jewish features of the "hybrid" Leon — such as poor eyesight, a repulsion for nonkosher animals and food, and his dread of being exposed naked in the Chadwick bathroom[19] — with his other side: his distaste for family secrets and "white lies" (which renders him hapless as an estate agent), his lack of business sense, and his failure to settle and procreate like his brothers. Leon feels drawn to the sensual and voyeuristic Madeleine, whose assertion that windows "fulfill a real need" and "allow you to see and be seen" resonates with him, as does her view that net curtains, which represent Sidney's petit bourgeois trade and stand for an unnecessarily veiled or hidden existence, stop "people enjoying the window from both sides." Madeleine fails, however, to ever position herself on the other side and develop respective sensibilities. As a consequence, Leon also remains fond of the young Jewish woman Lisa (Gina Bellman), but for her he is too familiar (that is, too Jewish). She has turned to Eastern spirituality in her search for excitement through difference.

It is through Lisa and Leon's relationship and the pig-sheep that the film is brought to its conclusion. The animal has remained offscreen throughout but has nevertheless triggered responses from the other characters: The veterinarian considers it an abomination; the rabbis disagree on its Halachic status; Brian first proposes its isolation and later, when vying with Sidney for Leon's filial attachment, its commodification. The responses toward mixed-race identity cover the ground of racial purity, religious doctrine, social models of segregation, and exoticization for profit.

It is only Leon who engages directly and emotionally with the creature, the foil of his own predicament. To him, the pig-sheep looks "happy" and is "getting on very well with the other pigs." When he fears for its life, he takes it away and releases it into the wild. Only Lisa wants to know what made him decide "to run away with the pig." Having given up a twenty-four-hour chant, she reflects on her fellow chanters and, implicitly, her own desire: "All just trying to be different." Leon complements her statement: "Without knowing why." Although Leon reminds Brian that something "good" can come from "crossbreeding," becoming Leon the Pig Farmer is not an option for him at the end of the film. The accident of his birth is not equated with social or cultural reorientation. Leon spiritually reconnects with the Jewish community when a fiddler plays "Hava Nagila" in a restaurant, while the pig-sheep remains an anomaly that fends for itself in the English countryside. The latter's future prospects are unclear, but the film leaves the Gellers and the Chadwicks at the beginning of a friendship beyond mutual stereotypes and presents Lisa and Leon as the made-for-each-other romantic couple.

Leon's narrative gambit of diasporic infertility alludes to the (perceived) crisis of community continuity, which dominated the discourse of the then chief rabbi, Jonathan Sacks, in the 1990s. It found expression in a new organization for community development, Jewish Continuity (1993–98), and underpinned much of the subsequent social research into British Jewish demographics, attitudes, and lifestyle choices.[20] Through the insemination plot, the film offers a subversive rejoinder to this alarmist stance. Rather than dwell on anxieties associated with biological, genetic, and ethnoreligious succession, the filmmakers espouse an understanding of genealogy that sees hybridity and heterogeneity in a positive light. Despite its critique of purism and sympathies for cross-cultural exchange, however, *Leon* is critical of disowning cultural specificity. The comedy also utilizes the reproduction narrative to assert Jewish identity (and masculinity, in particular) and to present it as enduring in its own right. The relationship with Madeleine is treated as an interlude, and no plotline is developed relating to the prospects of intermarriage, which is frequently regarded as the single biggest threat to cultural (and, to a lesser extent, biological) Jewish survival in the post-Holocaust age.

Sarah Franklin contends that "new reproductive technologies not only create new persons; they create new relations, in both senses of the term."[21] In Leon's case, these relations are established between an increasingly assertive British Jewry and a reasonably tolerant non-Jewish majority in need of awareness and insight. *The Infidel* is more aligned with the wider category of multiculturally informed narratives around the turn of the twenty-first century as described by, among others, Sander Gilman, Efraim Sicher, and Linda Weinhouse.[22] Nearly two decades after the 1992 release of *Leon the Pig Farmer*, cultural diversity in Britain has been further normalized but also unsettled by both a rise in antisemitism and a preoccupation with Islam and the Middle East after the events of 9/11 in New York and 7/7 in London. The 2010 film *The Infidel* responds to these modified coordinates by shifting the focus to interdiasporic relations between Muslims and Jews in a narrative that relegates white English Christian ethnicity to the sidelines.

The Name of the Father: Transracial Adoption and the Subversion of Ethnic Matching

In *The Infidel*, it is the main character's Muslim identity that is called into question when he finds out that he is an adoptee, a fact that had been concealed from him until the death of both adoptive parents. While adoption, unlike artificial insemination, does not involve bodily intervention, it nevertheless "figures among the technologies conjoined in the generation of families and is arguably a form of assisted reproduction."[23] Like other reproductive technologies, it occupies, in religious and social discourse, a dominant position in debates around genealogy. Judaism shares with Islam the concern with lineage and ancestry, but before *The Infidel* turns to questions of Mahmud's newly discovered Jewishness, the complexity of social parenting in Muslim families is introduced as a further dimension of the adoption plot and its associated myth of hidden identities.

After establishing Mahmud's family and diverse aspects of modern British Muslim life (including work, religious practice, dress codes, and media representation), the film introduces the adoption theme by drawing attention to the role that looking after orphaned and abandoned children plays in Islam. When packing up the belongings of his dead mother, Mahmud is touched by the words of a hadith displayed in a frame on the wall. It relates the Prophet Muhammad's saying, "He who looks after an orphan, shall be in paradise."[24] Mahmud, who lost his (adoptive) father when he was a child, is now parentless, and in the ensuing exchange with his son, Rashid, the connection is made with Muhammad, whose father died before he was born and whose mother died when he was six. The Prophet grew up with several (foster) carers and, later in life, adopted a freed slave as his son, whom he initially gave his name: Zayd ibn Muhammad. This adoption was eventually dissolved in response to the revelations that were to be compiled in the Qur'an: "NEVER has God . . . made your adopted sons [truly] your sons. . . . [As for your adopted children,] call them by their [real] fathers' names: this is more equitable in the sight of God . . ." (Surah 33, Ayat 4 and 5). The pre-Islamic practice of adoption was replaced by *kafala*, a form of fostering, which "involves the obligations of guardianship and maintenance without the creation of legal ties" and "does not sever the biological family bonds of the child or alter the descent lines for the adopting family."[25]

In *The Infidel*, Mahmud's adoption is based on a secular legal process. It is a closed adoption, and no link between birth and adoptive family is maintained. This is in conflict with *kafala*, which rejects "obliterating lineage" and "dissimulation through naming."[26] Mahmud, who feels he has been deprived of his biological identity and family name, demands immediate access to his case file from a reluctant social worker, explicitly referring to Islamic patriliny: "Please, in my culture, a man's name is really important to him." With the revelation of Solly Shimshillewitz as Mahmud's preadoption name, however, a dramatic shift occurs: the issue of family lineage is replaced by the question of collective descent. Just as in *Leon the Pig Farmer*, a transethnic component challenges automatic assumptions about the link between biology and ethnoreligious identity and subverts the (normalized) principle of ethnic matching. After forcefully gaining access to his adoption record, the patronymic Shimshillewitz confirms not only Mahmud's non-Muslim roots but also improbable (and thus funny) cross-cultural relations between Jews and Muslims in Britain. As the social worker explains, "In common with many people living in this area at the time you are by birth Jewish."

Solly Shimshillewitz therefore stands for biological descent ("by birth") and ethnic overdetermination (Lenny says: "Why didn't they just call you 'Jew Jew Jew Jew Jew' and be done with it?"), but the social worker's line goes further by localizing ("in this area") and historicizing ("at the time") the fictional event. The un-Anglicized surname and the anachronistically dubbed Whitechapel Branch of the Waifs and Strays' Society,[27] which administered the placement, conjure up the image of a historical East End. Although the screenwriter does not provide a backstory for the migration background and circumstances of Mahmud's birthparents, at least the British Jewish viewer will associate the Whitechapel ward in East London with Jewish migration and settlement in England. In modern history, Whitechapel absorbed thousands of Eastern European migrants arriving between the 1880s and 1914, refugees fleeing Nazi persecution, a smaller number of young survivors who came in 1945, and Polish Jewish soldiers who had fought under the British High Command in the Second World War. As the *Kindertransport* statue by Frank Meisler, located outside Liverpool Street Station, commemorates, the borough also received many of the ten thousand namesake *Kinder* (children) who escaped to Britain in 1938 and 1939. The Jewish child refugees experienced separation, displacement, and orphaning as well as transnational and, in some cases, transethnic adoption and fostering. At the same time, the 1939 British White Paper restricted Jewish migration to Palestine and, from 1940 to 1941, male adult Jews without British citizenship were among those interned as "enemy aliens."[28] It was against this background that Jewish migrants eventually made new lives in Britain, and established British Jews negotiated their Britishness and Jewishness, some of whom lived in the East End of London, which had been a bombing target during the Blitz.

The Infidel's imagined placement of a child born to Whitechapel Jews in a Muslim shopkeeper's family in the 1960s (the same period as that of the insemination in *Leon*) therefore points to a Jewish heritage but also to (post)colonial migration after 1945 and further demographic change. Implicit is not only the notion of similar diasporic histories but also belonging to a lower socioeconomic class. In 2010, Mahmud's birth father lives in a care home in Golders Green, which stands for the social mobility of Jewish Britons and their suburban self-invisibilization,[29] whereas Whitechapel and the East End, while remaining sites of continuing high migrant and diasporic visibility, have become predominantly Asian and Muslim.

This historicity of place and populations is mainly a subtextual effect evoked by the dialogue in the adoption services scene. Location shots are limited, with the exception of a multicultural sequence filmed at Walthamstow Market in East London. More striking for the audience is the (unlikely) establishment of Jewish-Muslim kinship through adoption. As in *Leon*, assisted reproduction is presented as additionally charged when it involves what is perceived as ethnoreligious transgression. While adoption has been common throughout history, it has also been stigmatized as falsehood, associated with social risk and thus often hushed up. The practice of transracial adoption has been particularly controversial. Adoption across national, religious, ethnic, and racial boundaries became more widespread after the mid-twentieth century as a humanitarian response to concerns about the welfare and opportunities of children in the care system or those orphaned or abandoned due to war, persecution, famine, natural disasters, ill health, poverty, and gender bias. Historically informed arguments against such placements foreground instances of authorized domination and/or child removals built on racial hierarchies.[30] Critics also suggest that even consensual adoptions are based on ethnic and class inequalities within nation-states and, in international adoption, on global inequities. Placing minority ethnic children into families representing a dominant culture has been interpreted as a threat to the cultural continuation of respective communities, an argument that is notably also voiced against intermarriage. From a social position, it has been argued that ethnic (and religious) matching is a better enabler of identity formation in adoptees than transplacements where children have to negotiate their place in mainstream culture *and* develop a positive sense of their ethnic (and/or religious) birth identity.

Read culturally and against *The Infidel*'s adoption plot, the latter positions once again emphasize a threat to community autonomy and survival. Mahmud's adoption suggests the notion of an "unlived past or heritage,"[31] albeit one that is not automatically suppressed by assimilation into a majority culture. A different reading sees adoption as the manifestation of a "common humanity" model[32] and not as an interaction between competing social, ethnic, and religious groups. Just like the intermingling of seeds and genes, adoption can "inform the way we read other social relations and the regulatory mechanisms, policies, and practices that allow us, as individuals and society, to recognize and connect with one another."[33] Understood in this way, Mahmud's case offers a number of new narrative and conceptual possibilities. Central is the possibility to swap or rather double perspectives and thus bring into contact two diasporic minorities of unequal size, differing traditions, and conflicts of interest and affiliation.[34]

The generative moment is Mahmud's interpellation as a Jew. In Louis Althusser's conception, the unborn child is already ideologically constituted because of the certainty that it "will bear its Father's Name."[35] Adoption subverts this certainty by way of the ambiguity outlined earlier. In Judith Butler's words, "being called a name is . . . one of the conditions by which a subject is constituted in language."[36] Notably, Butler refers, among others, to adoption papers as a source for an "interpellative name."[37] Mahmud is called quite literally by the name of his biological father, but he is also labeled as a Jew, a contextually contentious ascription. In her analysis of "injurious" speech, Butler approaches interpellation in a way that echoes the dual reading of adoption. She states that

> one is not simply fixed by the name that one is called. . . . The name holds out another possibility as well: by being called a name, one is also, paradoxically, given a certain possibility for social existence. . . . Thus the injurious address may appear to fix or paralyze the one it hails, but it may also produce an unexpected and enabling response.[38]

Initially, being called a Jew means that Mahmud has to actualize and be faced with stereotypes. The adoptee, who is removed from the social worker's office after forcefully gaining access to his file, lays claim to an instant racialization when he transforms from Mahmud to Solly: "You find out you're Jewish, and suddenly a bloke in a uniform is leading you away. Ridiculous." Jewishness is associated here with state-sanctioned maltreatment, and a comic effect is achieved by drawing on the popular knowledge of Nazi Germany's antisemitic practices and superimposing them on a scene unrelated to matters of ethnicity. The scene also suggests an automatic Jewish persecution complex rooted in memory and history rather than present-day experience. In the course of the remaining screen time, Mahmud encounters further moments of paranoia, but he is also confronted with the spectrum of old and new (or repackaged) stereotypes, even setting off a few of them himself to test the attitudes of his British Muslim colleagues. His "hailing" continues in a dream sequence wherein Mahmud mishears his family members' words and imagines that they "Jew" him linguistically. He also visualizes his new identity through images of himself as a Haredi Jew, a concentration camp inmate, and an effeminate entertainment performer.[39] Mahmud's online research via the fictional search engine "Perplexed," named in direct allusion to Maimonides's twelfth-century *Guide for the Perplexed*, shows the ubiquity of antisemitic words and images by presenting numerous entries leading to conspiracy theory websites, caricature collections, neo-Nazi community platforms, and militant anti-Zionist propaganda. The presence of such antisemitic subcultures constitutes a persistent threat and leads to heightened vigilance within the British Jewish community. When Mahmud calls at the home where his birth father lives, his arrival has been anticipated. He is informed that Jewish care homes "share info" for protection. A swastika is sprayed onto Mahmud's house after he has revealed his adoption and Jewish descent, not only to his family but also—due to the film's eccentric plotline—on national television.

Mahmud's interpellation, however, also triggers the character's efforts to inhabit, embody, and put into practice his Jewishness. It becomes, in analogy to Butler's discussion of gender, "*a corporeal style*, an 'act,' as it were, which is both intentional and performative," externalizing through diegetic and extradiegetic (en)acting that "the body is always an embodying of possibilities both conditioned and circumscribed by historical convention."[40] This effect is further enhanced by the screen acting of the British Iranian Baha'i Omid Djalili, who performs the British Pakistani Muslim Mahmud, who performs the British Ashkenazi Jew Solly Shimshillewitz, drawing—as do the Chadwicks in *Leon*—on a set of iconic texts, behaviors, and practices. Blurring the boundaries between performance (as in acting a role) and performativity (as in assuming and constructing an identity) is part of a postethnic playfulness that is not restricted to Mahmud: the filmmakers deliberately cast a Jewish actor (Igal Naor, an Israeli of Iraqi descent) in the role of the Egyptian Muslim Arshad Al-Masri. This screen character claims to trace back his lineage to eighth-century Medina but is unmasked as the reincarnation of a 1980s English pop icon with racist leanings, who grew up in a white Scientologist family from Manchester and, infatuated with charismatic otherness, reinvented himself as an Islamic leader.

Adoption plots and the fantasy of unknown kindred and heritage abound in the English literary and popular imagination, particularly in the nineteenth century, and have been read as reflections on adoption per se and "as allegories for other issues."[41] George Eliot's title character of *Daniel Deronda* (1876) is English literature's canonical Jewish adoptee.[42] Also unaware of his Jewish descent at the outset, Deronda eventually encounters his birth mother, whose disaffection with Judaism led her to place her son with the wealthy Sir Hugo Mallinger. In contrast, Mahmud's meeting with his birth father (and mother) is forever deferred. He cannot connect with his Whitechapel Jewish heritage through his birth parent and thus needs to reconcile his own diffuse awareness of Jews and Jewishness, suggestibly acquired through British schooling, media coverage, and political Islam, with what Lenny has to offer. His mentor can be read as a parodic version of Deronda's cultural fosterer Mordecai.[43] Lenny has only limited knowledge of the foundations of Judaism and the Zionist project—still a utopia in Eliot's novel—but he has more mundane answers to Mahmud's questions about "Jews." Among others, he attempts to provide the wider context into which Mahmud has been interpellated:

> Let's start with me, the archetype: the American Jew. . . . Like my fellow countrymen, I didn't think there were any other Jews in the whole fucking world, especially not Britain. Britain, Land of Hope and Pork! A Jew in Britain, that's just weird! . . . But no, in London alone you've got your Hampstead liberal intellectual Jew, you've got your Pinner secular accountant Jew, you've got your Hendon Orthodox lawyer Jew, your scum-of-kosher-scum Essex Jew, of which heritage my recently ex-wife. . . . And then you've got your Israeli Jews, you know, Jews without angst, without guilt, so really not Jews at all.

Lenny here touches on the hegemonic role played by American Jewry after the Second World War, especially in the Anglophone world, and the lack of recognition for British Jews, despite their diasporic history that dates back to the medieval period.

The Infidel also addresses the low profile of Jewishness in British multiculturalism. In one of the film's media scenes, screenwriter and TV persona David Baddiel appears as himself in a fictional episode of Channel 5's topical debate show *The Wright Stuff*, dedicated to Mahmud's televised coming out as a Jew. Before Baddiel can respond to a question posed by the program's host about the footage, the other panel guest jumps in and appropriates the incident: "This guy is multiculturalism made flesh. He is a hero for our times. Somebody that we have to use." Who is included in the speaker's "we" remains open, but ignoring the Jewish voice may be indicative of the fact that "not only have Jews often been suspicious of multicultural discourse, [but] scholars interested in multiculturalism and minority issues in Britain have rarely considered the Jewish experience."[44] The public discourse of constructing the Jewish diaspora as a model community can act as a disincentive to draw attention to ethnic or religious particularity, dissent, and grievances,[45] but even where this is not the case, Jews may face, as Efraim Sicher argues, "a postcolonial agenda that has tended to exclude consideration of Jewish issues or anti-Semitism, while making 'Palestine' the center of political consensus."[46] Such silencing is counteracted by the film itself, however, which purposely unites Muslims and Jews rather than pitching minority experiences against the majority culture or each other.

In line with adoption's deconstruction of "naturalized versions of national, racial, and cultural belonging,"[47] the interpellative plot of *The Infidel* not only leads to identity adjustments, a new consciousness, and redirected sensibilities but also plays out the implications of a transethnic kinship on several levels. Mahmud shares physical features with Solly and can easily pass as either Muslim or Jew.[48] Further alignments include rituals and bodily manifestations (Lenny realizes that a circumcised penis would neither confirm nor dismiss Mahmud's claim to Jewishness), dress codes (Mahmud puts his taqiyah over the yarmulke he tried on earlier), and shared places of arrival (such as London's East End). Mahmud places Chumash and Qur'an next to each other when he sets out to challenge Al-Masri, and he addresses the similarities of belief, text, and language in his final confrontation. A further commonality is the—albeit split—vested interest in Israel/Palestine and respective diasporic loyalties and various community demands for solidarity. Mahmud feels obliged to attend a pro-Palestinian demonstration, but as Solly, he is also expected to support Israel. Self-identifying as a modern Sunni whose Muslim identity is easily compatible with multicultural coexistence; Mahmud feels more alienated when he performs an Israel-hating antisemitic act than when attempting to enact Jewishness.

Lenny and Mahmud eventually join forces against the dogmatists of religious purity, personified by the dying father's rabbi, whose guardianship lacks humanity, and by Al-Masri, who wants to prevent the marriage between Rashid and his stepdaughter Uzma (Soraya Radford). On the DVD commentary track, the filmmakers are outspoken about their critique of "gatekeepers" who lay claim to defining identities for others. They refer not only to their own film but also to institutions such as the Board of Deputies of British Jews and the Muslim Council of Britain. *The Infidel* deconstructs the hollow demands of agitators and the narrow-mindedness of the community establishment and favors the friendship and disputations of Lenny and Mahmud. The response to the task set for Mahmud by the rabbi ("Think what it means to be a Jew") is an affirmation and embrace of cultural and ethnic diversity and hybridity—based on humor that will continue to need stereotypes and adversity but clearly distances itself from British Jewish parochialism and itinerant Islamism alike.

A Cinema of Irregular Reproduction

Paul Morrison, the writer-director of two historical British Jewish films, *Solomon and Gaenor* (1999) and *Wondrous Oblivion* (2003), stated in an interview that having come of age in the late 1950s and early 1960s, his upbringing reflected the unease associated with the status of Jews in Britain as existing "on sufferance" and conditions of assimilation.[49] Morrison also described the "acute depression" in postwar British Jewry, situated "on the edge of the Holocaust," and what he later realized was the ambivalent part played by British Jewry in connection with British politics in the 1930s and 1940s. He remembers growing up in a "self-denying world," in which he was told "not to be a loud Jew," where "hiding" was a "big thing" and he had felt proud that he "could pass as a non-Jew." Unlike Morrison, the screenwriters of *Leon the Pig Farmer* and *The Infidel* belong to a generation whose formative years fell into the 1970s and whose protagonists are also products of the 1960s.[50] Director Josh Appignanesi, born even later, in 1975, underlines this significant generational shift. He draws attention to

> the notion that new generations are questioning those inherited prejudices upon which the continuity of communities has rested. What remains most radical here is perhaps the vexed and shifting notion of community itself, so closely allied to the idea of the family, but also, crucially for filmmakers, to the idea of the audience.[51]

Irregular reproduction serves as metaphor for the "new Jew" who emerges from hiding and who, despite some caveats, finds himself (or herself) in a Britain in which models of community and their survival can be challenged (*Leon*) and where shared diaspora space and histories can be imagined (*The Infidel*). The stories of empowered Jewishness without negation of a distinctive history and multicultural conviviality fall into step with the broader developments in British society during the 1980s and 1990s. Concepts of identity and community determined and circumscribed by genetics, biology, religion, race, or ethnicity are juxtaposed with more ephemeral, malleable, and flexible models of subjectivity. In the films' attempt to undermine foundational birth narratives, notions of impurity are presented as life-giving and thus relevant to the history and future of diasporic (British) Jews.[52]

This chapter's reading of *Leon* and *The Infidel* treats the two productions as representative of (British) Jewish and a wider diasporic (European) cinema, privileging an analytical approach that centers on religion and ethnicity. *Leon* and *The Infidel*, however, also belong to a growing number of international feature films about fertility, assisted reproduction, and adoption. Some of these are dystopian narratives that envision a collapsed biopolitical order of entire societies (*The Handmaid's Tale*, 1990; *Children of Men*, 2006); others address the psychological impact of infertility treatment (*Forget Paris*, 1995; *Maybe Baby*, 2000), stillbirth (*Return to Zero*, 2014), surrogacy (*Baby Mama*, 2008), miscarriage and adoption (*Then She Found Me*, 2008) on individuals. Irrespective of whether the films employ comedy, romance, social realism, or science fiction as styles, they invite reflection on contemporary lifestyles, bioethics, and the institution of the family. Furthermore, they position themselves vis-à-vis issues of race and class (*Secrets and Lies*, 1996), religion (*Kadosh*, 1999), sexuality (*Two Mothers*, 2013) and gender (*Mother and Child*, 2009).[53]

If *Leon* and *The Infidel* are read as contributions to this particular cinema, their most notable feature is, apart from the focus on British Jewishness, the masculinist approach they take throughout. Leon and Mahmud are driven to connect with their biological fathers. Leon's mother appears in the story, but more emphasis is placed on the father's reactions. Mahmud's adoptive mother has died, and his birth mother, usually a central figure in the adoption triangle, is never mentioned. While both films could be subject to a feminist critique for their eclipse of women's roles and experiences, the irregularity of their cinematic Jewish masculinity is productive in its own right. It exemplifies the "shift towards more subtle, nuanced, playful and even outrageous representations of the Jewish male body"[54] on the screen *and* offers a particular thematic variation, thus expanding the archive of the cinema of reproduction at large.

Notes

1. *Leon the Pig Farmer*, directed by Vadim Jean and Gary Sinyor (London: Leon the Pig Farmer Plc, 1992). *The Infidel*, directed by Josh Appignanesi (London: Infidel Films Limited, Slingshot, Met Film Ombudsman; developed in association with BBC Films, 2010). A musical version of *The Infidel* premiered at the Theatre Royal Stratford East in London in October 2014.

2. Alys Eve Weinbaum, *Wayward Reproductions: Genealogies of Race and Nation in Transatlantic Modern Thought* (Durham, N.C.: Duke University Press; Chesham: Combined Academic, 2004), 2.

3. Ibid., 2.

4. Ibid.

5. Howard Eilberg-Schwartz, "Introduction: People of the Body," in *People of the Body: Jews and Judaism from an Embodied Perspective*, edited by Howard Eilberg-Schwartz, 1–15 (Albany: State University of New York Press, 1992), 2.

6. Ibid., 1.

7. Deuteronomy 23:2 also excludes men who have not reproduced from serving as high priests or on the Sanhedrin. For a summary, see Anthony V. Hirsh, "Infertility in Jewish Couples: Biblical and Rabbinic Law," *Human Fertility* 1, no. 1 (1998): 14–19, 15.

8. Pronatalism is common to all religions, but the Jewish case in the State of Israel has generated special interest; see, for example, Susan Martha Kahn, *Reproducing Jews: A Cultural Account of Assisted Conception in Israel* (Durham, N.C.: Duke University Press, 2000).

9. Emil Fackenheim, "The 614th Commandment" (1967), in *The Jewish Thought of Emil Fackenheim: A Reader*, edited by Michael L. Morgan, 157–60 (Detroit: Wayne State University Press, 1987), 158.

10. Emil Fackenheim, *God's Presence in History: Jewish Affirmations and Philosophical Reflections* (1970; Northvale, N.J.: J. Aronson, 1997), 71.

11. Hirsh, "Infertility in Jewish Couples," 17.

12. Ibid., 18.

13. Ibid.

14. See Kahn, *Reproducing Jews*, chapters 2 and 3.

15. The contradictions of reproductive logics can be further exemplified here: Despite the overarching matrilineal principle, patriliny is found in the Torah and applies to the priestly castes of Cohen and Levi for whom ancestral descent is constructed through the male line. Paradoxically, patriliny can also feature in Reform and Progressive Judaism, where the Jewishness of either parent is considered to establish community membership. Nazism constructed its own version of Jewishness in a generational model based on a combination of religious identification and racialization.

16. In the mid-1980s, the Indonesian piglike animal babirusa was discussed as a food source that might be kosher. For more recent references to "kosher pigs" in the context of reproduction technologies, see David J. Bleich, *Bioethical Dilemmas: A Jewish Perspective*, vol. 2 (Southfield, Mich.: Targum, 2006), 31–32; Miryam Z. Wahrman, *Brave New Judaism: When Science and Scripture Collide* (Lebanon, N.H.: Brandeis University Press, 2002), 192–94.

17. On the DVD commentary track, *Leon*'s directors acknowledge their indebtedness to American Jewish culture, in particular film: "We only stole from other Jewish films." One example of citational reverence is the use of lobsters, which alludes to the well-known sequences in Woody Allen's *Annie Hall* (1977). *Leon the Pig Farmer*, DVD (London: Carlton Visual Entertainment, 2002).

18. Eugene Goodheart, "Jew d'Esprit," in *The New York Public Intellectuals and Beyond*, edited by Ethan Goffman and Daniel Morris, 35–43 (West Lafayette, Ind.: Purdue University Press, 2009), 42.

19. On the recurring bathroom trope in contemporary cinema, see Nathan Abrams, *The New Jew in Film: Exploring Jewishness and Judaism in Contemporary Cinema* (London, New York: I. B. Tauris, 2012), 183–206.

20. On the reflexive turn, strategy of insecurity, and initiatives for community enhancement in the 1990s, see Keith Kahn-Harris and Ben Gidley, *Turbulent Times: The British Jewish Community Today* (London: Continuum, 2010), 13 and 38–55. Findings of the Institute for Jewish Policy Research from the 1990s and 2000s can be accessed at http://www.jpr.org.uk/.

21. Sarah Franklin, *Embodied Progress: A Cultural Account of Assisted Conception* (London: Routledge, 1997), 4.

22. Sander Gilman, *Multiculturalism and the Jews* (New York: Routledge, 2006); Efraim Sicher and Linda Weinhouse, *Under Postcolonial Eyes: Figuring the "Jew" in Contemporary British Writing* (Lincoln: University of Nebraska Press, 2012).

23. Claudia Castañeda, "Incorporating the Transnational Adoptee," in *Imagining Adoption: Essays on Literature and Culture*, edited by Marianne Novy, 277–99 (Ann Arbor: University of Michigan Press, 2004), 278.

24. The quotation is taken from the film's dialogue. The full hadith in the Sahih al Bukhari (volume 8, book 73, number 34) reads, "The Prophet said, 'I and the person who looks after an orphan and provides for him, will be in Paradise like this,' putting his index and middle fingers together."

25. Muslim Women's Shura Council, *Adoption and the Care of Orphan Children: Islam and the Best Interests of the Child* (New York: American Society of Muslim Advancement, August 2011), 6.

26. Ibid., 8, 7.

27. Baddiel appropriates the name of the Waifs and Strays' Society, founded in 1881, which was renamed the Church of England Children's Society in 1946 and has been known as the Children's Society since 1982.

28. Screenwriter David Baddiel's novel *The Secret Purposes* (London: Harper Perennial, 2004) deals with the experience of German Jewish civilian internment in Britain during the Second World War.

29. Assimilation through deghettoization, economic and professional achievement, and sociocultural inconspicuousness have rendered large parts of British Jewry "invisible," making them less vulnerable to marginalization than other religious minorities, nonwhite or non-middle-class ethnic groups but also less vocal and interventionist in the larger debates around integration and social cohesion.

30. Children were taken from Eastern European countries for "Germanization" in Lebensborn homes between 1939 and 1945, from Aboriginal families in Australia in the years 1880–1970, and from Native American communities in the United States until the Indian Child Welfare Act of 1978.

31. Vincent J. Cheng, *Inauthentic: The Anxiety over Culture and Identity* (Piscataway, N.J.: Rutgers University Press, 2004), 68 and 178. See here also the wider discussion of transracial adoption and of Jewish "authenticity" in chapters 4 and 5.

32. Elizabeth Bartholet, *Family Bonds: Adoption and the Politics of Parenting* (Boston: Houghton Mifflin, 1993), 143.

33. Jill R. Deans, "'File It under "L" for Love Child': Adoptive Policies and Practices in the Erdrich Tetralogy," in Novy, 231–49, *Imagining Adoption*, 247.

34. The 2011 Census for England and Wales enumerated 263,346 Jews and 2,706,066 Muslims, at 0.5 percent and 4.8 percent of the total population, respectively.

35. Louis Althusser, "Ideology and the State" (1970), in *Lenin and Philosophy and Other Essays*, 127–86 (New York: Monthly Review Press, 1971), 176.

36. Judith Butler, *Excitable Speech: A Politics of the Performative* (New York: Routledge, 1997), 2.

37. Ibid., 34.

38. Ibid., 2.

39. As in *Leon*, some of these scenes make reference to *Annie Hall*.

40. Judith Butler, "Performative Acts and Gender Constitution: An Essay in Phenomenology and Feminist Theory," *Theatre Journal* 40, no. 4 (1988): 519–31; 521–22, emphasis in the original.

41. Marianne Novy, *Reading Adoption: Family and Difference in Fiction and Drama* (Ann Arbor: University of Michigan Press, 2005), 123.

42. Adoption must not be understood in legal terms here; the institution was not formalized in the same way as it is today.

43. The biblical Mordecai adopts — or fosters — his orphaned cousin Hadassah, who becomes Babylonian queen under the name of Esther (Esther 2:7).

44. Kahn-Harris and Gidley, *Turbulent Times*, 171.

45. See, for example, Prime Minister Tony Blair's speech on the occasion of the 350th anniversary of the resettlement of Jews in England: "Speech at the Bevis Marks Synagogue," *National Archives*, June 13, 2006, accessed November 2, 2015, http://webarchive.nationalarchives.gov.uk/20040105034004/http://number10.gov.uk/page9676.

46. Efraim Sicher, "The Image of Israel and Postcolonial Discourse in the Early 21st Century: A View from Britain," *Israel Studies* 16, no. 1 (2011): 1–25, 3.

47. Castañeda, "Transnational Adoptee," 284.

48. It is not uncommon for Jews in Europe to be mistaken for members of a (larger) Muslim minority. Baddiel reports his experience of having been beaten up twice, once for being Jewish and once for being Pakistani (DVD commentary). *The Infidel*, DVD (London: Revolver Entertainment, 2010).

49. Paul Morrison, interview by Claudia Sternberg, July 11, 2007. *Solomon and Gaenor*, directed by Paul Morrison (London: APT Films, APT Productions, Arts Council of England, 1999); *Wondrous Oblivion*, directed by Paul Morrison (London: APT Films, Met Film Production, Met Film, 2003).

50. Normand and Sinyor were born in 1958 and 1962, respectively; Baddiel was born in 1964.

51. Josh Appignanesi, "Unothering the Other: *Ajami/The Infidel*," *Jewish Quarterly*, July 23, 2010, http://jewishquarterly.org/2010/07/unothering-the-other-ajamithe-infidel/.

52. British Jewish author Clive Sinclair, who addresses Jewish reproduction in his own work (*Blood Libels*, 1985; *The Lady with the Laptop*, 1996; *A Soap Opera from Hell*, 1998), cites Primo Levi's *The Periodic Table* (first published in Italian; Turin, 1975) for whom impurity "gives rise to changes, in other words, to life." See Sinclair's short story "In Praise of Impurity" in *The Lady with the Laptop*, 175–83 (London: Picador, 1996), 176.

53. *The Handmaid's Tale*, directed by Volker Schlöndorff (Munich: Bioskop Film, New York: Cinecom Entertainment Group, 1990); *Children of Men*, directed by Alfonso Cuarón (Los Angeles: Universal Pictures, Strike Entertainment, Hit and Run Productions, 2006); *Forget Paris*, directed by Billy Crystal (Los Angeles: Castle Rock Entertainment, Face Productions, 1995); *Maybe Baby*, directed by Ben Elton (London: Pandora Cinema, BBC Films, 2000); *Return to Zero*, directed by Sean Hanish (Pasadena, Calif.: Cannonball Productions, 2014); *Baby Mama*, directed by Michael McCullers (Los Angeles: Michaels-Goldwyn, Relativity Media, 2008); *Then She Found Me*, directed by Helen Hunt (Los Angeles: Odyssey Entertainment, Killer Films, et al., 2008); *Secrets and Lies*, directed by Mike Leigh (London: Thin Man Films, 1996); *Kadosh*, directed by Amos Gitaï (Tel Aviv: Agav Hafakot, MP Productions, 1999); *Zwei Mütter/Two Mothers*, directed by Anna Zohra Berrached (Ludwigsburg, Ger.: Filmakademie Baden-Württemberg, ZDF, 2013); *Mother and Child*, directed by Rodrigo García (Los Angeles: Everest Entertainment, Cha Cha Cha, Mockingbird Pictures, 2009).

54. Nathan Abrams, "From Jesus to Jeremy: The Jewish Male Body on Film, 1990 to the Present," in *Mysterious Skin: Male Bodies in Contemporary Cinema*, edited by Santiago Fouz-Hernández, 15–29 (London: I. B. Tauris, 2009), 15.

MICHELE BYERS

On the Threshold
British Jewish Femininity in Suzie Gold *(2004)*

The 2004 British film *Suzie Gold* focuses on several months in the life of Suzie (Summer Phoenix), a twenty-three-year-old woman who has grown up in the heart of North London's Jewish community, as she navigates a secret love affair with Darren (Leo Gregory), a non-Jewish man. Complicating this new, illicit romance is the return of Anthony Silver (Iddo Goldberg), allegedly the most eligible Jewish bachelor in London, whose attentions have turned to Suzie. The film represents a rare, explicitly Jewish foray into British culture, one made by a number of young British Jews whose backgrounds are, by their admission, relatively similar to those depicted in the film.[1] Rebecca Green and Lisa Ratner, daughters of two wealthy and well-known British Jewish businessmen, developed the story. As described by Mark Palmer in the *Daily Telegraph*, "Like Suzie, both Rebecca and Lisa have powerful, energetic fathers. Both have sisters who have married Jews. Both have memories of Friday night dinners, when cousins, aunts and uncles would feast on roast chicken and stereotypical Jewish conversation tit-bits."[2] Ric Cantor was brought in to direct, because, as Green notes, "He's Jewish and understands that world but also questions all of it."[3] Thus, from its inception, *Suzie Gold* is rooted in the desire of these young people to tell stories about the world they come from, linking its specificity to more universal themes of family and belonging. As Cantor states, the film is "about coming of age; about living in a world that's slightly different to the greater world around you."[4]

Balancing the desire for specificity and universality was not easy, Green noted:

> Doing a film about a Jewish family is trickier than it seems — it's a very sensitive issue. I think it's part of being Jewish, I mean I feel it myself — we have this paranoia that is ingrained . . . that's just sort of been handed down to you, you can't get away from it. . . . no — a lot of the Jewish members of the industry were scared. And I think certain Jewish people may have that reaction when they see the film, it's close to the bone, sometimes it can be uncomfortable.[5]

These comments help situate both the production of the film and my reading of it within the context of the production team's understanding of contemporary British Jewish life.

In a recent essay, I explored *Suzie Gold* in relation to two other contemporary British films, both of which were released around the same time and which also prominently featured Jewish girls.[6] Unlike *Suzie Gold*, in the two other films — *Me Without You* (2001) and *Starter for 10* (2006) — Jewishness was largely constructed outside of a narrative that included antisemitism or World War II; the Jews represented in those films appeared without any explicit markers of Jewishness that might connect them to those historic events or to the communities of diaspora that grew out of them.[7] In contrast, in *Suzie Gold*, Jews are represented as somewhat different, somewhat socially and culturally separate from other parts of British society; the film links that space of difference more explicitly (although not exclusively) to the experience of antisemitism, diaspora, and displacement that are a legacy of World War II and the Holocaust. In that first essay, I asked why contemporary British Jewishness seems to exist, cinematically, as one of these two opposing points on the spectrum of identity and assimilation and why all three of the young heroines of these films found desire and "the future" embodied in white, often working-class, gentile males. Here, in comparison, by taking a narrower focus, I ask how *Suzie Gold* produces British Jewishness, paying particular attention to the way British Jewish identities are produced in relation to World War II, the Holocaust, and the history and legacy of British antisemitism. These processes are not specific to the Jewish community in Britain, as they reflect wider social and historical changes; however, it is the filmmakers' choice to marry these processes to a story of British Jewish life that makes them so relevant here.

Jewish Girlhood and British Film

All three of the films explored in my aforementioned essay construct British Jewishness in an explicit fashion. These are not crypto-Jews whose Jewishness we have to labor diligently to extract from inference and inflection.[8] But beyond that point of similarity their representations diverge. For the young Jewish heroines of both *Starter for 10* and *Me Without You*, being Jewish is part of the way they are represented as understanding themselves. They talk about being Jewish, and Yiddish words and Jewish cultural symbols are used regularly if not extensively in each text.[9] However, these characters exist in a world where, as Jews, they are relatively exotic; their Jewishness is rendered as part of what makes them special, desirable, and different. They are part of a community, but that community is almost exclusively gentile. In these cinematic renderings of Britain, there is no history of antisemitism and little or no memory of World War II as part of what constructs the contemporary experience of modern British Jewry. It may be significant that both films take place, at least in part, at universities in the south of England (Bristol and Brighton), a region that typically lies at the heart of the English pastoral imagination, that is, in an Englishness that is not rooted in the mills of Manchester, the workshops of Birmingham, or the factories of the northeast, but in the village inn, the church, and the cricket pitch of rural southern England.[10]

Suzie Gold is different. In this cinematic world, being Jewish, while still represented as different and desirable from an outsider's perspective, is also represented as being part of a broader Jewish community. That is, Jewishness is represented not only through a vague constellation of historical figures, mannerisms, and symbols but also as a living community of actual Jews. In fact, in *Suzie Gold*, the Jewish community is represented as central to the construction, maintenance, and policing of Jewish identity. The Jewish community represented in this film—affluent, urban, entrepreneurial—is rooted not only in cultural stereotypes and symbols (although these are prolifically on display) but also in an explicitly articulated idea of maintaining connection through identity and difference, rooted at least in part in the British Jewish experience of modern Jewish diaspora, World War II, the Holocaust, and an ongoing fear of British antisemitism. As Nathan Abrams has argued, Jews have tended to adopt the dominant models of citizenship found in countries of migration: "In the United Kingdom, where citizenship has not warmly embraced the notion of the hyphenate identity . . . one is not and perhaps cannot even be . . . a Jewish-Briton."[11] As a closed identity, which is claimed to have always already been constituted, Englishness is never entirely open to Jews. The Jews of England, according to Philip Dodd, "were invited to take their place, and become spectators of a culture already complete and represented for them by its trustees."[12] For Jews, English antisemitism could be met in two ways: "to wholeheartedly embrace Britishness" or to "embrace humility as an assimilationist strategy. . . . This was essentially to keep one's head down."[13] Watching *Suzie Gold*, one feels this tension in action as Suzie struggles with her desire for connection and emancipation.

The Holocaust is evoked explicitly and deliberately in *Suzie Gold*. The first example of this referencing comes relatively early in the film, as part of a longer scene I discuss in more detail later in the chapter. In that scene, the Gold family and their friends, including many young adult children, gather for Friday night dinner. A discussion begins about which celebrities are Jewish and devolves into a diatribe about the dangers of intermarriage. Joyce (Frances Barber), a close friend of the Gold parents, responds to Suzie's suggestion that not all gentiles are antisemites with the following: "And what makes you so clever? My family didn't go to the gas chambers just so that you could decide to throw away your heritage. And what happens when everyone's married out? And then there's no Jews left?" This is a key moment in the way the audience is positioned to read the characters in this film. It frames our understanding of the Golds within contemporary conceptions of Jewish identities and communities — it makes them knowable or locatable in particular ways; for example, as people who belong to an insular community in which "marrying out" is not only seen as "wrong" but as potentially devastating to the community — and gives us insight into the resistance to her interfaith relationship Suzie later anticipates receiving. It is particularly important to note the explicit link that is made here between the Holocaust and intermarriage. First, survival is framed as an obligation not to "break faith." Second, intermarriage is framed as representing a reiteration or extension of the Holocaust, in which the ultimate goal of eliminating every last Jew might finally be realized. We can relate this to Emil Fackenheim's conceptualization of the need for a 614th commandment after Auschwitz; "to cease to be Jews (and to bring up Jewish children)," Fackenheim asserts, "would be to abandon our millennial post as witnesses to the God of history."[14] The imperative nature of these words is particularly resounding in the context of the decline of the British Jewish community by close to half between the mid-1940s and the middle of the first decade of the twenty-first century, when *Suzie Gold* was made.

Suzie Gold is part of a cycle of Anglo-American/British/Canadian romance narratives about young people from "ethnic" communities falling in love with people from the dominant white, Anglo community — a cycle that includes *Bend It Like Beckham* (2002), *My Big Fat Greek Wedding* (2002), *Touch of Pink* (2004), and *Kissing Jessica Stein* (2001) — which are critical of the first post–World War II or immigrant (read parental) generation.[15] Although not all of these films are about Jews, many of them share a representation of the parental generation as xenophobic, paralyzed by fear of community criticism and the memory of persecution.[16] Suzie's parents and their friends are represented as particularly grotesque in this film. Although the film is not much more generous in representing Suzie's friends, the narrative suggests that what is grotesque about the young people is rooted in the fears and aspirations that their parents have passed on to them.

Defining British Jewishness

Jon Stratton, in his excellent volume *Jews, Race, and Popular Music*, notes that the premiership of Margaret Thatcher (1975–1990) was a period that saw both the rise of multiculturalism in Britain and the broader visibility of Jews in political life.[17] Jews, he argues, were "model" minorities because they had learned to stay in the background and not call attention to themselves. As producers, they provided capital and structure for art and political life, rather than take to the spotlight themselves as performers. The invisibility of Jews is something Janell Metzger identifies as evidenced in the existence of known crypto-Jews in England even during the period following their expulsion (1290–1665).[18] As long as Jews used their wealth in the service of nation and kept their Jewishness private, they were tolerated. However, in the contemporary period, when immigrants and refugees are more numerous and more diverse in Britain, particularly those from the Caribbean and the Indian subcontinent, the once marked difference of Jewishness has faded, allowing Jews to pass.[19] It is the possibility of seeing Jews as "white" that has allowed this to happen.[20] Sander Gilman offers a reading of Zadie Smith's multicultural novel *White Teeth* (2000) that is illustrative here. The novel weaves a complex story at whose core is the question of whether immigrants and those with hybrid identities can attain that elusive status: "Englishness." One of the key families followed are the Chalfens, who are Jewish and of a higher class status than most of the other characters in the novel. While the Chalfens want to believe in their attainment of insider status, they, and even their son Joshua, are—via Simmel—"'sojourner' children who remain different, as [their] origin is in history, not in geography."[21] Gilman continues, Marcus Chalfen "is English, but only from his own perspective and that of the other multicultural figures"; he and those like him "do not really belong to the true corridors of power in this world."[22]

Jacqueline Rose takes up the historical dilemma of English Jewry in her reading of the following scene from Dorothy Richardson:

> "It is sad for me, this first meeting with English Jews."
>
> "Perhaps you can make Zionists of them."
>
> "That is absolutely impossible. . . . It is useless to talk to these people whose first pride is that they are *British* . . . . What they do not see is that they are not, and never can be, British; that the British do not accept them as such."
>
> . . .
>
> "*Never*. England can assimilate anything."
>
> "No nation can assimilate the Jew."[23]

Rose illustrates an interesting tension that is visible in the idea that Englishness is, on the one hand, a preexisting, always already known, bounded identity, something knowable, and usually collapsible, into whiteness, "Angloness," and Christianity, and, on the other hand, something that is open, changeable, or, at least, something into which one might assimilate. Nathan Abrams argues that "Nick Lambert's study of British-Jewish identity in the twenty-first century described Englishness as 'closed and native,' 'regional and ethnic.' . . . Englishness is depicted as more stable, but also as more closed to the Jews than Britishness. Englishness lives inside cricket results, village teas, soap operas, pub culture; 'the English' are emotionally distant, no-nonsense, understated, practical people, who are socially-correct, upright, sporting and gentlemanly."[24]

In *Suzie Gold* the British Jew is precluded from the full measure of English identity because Jewish identity is constructed in opposition to all things English: Jews being (represented as) overly emotional and dramatic, rather silly, overstated, impractical, impolite, overdressed and made up, ostentatious, unscrupulous, lazy, and rude.[25] It is worth noting again that, in general, the characters that most intensely embody these characteristics are the parents rather than the young adult characters; that is, Suzie's parents rather than Suzie herself. This characterization might suggest a generational shift, reflecting the point of view of the young Jews who are at helm of this project, in which the younger generation is becoming more English. But this shift is never complete, and the film itself, with its ambiguous ending, points to the ambivalence of Jewish assimilation in Britain even today. As Stratton offers, in his reading of British Jewish writer Linda Grant, "Grant remarks how remote the two generations are from each other. She means her own, fully English and assimilated . . . and her mother's generation. This she portrays as unsettled, 'those children of immigrants who had in their heads two worlds, the one they lived in and a partial, incomplete place that their parents handed on to them.'"[26] Stratton argues that Grant undermines this dichotomization when she herself slips into a discourse of genocidal anxiety characteristic of what she identifies as her mother's generation. And while the young characters in *Suzie Gold* are not portrayed as having this particular anxiety, they nonetheless appear to buy into many similar concerns: the fear of being persecuted, of the need for two Jewish parents to create Jewish children, and so on.

Postcolonial critic Homi Bhabha argues for a reading of the stereotype as characterized by ambivalence and excess, as "a complex, ambivalent, contradictory mode of representation, as anxious as it is assertive."[27] *Suzie Gold*'s representations of Jewish stereotypes present just such an ambivalence, moving constantly from the extremely crass to the thoughtful and moving. The sympathy exemplified in the invocation of the Holocaust is contradicted by the representation of Suzie's parents' generation through constant stereotypes of excess:[28] everything about them is too much, too loud, too big. And yet none of their wealth and success is enough to squelch the feeling that they do not belong, that gentiles are ultimately antisemitic, and that the end of their culture and community is right around the corner.[29] Their nouveau riche status reinforces the uncertainty of their position in a class-bound British society that frowns on Jews as parvenus, even in the early twenty-first century. Furthermore, given the decline in both numbers and observance of the postwar British Jewish community, their fears may very well feel justified. In contrast, the young(er) Jews are represented as either completely complacent in their assumption of the economic power won by their parents or equally entitled, but without any sense of their own intrinsic value. These young people have already inherited (or are in the midst of inheriting) their parents' class and social position. Because this system is represented as highly gendered, Suzie and her girlfriends' inheritance depends on their finding the right (Jewish) man. As Suzie articulates explicitly, "I mean, my best friend was about to slit her wrists because some boring, fat-assed lawyer wouldn't marry her. And Joanna hadn't eaten a meal in 18 months because some boring, fat-assed lawyer did marry her. . . . Something had to give."

Bhabha observes that "to be Anglicized is *emphatically* not to be English."[30] That is, just because a subject is colonized—and whether this colonization is effected through imperial conquest or by the arrival (often through forced migration) of various peoples to British soil—and has learned to become an exemplary mimic of the dominant culture, it does not mean that the subject has really become part of that culture. It suggests that in relation to British Jews, this has been expressed as a tension between conservative and liberal antisemitism: discourses of expulsion versus discourses of tolerance for the Other who can never be assimilated. In *Suzie Gold*, British Jewry can be read through a conservative paradigm of radical difference, where Jews are bad mimics and where the possibility of violent expressions of antisemitism (individual or more broadly) appears to lurk around every corner.

British Jewishness in the Wake of World War II

Suzie Gold strongly differentiates itself from many other film texts by representing Jews as members of a community. Jewishness is constructed not only through the individual and the single family, but as a multigenerational, close-knit, enclave-like community. It is a community in which Jewishness is constructed in relation to contemporary histories that include direct or familial experience of the Holocaust and a continued concern with antisemitism as a (perceived) reality for British Jews.

The text directs our attention to the centrality of both memories of World War II and continued fears of persecution in shaping the characters, their relationships to one another, and their community. It suggests that it is precisely these fears that push Suzie toward Darren; the insularity of the community, propelled by memories of the war, the Holocaust, and fears of antisemitism, creates a context that Suzie cannot help but want to escape. The stage is set in the opening scene—a flash-forward to Suzie's sister Sophie's wedding—and then cemented later over dinner. In the first scene, Suzie, in voice-over, explains, "This is my world. A world where everyone can be defined by which table they're at, at a wedding." She notes, "Out on the edges are C-list guests, the people with non-Jewish partners, the married-out table." It is a throwaway line at this point in the film, tucked into a rather long voice-over sequence and squeezed in among several other points about "young eligibles," kosher hypocrisy, and napkin rings.

The fact that the "married-outs" become C-list guests at family weddings and community events signals the boundaries of the British Jewish community to which Suzie belongs. Because the dominant form of affiliation depicted in the film is mainstream orthodoxy, as represented by the United Synagogue, those who have "married out" are marginalized and set apart, even if the married-out partner is female and hence her children remain Jewish. This also indicates how high the stakes may be for Suzie in her pursuit of Darren: she knows she may be ostracized by her family and community if things become serious with him. The fear of the C-list helps explain why Suzie is surprised to find herself attracted to Darren, is afraid to come clean to her friends and family, and is so willing to contemplate letting him go.

The C-list becomes a rather marginal fear, however, when a link is drawn between intermarriage and Jewish extermination. Here is the longer version of the scene described in the introduction to this chapter, one involving a conversation between Suzie's parents, Barbara (Rebecca Front) and Irving (Stanley Townsend) and their friends, Joyce and Leo Spencer (Steve Jameson) during a Friday night dinner at the Gold house:

> JOYCE: I read this week in the *Jewish Chronicle* that 3 out of 4 young people marry out now.
>
> BARBARA: It's terrible. I blame the parents.
>
> LEO: It's one thing marrying out; it's the children I feel sorry for, they don't know who they are or where they're going.
>
> JOYCE: It never works. There's no common ground. Oil and water don't mix.
>
> SUZIE: Well, what happens if you fall in love?
>
> JOYCE: Ha. Yes, and then when you fall out of love they're the first to turn 'round and call you "Jew."
>
> SUZIE: I don't think every non-Jew's antisemitic.
>
> JOYCE: And what makes you so clever? My family didn't go to the gas chambers just so that you could decide to throw away your heritage. And what happens when everyone's married out? And then there's no Jews left? [*She leaves, weeping.*]
>
> BARBARA: Are you happy now?
>
> SUZIE: What did I do?
>
> LEO: We just found out Danny is going out with a non-Jewish girl, and it looks serious.
>
> IRVING: I'm sorry. That's terrible.

This scene conveys the insularity of the North London community from which Suzie originates. In this world, Jews are only safe with other Jews, Jews only marry other Jews, and, in a stretch, Jews only know other Jews. Even more significantly, however, the scene suggests that love outside the bounds of faith is not only difficult ("oil and water") but ultimately a form of violence. Choosing intermarriage is compared to the extermination of the Jewish people, and, as mentioned earlier in this chapter, to Fackenheim's notion of the 614th commandment required of Jews after World War II. There is no space, in this worldview, for conceptualizing the child with one Jewish parent (even, it would seem, a Jewish mother) as Jewish or as being able to grow up with a strong sense of a Jewish self.

The scene creates a context for understanding the peculiarity of this British, Jewish space. Julia Magnet, an American living in London at the time of the film's release, noted, "Jewish culture is at the edge of British society. . . . There are plenty of Jews in London, though they keep a low profile."[31] She continues, "I believe this isolation is the dark subtext of the charming British comedy *Suzie Gold*."[32] Magnet notes that the long history of Jewish presence in Britain is eclipsed by the way Jews are represented in this film, their being taken up here as an exclusively immigrant (postwar) community. What is interesting, she observes, is that the anxieties that pervade *Suzie Gold* are ones expressed by Magnet's friends in London, who ask her such questions as, "Would you really marry a non-Jew? What would your parents say?" This dynamic, she claims, is not visible in mainstream American representations of Jewishness, pointing to the cultural specificity of this film as Britishly Jewish or Jewishly British. The xenophobic fears of the Jews in *Suzie Gold*, and the critique of the insularity it produces in the British Jewish community as represented here, is reiterated many times throughout the film.

In some ways, *Suzie Gold* is a story of three generations of British Jews defined in relation to World War II. Indeed, the movie seems to suggest, in focusing its attention on characters who are postwar immigrants to Britain — in contrast, it would seem, to the Jewish characters in other films, such as *Starter for 10* and *Me Without You* — that these characters and their behaviors are a direct effect of the legacies of the Holocaust.[33] As a gendered subject, Suzie is contrasted with her mother, Barbara, who exemplifies the stereotype of the Jewish mother as loud, nasty, pampered, controlling, and shrewish. Although not entirely one-dimensional, she is ultimately presented as caring more about appearances than about her daughter's happiness. Indeed, the women of Suzie's mother's generation are largely portrayed as emerging from this mold. Frances Barber as Joyce Spencer is always overdressed, garishly made up, with her clothes overly tight and her breasts spilling out. In one scene, after discovering she is having an affair with his best friend, her husband kicks her into their lavishly appointed swimming pool as she speaks into her mobile phone. The father and other men of that generation are equally true to stereotype: loud, unattractive, heavy, hirsute, garish, cigar-smoking, and uncouth.

The next generation fares little better, largely represented as obsessed with money and status and with finding suitable mates to continue not culture but lifestyle. Anthony Silver, for example, explicitly describes marriage as a merger between corporations.[34] The girls are represented as having few aspirations beyond being married to men as wealthy as (or wealthier than) their fathers. The need to be married to find one's place in the social order (the A-list alluded to in the first scene of the film) is represented as the central quest in the life of young Jews, particularly young women. Suzie's best friend, Debbie Levine (Sophie Winkleman)—whose brother Richard (Daniel Mendoza) is marrying Suzie's sister Sophie (Ariana Fraval)—frames the fear of waiting for her lawyer boyfriend to propose thus: "I'm now twenty-three, time is running out, my tits will be on the floor, out the window and down the high street, and into the bagel shop." Debbie constructs herself primarily as a body with the horrifying expiration date of age twenty-three. The anxiety of expiring (another metaphor for annihilation in the film) is something that these girls share with their parents, something that undergirds the grotesque stereotypes of Jewish identity they perform. Suzie is constructed through and against these types: she is the gentle Jewish princess, composed and with style, striking out beyond the confines of the world her parents built and of which her sister and friends are so desperate to be a part.[35]

If Jewish stereotypes are located most explicitly in the first generation of British Jews born and/or raised after the Holocaust, and these stereotypes are shown to have trickled down into the second generation, the immigrant generation largely escapes these characterizations in the film. Suzie's Nana Sadie (Miriam Karlin) represents the generation of Holocaust refugees. She comes from Poland, speaks with a strong Yiddish accent, and offers a familiar continuity with other images of the *Yiddische Mama*.[36] Sadie is represented, in large measure, as genteel and sophisticated. She is aspirational, but in an equal-opportunity way. Sadie, the Polish immigrant, has bourgeois aspirations for her granddaughter, in that she imagines her access to education and career as offering a route to freedom and emancipation that is represented as being of little value to Suzie's parents, siblings, or friends. While the world Sadie grew up in has disappeared, that world appears to have provided her with a sense of Jewish selfhood and identity that is not brutalized by fear. This is something that could not be transmitted to her children's generation, even though they were born in the relative safety of British citizenship and (ostensible, legal) belonging. And it is also worth considering that the parents, who are represented as a grasping, venal generation, provide a commentary on the generation most closely associated with Margaret Thatcher's Britain. Their children, raised on the legacies of loss *and* of Thatcherism but outside them, are the ones the film holds out as the hope for the future.

Sadie is a marker of an Ashkenazi Jewish past that is transnational in character. Her voice is a Yiddish voice — she mentions several times the Yiddish inflection she retains and how she only leaned to say "Shabbat" (rather than "*Shabbes*") when she came to England — a voice without the northwest London inflection of the other Jewish characters. At her funeral, the rabbi says, "She once told me she so wished that she could see her family that never made it out of Poland. Well Sadie, now you can." Sadie's loss is specifically linked to antisemitic violence and the Holocaust. It is Sadie's death that moves Suzie to break up with Darren and go back to Anthony, the boy who represents the safety and familiarity of her community. But *Suzie Gold* resists a reading in which the audience would laud Suzie's choice of Anthony. The film positions Darren as a better lover and a better person (with a better family) than Anthony. It suggests, ultimately, that Suzie will only grow into the best person she can be if she moves outside of the gilded enclave in which she was raised and finds a truer and more complicated sense of her British Jewish self.

Jewish Girl as Jewish Princess

In one of the early scenes in the film, we find ourselves at the Gold family's huge North London home. Suzie intones in voice-over, "My sister had just announced her engagement, which meant I was going to be left on the shelf . . . forever. But that Friday night things were looking up . . . you see, the Silvers were coming for dinner. And rumor had it Anti was back in town." Anti is Anthony Silver, London's most desirable Jewish bachelor, on whose shoulders Suzie's hopes for a wedding of her own reside, as well as the community's hopes for its future continuity in the wake of the postwar decline in numbers. Sue Vice suggests the importance of the voice-over, of whose voice frames the narrative.[37] In *Suzie Gold*, it is Suzie's voice that guides our reading. Suzie's lengthy opening monologue takes us on a tour of the sociopolitics of a London Jewish wedding, explaining, "This is my world. A world where everyone can be defined by which table they're at, at a wedding." In Suzie's demeanor, and her inner monologues, we see her "fit" into this world, as well as her increasing confusion as she struggles to navigate her ambivalent desire to remain part of and yet to leave the only world she has ever known. The key figure in this ambivalence is Darren, the young non-Jewish man Suzie meets at her first job at a TV studio soon after the night of the fateful Shabbat dinner described earlier. Her feelings for Darren — a man we are told often she should not desire — are what open the gate for her to begin to question whether she truly wants to fit so seamlessly into the world of her childhood and young adulthood.

What appears to initiate Suzie and Darren's desire for each other is difference. Not just Suzie's curiosity about Darren as an outsider from her sheltered community, but his curiosity about her:

> SUZIE: Okay, I've got one for you. Rachel, Monica, or Phoebe?
> DARREN: From *Friends*, yeah? Okay. Kill Monica? Shag Phoebe and marry Rachel.
> SUZIE: You'd marry the spoiled Jewish princess?
> DARREN: Yeah, then I could shag her every day.

This moment draws our attention to the centrality of American popular television as a language through which identities are transnationally and transethnically constructed. It is startling (or it was to this viewer) that Darren immediately knows what Suzie is asking. His comment about Rachel's desirability offers a counter discourse to the assumption that "Jewish princesses" are not desirable. While Suzie's comment appears to be flippant, I wonder: Is she testing him to see if he picks Rachel, who she knows is "like her"? Does she assume he will not recognize Rachel or herself as Jewish (princesses)? Darren's reaction surprises Suzie because it suggests that Rachel's identity is visible and knowable even to him (someone without insider knowledge) and might, in fact, be part of her appeal.

If the Jewish princess is as exotic as an episode of *Friends*, to the somewhat cloistered Suzie, it is Darren who appears exotic.[38] When her best friend, Debbie, finds out about their relationship, the following exchange takes place:

DEBBIE: Well, I want to pause for one second. Where is this going with this guy? What happens if it gets serious? Your parents will go mental.

SUZIE: My parents are not going to find out. And you're not going to tell anyone. I've got enough on my plate right now without the whole family finding out.

DEBBIE: Well, when the foreskin fetish has worn off and you're sitting in your Wallace cardigan in your council flat with your six snotty-nosed kids waiting for some *goyische* [non-Jewish] fella to come back from the pub and beat you up . . . I'll try very hard not to say "I told you so."

Debbie explicitly frames Suzie's attraction to Darren as desire for the Other ("foreskin festish"). But this sexuality is also linked to stereotypical characteristics associated with the white British underclass ("Wallace cardigan," "council flat") and its gender role stereotypes (alcoholism and domestic abuse). Debbie implies that while Darren might be able to provide for her sexually, he cannot provide the princess with the type of bourgeois life to which she is accustomed. How could any life with Darren compare with the life Suzie could have with Anthony Silver?

There are two things Anthony cannot offer Suzie. One is good sex (and a foreskin); the other is a glimpse of life outside her "gilded ghetto." It is Darren who offers a glimmer of a different life. About halfway through the film he takes Suzie to his mother's home, an apartment in a high-rise block of flats. His mother (Gwyneth Strong) is quite young looking, casual, and not made up; there is no father. The scene is clearly intended to offer a stark contrast between Darren's family and Suzie's, contrasting the strong family-centered nucleus of Jewish life with the fatherless mode of the British underclass. However, undercutting this stereotype is Darren's mother, who has cooked a vegetarian meal because she is unsure whether "Suzie practiced kosher or not." The fact that Darren's mother knows that Suzie is Jewish (and possibly observant), knows about kashrut, and is both comfortable and willing to go out of her way to make Suzie feel comfortable is decidedly different from the depiction of Suzie's family and circle of friends. Here it is the "immigrant" family that is represented as unwilling to tolerate difference, which is confirmed by the South Asian wife (Pooja Shah) of Darren's brother (Nick Haverson), who suggests that she also finds Darren's family nicer and more accepting than her own.[39] Where Darren's mother makes Suzie vegetarian food, Suzie's mother calls Darren a "yobbo," and her best friend assumes that marrying him is equal to a life of loneliness, tedium, and squalor. This representation is significant because it goes against the grain; it is usually the gentile family that is constructed as cold and unwelcoming, as we have seen in previous chapters, with regard to Jack Rosenthal's *The Evacuees*.

The problem of Suzie's simultaneous desire for continuity and for change, to be the dutiful daughter while also finding herself, remains an unresolvable tension in this film. The tension is perhaps most visible in the Yom Kippur scene. Suzie is sitting in the women's section of the Orthodox synagogue she attends with her family, which is located in an upstairs gallery. She imagines she sees Darren walk in and attempt to blow the shofar. Of course he fails. Suzie looks away but looks back when she hears the shofar being blown by Anthony. As Suzie admits, "Going out with Anthony was like coming home. . . . This was real. It wasn't a fantasy." But in fact Anthony is a fantasy, as Suzie herself admits; he is "the kind of boy I imagined I'd end up with . . . when I was twelve." Anthony is presented as the fantasy of convention, the fantasy of a young girl and not a woman. But the film also refuses Suzie a fantasy in which Darren enters the synagogue and blows the shofar, which would have hinted at his ripeness for conversion and her world's acceptance of him through his ultimate assimilability.

Suzie wants to escape her family's overbearing demands for her conformity but not her own identity. She is burdened by the specific parameters that her family and community have established for her happiness, by the only blueprint they seem to have for the way to live her life. In *Suzie Gold*, desire for what is different from the self underscores a desire for distance from one's own intrinsic Otherness. Marriage into the dominant order is often represented as a desire for assimilation. But Suzie is not assimilationist; she is in no great rush to abandon her name and what that name represents or to relinquish her ties to the customs of her community. In her willingness to explore her desire for Darren, she begins to rewrite the boundaries of her own Jewishness, of what is possible within that identity.

In similar films containing interethnic romance narratives, the romance plot underscores "the coincidence of happy objects."[40] In *Suzie Gold* desire is almost exclusively linked to the romance plot. There is nothing apparent that Suzie wants, aside from being free to choose Darren over Anthony. Suzie does not appear to even dream in broader categories. Her grandmother's allegory about Suzie's choice between Darren and Anthony—"Life is complicated. When you put on a red dress you feel different than when you put on navy trousers. The important thing is how you feel with no clothes on."—does not appear to sink in. Maybe Suzie cannot imagine herself naked, that is, as a self whose mastery comes from within rather than through subjection to the lover or Other. Her character is not offered a narrative complicated by a third choice, one that stands outside of romance. In other films the romance narrative is an anchor and ultimately offers pleasurable resolution, but desire is not limited to that sphere, the girls want more, and that more is presented as central to their happiness and growth.[41] For Suzie, by contrast, her most essential and enduring characteristic is ambivalence.

The ambivalence Suzie feels and embodies is reflected in the filmmakers' choice to deny us a glimpse of Suzie's future. While she ultimately refuses to marry Anthony and confronts her parents about Darren, the last scene shows her at the door, outside of the pub (as if realizing Debbie's class-prejudiced prediction) where Darren is with his friends. This is quite different from the resolution offered in other films about interethnic romance. In *Bend It Like Beckham*, for example, the film ends not with the image of Jas (Parminder Nagra) and her Irish boyfriend, Joe (Jonathan Rhys Meyers) kissing in front of her parents, but with the image of that boyfriend with Jas's father (Anupam Kher) and other members of the Sikh community, playing cricket. The film implies a shift in the community that will allow space for Jas to have a relationship with Joe without the dissolution of Jas's connection to her family and culture of origin. Likewise, in *My Big Fat Greek Wedding*, it is the WASP Ian (John Corbett) who converts to the Greek Orthodox Church and whose family is ultimately assimilated into the world of his Greek in-laws. The film ends not with the wedding but with Toula (Nia Vardalos) and Ian living next door to Toula's parents and Ian encouraging their daughter off to Greek school. No such ending is intimated in *Suzie Gold*, suggesting that the union of Jew and gentile, within the context of British Jewry, is still not quite within the realm of representation.

In *Suzie Gold*, love and cultural hybridity—which comes from leaving one's community or family of origin without abandoning them or cutting ties completely—are positioned as the pivot points around which good feelings potentially spring.[42] Because this is in large measure a romance narrative, as well as a coming-of-age story, good feelings come from making the right choice in a romantic partner. But the freedom to make this choice and the consequences of doing so are different for Suzie than for many Jewish characters in other films because her Jewish identity is so closely tied to a deeply connected, insular community. For Suzie, intermarriage is a huge risk. At the same time, in *Suzie Gold* marriage to the "right" — read Jewish — boy is represented as the lesser of the choices offered, the one that offers less freedom, less optimism, less growth.

While there are moments of warmth and pathos between members of the Gold family and those close to them, the film ultimately suggests that the best choice for Suzie and other members of her generation is one that leads beyond the exclusive walls of their community — toward the Darrens, not the Anthonys — without in any way suggesting that they ought to jettison their Jewish identities, families, or communities in doing so.

Jewishness in *Suzie Gold* is rooted in the specificity of British Jewish history and cultural experience. Perhaps the most significant thing about the film is that it produces a world in which Jewishness is anchored explicitly to the past, in particular Jewish survival and continuity in the wake of the Holocaust and post–World War II decline. In *Suzie Gold*, we have the urban enclave and resounding stereotypes of what almost feels like an earlier generation of American cinematic representation. Indeed, the film suggests that residual fears of persecution and memories of genocide are central to the production and reproduction of the community itself and perhaps account for its most toxic stereotypes. In this way, the Jews of *Suzie Gold* locate themselves within a model of conservative antisemitism, in which the possibility of expulsion and extermination remains ever present.

Notes

The author would like to thank the Social Sciences and Humanities Research Council of Canada (SSHRC) for its ongoing support of her work, as well as the blind reviewers of this essay and Nathan Abrams, patient and generous editor always.

1. Caroline Westbrook, "There's Something about Suzie," *Something Jewish*, last modified March 2, 2004, accessed November 3, 2015, http://www.somethingjewish.co.uk/articles/848_there_s_something_ab.htm.

2. Mark Palmer, "'British Jews Need to Laugh at Themselves,'" *Daily Telegraph*, March 1, 2004., http://www.telegraph.co.uk.

3. Rebecca Green quoted in "Suzie Gold," *The Writing Studio.*, accessed March 28, 2014, (article no longer available).

4. Ric Cantor quoted ibid.

5. Rebecca Green quoted in Westbrook, "Something about Suzie."

6. Michele Byers, "Jewish Girls in British Cinema," *Journal of European Popular Culture* 3, no. 2 (2012): 169–80.

7. *Me Without You*, directed by Sandra Goldbacher (London: Fireworks Pictures, 2001); *Starter for 10*. directed by Tom Vaughn (London: BBC Films, 2006).

8. See, for example, Maurice Berger, "The Mouse that Never Roars: Jewish Masculinity on American Television," in *Too Jewish? Challenging Traditional Identities*, edited by Norman L. Kleeblatt, 93–107 (New York: Jewish Museum; New Brunswick, N.J.: Rutgers University Press, 1996); Vincent Brook, *Something Ain't Kosher Here: The Rise of the "Jewish" Sitcom* (New Brunswick, N.J.: Rutgers University Press, 2003); David Zurawik, *The Jews of Prime Time* (Hanover: Brandeis and UPNE, 2003).

9. Rosalin Krieger, "'Does He Actually Say the Word Jewish?'—Jewish Representations in *Seinfeld*," *Journal for Cultural Research* 7, no. 4 (2003): 387–404.

10. Nathan Abrams, personal communication, August 13, 2013.

11. Nathan Abrams, "Hidden: Jewish Film in the United Kingdom, past and present," *Journal of European Popular Culture* 1, no. 1 (2010), 59.

12. Philip Dodd, "Englishness and the National Culture," in *Englishness and Culture 1880–1920*, edited by Robert Colls and Philip Dodd, 22 (London: Croom Helm, 1986). See also Bryan Cheyette, "'Ineffable and Usable': Towards a Diasporic British-Jewish Writing," *Textual Practice* 10, no. 2 (1996): 295–313.

13. Abrams, "Hidden," 61–62.

14. Emil Fackenheim, "The 614th Commandment" (1967), in *The Jewish Thought of Emil Fackenheim: A Reader*, edited by Michael L. Morgan, 157–60 (Detroit: Wayne State University Press, 1987), 158.

15. *Bend It Like Beckham*, directed by Gurinder Chadha (USA: Kintop Pictures (presents), London: The Film Council (in association with), Hamburg: FilmFoerderung Hamburg (in association with) 2002); *My Big Fat Greek Wedding*, directed by Nia Vardalos (USA: Gold Circle Films, 2002); *Touch of Pink*, directed by Ian Iqbal Rashid (Iver Heath: Martin Pope Productions, Toronto: Sienna Films, 2004); *Kissing Jessica Stein*, directed by Charles Herman-Wurmfeld (Hollywood: Fox Searchlight Pictures, 2001).

16. *Kissing Jessica Stein*, the other film listed here in which the title character is Jewish, breaks with this tradition. Although the mother here is not altogether different from the mother in *Suzie Gold* (physically, and in terms of style of dress and hair, they are really quite similar), the mother in *Kissing Jessica Stein* is much more refined and insists on her desire for Jessica to be happy, whether that means being with a gentile woman or a Jewish man.

17. John Stratton, *Jews, Race, and Popular Music* (Farnham, U.K.: Ashgate, 2009).

18. Mary Janell Metzger, "'Now by My Hood, a Gentle and No Jew': Jessica, *The Merchant of Venice*, and the Discourse of Early Modern English Identity," *PMLA* 113, no.1 (1998): 52–63.

19. At the same time, and as a consequence, Jews are allowed to publicly claim and even showcase their difference to demonstrate the tolerance of the nation, diverting attention away from practices of intolerance aimed at other marginalized groups.

20. See, for example, Sander Gilman, *Multiculturalism and the Jews* (New York: Routledge, 2006).

21. Georg Simmel quoted ibid., 161.

22. Ibid., 161, 159.

23. Jacqueline Rose, "Dorothy Richardson and the Jew," in Cheyette, *Between "Race" and Culture*, 123.

24. Abrams, "Hidden," 60.

25. The film's director himself makes this point: "Americans and Jewish people have something in common in that they're not polite and reserved in an English way, they're loud and cheeky." See Byers, "Jewish Girls in British Cinema."

26. Jon Stratton, *Coming Out Jewish* (London: Routledge, 2000), 91.

27. Homi Bhabha, *The Location of Culture* (London: Routledge, 1994), 70.

28. Given the time frame of the film, we can assume these Jews are mostly British/ postwar born.

29. Given the decline in both in-marriage and observance, it is possible to read this last, at least, as a real fear for a community that defines itself in these ways.

30. Bhabha, *Location of Culture*, 87, emphasis in the original.

31. Julia Magnet, "You're Strictly a London Girl, Suzie Gold, You'd Be a Foreigner in New York," *Times* (London), March 15, 2004.

32. Ibid.

33. Whether all the characters are meant to be first- and second-generation British born is unclear. However, much is made of Suzie's grandmother Sadie (her father's mother) who talks about immigrating to England and speaks with a Yiddish accent.

34. When he asks Irving if he can marry Suzie, the first thing Irving does is ask if he will get a break on the catering, given that Anthony and his family run the business.

35. Please note that I use the term "Jewish princess" deliberately and with a full understanding of the problematic nature of the term, having written about it elsewhere. See Michele Byers, "The Pariah Princess: Agency, Representation, and Neoliberal Jewish Girlhood," *Girlhood Studies: An Interdisciplinary Journal* 2, no. 2 (2009): 33–54; "Bat Mitzvah," in *Girl Culture: An Encyclopedia*, vol. 1, edited by Claudia Mitchell and Jacqueline Reid-Walsh, 165–69 (Santa Barbara, Calif.: Greenwood Press, 2008); "Not Just a Princess: Beyond the JAP in Jewish Girlhood," *Conference Summary Report: What Are We Holding in Our Hands Now?* (Montreal: PowerCamp National/ Filles d'Actions, 2004), 63–65. The literature on the Jewish princess as a particularly raced, classed, and gendered cultural stereotype is extensive; most notable is the work of Riv-Ellen Prell, in particular her *Fighting to Become Americans* (Boston, Mass.: Beacon Press, 1999). I would also note that the script of *Suzie Gold* explicitly invokes the specter of the Jewish princess, linking it to American culture via the invocation of the TV sitcom *Friends*—discussed in this chapter—but also in the way that Suzie and her girlfriends are constructed in the film. As I have written elsewhere, drawing on the work of Alana Newhouse, the princess figure, today, is more marked by ambivalence than derision, and Jewish girls may choose quite consciously to cultivate this persona rather than see it as something imposed upon them by others. See Alana Newhouse, "The Return of the JAP," *Boston Globe*, March 13, 2005, and "The JAP: Reclaim Her or Reject Her?" *Lilith* 30, no. 2 (2005): 28–39; Rhonda Lieberman, "Jewish Barbie," in Kleeblatt, *Too Jewish?* 108–14.

36. Joyce Antler, *You Never Call! You Never Write! A History of the Jewish Mother* (Oxford: Oxford University Press, 2008).

37. Sue Vice, *Jack Rosenthal* (Manchester, U.K.: Manchester University Press, 2009).

38. *Friends* (Los Angeles: Warner Bros. Television, 1994–2004).

39. It is worth noting that "Darren" appears to have been a name chosen intentionally, as marking a Jew's idea of a very working-class British name.

40. Sara Ahmed, "Happy Objects," in *The Affect Theory Reader*, edited by M. Gregg and G. J. Seigworth, 29–51 (Durham, N.C.: Duke University Press, 2010), 46.

41. Ibid.

42. Ibid.

SUE VICE

Christmas Trees and Hanukkah Bushes

The "Emancipation Contract" in the Contemporary British Television Dramas Hebburn *and* Friday Night Dinner

In "Kosher," an episode of the BBC Radio 4 radio sitcom *House on Fire* (2010–13),[1] the hapless Matt South (Jody Latham) decides that he wants to convert to Judaism. Matt's wish is inspired by the apparently happy-go-lucky, song-filled life of Tevye (Topol) in *Fiddler on the Roof* (1971).[2] He is driven to watch the movie by his distaste for the reality television show *The Great British Bake-Off*,[3] in which everyone else in his family is engrossed and which he clearly considers unexcitingly middle-of-the-road in terms of ethnicity as well as class. Indeed, it is their immersion in this show that results in Matt's parents' lack of concern at their son's decision, which he announces enthusiastically while they are watching it:

> MATT: I've become a Jew!
> MUM (Janine Duvitski): That's nice, dear.

Yet, although he throws out the nonkosher food of his housemate (Emma Pierson) and disables the household electrics on Fridays to observe Shabbat, the episode's punch line is that Matt cannot go through with his stated wish to become a Jew. This is because, in order to do so, he would have to be circumcised. While the "conversion of the Jews" may no longer be a central element in the project of English self-definition, as Michael Ragussis argues is the case in nineteenth-century society and literature,[4] the reverse transformation, of Englishman into Jew, is still too dangerous to be represented here. Such a conversion is a threat that would represent too permanent a change in the static world of a sitcom, which the BBC guidelines for prospective writers describe as taking place "in a set-up that remains unchanged" throughout its run,[5] as well as a dangerous blurring of identity boundaries in the plot. The comedy of Matt's mother's low-key, and stereotypically English, response to her son's declaration lies precisely in its failure to react adequately to such a threat.

Through the trope of conversion, then, "Kosher" raises issues about the encounters between Jewishness and Britishness in contemporary U.K. television drama that will be my focus. Specifically, I will explore two series that enact the relationship between Jewish and non-Jewish Britons from opposite perspectives. In both programs, the clash between a tolerance that entails ignorance on the British side and assimilated difference on that of the Jewish is represented to comic effect. Whereas *Hebburn* concerns the introduction of the protagonist's Jewish wife to his Catholic family, *Friday Night Dinner* (*FND*) is, in part, about a Jewish family as viewed by its non-Jewish neighbor. Both series register the implications of a contemporary "emancipation contract" established between a host nation and its Jewish citizens, which offers the promise of full membership in exchange for assimilation.[6] Underlying these encounters is evidence of evolving British Jewish cultural formations, as well as the "indelible" memory of recent European Jewish history.[7]

Where earlier representations of Jews in British society emphasized "painful tensions" rather than "harmonious fusions,"[8] *Hebburn* and *FND* humorously exploit tensions and eschew fusions, such that their acknowledgement of any underlying pain is represented more obliquely. Similarly, in the "Kosher" episode of the radio drama *House on Fire*, explicit confrontation between Britishness and Jewishness is itself the source of comedy, apparent in such details as Matt using a paper doily to cover his head since he does not possess a yarmulke. Any suggestion of alien religious fervor in the invocation of a yarmulke is tempered here by the presence of the doily, an archaic signifier of British "suburban gentility" but one which (surely unbeknownst to Matt) British Jewry has itself adopted, perhaps to signal a Jewish arrival in both class and assimilatory terms.[9] "Kosher" offers an image of Judaism and Jewishness that does not take the form of religion or ethnicity, and the non-Jewish characters do not respond to it as such. Instead, Jewishness is incorporated into the more familiar discourses of class stratification and social nuance, the comedy arising from their transgression. Thus British uncertainty about how to respond to Jews takes on the accidental appearance of "postethnicity" by detaching Jewishness from conceptions of racial difference.[10] Even in those examples where a self-contained, self-defining Jewish world is represented in television drama — for instance, in Simon Amstell's series *Grandma's House* and Jack Rosenthal's earlier play *Bar Mitzvah Boy* — references to historical or political realities such as the Holocaust and the State of Israel appear in only minimal form, including instances where, as in Rosenthal's play *The Evacuees*,[11] the action takes place during World War II. However, various kinds of reference to the wartime Jewish tragedy appear in all the examples under discussion here, including "Kosher," where Matt's wish to embrace the apparently joyful shtetl life of Tevye is based on what could be called a "fetishistic" narrative. Matt has unquestioningly accepted the rose-tinted version of Jewish existence in czarist Russia represented in *Fiddler on the Roof*, although the film hints at the loss of traditional ways of life and represents the violence of pogroms and expulsion. Yet Matt has "expunged" any awareness of these "traces of the trauma or loss that called the narrative into being in the first place," in Eric Santner's phrasing.[12] Indeed, Primo Levi invokes the shtetl figure of Tevye as the very embodiment of historical rupture in his collection of essays *The Search for Roots*. There he argues, of Sholem Aleichem's original nineteenth-century short story "Tevye the Milkman" on which *Fiddler on the Roof* is based, that "Tevye exists no longer: the gas of Auschwitz and Stalin's camps have destroyed him."[13] The humor in "Kosher" relies on Matt's substituting temporary enthusiasm about Judaism for knowledge or conviction, and his disavowing any knowledge of antisemitism forms as much a part of such substitution as does his overlooking the religious imperative of circumcision.

Similar structures are evident in *FND* and *Hebburn* in relation to the threat of conversion and the repudiation of genocide, respectively. In *FND*, the eager insistence by the non-Jewish Jim (Mark Heap) that, using a comically old-fashioned British term of praise, Judaism is a "super" religion, is followed by his fervent, "How do I join?" — a question treated as thoroughly rhetorical by his neighbors, the Goodman family, and the audience alike. In *Hebburn*, Pauline Pearson (Gina McKee) is mortified to be found cooking bacon when she learns that her daughter-in-law Sarah (Kimberley Nixon) is Jewish, and insists, over a close-up of an overflowing frying pan, that the "forbidden" smell of bacon be wafted away: "Her people have been through enough," she says reproachfully to her husband, Joe (Jim Moir), at the stove. This apparent hint at the reality of millennia of persecution is acknowledged, only to be dispelled by a reversion to the topic of food, as Pauline instructs Joe to make Sarah feel at home by creating bagels for her that are, as their daughter Vicki (Lisa McGrillis) exclaims, just "buns with the middles cut out." Yet the specific referent of Pauline's reproach, what exactly it is that Sarah's people have "been through," is left comically vague. This signals Pauline's own uncertainty about the detail of Jewish history and allows her remark to refer to a "lachrymose" conception of Jewish history in general, to the Holocaust, and even to the history of the Jews of Britain, since Sarah's hometown is York, the site of a massacre in 1190 that is "the most notorious anti-Jewish atrocity" in British history.[14]

While subliminal reference to Jewish history and invocation of Jewish stereotypes occur in *Hebburn* on the part of the gentile characters, in *FND* the Jewish characters reveal their location between two narratives: a history of Holocaust genocide and loss versus the British national myth of wartime triumph. In each of the examples that follow, I will analyze how Jewishness and Britishness are shown to interact and how comedy arises from both their copresence and their difference. While British "tolerance"[15] may be present in Mrs. South's response to her son's declaration of Jewishness in "Kosher," it also resounds with the lack of awareness and confusion on the part of non-Jewish Britons that serve as the source of comedy in *Hebburn* and *FND*. Such obliviousness to Jewish difference can be seen as a contemporary legacy of the British "emancipation contract," a milder local version of the "assimilatory pressure" exerted on Jews as they gradually attained legal equality elsewhere in Europe in the eighteenth and nineteenth centuries, accompanied by "resentment" when assimilation was not sufficiently thorough.[16] In both these television series, Jewishness is made manifest most clearly not on its own terms but when it comes into contact with non-Jewish Englishness. Although the non-Jewish characters who encounter their Jewish in-laws and neighbors react with delighted amazement to their presence, their very surprise and the degree of their unfamiliarity with Judaism testify to a barely formulated suspicion that these close Jewish associates might not really be "English at heart."[17]

"She's Jewish, for Christ's Sake!": *Hebburn*

Hebburn is set in the eponymous small town on England's northeast coast near the city of Newcastle, and it focuses on the situation comedy staples of family interaction alongside class and regional difference. Since losing his job in Manchester, the series' protagonist Jack Pearson (Chris Ramsey) has returned to live with his parents, thus introducing those elements of entrapment and thwarted aspiration that have long characterized British sitcoms.[18] Yet *Hebburn*'s apparently conventional format includes an unusual element in the form of Jack also bringing his Jewish and middle-class wife, Sarah, to live with his Catholic and working-class family. For the series' writer, Jason Cook, such an overdetermined clash of cultures was simply "a useful comic device."[19] Sarah is not in herself a figure of fun, since "The real comedy comes with how people cope with her"[20]: here, "people" is taken to mean the non-Jewish local residents. The elements of food, "foreign" discourse, and circumcision are taken to sum up Judaism in *Hebburn*, just as they were in the "Kosher" episode of *House on Fire*. Indeed, Sarah's identity offers the occasion for the appearance of the British sitcom features of misunderstanding, talking at cross-purposes, double entendres, and social gaffes. This structure also appears in *Friday Night Dinner*, as we shall see, where the non-Jewish Jim cannot distinguish the Goodman family's eccentric habits from religious rites. Thus in both cases, the British sitcom format is filled with a Jewish content.

The phlegmatic response to the specter of Jewishness on the part of Matt's mother in "Kosher" is also evident in that of Jack's mother, Pauline, in *Hebburn*. Pauline is relieved to learn that Sarah's reason for refusing an offer of a bacon sandwich is because she is Jewish rather than a vegetarian: "we're in the clear—she can stay," Pauline says, as if to reassure the viewer that on this occasion rejection is reserved for others. The Pearsons' response to Sarah is presented in terms of a montage of clichés, each of which is subverted within the narrative, often without Sarah herself being required to answer back. On hearing that Sarah's parents sell shoes, Pauline wonders if they "live above the shop" and whether Sarah will "get extra points" for putting a cup of tea on a coaster featuring the pope's face, implying that this religious symbol for her Catholic hosts is target practice for Sarah. Pauline's remarks reveal anachronistic thinking and a blurring of Judaism with Protestantism: her image of the shopkeeper who lives on the premises comes from an earlier period of Jewish life in Britain,[21] while her assumption of antipapal sentiment is one drawn from Christian sectarian conflict. Pauline's persistence in seeing religious difference in terms of the sporting rivalry of "points" continues when she asks Sarah whether Jack will have to "convert to your side"; and she expresses concern that her husband's heart is unlikely to be able to "take [Jack] being circumvented." Thus the audience here, Jewish and non-Jewish alike, is invited to share Sarah's perspective, such that it is the gentile Pauline who is the object of the jokes, and within the narrative even her own family is amused by her malapropism for "circumcised." This is gentle irony at Pauline's expense, since we know that she considers Sarah's Jewishness to be "wonderful" and is simply motivated by "panic about not knowing anything about Judaism"[22] — although enough to invoke once more the trope of circumcision as a figure for conversion's impossibility. The implied spectator is one who is sufficiently familiar with the details of Jewish life to be able to recognize Pauline's errors, implying that such an extreme confusion arising from the emancipation contract's imperative of Jewish assimilation is perhaps outmoded.

The younger generation of Hebburn's local residents — those "people" whose ability to "cope" with Sarah is initially the series' comic core — embark on different kinds of misunderstanding in their relation to her. Each instance is predicated on the recognition of difference alongside the inability to understand its significance. In place of Pauline's food-related efforts, Jack's sister Vicki and his former girlfriend Denise (Victoria Elliott) identify Jewishness with sexuality. While Vicki wonders if a former boyfriend's distinctive private parts are enough to make him "proper kosher," Denise greets the news of Sarah's Jewishness with a question to Jack that implies her religious allegiance is his sexual preference: "Is that what you're into these days?" Confusion on the part of both women — Vicki claims never to have met anyone "fully Jewish" before — means simply that their own concerns are expressed by means of this new notion. On their second meeting, Denise's question to Sarah, "Are you still Jewish?" accidentally implies a utopian mutability, in its expression of a wish that such a change on Sarah's part might cause Jack to lose interest in her and be free for Denise again. Such unexpected versions of stock responses are also evident in relation to Sarah's sister (Verity-May

Henry), who has changed her name from Miriam to Marial. This might suggest a wish to hide her name's Hebraic origins but seems rather to be a choice made to fit her hippie lifestyle.[23] Denise's question to Marial, "Are you Jewish too?" is equally double-voiced. Its humor lies in Denise's seemingly postethnic failure to understand the conventional matrilineal transmission of Judaism, to which Marial responds, with philosophical literalness, that she does not adhere to any doctrine. The greeting by Jack's friend Ramsey (Jason Cook) to Sarah, on learning of her Jewishness, "I've never met anyone from overseas before," reveals in his confusion of religious with national difference an overlap between comic ignorance and a less humorous stereotype, that of the Jew's divided loyalties and unreliable national allegiance.[24]

Yet no such suspicion of negative stereotyping can be upheld. Neither Sarah's religious nor her regional identity—since she is from York, in "the south"—is constructed in any overt way.[25] Her accent is the standard English one of Received Pronunciation, which is unmarked by region, while Pauline comments simply on how "gorgeous" her young, blonde daughter-in-law looks. Indeed, withholding any stereotypical signifiers of either Jewish appearance or accent is in itself subtly comic, particularly in contrast to the non-Jewish characters, who are characterized visibly and audibly in overdetermined ways. Pauline, for instance, is unmistakably identified in terms of both religion and region in that she wears a crucifix and is performed by Gina McKee using the "strong" version of her native Geordie, or Tyneside, accent.[26]

However, by contrast to its Geordie elements, Sarah's Jewishness is not represented in a sustained way in *Hebburn*. Later in the series, Judaism's role in providing the opportunity for comic misunderstanding is overtaken by different discourses, and various kinds of otherness are used to make evident Pauline's parochial good-heartedness. These include Marial's new-age and therapeutic utterances, such as her use of the Hindu greeting "Namaste"—which prompts Pauline's effusive, "Of course you can stay!"—and her diagnosis of Jim and Pauline's relationship as "symbiotic," to which the latter defensively responds, "Oh, he's never hit us!" The same diffusion is evident in relation to the series' deployment of kosher food laws for comic effect. In all the examples mentioned here, non-Jewish awareness of the food associated with Jewish traditions may appear to act as a substitute for a more profound knowledge but also, perhaps unwittingly, honors something of its spiritual significance. As Gil Marks puts it, "Through food Jews internalize each holiday,"[27] as well as observing by such means commandments and rituals and acknowledging the detail of Jewish history. However, despite Sarah's refusal to eat bacon in *Hebburn*, no such comic mileage is derived from her being offered scampi at the local pub, which she consumes without comment; this inconsistency suggests that the full implications of the kashrut laws, which also forbid the consumption of shellfish, are too arcane for mainstream British humor. It also signals a shift in the narrative from religion to class, since the scampi are invoked as déclassé rather than as nonkosher. Even the significance of pork itself changes during the course of the series. Joe must forgo pork pies for the sake of his health, but despite Jack's description of this foodstuff as "the forbidden pie," no reminder is given of the earlier consternation caused by having such nonkosher food in the house. The pork pie has taken on a different meaning—that of masculine pleasure denied.[28] Along with the word "forbidden," pork has been recuperated back into the series' unitary British narrative, its Jewish strand suppressed.

Even Pauline's preference for Jews over implicitly middle-class vegetarians is explicable in terms of the insignificance of religion where class is concerned. Such a move from religion to class is most obvious in the encounters between Sarah's and Jack's respective families. Pauline's efforts to welcome Sarah's parents appear to center on religious and cultural difference, since they include playing klezmer music at top volume and greeting the couple in Hebrew ("I've shalomed them," she reports to Joe). A conversation full of Yiddish malapropisms—"you must have been a klutz when you fell for Susan," she tells Ben (Phil Nice)—is followed by Pauline's more accurate lament to her husband about Susan (Jan Ravens): "I'm a mensch but that yenta's treating me like a schmendrick!" Yet Pauline's ethnically directed efforts have a regionally and class-based equivalent on the part of the Jewish women. Marial tries out a local Geordie greeting ("Howay," she says to Big Keith, played by Steffen Peddie), and Sarah cements an agreement with Denise by describing it as one between "two big lass mates." This reversion to class is even clearer in the value-laden representation of Sarah's mother Susan's response to her environment: she is incredulous that Newcastle has a university and wonders with distaste if the description by Grandma Dot (Pat Dunn) of hiding money in her "Tigger," a china tiger, is "Geordie slang" for a bodily location. While Pauline's blunders are expressive of her generosity, Susan's reveal her condescension. The same is true of the Christian nature of Jack and Sarah's nuptial blessing, one that passes almost entirely without comment, apart from the offer by Gervaise (Neil Grainger) to contribute a "Jewish element" to it in the form of Barry Manilow songs. Susan tries to insist that the ceremony take place in York, yet there is apparently no contest about its more specific location in a church and the priest's blessing of the couple, all of which goes unquestioned. When Susan declares first the wedding itself and then the spectacle of Marial kissing Big Keith to be her "worst nightmare," she is objecting to social, rather than religious, shame. Thus class fully trumps ethnicity as the source of the "conflict and prejudice"[29] on which situation comedy relies. Since British Jews are considered to be "marginal but not marginalized," in David Baddiel's phrase, as a minority but most often a middle-class one, Jewish characters have not often been seen as sitcom fare.[30] In *Hebburn*, the class and religious conflict embodied by Sarah's role is smoothed away by the series' conclusion, along with her religious identity itself, to allow the drama to resume its primary identity as a comedy about a Tyneside working-class family. Indeed, just as she comes to "love" Hebburn, Sarah describes Jack's family, in a moment of drunken sentimentality, as if it is they who are the stereotypical Jews: "these are good people; they take care of their own."

"I Understand Your Traditions": *Friday Night Dinner*

Robert Popper's television series *Friday Night Dinner* also dramatizes an encounter between Jewish mores and a representation of enthusiastic but baffled Britishness. It concerns the weekly coming together of the Goodman family in their north London home, the mishaps that befall the parents, Jackie (Tamsin Grieg) and Martin (Paul Ritter), and their twentysomething sons, Adam (Simon Bird) and Jonny (Tom Rosenthal), who regress to childlike behavior once they are inside the family home, as well as those that result from the appearance of visitors at the house. The power relations between Jewish and British life are ostensibly reversed, since in this case it is Jim, the gentile neighbor, who wishes to enter and dine in a Jewish household but is constantly kept out, in contrast to Sarah's introduction to the Pearsons' non-Jewish home in *Hebburn*. In *FND*, Jim's wish for acceptance reveals the overlap between sitcom staples and the series' specifically Jewish content. His weekly appearance on the doorstep, along with his yearning to be invited in for Friday night dinner, to count himself as a family member, and his badly concealed crush on Jackie, are plot-driving personal eccentricities that equally entail an urge for proximity or merger with Jewishness, as his apparent desire for conversion suggests. In this way, Jim is a figure for the implied British spectator, an onlooker forever barred from full entry into the Goodmans' home, as suggested by the frequent shots of all four family members filmed from the point of view of an outsider at whom they are staring in puzzlement. Thus Jim attempts to negotiate, yet invariably confuses, the difference between what Zygmunt Bauman calls the conceptual and the empirical Jew: the one constructed from stereotypes and misinformation and the one who lives next door.[31]

Critical opinion of *FND*, in both the Jewish and non-Jewish British press, suggests that it attempts to pass as a mainstream sitcom about an eccentric family. It does so at the expense of expressing a true "Jewish self-consciousness," in Todd Endelman's phrase, which might have included representation of "the distinctive products" of Jewish life, such as "Jewish learning, culture, philanthropy and piety."[32] Such a view holds that although the series' Shabbat evening setting is evident in a variety of ways, ranging from the characters' dialog to the mise-en-scène and title, it has effectively de-Judaized itself for the sake of a wider audience and higher ratings. The series author Robert Popper's own commentary on the drama, along with that of reviewers, has supported such an estimate. For instance, in an interview with Popper, Marc Lee claims that "it's not obvious it's a Jewish family, is it?"[33] Popper himself argues that, although it is based on his own Jewish family life, "it's not a Jewish family sitcom. It's a sitcom about a family who just happens to be Jewish,"[34] and who come together on Friday evenings for a Shabbat meal that is not identified as such. If there is indeed a need of this kind to downplay the Goodmans' Jewishness, it could be ascribed to Popper's awareness of a British fantasy of homogeneity. Although Jewishness is present in *FND*, its minimalized presence exists in response to the fact that "Jews in England . . . are terrified about being seen as *making a fuss* about being Jewish."[35] Such an impetus toward homogeneity persists even in the face of the real-life diversity of Britain, particularly from the second half of the twentieth century onward, reflected in such multicultural televisual material as, for instance, the comedy series *Citizen Khan*.[36] This is the BBC's first sitcom with a South Asian related theme, set in what its eponymous protagonist calls "the capital of British Pakistan"—that is, the Midlands city of Birmingham. The very title of this drama places the notion of British citizenship alongside a name that signifies a Muslim identity, as if the two are definitionally at odds, while also bathetically alluding to the extraordinary, and white, American citizen of Orson Welles's 1941 film *Citizen Kane*.

However, the case with *Friday Night Dinner* is rather different. The series' title so clearly refers to a religiously specific practice that it seems paradoxical to argue that, so reduced is its Jewish detail, it could instead have been called *Sunday Lunch*.[37] As the narrator in Francesca Segal's novel *The Innocents* puts it, "'Friday night dinner' is one of the most evocative phrases in the vocabulary of any Jew—up there in significance with 'my son the doctor' and 'my daughter's wedding.'"[38] In an opposite pattern to that of *Hebburn*, the plot of *FND* represents increasingly explicit Jewish elements as the series progresses. This plot development takes the form of invocations of Jewish religious practice, a conflict between British and Jewish discourses about the Second World War, and even Jewish attitudes toward the crucifixion of Jesus Christ. The overt representation of Jewish life in Britain is made clear, at least to those who know,[39] in the repetition of such details as the family's fondness for a nearby Chinese restaurant and unfamiliarity with the local pub. Indeed, the two locations are contrasted: while the Goodmans feel at home in the Chinese restaurant, the pub is shown from their viewpoint as an alienating and excessively English environment, decked out in the flag of Saint George and named "The Black Boy." Although the image of an African youth displayed outside this particular pub suggests that it has been so called in a spirit of racist imperial nostalgia, the name originates rather in seventeenth-century references to the dark complexion of King Charles II. Yet both meanings of the term are comically exclusive, constructing Englishness as at once racist and ancient, predating Jewish immigration. In their preference for Chinese restaurant over local pub, the Goodmans appear to eschew a British social institution in favor of a cuisine that has become a "New York Jewish family tradition"[40] and is thus multiply non-British. Although Simon Bird, who plays the older son, Adam, may be correct to distinguish the series from U.S. sitcoms on the grounds that "our [British] humor is not infused with Jewish humor," this also means that Popper's series is able to construct its own representational mode. In this way, despite initial appearances, *FND* does not profoundly resemble *Citizen Khan*, since its characters are marked by eccentricity and class rather than by "racial" difference: Jewishness is expressed in British terms.

This particular representational technique is apparent in a series of jokes that relies on the Goodmans' neighbor Jim's enthusiastic but uninformed attitude toward Jewish "tradition," a term that comes to signify its precise opposite: that of spur-of-the-moment invention and trickery. It is evident in the episode "The Mercedes," which takes place on Adam's birthday. Here, Jonny plays a trick on his brother Adam by telling Jim about the birthday practice of "schmoigel": "It's traditional to give a big basket of fruit to the oldest son of the family," to include "only green-colored ones." Jonny elaborates that, following the rules of "schmoigel," kiwi fruit is "allowed" while pears are "forbidden." Jim does indeed present a bemused Adam with a basket of this kind. Revealingly, Jonny's conversation with Jim concludes with an affirmation of their different notions of "tradition." For the philosemitic Jim, the word signifies cultural practices that are enviably characterized by "great antiquity" and mystery;[41] for Jonny, it is simply an empty term that allows him to play a surreal joke on his brother:

> JIM [*earnestly*]: I understand your traditions.
> JONNY [*with irony*]: Traditions, yeah.

The "schmoigel" joke relies on the same features that were taken to be metonymic of Jewish life in the "Kosher" episode of *House on Fire* and in *Hebburn*, including Yiddish phrases, kosher food laws, and the following of apparently arbitrary strictures, to hoodwink Jim—and potentially the spectator, too. Viewers' online questions about "schmoigel," including whether it is a reference to the Bible or virginity, or an insult, might suggest that it functioned successfully as a practical joke extradiegetically too. Yet it seems that only an inattentive viewer could have missed intradiegetic signs that the practice of "schmoigel," and the term itself, is a joke at Jim's expense. These signs include the term's following on from Jonny informing Jim that "Pus-face," his epithet for Adam, is a "Jewish nickname," and its later being matched by Jonny pressing Jim to go home by means of the "final Jewish prayer" of the evening that the latter asked to hear:

> JONNY: Thank you, Lord, for the delicious meal, but now we must all go home to our sacred beds as soon as the Lord can send you. On your marks, get set, go! Amen.

In this "prayer," the phraseology of everyday urgency is couched in the form of a cod-benediction, although this joke, like "schmoigel," does have roots in Jewish practice, in the form of the commandment in Deuteronomy 8:10 to bless God after eating food, part of the prayer "Birkat ha-mazon." Both "schmoigel" and Jonny's parodic after-dinner grace are instances of the way in which surrealism, trickery, and regressive name-calling can all be naturalized as "tradition" by the unsuspecting non-Jew.

Indeed, such a pattern of allowing for or encouraging a confusion of "familyisms"[42] and eccentricity with Jewish practice is evident throughout *FND*, most strikingly so in the second season, in the episode "The Mouse." Jim's role as the naive gentile mediator of Jewish practice, from whom viewers can surely only wish to distance themselves, reaches its apotheosis when he succeeds at last in joining the Goodmans for dinner on Friday night. Although antisemitism has been ascribed to fear born of malicious "parochial ignorance,"[43] here it is an idealizing version of such ignorance that allows for Jim's self-inflicted status as dupe. At first this takes the same form as the "schmoigel" gag, in which Jim interprets everything in terms of Jewish significance, as revealed by his alarmed reaction to Martin's customary mealtime joke:

> JIM: This is the first time I've ever eaten Jewish food!
> JACKIE: It's all quite ordinary.
> MARTIN [*appreciatively*]: Lovely bit of squirrel!

However, Jim's other errors in this episode have their origin in garbled versions of real Jewish practice, and they function to make his mistakes, rather than the rituals themselves, the object of comedy. Jim's dinnertime behavior in suddenly throwing a plate at the wall is initially inexplicable, although illuminated when he insists once more, "It's tradition!" The act of violence is recuperated as his mistaking Greek dining habits for Jewish ones,[44] thus substituting one stereotype and one "otherness" for another. Jim takes the boys' mealtime joke, established, like Martin's squirrel mantra, over the duration of all three seasons, in which they trick each other into drinking salted water, to be a ritual he too must follow, and he insincerely praises the "refreshing" nature of this "traditional . . . Hebrew water." Like Matt in "Kosher," Jim improvises his own yarmulke out of a domestic object, this time a circle of cloth cut from his shirt. Just as Jim's "Jewish hat," as he puts it, is a simulacrum of the real object, so we gain a glimpse of the actual practices that constitute his errors. These include the kosher food laws that also underlie "schmoigel," the salt water used for dipping at a Passover meal that is the subtext for the salty drinking water, or the breaking of a glass at a Jewish wedding that seems in part to have inspired the shattering of a dinner plate. Yet it is Jim himself who is positioned as "other," not his Jewish hosts. It is he who, in the manner of Zygmunt Bauman's "allosemite," patently wishes for and constructs otherness. Jim embarrasses the Goodmans by repeating Pauline Pearson's gesture of insistently greeting everyone with "shalom," asking hopefully if the one he attends will be "a very religious dinner" and whether the menfolk have been circumcised together "as a set"; while his effort at conforming by smashing a plate provokes an unequivocal outburst from Martin: "You buggering lunatic!" Just as it is his behavior and not Jewish practice that is shown to be outlandish, so the arcane nature of Jim's own mealtime rituals exceeds that of any of the religious ones that he has imagined: he tears up his food with a spoon and douses it with vinegar. Indeed, Jim's inability to distinguish religious practice from family idiosyncrasy constructs him throughout the series as a comic version of what Kristin Bluemel has called the Jews' "gentile problem."[45] Such an effect is even more pronounced in *FND*'s season three, in which comic subplots rely on Jonny being able easily to delude Jim into believing that Jewish custom includes the consumption of foxes and, even more uncomfortably, the practice of under-age marriage.

Although it may appear that *FND* takes place in an ahistorical and timeless sitcom setting from which topical reference of any kind is absent, the series does invoke recent Jewish history. This acknowledgment takes the form of Martin's conflation of the British national conception of the Second World War, one of successful and heroic battles against moral evil both overseas and on the home front, with knowledge of the murder of European Jews that Britain was unable to prevent. Once more, such comically presented confusion on Martin's part occurs with increasing explicitness as the series progresses, and it reaches its fullest expression on Adam's birthday. It may be far-fetched to interpret Martin's eccentric humor as an example of Holocaust consciousness. Yet his penchant for expressing subliminal aggression toward his wife takes such a form. For instance, Martin starts a bonfire in the garden at Jackie's insistence, to get rid of his back collection of *New Scientist* magazine, and responds to his sons' question about what he is burning thus: "Your mother!" He replies to Jackie's demand that he take off his outdoor boots in the house with, "Yes, mein Führer!" And on other occasions Martin's resistance to household chores is expressed by his addressing Jackie as "mein Kapitän" and "my little Reichsführer." In this way, Martin expresses an inwardly turned version of extreme Jewish paranoia about the Nazis' return. Just as his sons express disapprobation of their grandmother's suitor, Mr. Morris (Harry Landis), by describing him as, "horrible . . . Hitlerish," so Martin uses the discourse of Nazism to express dissent from domestic arrangements, as in the case of his low-cholesterol diet:

> MARTIN: We've been eating fruit salad for dessert. It's like living in Nazi Germany.
> ADAM: Isn't that a bit of an exaggeration?
> [*Fruit salad is served*]
> MARTIN: What did I tell you? Nazi Germany!

Such references simultaneously evoke the specter of European history and transform it into a system of comically hyperbolic utterances. Only a British Jewish subject position can allow for this effect, combining the bystander status of both Britain and its Jews in relation to Nazi occupation and genocide, respectively.

Yet the two positions are more often at odds. In "The Mercedes," Martin's birthday gift to Adam is an illustrated book entitled *Warriors of War: The SS*. Although his family responds to the book as Jews, pointing out its focus on atrocities and glorification of the "weapons" and "heroes" of the SS, Martin explains his choice in terms that might rather be used by a British military buff: he claims that Adam "used to love the war, remember?" It is Jackie who points to the difference between a British narrative of wartime triumph and a Jewish one of loss:

> JACKIE: You said you were getting him a book about the war!
> MARTIN: It *is* about the war!
> JACKIE: Wonderful present for a Jewish son!

This dialogue, in its opposed uses of the word "war," enacts an example of the "rival" memories characterizing Jewish and British perspectives on the Second World War.[46] Jackie's warning "not to let my mother see [the book]" is an apparent reminder of what the war and the Holocaust might mean to someone of an earlier generation, but her mother's unexpected reaction marks a reversion to surrealism. "Oh, the SS," she says to Adam, on catching sight of the book, "you lucky boy!"

In this same episode the wartime subtext of such humor becomes clearer. The episode focuses on the eponymous Mercedes car, which belongs to Martin's former girlfriend Sheila Bloom (Frances Barber), who uses her car as a means of establishing her superiority over the Goodmans and their lowly vehicles. In a trajectory of an opposite kind to that in *Hebburn*, the narrative here is one of class snobbery but which has a subtext that concerns Jewish history. The Goodmans greet every mention of Sheila's car brand with irrepressible outbursts of satirical laughter and ultimately violence when Martin reverses his car into the Mercedes with predictably damaging results. It is tempting to see these reactions as arising from an unuttered awareness on the Goodmans' part of the company's role during the war: Mercedes-Benz was the major arms manufacturer in Nazi Germany and an exploiter of Jewish and other kinds of slave labor.[47] In contrast, the implicitly Jewish yet unconcerned Sheila allows present-day materialism to blot out knowledge of a compromised history even as it might affect her.

The relationship between Jews and gentiles in *FND* is made explicit in relation to another British institution, that of the series's "Christmas Special."[48] The title gives a double-voiced frame to the episode; literally so, since it opens with Adam's arrival at the family home in a sequence where he is viewed from beneath a tree branch laden with silver baubles.

The presence of a menorah and a Hanukkah card in the Goodmans' dining room in this episode acts as a pointed version of the series's deployment of what Nathan Abrams has called "ethnic wallpaper."[49] In *FND* it customarily takes the form of showing items such as Shabbat candles and challah that are fitting for a Friday night meal but which are neither mentioned in the dialogue nor foregrounded in the mise-en-scène. The series's title is itself an example of such "wallpaper," which is legible and crucial yet takes the form of a backdrop.

In the "Christmas Special," there is something of a dialectical structure to the representation of Jewishness: at first it is conspicuous by its absence, as the family members gather for Christmas Day, then the contradictory nature of such a celebration is debated between Jackie and Adam ("Why is it weird?" "Maybe because we're . . . *Jewish*?"), and at last the danger posed by Jewish difference in such an overdetermined setting appears to be neutralized by Jim, who sings a Christmas carol that reduces Jackie to tears. Although it is Jackie who is the bearer of changing attitudes toward Christmas "tradition," as she puts it, in this episode, the Jewish ambivalence of attraction and repulsion toward the festival, and towards gentile life more generally, is registered by other characters, too. Martin urges his sons to accompany him to the shed, where a "surprise" is hidden:

> JONNY: Have you got Rudolph in there?
> MARTIN: Yes, Rudolf *Hess!* [*sardonic laughter*]

Martin's joke, like his birthday gift of a book about the SS, effects something of a return of the historical repressed, as well as a daring post-assimilatory confidence in expressing humor about the Second World War. In this Christmas setting, the conflation of Rudolph, the Red-Nosed Reindeer, with Rudolf Hess, the wartime commandant of Auschwitz, is ostensibly an expression of Martin's eccentricity, but it also implies a link between two kinds of antisemitism: that of the Nazis and that of the Christian church that helped justify genocide. Indeed, Jackie's defense of honoring Christmas as a "tradition" falters in the face of the "surprise" Martin has hidden in the shed, a giant tree that barely fits into the house and of which she declares, "We've *never* had a tree before. . . . It's *wrong*." Jackie instinctively recognizes a difference between the Christmas tree, in its guise as an "evergreen" reminder of the Crucifixion, and the festival's less religious elements of turkey and crackers that cause her no demur. Jackie's wish to redesignate the Christmas tree as a "Hanukkah bush" is not simply a comic reversal of David Ruderman's notion of the "Englishing" of Jewishness[50] but also a substitution of the symbol of God's appearance in the form of a burning bush from the Hebrew Bible for that of the New Testament story of Jesus's birth and death. The subversive nature of Jackie's rebellion against the imagery of Christmas is simultaneously dramatized yet undermined, since its strongest association is with "Horrible Grandma," Martin's mother, Cynthia (Rosalind Knight). As well as acting dismissively toward her daughter-in-law and grandsons, it is Cynthia who explicitly deplores "all this fuss for a Christian holiday; we're supposed to be Jewish," thus discrediting such a viewpoint. Yet even Cynthia is emotionally moved by Jim's final rendition of a carol to the extent that for the first time she acts lovingly toward her son's family.

In the "Christmas Special," Jim's first incursion into the Goodman household is as a carol singer. Jackie interrupts his doorstep rendition of "Away in a Manger" to observe that, "We don't really do carols, because we're—you know—Jewish." Her invocation of Jewishness is in part pragmatic, since it is designed to get Jim to leave, but also an element in Jackie's inconsistent attitude toward Christmas celebration: here, she repudiates it. Jackie's later invitation to Jim to sing is likewise partly pragmatic, since it is intended to prevent the need for small talk, and he chooses "Silent Night." Although the latter may seem at first to be less overtly Christian than "Away in a Manger,"[51] it too celebrates the birth of Jesus that Adam had reminded Jackie, in the face of her denial, was the Christian foundation of the festival. Both the outsider Jim and the carol become acceptable together; it seems that only a Christian message can unite the family members and cause the feuding grandmothers to agree on something: that Jim's singing of the carol is "really beautiful." Yet in this sequence it is comic subversion that has the effect of "wallpaper," in the sense of an understated backdrop that nonetheless fundamentally alters the meaning of what is represented in the foreground. Throughout the episode the use of "Jesus" as an expletive rather than an appellation serves as an ironic counterpoint to the action; for instance, in Jonny's outburst of frustration while Martin and the boys attempt to make the enormous tree stand upright in the dining room. Jim's entrance in the final carol-singing scene is heralded by a similar joke, one that parodically transforms him into Jesus Christ:

> ADAM: You're dressed as . . .
> JONNY [*shocked*]: *Jesus!*
> JIM: No, Father Christmas.

Even more daringly, the episode does not conclude with the sentimental success of Jim's singing "Silent Night." The last words of dialogue consist of Adam's address to his grandmother Cynthia, who for the first time responds warmly to her grandson, to draw her attention to the final stage in a story of resurrection, albeit of a canine variety:

> ADAM: Grandma?
> HORRIBLE GRANDMA [*smiling fondly*]: Yes?
> ADAM: Your dog's died again.

The first "death" of Cynthia's dog Boadicea was caused by the tree, which toppled over just as Martin succeeded in causing his mother to laugh, as if the tree's Christian symbology, as Christmas icon or signifier of the cross, was marking laughter out as profanity. The dog's name itself, as that of the queen of a British tribe who led an uprising against the occupying Roman forces around 60 CE, signals in double-voiced fashion both the rebellion against conformity that a Jewish Christmas implies and an ancient, pre-Roman Britishness. "Boadicea" contrasts with the name of Jim's dog, "Wilson." While this might seem to make the dog into the namesake of a more mundane historical figure in British history, the Labour prime minister Harold Wilson, it is also the name of the brand of volleyball which acts as a companion to Chuck Noland (Tom Hanks) in *Cast Away* (Robert Zemeckis, Twentieth Century Fox, 2000). The echo here of the "Wilson" brand volleyball emphasizes the fact that both dog and ball assume the role of a nonhuman interlocutor for a man living in isolation.[52] Cynthia's description of Boadicea's life of "suffering" is followed by the dog's miraculously returning to life, only to die again at the episode's conclusion. It is tempting to see these two parodic incarnations of Jesus, in the form of Jim in his Father Christmas costume and the canine Boadicea in her reborn state, as the final expressions of

Jewish ambivalence, in the Bakhtinian sense of simultaneous assertion and denial,[53] toward the gentile, British world in this "Christmas Special."

In her account of representations of Jews in British children's fiction, Madelyn Travis declares her focus to be on "Jewish characters and Jewishness" rather than "'Jewish literature' as a genre," although she also invokes the notion of "authorial intention" and the author's relation to his or her material as a means of identifying the Jewishness of fictional characters.[54] In the examples I have analyzed, the author's personal connection to his or her material is often made public, both to impart authenticity to the text and to guard against charges of stereotyping where comedy is concerned. The particular relation of author to topic in the examples I have discussed here in part explains the different fate of the Jewish elements, which are gradually replaced by a comic concern with class in *Hebburn* yet remain, by contrast, central to the conception of *Friday Night Dinner*. While Jason Cook explains that the character of Sarah in *Hebburn* is based on that of his Jewish wife, Clare, after whom the character was originally named, Robert Popper claims to have drawn on his own family life in *Friday Night Dinner*. Even Chris Sussman notes of his radio sitcom episode "Kosher" that his "fairly strong and varied experience of what it's like to be Jewish" arises from being "born into a Liberal Jewish family."[55] In the case of each of these dramas, the comic clash between Jewishness and Britishness itself has an autofictional role, accounting in part for the ratio and nature of the Jewish-related material in each of these works.

Both *Hebburn* and *FND* support in dramatic form several truisms about British Jewry. These include the fact that the small size of the community and its presence in a nation whose identity was "formed centuries earlier" than the large-scale Jewish immigration of the nineteenth century[56] mean that its members are received with toleration, as long as they do not advertise their difference. The history of the Jews in Britain differs from that of North America, a culture of immigrants in which a figure such as Saul Bellow's Augie March can be an "everyman," but equally British Jews are only on the periphery of Europe's twentieth-century history of discrimination and murder.[57] Set against such a background, form and content in both *Hebburn* and *FND* are closely allied in particular ways. In *Hebburn*, Jewishness is boldly introduced but then gradually disappears from the plot, echoing the notion of an emancipation contract by means of which British tolerance is won at the price of Jewish reticence and assimilation. In this way, over the duration of its first season, *Hebburn* resembles descriptions of the British liberal state, which eschewed antisemitism but, at the same time, allowed little room for "a distinctively Jewish population."[58] As I have argued, Sarah is met with enthusiasm by her in-laws, and the only suggestion of antisemitism in *Hebburn* arises from the Pearsons' uncertainty about which discourse to use in relation to her: that of religion, ethnicity, nationality, or even gender. On the other hand, none of these categories of Jewishness survives as Sarah becomes acculturated into the family.

In *FND*, the opposite trajectory takes place, and Jewish concerns become more, rather than less, prominent in what seems almost to be a spirit of comic defiance in the face of the British emancipatory bargain. Although the novelist Linda Grant insists on the difficulty for British Jewish artists of establishing a distinctive "ethnic voice,"[59] in Robert Popper's series it is precisely the elements of gentile Britishness, including Christianity and the national myth of the war, that are used to construct a Jewish artwork. In both dramas, Jewishness is known only through the individual Jews who are taken to embody it, and stereotypical or imagined details replace any sense of its self-defining "group habits, values, attitudes and sentiments"[60] for its onlookers. Yet in *Hebburn* and *FND*, the conundrum of Jewish particularity in the face of a homogenizing Britishness in the twenty-first century is not only acted out in dramatic form but also satirized and questioned.

Notes

Thanks to Nathan Abrams, David Forrest, Phyllis Lassner, and Pete Lyons for their suggestions in relation to this chapter.

1. *House on Fire*, written by Dan Hine and Chris Sussman (London: Pacificus Productions, 2010–2013). Broadcast on BBC Radio 4.

2. *Fiddler on the Roof*, directed by Norman Jewison (Beverly Hills: Mirisch Production Company, Cartier Productions, 1971).

3. *The Great British Bake Off* (London: Love Productions, BBC2, 2010).

4. Michael Ragussis, *Figures of Conversion: The "Jewish Question" and English National Identity* (Durham, N.C.: Duke University Press, 1995).

5. BBC Writers' Room, "TV Comedy Series," accessed August 12, 2013, http://www.bbc.co.uk/writersroom/send-a-script/medium-and-format-guidelines (no longer available).

6. Todd M. Endelman, *England — Good or Bad for the Jews?* Jubilee Parkes Lecture,

May 2002, Parkes Institute Pamphlet no. 3 (Southampton, U.K.: University of Southampton, 2003), 12.

7. Annette Insdorf, *Indelible Shadows: Film and the Holocaust* (Cambridge: Cambridge University Press, 2003.

8. Nadia Valman, *The Jewess in Nineteenth-Century British Literary Culture* (Cambridge: Cambridge University Press, 2007), 218.

9. David Wilkes, "Tell Hyacinth the Doily is Dead," *Daily Mail*, May 17, 2007.

10. Eli Lederhendler, preface to *Ethnicity and Beyond: Theories and Dilemmas of Jewish Group Identity: Studies in Contemporary Jewry XXV*, edited by Eli Lederhendler, vii–x (Oxford: Oxford University Press, 2011), vii.

11. *The Evacuees*, directed by Alan Parker, written by Jack Rosenthal (London: BBC, 1975).

12. Eric Santner, "History Beyond the Pleasure Principle: Some Thoughts on the Representation of Trauma," in *Probing the Limits of Representation: Nazism and the "Final Solution,"* edited by Saul Friedlander (Cambridge, Mass.: Harvard University Press, 1992).

13. Primo Levi, *The Search for Roots: A Personal Anthology*, translated by Peter Forbes (1981; repr., Harmondsworth, U.K.: Penguin, 2001), 148. Thanks to Victoria Nesfield for this reference.

14. The term "lachrymose" is that of the historian Salo Baron: see Robert Liberles, *Salo Wittmayer Baron: Architect of Jewish History* (New York: New York University Press, 1995), 117. York massacre quotation in Sethina Watson, "Introduction: The Moment and Memory of the York Massacre of 1190," in *Christians and Jews in Angevin England*, edited by Sethina Watson (London: Boydell and Brewer, 2013).

15. Todd M. Endelman, *The Jews of Britain, 1656 to 2000* (Berkeley: University of California Press, 2002), 69.

16. Endelman, *England*, 12–13.

17. Bryan Cheyette, "Jewish Stereotyping and English Literature, 1875–1920," in *Traditions of Intolerance: Historical Perspectives on Fascism and Race Discourse in Britain*, edited by Tony Kushner and Kenneth Lunn (Manchester, U.K.: Manchester University Press, 1989), 29.

18. See Barry Langford, "'Our Usual Impasse': The Episodic Situation Comedy Revisited," in *Popular Television Drama: Critical Perspectives*, edited by Jonathan Bignell and Stephen Lacey (Manchester, U.K.: Manchester University Press, 2005), 21–23.

19. Jason Cook quoted in Simon Round, "*Hebburn*: A British Sitcom that Avoids Jewish Clichés," *Jewish Chronicle*, October 19, 2012.

20. Ibid.

21. The historian Cecil Roth identifies shopkeepers as part of middle-class Jewish life in nineteenth-century London, in distinction to those with less education or capital who were artisans, or, with even fewer means, peddlers. See his *A History of the Jews in England* (Oxford: Oxford University Press, 1941), 228.

22. Morgan Jeffrey, "Kimberley Nixon 'Hebburn' Q&A: 'The North East Was a Mystery to Me,'" *Digital Spy*, October 18, 2012, accessed November 5, 2015, http://www.digitalspy.co.uk/tv/interviews/a431699/kimberley-nixon-hebburn-qa-the-north-east-was-a-mystery-to-me.html.

23. The name "Marial" also signals an intertextual debt to the television sitcom *Hunderby* (2012), released three months earlier than *Hebburn* by the same production

company. Verity-May Henry's character has the same name in both series, as do those of her parents, Susan and Ben, who are played by the same actors.

24. See Ann Pellegrini, *Jews and Other Differences: The New Jewish Cultural Studies* (Minneapolis: University of Minnesota Press, 1996).

25. It should be noted that York is approximately seventy miles south of Newcastle.

26. The term "Geordie" refers both to a native of Newcastle upon Tyne and to the surrounding urban area of Tyneside, as well as to the speech of those inhabitants. The entry on McKee in Sue Terry's voice-over agency website describes her accent as, "Neutral. Just a hint of Geordie," and elaborates, "Born in Durham so has a natural Geordie/North Yorkshire accent that she can strengthen or weaken as desired." "Gina McKee," *SueTerryVoices*, last updated 2014, accessed November 5, 2015, http://sueterryvoices.com/profile/gina-mckee/. In *Hebburn*, McKee's character is constructed by means of the "strengthened" version of this accent, in contrast to Sarah's lack of any such markers.

27. Gil Marks, introduction to *Encyclopedia of Jewish Food* (New York: Wiley, 2001), ii.

28. See, for instance, the appearance of the pork pie in such terms in *Withnail and I* (1987), in the description provided by Withnail (Richard E. Grant) of a lads' evening out with Marwood (Paul McGann) at the pub: "We get in there and get wrecked, then we'll eat a pork pie, then we'll drop a couple of Surmontil-50's each."

29. Phil Wickham, "Sitcom," *BFI Screenonline*, accessed November 5, 2015, http://www.screenonline.org.uk/tv/id/445368/.

30. David Baddiel, "My Identity Is in My Bones—but Let's Not Make a Big Deal Out of It," *New Statesman*, May 28, 2012, 70. For more on late twentieth-century Jewish upward mobility in Britain, see Endelman, *Jews of Britain*, 229–56.

31. Zygmunt Bauman, "Allosemitism: Premodern, Modern, Postmodern," in *Modernity, Culture and "the Jew,"* edited by Bryan Cheyette and Laura Marcus (Cambridge: Polity Press, 1998), 148.

32. Endelman, *England*, 11, 23.

33. Marc Lee, "Interview: Friday Night Dinner Creator Robert Popper," *Daily Telegraph*, February 25, 2011, http://www.telegraph.co.uk/culture/tvandradio/8345307/Interview-Friday-Night-Dinner-creator-Robert-Popper.html. See also Ruth Gilbert, "My Big Fat Jewish TV Dinner: Reflections on British Jewishness in 'Friday Night Dinner' and 'Grandma's House,'" *Jewish Film and New Media* 2, no. 2: 181–200.

34. Christina Radish, "Simon Bird and Robert Popper Interview: Friday Night Dinner," *Collider*, July 30, 2011, accessed November 5, 2015, http://collider.com/friday-night-dinner-simon-bird-robert-popper-interview/106717/.

35. Baddiel, "Identity in Bones."

36. *Citizen Khan*, directed by Nick Wood, written by Anil Gupta, Richard Pinto, and Adil Ray (London: BBC One, 2012).

37. Jessica Elgot, "Interview with Robert Popper," *Jewish Chronicle*, February 24, 2011, http://www.thejc.com/arts/arts-interviews/45724/interview-robert-popper.

38. Francesca Segal, *The Innocents* (London: Chatto and Windus, 2012), 167.

39. See Henry Bial, *Acting Jewish: Negotiating Jewishness on the American Stage and Screen* (Ann Arbor: University of Michigan Press, 2005), chap. 6.

40. Gaye Tuchman and Harry Levine quoted in Nathan Abrams, "Digesting Food and Foodways in the Movies of Woody Allen," in *Woody on Rye: Re-examining Jewish-*

ness in the Films and Plays of Woody Allen, edited by Vincent Brook and Marat Greenberg (Waltham, Mass.: Brandeis University Press, 2013), 225.

41. Adam Sutcliffe and Jonathan Karp, "Introduction: A Brief History of Philosemitism," in *Philosemitism in History*, edited by Jonathan Karp and Adam Sutcliffe (Cambridge: Cambridge University Press, 2011), 13.

42. Robert Popper, "Television Guide," *Guardian*, February 19, 2011.

43. Howard Lupovitch, "Ordinary People, Ordinary Jews," in Karp and Sutcliffe, *Philosemitism in History*, 132.

44. Matt makes the same category error in "Kosher" but approaches closer to the actual practice when he refers to the "breaking of plates" at "Jewish weddings."

45. Kristin Bluemel, "The Urban Geography of English Antisemitism and Assimilation: A Case Study," in *Antisemitism and Philosemitism in the Twentieth and Twenty-first Centuries: Representing Jews, Jewishness and Modern Culture*, edited by Phyllis Lassner and Lara Trubowitz (Cranbury, N.J.: Associated University Presses, 2008), 176.

46. Tony Kushner, "Loose Connections? Britain and the 'Final Solution,'" in *Britain and the Holocaust: Remembering and Representing Genocide*, edited by Caroline Sharples and Olaf Jensen (Basingstoke, U.K.: Palgrave, 2013), 51–70.

47. See Bernard P. Bellon, *Mercedes in Peace and War: German Automobile Workers, 1903–1945* (New York: Columbia University Press, 1990).

48. *Hebburn*'s "Christmas Special," broadcast on December 22, 2013, also took the opportunity to represent a comic clash between Jewish and gentile expectations by bringing both families together for this "winter festival." However, in place of the Jewish subversion apparent in the conclusion to *FND*'s "Christmas Special," here the only Jewish grandmother is a "horrible " one (played by Miriam Margolyes) and is left isolated by everyone at the episode's end, suggesting the triumph of non-Jewish culture.

49. Nathan Abrams, comment at the seminar "Hidden? Representing Jews in British Film and Television" (Bangor University, Wales, May 25, 2011).

50. David Ruderman. *Jewish Enlightenment in an English Key: Anglo-Jewry's Construction of Modern Jewish Thought* (Princeton, N.J.: Princeton University Press, 2000), 240.

51. For instance, the "Christmas historian" Bill Egan describes "Silent Night" in such terms as a "powerful message of heavenly peace [that] has crossed all borders and language barriers, conquering the hearts of people everywhere." Bill Eagan, "Silent Night: The Song Heard 'Round the World," accessed November 5, 2015, http://silentnight.web.za/history/.

52. It is worth noting that Harold Wilson is a figure with interests akin to Jim's, since he was well known as a friend of Israel and advocate of Soviet Jewry's cause.

53. Mikhail Bakhtin, *Rabelais and His World*, translated by Hélène Iswolsky (1965; Bloomington: Indiana University Press, 1984), 12.

54. Madelyn J. Travis, *Jews and Jewishness in British Children's Literature* (London: Routledge, 2012), 4–5.

55. Jason Cook quoted in Catriona Wightman, "Vic Reeves, Kimberly Nixon for BBC Two Comedy 'Hebburn,'" *Digital Spy*, March 6, 2012, accessed November 5, 2015, http://www.digitalspy.co.uk/tv/news/a369619/vic-reeves-kimberley-nixon-for-bbc-two-comedy-hebburn.html; Elgot, "Interview with Robert Popper." Sussman adds, "I should also point out that the producer and commissioner of 'House on Fire' are Jewish as well"; Chris Sussman, personal correspondence with author, June 19, 2013.

56. Linda Grant, "Background Noise," *New Statesman*, May 2012, 51.
57. Ibid.
58. Tony Kushner, "The Impact of British Anti-Semitism, 1918–1945," in *The Making of Modern Anglo-Jewry*, edited by David Cesarani (Oxford: Basil Blackwell, 1990), 205.
59. Grant, "Background Noise," 51.
60. Endelman, *England*, 26.

NIR COHEN

Love and Betrayal

Politicized Romance in Peter Kosminsky's The Promise *(2011)*

The Promise (2011) is an epic British TV drama that attempts to recount the story of the Israeli–Palestinian conflict in two parallel narratives situated in two eras: 1945–1948 and 2005. The first focuses on the experiences of Leonard (Len) Matthews (Christian Cooke), a British soldier serving in the post–World War II British mandate in Palestine. The second follows Len's granddaughter, a young British woman named Erin Matthews (Claire Foy), who is retracing his footsteps. In so doing, Erin learns about her grandfather's tormented psyche, the region's conflicted past and present, and Britain's role in it immediately after the war itself.

The 1940s narrative consists of pivotal historical events, such as the liberation of the concentration and death camps in Central and Eastern Europe and the subsequent mass immigration of Jews to British-ruled Palestine; the strict immigration policy of the mandate administration, decided by the Colonial Office and His Majesty's Government, and enforced by the British army, to ease the tension between Jews and Arabs; the United Nations decision on the partition of the land between the two peoples; and finally, the establishment of the Jewish state and, with it, the British army's withdrawal and the unfolding of the Nakba ("catastrophe"), the Arabic name given to the uprooting and expulsion of hundreds of thousands of Arabs from their homes and land.

The modern-day narrative focuses on the Israeli occupation of the West Bank and Gaza, the mistreatment of Arab citizens of the state of Israel, and the internal conflicts that split Israeli and Palestinian societies.

On the Israeli side, the drama represents illegal, ultrareligious settlers who hold messianic views about Greater Israel and secular, left-wing activists who fight to end the occupation and to open communication channels with their Arab counterparts. On the Arab side, the drama hints at the tension between Fatah and Hamas activists in Gaza—with each group vying to represent the whole of the Palestinian people—as well as at the different legal, economic, and political status of Palestinian citizens of Israel compared to that of Palestinians who live on the other side of the wall. Whereas in the Israeli camp conflicts are mostly a corollary of clashing ideologies, among the Palestinians, separation—at least as it is portrayed in *The Promise*—is in part a consequence of the force of occupation, an almost arbitrary act of redrawing lines by a foreign, hostile army. In the modern-day narrative, notable events include a suicide bombing in a Tel Aviv café followed by the demolition of a terrorist's family's house by the Israel Defense Forces as a reaction to yet another suicide bombing in Tel Aviv. Verbal and physical abuse of Arab residents by neighboring Jewish settlers are also shown, and at least one of the incidents is based on actual footage showing a female Jewish settler repeatedly calling an Arab woman enclosed behind a fence "a whore" and ordering her to lock herself in "her cage."[1]

The lavish production—the estimated budget was seven million pounds, or approximately 10.5 million dollars (the majority of which, approximately five million pounds, was given by Channel 4, topped up by Canal + and the EU Media Fund)—of *The Promise*, which was shot entirely on location in Israel,[2] fits with the immense task the serial attempts to tackle. The two narratives are carefully interwoven into one story of two peoples over the course of six decades, compressed into four episodes totaling 350 minutes. The serial begins with actual documentary footage of the liberation of the concentration and death camps, presented as the rationale for granting a national home in Palestine to the Jews. This footage is followed by a dramatization of the bombing of the King David Hotel by the Irgun on July 22, 1946, in which ninety-one people of various nationalities were killed; the Sergeants' Affair, the kidnapping and killing of two British soldiers by the Irgun in July 1947; the massacre in the Palestinian village of Deir Yassin, carried out by paramilitaries from the Irgun and Lehi groups on April 9, 1948, and portrayed in the serial as a clear case of "ethnic cleansing"; and the Nakba. While both the Irgun and Lehi (also known in English as "the Stern Gang," a militant Zionist group led by Avraham ["Yair"] Stern), two of the three Zionist underground paramilitary groups that operated at that time, are mentioned, it is important to note what seems to be *The Promise*'s intentional omission of the third group, the Haganah. This omission occurs despite the fact that the Haganah was larger in size and influence than either the Irgun or Lehi and far more consensual. Thus, although *The Promise* comes across at times as a lesson in the history of Israel-Palestine for beginners, it strangely omits that very history.[3]

With Peter Kosminsky serving as both the director and writer of the serial, his vision of Israel and Palestine both in the 1940s and today is one that is mirrored by the conflicted emotional lives of the serial's protagonists. Indeed, love and relationships in *The Promise* are often marred by violence and betrayal and undermined by a national cause. While discussing *The Promise* in broad terms, I will focus my observations around the portrayal of its main characters' emotional lives. Although attempts to form romantic relationships are abundant in *The Promise*, expressions of true love and affection seem to be missing. Instead, romance is yet another tool in a system whose role is to monitor, control, and conquer; lovers are often enemies; and relationships are motivated not just by emotions but also by political ambitions.

As the notion of love — romantic or otherwise — is challenged, tested, and ultimately dismissed in the serial, it is probably appropriate that one of the first words uttered in *The Promise* is actually the verb "hate." When Erin, the young female lead, is taken against her will to visit her grandfather in a hospital in the northern English city of Leeds, she protests to her mother, "I don't know why we're doing this; you hate him." Indeed, it is not only the mother who hates her own father but, at this point at least, also the granddaughter who hates her grandfather. And the reason for that, as we quickly learn, is the grandfather's own feeling of self-hatred and misery, which affected his relationships with both daughter and granddaughter. The motif of hate runs through the serial and plays an important part on both personal and national levels: It is the Jewish community that hates both the British and the Arabs; the Arabs who hate the Jews; Eliza (Perdita Weeks), Erin's best friend, who hates her brother Paul (Itay Tiran); and Paul, who hates his parents' faux-liberal beliefs. And maybe most important, it is if not hate exactly, then definitely disaffection that the audience — and here I am taking the liberty to express my own feelings as a viewer — feels toward the lot of them. Indeed, *The Promise* is quite remarkable in its failure to produce hardly any likable characters. Yet despite this failure, these characters do love in the serial, or at least purport to be engaged in the labor of loving. But how exactly do they love? And, more crucially, to what end?

The Promise portrays romantic and sexual relationships as false, abusive, or transgressive. As will be demonstrated in this chapter, the viewer learns early on to expect every romantic gesture to be undermined by political strife. Love is never the ultimate goal in the serial but a mechanism through which political alliances are being either established or broken. The main — and most treacherous, perhaps — love story in the show is that between British sergeant Len and his German-born Jewish lover, Clara Rosenbaum (Katharina Schüttler). On the face of it, it is the way this romance ends that reveals its questionable beginnings: Clara turns out to be an Irgun mole, an extremist who takes an active part in the Deir Yassin massacre in 1948, an assault carried out by Jewish militia in which more than one hundred Palestinian villagers, including women and children, were killed. Her love affair with the naive and righteous Len is no more than a sham. Clara's attempt to claim that her love for Len has been real comes across as hollow and insincere. However, the beginning of their relationship at a city hospitality club sheds some light on what is to follow: the flirty conversation between the two posits Clara in the role of a prostitute who offers her services to the handsome sergeant. In a way, this is not too far from the truth with which the narrative presents us: Clara may be truly attracted to Len, she may even see herself as falling in love with him, but her affection and sexual favors come at a price. She is paid twice — once by the Irgun, who employ her to befriend and charm British soldiers like Len so they would side with the Jews, and then also by Len himself, who unwittingly gives her top-secret information about future operations of the British army. The love affair between Len and Clara is just one brief example of the ideological use of the concept of love in the serial. Other relationships follow the same path in the way that they are invested in political interests. But before I go further, I would like first to discuss *The Promise* as a whole.

A British Spirit

Given the central place that the Israeli–Palestinian conflict occupies in the lives and minds of millions of people inside and outside the Middle East, it is surprising that only a few films and TV programs have so far dealt with this issue. The majority of those few productions of recent years are either Israeli or Palestinian. Since they have received little exposure in the European and American markets, they have left little impression on those who may have general interest in world politics but are not necessarily especially engaged with the Middle East's unresolved drama. This is why the British TV drama series *The Promise*, directed and written by veteran Peter Kosminsky and broadcast on Channel 4 in early 2011 in its Sunday prime-time slot (promoted by a billboard campaign and wide media coverage), is so noteworthy.[4]

Despite British involvement in Palestine and the focus of *The Promise* on its two main British protagonists — namely, the young granddaughter in the 2005 narrative and the grandfather as a young British soldier in the 1940s narrative — the series is still a TV drama about the Middle East made by people who are not directly part of the conflict. The power of such a drama lies in its potential to offer a much-needed critical distance and perspective that are often missing from films made by Israeli or Palestinian directors and writers. Whether the series realizes this potential is debatable.

The Promise was an unusual production in the contemporary landscape of British TV, one where Israel as a subject is largely avoided beyond news and documentary programs. However, for Kosminsky, who came up with the idea in the early years of the twenty-first century, making *The Promise* was a rather natural career progression. His previous projects — including *The Government Inspector* (2005), which told the story of the search for weapons of mass destruction in Iraq, and *Britz* (2007), on the life of second-generation Muslims in Britain today — explored, much like *The Promise*, highly charged political issues.[5]

The Promise proved to be controversial and divisive: while supporters praised its bold take on the political situation in the Middle East, opponents — many of whom were members of the British Jewish community — linked the series to what they saw as a manifestation of broader anti-Israeli (often conflated with antisemitic) sentiments in the

United Kingdom and Europe.[6] Indeed, *The Promise* emerged at a time when the United Kingdom was increasingly being labeled by some pro-Israeli groups as the center of a global anti-Zionist conspiracy with recurring calls for an academic boycott of Israel, for instance, or the 2012 campaign to boycott the U.K. tour of the Israeli dance company Batsheva. The fact that Kosminsky is a British Jew did not help assuage those heated feelings and maybe even exacerbated them. Kosminsky himself, it seems, was fully aware of the impact that his Jewishness had on the reception of his serial, at least in Jewish, pro-Israeli circles in Britain. Choosing to be interviewed on a question-and-answer session hosted by the Qatari TV news channel Al-Jazeera, which itself has been accused of antisemitic bias, Kosminsky said, "If you seek to comment on the domestic or international policy of Israel, particularly if you are Jewish, you open yourself up to accusations of antisemitism. I get very nervous about the light use of the racism label."[7] Given that the production is based in the United Kingdom, in both narratives British protagonists serve as intermediaries between the Arabs and the Jews. In the 1940s narrative it is Len Matthews, a British sergeant who is posted in Palestine after serving in the liberation of Bergen-Belsen. His professional involvement with the two warring parties soon turns personal: he becomes romantically involved with the Jewish Clara and, around the same time, befriends his Arab servant, Abu-Hassan Mohammed (Ali Suliman). Both Clara and Mohammed are deeply invested in the political drama around them. Whereas Clara is a devout and active member of the Irgun, Mohammed's involvement in the conflict is passive: it is forced on him as he and his family are driven out of their home in the village Ein Hwad[8] near Haifa in 1948.

In the 2005 narrative, Len's past role as the British broker is reenacted by his granddaughter, Erin. Erin finds herself accompanying her friend Eliza Meyer to Israel. Eliza has dual citizenship, and while she was schooled in Britain, her family now lives in the town of Caesarea. Eliza travels to Israel to enlist in the army, an act to which she does not seem to attach any political meaning; like many other young Israelis, she perceives it as an obligatory rite of passage, an essential but also perhaps an almost innocent declaration of belonging to Israeli society (the Israeli army has been known as the state's "melting pot" or the "people's army," and enlistment has social and cultural importance that goes beyond the defense needs of the state). Erin joins her for no other reason than to spend the summer under the Mediterranean sun at Eliza's parents' poolside. Her plans, however, take an unexpected turn as she becomes increasingly caught up in the intricate realities of the region.

Her interest is prompted by the journal that her grandfather kept while in Palestine in the 1940s, a journal she salvages from his home just before embarking on her trip. The journal will prove to be the missing link between past and present, a key document that sheds light on the origins of a decades-long conflict. The journal will also allow Erin to intimately get to know her grandfather, to whom, we learn, neither she nor her mother — Len's daughter — were particularly close. Reliving his life experiences will allow Erin to better understand — and even empathize with — his conflicted psyche. It will also guide her in completing the mission that her grandfather could not achieve, after he was imprisoned for desertion and taking sides with the Arabs. That mission is to return the house key, attached to the back of the journal, to the surviving relatives of its former owner, Abu-Hassan Mohammed, Len's servant. This is the key to the house from which the family fled in 1948 as well as a symbol of the unremitting Palestinian hope of return. There are many just like it, preciously kept by Palestinians who are scattered in their diasporas but hoping to go back, one day, to their former homes. Erin succeeds in returning the key to Mohammed's ailing daughter, Jawda (Hiam Abbass), who now lives in Gaza in a house that is about to be torn down by the Israeli army.

The completion of Erin's mission is also her cue to return to the United Kingdom. The serial, therefore, completes a full cycle: the character of Len personifies long, deep feelings of guilt for the way the British army abandoned the defenseless Arab population in 1948. The character of his granddaughter personifies a British urge to amend its alleged past mistakes. By returning the key to the family of her grandfather's servant and friend — surmounting on her way numerous metaphorical and literal obstacles — Erin clears both her grandfather's and her nation's conscience regarding the fate of the Palestinians.

The serial does not show similar understanding toward the plight of the Jews in Palestine, except for the necessary mention of the Holocaust and Jewish illegal immigration to Palestine in the first half of the first episode. For the rest of the serial, the Jews are portrayed mostly as agents of uncontrolled aggression, destruction, and betrayal. Even the Holocaust imagery, conjured up earlier on, is employed at a later stage to describe Jewish accountability for the tragedy of the Nakba. An old Arab man tells Erin, "When the Jews came in '48, I was five years old. They rounded us up and took us to a prison camp." This speech, with the description of the act of "rounding up" and the prison camp, deliberately evokes Holocaust iconography. In *The Promise*, it would seem, the Jews' desire for their own land is judged not so much in relation to their past and their agreed-upon right to it but rather in relation to their actions to secure it—actions that, for the most part, are described as evil and inhumane. Did the Jews deserve a state after all? The verdict, given by Len in a diary entry at the end of the final episode, is that no, they did not. Efraim Sicher argues, in an article exploring the ways in which Israel is perceived and portrayed in Britain, that an "insidious example of anti-Zionist treatment of Israel is the premise that, in view of the suffering of Palestinian Arabs, the establishment of the State of Israel was a historical mistake, from which the logical inference is drawn that the State of Israel should be 'dismantled,' something that is sometimes presented as a benign regime change."[9] Len's opinion, scripted by Kosminsky, can be seen as a clear manifestation of this line of thought. This is also Erin's verdict when asked by Eliza's brother, Paul, if she will ever come back to Israel. "No," she replies dryly, "What's the point?"

The parallel journey—both physical and emotional—that grandfather and granddaughter experience during their time in Palestine/Israel is a key element in *The Promise*. The background may consist of some dramatic events in the mid-twentieth and early twenty-first centuries, but it is Erin's growing understanding of Len, her distant grandfather, that occupies a central role in the unfolding drama. From an estranged old relative to whom she pays little to no attention, he becomes a captivating young man who fills Erin's fantasies, even her sexual ones: it is in a reverie while on the bus to Hebron that she dreams of a young Len making love to her. Overwhelmed by this transgression, she wakes up. "Just a bad dream," she explains to Omar Habash (Haaz Sleiman), her traveling companion. When Erin, who suffers from epilepsy, reads in her grandfather's journal about his own epileptic fit, a troubling incident he could not identify as such himself, their shared destinies become even more palpable to her.

In a sense, Len and Erin become one in the serial, a single entity that embodies the spirit of Britain, past and present. Here transgressive love—namely, the incestuous lovemaking scene between Erin and Len—is used, or rather misused, as a tool to express an explicit political statement. It is the lost youth of Len—a formerly handsome, courageous, and, above all, moral soldier who is now moving in and out of consciousness—that stands for the waning days of the British Empire, from its moribund state in the mid-1940s to its final decline soon afterward. But the representation of the young Erin as valiant and virtuous, just like her grandfather used to be, helps revive and even relive, for the viewer, Britain's past glories. Kosminsky has argued that he "wanted to remind British people that we have some culpability in one of the most tragic and intractable conflicts of our age," but his drama suggests otherwise.[10] The focus on the relationship between Erin and Len, both real and fantasized at once, means that the serial is primarily a means of exculpating Britain's sense of responsibility for the current situation in Israel and Palestine as well as repairing its bruised national pride. In short, *The Promise* says more about how Britain would like to perceive itself than it does about the contentious politics of the Middle East (or perhaps about the way Kosminsky believes the British people would like to think of that chapter in their history).[11]

The Ravished and the Ravisher

While in Israel, Erin, like her grandfather, gets personally involved with Israelis and Arabs. On the Israeli side, there are the Meyers, her host family, who live a life of luxury in one of Israel's richest areas. Some of the white walls of their house are decorated with expensive-looking Oriental rugs, a small yet significant nod to their—perhaps not fully conscious—colonial tendencies and taste. Politically at least, the family itself cannot be seen as a unified unit, although all of its members can be broadly identified with the Israeli left in their opposition to the occupation (but not in the solution to it). Whereas the parents seem to hold moderate views, their son, Paul, is an active member of a joint Israeli-Palestinian group called Combatants for Peace. Of the center-left camp in Israel he says to Erin with contempt, "It makes you think Israel is a society like yours. That's how protests help the occupation, by making the world think that this is a functioning democracy, that you can change anything here by political action." To him, even the so-called liberals in Israel, such as his father, are racists and bigots in disguise. Omar, a Palestinian citizen of Israel, is also a member of Combatants for Peace, and he is Erin's link to the Palestinian world about which she is so eager to learn. It is through Paul and Omar that Erin will gain her knowledge of present-day Israel/Palestine, which will transform her from a passive observer to a proactive agent of change. Throughout the serial, and in the many encounters Erin has with the locals, she is asked what brought her there, a question that remains without a clear answer. It is only toward the very end—the end of the serial as well as the end of Erin's quest in Israel and Palestine—that she replies, "I don't know. I'm from England. I suppose I'm trying to help." This is a stance not unlike Len's, and by extension that of the British Empire he represents; namely, an inherent feeling of moral superiority and a staunch—colonial—belief in their right to play a role in foreign lands.

The events that have inspired the modern-day narrative of *The Promise* take place on a piece of land that has been crisscrossed with numerous checkpoints and the West Bank barrier Israel has built. Indeed, the modernity that Israel represents does not provide Israelis or Palestinians with the freedom both sides long for. Paradoxically, the 1940s prestate years, as they are reconstructed in *The Promise*, despite the killings on all sides—Arab, Jewish, and British—are invested with a much greater visual and dramatic charm. The elegance of the hospitality clubs and teahouses, the refined clothes and hairdos, and the impeccable manners are symbols of a bygone era, one associated with classical Hollywood and British films. Rachel Cooke correctly observed in the British leftist publication *New Statesman*, "In the sections set during the Mandate, you can almost smell the orange blossom, heady on the breeze; and 21st-century Israel feels clenched, like a fist. Even the dazzling white houses of Caesarea, the country's richest city and where Eliza's family lives, have an air of watchfulness."[12]

If indeed there was an effort to approach this project with an objective, unprejudiced perspective—"I set out to try to be balanced," Kosminsky told the *Jewish Chronicle*[13]—this ambition, in my mind at least, has failed. Too often it seems that Kosminsky struggles to portray the Jews of Palestine and modern-day Israelis as nothing more than intruders into someone else's land who are willing to inflict pain for political gain, or are just plain nasty and treacherous. Here I quite naturally go back to the love story between Len and Clara with which I opened: Clara's betrayal of her lover, Len, echoes that of Jesus by his disciple and good friend Judas Iscariot. Clara's love for Len, it seems, is just one of a series of lies she tells to gather confidential information about the plans of the British army. To this end, she goes as far as feigning a cruel attack on herself, supposedly carried out by her fellow Irgun members, and presenting it as a punishment for her relationship with Len. Len finds her covered in tar and feathers, her long, beautiful locks shorn. Later on, the viewers, together with Len, find that this was a ploy to get Len to divulge information. The sensitive information he gives her not only will harm the plans of the British army as an institution but will also lead to the kidnap of Len and two other soldiers by the Irgun; their incarceration in a tiny, airless cell for more than two weeks; and the eventual hanging of Len's fellow soldiers (Len is released thanks to Clara's efforts on his behalf). More than any other act of violence depicted in the serial, it is the abuse these British soldiers endure at the hands of the Jews — based roughly on the aforementioned Sergeants' Affair — that manages to truly shock and resonate.

It is important to note here that although the love affair between Len and Clara occupies a central place in the serial, it is by no means the only one. At least one other love story between a British soldier and a beautiful, European-looking Jewish woman blossoms, and in this case the soldier is "turned" — an act that emphasizes the true value of the love between them. It may be libidinal, but it is the political aspect that really matters.

The love story between Len and Clara brings to mind Roland Barthes' assertion that

> language (vocabulary) has long since posited the equivalence of love and war: in both cases, it is a matter of conquering, ravishing, capturing, etc. Each time a subject "falls" in love, he revives a fragment of the archaic time when men were supposed to carry off women (in order to ensure exogamy): every lover who falls in love at first sight has something of a Sabine Woman (or of some other celebrated victim of ravishment). However, there is an odd turnabout here: in the ancient myth, the ravisher is active, he wants to seize his prey, he is the subject of the rape (of which the object is a Woman, as we know, invariably passive);

> in the modern myth (that of love-as-passion), the contrary is the case: the ravisher wants nothing, does nothing; he is motionless (as any image), and it is the ravished object who is the real subject of the rape; the *object* of capture becomes the *subject* of love; and the *subject* of the conquest moves into the class of loved *object*. (There nonetheless remains a public vestige of the archaic model: the lover—the one who has been ravished—is always implicitly feminized.)[14]

Indeed, Clara is the original ravished object that becomes the ravisher—Len falls in love with her almost instantly, and she manipulatively enchants him into fulfilling her secret wishes; namely, revealing classified information to her. In contrast, the feminized Len turns into the passive ravished object. Having been manipulated by Clara, incarcerated by her fellow fighters, and then saved by her from certain death, he is the "*subject* of the conquest" who "moves into the class of loved *object*." Almost to the end, Len remains at Clara's mercy, a situation he fights but fails to change.

Clara, as the ravisher, stands for modern-day ravishing, aggressive Israel. The Deir Yassin massacre scene is the culmination of Clara's—and her nation's—violent, conquering tendencies. In the same way that Len and Erin personify purportedly moral, neutral, and fair Britain, Clara personifies Israel's aggressive and perfidious nature. In a side story, it is interesting to learn that Clara's absent mother was not murdered in the Holocaust as Len, and the viewers, suspect at first, but rather has left her father for another man she met in the camps and has moved with him to Italy. The Holocaust, as Clara bitterly notes, has provided her mother with a happy ending. Here Kosminsky undermines the importance of the Holocaust to the Zionist and Israeli cause that he acknowledged at the beginning of the serial. Instead, he renders it as an event in which Jews were given yet another opportunity to betray those who care for and love them.

Erin's Forbidden Love

Erin herself seems to be lost in love, swaying from British Israeli Paul, with whom she sleeps once, to Palestinian citizen of Israel Omar, with whom she flirts. It is Omar who truly attracts her, and their only partially realized love story evokes the British romantic notion of and fascination with the Orient—a fascination that sees in the Arab, in Edward Said's words, "that impossible creature whose libidinal energy drives him to paroxysms of over-stimulation—and yet, he is as a puppet in the eyes of the world, staring vacantly out at a modern landscape he can neither understand nor cope with."[15] As a British citizen, Erin does not belong to either of the two opposite camps but rather represents a neutral presence; she could have easily enjoyed an affair with the Arab Omar without being suspected of treason (unlike the case for Israelis, who are strongly discouraged from forming relationships with Palestinians). However, their love story is framed right from the start as "forbidden." Erin's Israeli hosts, the Meyers, are the ones who are responsible for this framing.[16] By hosting Erin, they expect her to adjust to their own way of living and to agree with their understanding of the Palestinian–Israeli situation. And their perspective, although self-appointedly liberal and progressive, still sees in Omar a threat. I should also point out that the Meyers' portrayal, like that of Clara in the 1940s, is intensely one-sided, as it focuses predominantly on their wealth and purchasing power; they thus are not representative of the average Israeli (in fact, this is a replay of a prototypical antisemitic canard). One scene in particular illustrates two of the Meyers' traits: their love for consumer goods (which the serial depicts as greater than the love the couple has for each other) and their expectation that Erin understand her infatuation with Omar as a dangerous violation of some unwritten rule.

In a telling scene, Max and Leah Meyer return to their home earlier than expected and surprise Erin and Omar, who are leisurely paddling in their pool. Erin's innocent invitation of the Palestinian Omar to the Meyers' house is treated as a gravely serious breach of confidence on her part. But beyond the not-so-subtle message of the impossibility of Palestinian citizens of Israel and Jews ever mixing together (which is here extended also to British Erin, who is expected to fully accept and sympathize with this Israeli Jewish anxiety), there is another significant detail in the scene: the Meyers enter the frame holding numerous shopping bags. We do not get to know much about Leah and Max Meyer—their occupations, for instance, remain unspecified—except that they like to shop and consume. (In another scene, Max Meyer is seen with a cigar in his mouth at a fancy party in his house.)

This awkward scene is followed by yet another, in which the Meyers are eating dinner with Erin and Omar. The family's servant serves dinner—a rare if not completely absent sight in contemporary Israeli homes. The servant is hardly addressed by the family members but is uncomfortably thanked by Omar. In this instance, Omar's compassion in acknowledging the attendant as his equal is shown to express the Meyers' lack of any shred of humanity. Also in this highly charged scene, Max Meyer asks Omar where his family is originally from. Omar then addresses the same question to Max, who tells him that he was born in Manchester, England. Omar then asks Leah Meyer about her country of origin. She simply answers "from over here," indicating a sense of entitlement to the land (or her birthplace). But when Omar investigates further, she admits her father emigrated from Hungary to Palestine. For Kosminsky, the "Europeanness" of the Jews of the 1940s narrative undermines their right to the land: they are not "native," unlike their Arab neighbors. Similarly, the Meyers' European origins as well as their dual Israeli-British citizenship weaken their right to live within the 1967 Israeli borders. Furthermore, contributing to this powerful impression is the Meyers' extreme wealth: their pool, their servant, and their shopping bags all contrast with the squalid conditions in which the Palestinians live, highlighting how Kosminsky has taken a clear stance on the matter. Through his artistic and aesthetic choices, Kosminsky has chosen to portray a specific view of Israeli reality.

Andrew Anthony stated in a review in the left-wing daily newspaper the *Guardian* that

> it's worth noting . . . that the problem with the difference in treatment of the two sides is not, as some may claim, that it favours the Arab cause but that it does a disservice to Arabs themselves. We glimpse the psychological complexities of the English observers and their Jewish Israeli hosts, but the Palestinian Arabs are largely ciphers on whom western guilt can be readily projected. They remain, in other words, what critics of orientalism like to call "other." We're not privy to the doubts and conflicts of their beliefs, and consequently as characters they're not quite as worthy of our belief.[17]

Indeed, for the most part, the Arabs in *The Promise* merely illuminate the flaws of the Jewish protagonists. In the 1940s narrative their passivity and naïveté are contrasted with the Jews' acts of aggressions and cunning operations. With no mention of the 1936–1939 Arab revolt in Palestine or of the Arab riots in 1920 and 1929, the Arabs of that time are portrayed as helpless victims who depend on the kindness of others — that of either the British soldiers or the surrounding Arab countries. However, those others cannot or do not want to help them, and the Nakba turns into an almost inevitable historical fact.

Omar is perhaps the only Arab character who is more than a mere symbol of suffering. We get to know a little bit more about him, apart from the fact that he belongs to the victims' camp. However, his character is still underdeveloped compared with his British and Israeli counterparts, whose aggressions, frustrations, and motivations are presented openly to the viewer. An interesting point about Omar is that although he is Palestinian, he is not a Muslim but rather a Christian. What may seem at first a negligible detail is in fact of great import: by making Omar Christian, Kosminsky still posits him as the Oriental Other but not as the enemy. Still inherently different to Erin, Omar's Christianity marks his otherness as harmless, as a source of romantic fascination rather than terror.

In both narratives the humanity of the Arabs is contrasted with the Israelis' callous nature. The unacknowledged themes that run through the servant scene at the Meyers' mansion, touched on before, are evident throughout the serial. In the first episode, for instance, shortly after Eliza and Erin's arrival in Israel, the two women go out dancing. The strobe lights at the discotheque trigger Erin's epilepsy, and she drops to the floor in a seizure. As it takes Eliza a few minutes to notice her friend from across the room, a crowd of fellow partygoers circle her and start laughing viciously. Nobody offers help, and they let Erin's body contort until Eliza comes to the rescue. If Kosminsky hopes to show by this how the violence of the occupation seeps through all layers of life, he is doing so in what can be described as a heavy-handed — and often prejudiced — manner. Even the token "good Israeli" of the serial, Paul, Eliza's tormented brother, comes across at times as no more than a robotic being, whose dogmatic way of thinking is not unlike that of the zealot illegal settlers in the Israeli-occupied territories featured in episode 3. Paul's unreserved sympathy for the Arab suicide bombers who attempted to kill him at the end the first episode is a case in point. Lying in his bed, injured and unable to move, he condones the actions of those who were sent to murder him. His unequivocal political stance is both psychologically incoherent and tendentious, and it merely takes away his humanity.

Not unlike the Arabs, the British too are portrayed as hapless victims of a situation in which they have accidentally found themselves trapped. Did the British army have any strategic ambitions in regard to Palestine and the Middle East in general? *The Promise* does not suggest it had. The British military presence is merely stated as a fact. Jews may call the British who govern them "Nazis," but the Jewish acts of violence, torture, killing, and betrayal are what make a lasting impression on the viewer. In fact, the way the British are portrayed in *The Promise* calls to mind the Hebrew phrase *yorim u'bochim* — "shooting and crying" — that is so often used to describe the double standard ingrained in the actions of the Israeli army against its perceived enemies, the hypocritical sorrow over actions that could have been avoided. In *The Promise*, the acts of aggression toward the British army take its soldiers by surprise, as if they had little basis or rationale.

When Erin first glimpses the life the Meyers lead, she exclaims that Israel is "just not what I expected. . . . It's like paradise." But soon afterward she realizes Israel is not the paradise she initially thought it was. The use of "paradise" as a metaphor recurs also in the choice of name for the café that is blown up at the end of the first episode: it is called Eden. The point Kosminsky tries to get across is loud and clear: Israel and Palestine may have had the chance to become paradise, but they have missed it. Just as Adam and Eve were expelled from Eden for Eve's transgressive taking of knowledge (Genesis 3), so — in Kosminsky's eyes — the Jews will be expelled for their land grabbing. And it is primarily the Zionist movement and the Israeli state that are to blame. As Len concludes in his diary, in an entry I mentioned earlier, "What about the Jews and their bloody state for which they've fought so hard? Three years ago I'd have said give 'em whatever they want. They deserve it after all they've been through. Now, I'm not so sure. This precious state of theirs has been born in violence and in cruelty to its neighbors. I'm not sure how it can hope to thrive."

The Promise is frustrating precisely because it does not reflect any side accurately: certainly not the Israelis, but also not the Palestinians — whether Israeli citizens or not — whom I doubt would recognize themselves on-screen; have they really been so passive in their quest for national self-determination? Again, the portrayal of the Arab community in Palestine as passive is not only inaccurate, given the various Arab riots in Palestine from 1920 to the 1936–1939 revolt, but also redolent of Orientalist sentiments. Without the ability to identify with the characters and situations described in *The Promise*, there is not much left for a serial that strives to be politically relevant and thought provoking. As an Israeli living in Britain, I found it interesting to see how acclaimed the serial was among U.K. critics — Andrew Anthony's review being the exception — and viewers: with *The Promise* Kosminsky may have hoped to help viewers make sense of the mess in the Middle East, but its didactic, heavy-handed, and often uneven portrayal abates its effect.[18] To me it is, regrettably, a promise unfulfilled. As expected, the series was not broadcast in Israel but was shown once at the Tel Aviv Cinematheque in April 2012. It received some media coverage, mostly negative, before that screening.[19]

So what has love got to do with this? Everything and nothing at all. The notion of love in *The Promise* is removed as can be from real emotion and comes to serve a purpose unrelated to the characters' wish for romance and affection: Clara can let herself love and feel loved only when those emotions, either real or imagined, also serve the national cause, while for Len, his affair with Clara paves the way to a total identification with the Arab side. His other platonic, homosocial love affair with his Arab servant and his son — today it would be described as a "bromance," a term used to describe an intimate, close relationship between two men — is a manifestation of that. Erin's confused emotions about both Paul and Omar reflect her confused political agenda. But her obvious infatuation with Omar is, as in the case of Len, a declaration of loyalty to the Arab side. It could be argued that the Gaelic origin of her first name — evoking the Irish Catholic struggle against the British and Protestantism, which can be compared with the Palestinians' against Israel — may have suggested her allegiance right from the start. It is through Omar that Erin manages to find the daughter of Mohammed in Gaza and to return the key to her. Thus Omar becomes a mechanism by which Erin can complete a full circle for her grandfather and, by extension, her nation as well.

Notes

1. The link to this footage is https://www.youtube.com/watch?v=qdeqXQPW7TM).

2. Shooting in Israel was a challenging experience, as Kosminsky explained to Rachel Cooke in the *Observer*: "It wasn't without its problems. . . . Every time we applied to shoot in a public building, permission was always denied, and no reason was ever given." Rachel Cooke, "Peter Kosminsky: Britain's Humiliation in Palestine," *Observer*, January 22, 2011, http://www.guardian.co.uk/tv-and-radio/2011/jan/23/peter-kosminsky-palestine-mandate-drama.

3. Naomi Shepherd writes about the Irgun and the active part it took in planning and carrying out terror acts during the last years of the British mandate in Palestine: "Until 1944, although there were Jewish extremists who challenged the authority of the Jewish Agency, the administration had been able to live with—and make use of—the Hagana. But rival militias had been set up by right-wing Jewish political groups, who now called for open rebellion against their British rulers and targeted the Arabs and the British alike. The Jewish Agency had no control of these militias, chief among them the Irgun . . . and the breakaway Stern Gang. . . . From the time of the Arab Revolt, the Irgun had rejected the Jewish Agency's policy of restraint, carried out indiscriminate revenge bombings and killed Arabs. Now they raided RAF [Royal Air Force] airfields, stole arms from military bases, killed British soldiers, and kidnapped British officers whom they held as hostages, hoping that death sentences on their own men would be commuted." Naomi Shepherd, *Ploughing Sand: British Rule in Palestine 1917–1948* (London: John Murray, 1999), 223–24.

4. The drama was first pitched to and accepted by the BBC, as reported by the *Guardian* in 2006. See Ben Dowell, "Kosminsky to Film Palestinian Drama," *Guardian*, January 12, 2006, http://www.theguardian.com/media/2006/jan/12/television.bbc. However, when Kosminsky's production company moved its "first look" deal from the BBC to Channel 4, Kosminsky took *The Promise* there. Channel 4, established in 1982, is a publicly owned but mostly commercially self-funded British television broadcaster with a reputation for innovation. In an interview with *GQ* in 2009, Kosminsky explained, "I don't think we can say the BBC bottled it. . . . Having said that, I am sad it seems to have lost its nerve for making challenging drama. And I don't just mean 'edgy' crime drama, but drama that gets it into political and legal hot water." Stuart McGurk, "Whipping Up a Desert Storm," *GQ*, February 18, 2011, http://www.gq-magazine.co.uk/entertainment/articles/2011–02/18/gq-tv-the-promise-channel-4-peter-kosminsky. Similarly, in an interview with Rachel Cooke in the *Observer*, he said, "'I spent a long time trying to make it work at the BBC, but then three projects I developed over many years were canned, which made me pretty cross.' According to Kosminsky, film-makers like him no longer see 'that flash of mischief' in the eyes of commissioning editors when they turn up at the BBC to pitch ideas" (Cooke, "Peter Kosminsky").

5. *The Government Inspector*, directed Peter Kosminsky (Strasbourg: Arte France; London: Mentorn Productions, 2005); *Britz*, directed Peter Kosminsky (Strasbourg: Arte France, 2007).

6. In a letter sent to David Abraham, chief executive of Channel 4, Vivian Wineman, president of the Board of Deputies of British Jews, wrote, "*The Promise* draws a totally one sided conclusion. Instead of seeing the conflict as the result of the incompatible aspirations of two peoples in one land it becomes a function of the violence and cruelty of the Jews so extreme as to deprive them of the sympathy for their past suffering.

The reference to neighbours skates over the fact that those neighbours invaded Israel the day after it declared independence with a view to wiping it off the map." Vivian Wineman, "'The Promise'—Letter to Channel 4," Board of Deputies of British Jews, March 3, 2011, accessed November 4, 2013, http://www.bod.org.uk/live/content.php?Item_ID=68. As reported by Marcus Dysch in the *Jewish Chronicle*, Abraham—who is, incidentally, Jewish—dismissed Wineman's concerns, arguing that Channel 4's Jewish-themed sitcom *Friday Night Dinner* "was an example of 'balance' in the station's programming." Marcus Dysch, "Promise Critics: Stop Moaning, You Have Friday Night Dinner," *Jewish Chronicle*, April 7, 2011, http://www.aijac.org.au/news/article/the-promise).

7. Sherry Ricchiardi noted, "For years, critics have assailed what they see as antisemitic, anti-American bias in the channel's news content. In the wake of 9/11, Al Jazeera broadcast statements by Osama bin Laden and reported from within the ranks of the Taliban, earning a reputation as a mouthpiece for terrorists. In October 2001, a *New York Times* editorial took Al Jazeera to task for reporting Jews had been informed in advance not to go to work at the World Trade Center the day of the attacks. The Bush administration was openly hostile to the news organization. Missteps over the years have fueled concern about the network's agenda. An often-repeated example involves an on-air birthday party organized by Al Jazeera's Beirut bureau chief for a Lebanese militant convicted of killing four Israelis, including a four-year-old girl. Al Jazeera greeted Samir Kuntar, released in a July 2008 prisoner swap, as a hero. . . . Al Jazeera later apologized to Israel for the 'unethical' coverage, but the damage had been done." Sherry Ricchiardi, "Al Jazeera Effect," *American Journalism Review*, April 21, 2011, http://ajr.org/Article.asp?id=5077. Kosminsky quoted in Marcus Dysch, "Peter Kosminsky Says He Kept Promise," *Jewish Chronicle*, January 24, 2011, http://www.thejc.com/news/uk-news/47277/peter-kosminsky-says-he-kept-promise.

8. Today the Israeli artists' colony Ein Hod.

9. Efraim Sicher, "The Image of Israel and Postcolonial Discourse in the Early 21st Century: A View from Britain," *Israel Studies* 16, no. 1 (2011): 10.

10. Dysch, "Peter Kosminsky Says He Kept Promise."

11. It should be noted that Kosminsky is not entirely oblivious of that fact. In an article in the right-wing daily newspaper the *Daily Telegraph*, days before *The Promise* first aired on British TV, he wrote, "At its simplest level, in telling this story in drama form, I'm just responding to a suggestion written in a letter over a decade ago. But, in imagining a character based on the veterans of the Palestine campaign, in interviewing old men still brooding half a century later on those three dark years of their lives, I've found myself moved and incensed in equal measure. In 1945, while Britain was focused on postwar bankruptcy and independence for India, these men traded a demob [demobilization] suit and family reunions for a bitter conflict in Mandate Palestine. They were carrying out British policy, even if it's a policy we would now like to quietly forget. They deserve our gratitude, our respect and, above all, their national memorial." Peter Kosminsky, "Peter Kosminsky on The Promise, His Drama about Palestine," *Daily Telegraph*, February 4, 2011, http://www.telegraph.co.uk/culture/tvandradio/8303231/Peter-Kosminsky-on-The-Promise-his-drama-about-Palestine.html.

12. Rachel Cooke, "The Promise," *New Statesman*, February 17, 2011, http://www.newstatesman.com/television/2011/02/israel-promise-eliza-palestine.

13. Dysch, "Peter Kosminsky Says He Kept Promise."

14. Roland Barthes, *A Lover's Discourse: Fragments* (1979; repr., London: Vintage, 2002), 188–89.

15. Edward W. Said, *Orientalism* (1978; repr., London: Penguin, 2003), 312.

16. The fear of mixing blood was prevalent in colonial Europe as much as it is prevalent in modern-day Israel. As Yosefa Loshitzky argues, "stories of 'forbidden love,' dealing with mainly with interracial romances, are a recurring theme in Western culture. European colonizers and their settler descendants have always been terrified by the prospect of miscegenation." Yosefa Loshitzky, *Identity Politics on the Israeli Screen* (Austin: University of Texas Press, 2001), 13.

17. Andrew Anthony, "Rewind TV: The Promise; Mad Dogs; Outcasts," *Guardian*, February 13, 2011, http://www.guardian.co.uk/tv-and-radio/2011/feb/13/promise-kosminsky-mad-dogs-review.

18. In the left-of-center daily newspaper the *Independent*, Hugh Montgomery wrote, "*The Promise* finds him [Kosminsky] back at his thought-provoking best. . . . Kosminsky balanced the demands of big-picture history and intimate human drama with a quite remarkable assurance." Hugh Montgomery, "*The Promise*, Channel 4, Sunday Mad Dogs, Sky 1, Thursday," *Independent*, February 13, 2011, http://www.independent.co.uk/arts-entertainment/tv/reviews/the-promise-channel-4-sundaybrmad-dogs-sky-1-thursday-2213036.html. Rachel Cooke exclaimed in the *Guardian*'s sister Sunday paper, the *Observer*: "Was it worth it? I think it would have been worth it if it had taken him twice as long. *The Promise*, which will be screened in four parts, and runs to some seven and a half hours, is the best thing you are likely to see on television this year, if not this decade. It is not only that it is so exciting, moving, and full of exquisite performances; it's also that the extraordinary detail and thoughtfulness of it—the sheer scale of the canvas on which its director works—subtly imparts so many emotional and factual truths that you feel your own allegiances, whatever they may be, suddenly shifting uneasily, sometimes on a minute-by-minute basis. Revelatory is an overused word, but *The Promise* is exactly that: the power of its storytelling will open eyes more effectively than any leaked document, any piece of rhetoric, any news bulletin" (Cooke, "Peter Kosminsky"). Even James Delingpole of the British conservative weekly magazine the *Spectator* found the serial "looking very . . . promising," although he did comment on "how intensely bloody annoying and leftie the end product is." James Delingpole, "Grandfather's Footsteps," *Spectator*, February 12, 2011, http://www.spectator.co.uk/arts/television/6684893/grandfathers-footsteps/.

19. The reviews in Israel, as expected, were not as flattering. In an article published in the left-wing *Ha'aretz* prior to the screening of the serial at the Tel Aviv Cinematheque in April 2012, Ruta Kupfer wrote that "its inaccurate portrayal of Israel is sure to offend" and that the "first episode romanticizes Israeli discourse. The son, Paul, a Peace Now activist, upbraids his father's liberal outlook, claiming that it perpetuates the conflict. It is as though the spectrum of politics among Jews in this country runs between the Meretz and Hadash parties. . . . In today's Israel, which is all about death, a Tel Aviv cafe looks like a cage surrounded by security forces. There are as many security guards at the cafe as there are at an airport. As it happens, the cafe filmed in this sequence is located in my own neighborhood; it has never looked the way it is made to appear in *The Promise*." Ruta Kupfer, "Controversial Film on British-controlled Palestine Comes to Tel Aviv," *Haaretz*, April 16, 2012, http://www.haaretz.com/news/features/controversial-film-series-on-british-controlled-palestine-comes-to-tel-aviv-1.424502.

Amir Ofek, press attaché at the Israeli embassy in London, went further by stating in an interview with the *Jewish Chronicle* that *The Promise* had "created a new category of hostility towards Israel. . . . In my 15-year career I have never seen anything like it in the western media. I'm aware of artistic freedom, but nevertheless I feel this is worse than anything I've seen." Marcus Dysch, "The Promise Has an 'Anti-Israel Premise,'" *Jewish Chronicle*, February 24, 2011, http://www.thejc.com/news/uk-news/45709/the-promise-has-anti-israel-premise.

CONTRIBUTORS

Nathan Abrams is Professor of Film Studies at Bangor University in Wales. He has written widely on the Jewish contribution to film and cinema, particularly in the United Kingdom and United States. He is the founding coeditor of *Jewish Film and New Media: An International Journal*, and his most recent book is *The New Jew in Film: Exploring Jewishness and Judaism in Contemporary Culture* (Rutgers University Press, 2012). He is currently working on a major archival-based project exploring the ethics and ethnicity of the work of Stanley Kubrick.

Lawrence Baron held the Nasatir Chair of Modern Jewish History at San Diego State University from 1988 until 2012 and directed its Jewish Studies Program until 2006. He received his Ph.D. in modern European cultural and intellectual history from the University of Wisconsin, where he studied with George L. Mosse. He taught at St. Lawrence University from 1975 until 1988. He has written and edited four books, including *The Modern Jewish Experience in World Cinema* (Brandeis University Press, 2011) and *Projecting the Holocaust into the Present: The Changing Focus of Contemporary Holocaust Cinema* (Rowman and Littlefield, 2005).

Michael Berkowitz is a professor of modern Jewish history at University College London. His books include *The Crime of My Very Existence: Nazism and the Myth of Jewish Criminality* (University of California Press, 2007); *The Jewish Self-Image: American and British Perspectives, 1881–1939* (Reaktion Press, 2000); *Western Jewry and the Zionist Project, 1914–1933* (Cambridge University Press, 1997); and *Zionist Culture and West European Jewry before the First World War* (Cambridge University Press, 1993).

Michele Byers is a professor in the Department of Sociology and Criminology at Saint Mary's University, Halifax, Canada. Much of her current work focuses on television and ethnicity, with a particular interest in Jewish identities. Published recent work includes *QSE*, *European Journal of Popular Culture*, *Canadian Ethnic Studies*, *Reconstruction*, and *Critical Studies in Television*, as well as the edited collections *Critical Canadian Studies* and *Canadian Television: Texts and Contexts*.

Nir Cohen is the author of *Soldiers, Rebels and Drifters: Gay Representation in Israeli Cinema* (Wayne State University Press, 2011) and coeditor of *Jewish Film & New Media: An International Journal* (also published by Wayne State University Press).

Rachel Garfield is an associate professor in art at the University of Reading. An artist, she has exhibited widely, most recently in a group show in the Hatton Gallery, Newcastle, and screening work at the Institute of Contemporary Arts as part of the London Short Film Festival (2012). Garfield also writes about video art and the modern and contemporary representation of Jews in art and popular media. Recent publications include "Questioning Perceptions of Jewish Identity in the Work of Ary Stillman," in *Ary Stillman: From Impressionism to Abstract Expressionism*, edited by James Wechsler; "Playing with History: Negotiating Subjectivity in Contemporary Lens Based Art," in *Routledge Handbook to Modern Jewish Cultures*, edited by Nadia Valman and Laurence Roth; and "Imagining Multicultural London: Containment and Excess in *Snatch*," published in *European Judaism* 47:2 (Autumn 2014).

Phyllis Lassner is a professor in the Crown Family Center for Jewish and Israel Studies, teaching in the Gender Studies and Writing Programs at Northwestern University. In addition to articles on interwar and World War II women writers, she has written *British Women Writers of World War II*, *Colonial Strangers: Women Writing the End of the British Empire*, and most recently, *Anglo-Jewish Women Writing the Holocaust*, as well as two books on Elizabeth Bown. She has also coedited *Antisemitism and Philosemitism in the Twentieth and Twenty-First Centuries: Representing Jews, Jewishness, and Modern Culture*, and *Rumer Godden: International and Intermodern Storyteller*.

Alexis Pogorelskin is an associate professor at the University of Minnesota-Duluth. She has published extensively on the opposition to Stalin as well as nineteenth century Russian liberalism with Cambridge University Press and in such journals as *Oxford Slavonic Papers, Slavic Review,* and *Journal of Finnish Studies*. She is the editor of *The NEP Era, Soviet History, 1921-1928*. Her monograph on *The Mortal Storm* is under contract with Northwestern University Press. She was most recently Vera Brittain Fellow on Women and War at Chawton House, U.K.

Gavin Schaffer is a professor of modern history at the University of Birmingham. He has published widely on the concept of race, Jewish history, and race relations and immigration. Schaffer is the author of *Racial Science and British Society* and editor of *The Lasting War and Racializing the Soldier*. His newest book, *The Vision of a Nation: Making Multiculturalism on British Television* (Palgrave, 2014), is on race relations and television.

Claudia Sternberg is a senior lecturer in cultural studies at the University of Leeds. Her research has focused on screenwriting; black, Asian, and Jewish British literature, film, and television; and media representations of the First World War. She coedited *European Cinema in Motion: Migrant and Diasporic Film in Contemporary Europe* (with D. Berghahn, 2010) and is coauthor of *Bidding for the Mainstream? Black and Asian British Film since the 1990s* (with B. Korte, 2004). She guest-edited "Jewish Cultures," a special issue of the *Journal for the Study of British Cultures* (2009), and currently works on cultural memory and the World War I centenary

Gil Toffell is currently conducting research on twentieth-century Jewish communal institutions in the East End of London for the Leverhulme Oxford Diasporas Programme. He also teaches a course on film audiences at Queen Mary, University of London. His book on Jews, cinema, and public life in interwar Britain is forthcoming from Palgrave. From 2009 to 2011 he worked on a two-year Leverhulme Trust–funded research project entitled "Jewish Cinema Culture in Interwar Britain" at Queen Mary.

Sue Vice is a professor of English literature at the University of Sheffield. Her most recent books are *Jack Rosenthal* (2009), *Shoah* (2011), the volume, coedited with Jenni Adams, *Representing Perpetrators in Holocaust Literature and Film* (2012), and *Textual Deceptions: False Memoirs and Literary Hoaxes in the Contemporary Era* (2014). She is currently completing a critical study of the work of the novelist and screenwriter Barry Hines, cowritten with David Forrest.

Donald Weber is Lucia, Ruth and Elizabeth MacGregor Professor of English at Mount Holyoke College. He is the author of *Haunted in the New World: Jewish American Culture from Cahan to The Goldbergs* (Indiana University Press, 2005). His essays and reviews on Jewish American literature and popular culture have appeared in a range of publications, including the *Forward*, *Tikkun*, and the *Chronicle Review*.

INDEX